R

D

William T. A

01   12-0-0   yale (w)

05   8-2-1   yale (L)

06   10-1-0   yale (L)

(3)   30-3-1   1-2

Writing
noted
5/4/12 -

Sport and Society

Series Editors

Benjamin G. Rader
Randy Roberts

*A list of books in the series
appears at the back of this book.*

Big-Time Football at Harvard, 1905

Big-Time Football at Harvard, 1905

The Diary of Coach Bill Reid

Edited by Ronald A. Smith

University of Illinois Press
Urbana and Chicago

To Thomas Stetson, Bill Reid's grandson,
for preserving the papers of Bill Reid.

This book is printed on acid-free paper.

Library of Congress Cataloging-in-Publication Data

Reid, Bill, 1878–1976
    Big-time football at Harvard, 1905 : the diary of Coach Bill Reid
/ edited by Ronald A. Smith.
       p.   cm.
    Includes index.
    ISBN 0-252-02047-2 (alk. paper)
    1. Reid, Bill, 1878–1976. 2. Football—United States—Coaches—
Biography. 3. Harvard University—Football—History. I. Smith,
Ronald A. (Ronald Austin), 1936– . II. Title.
GV939.R45A3   1994
796.332'092—dc20
    [B]   93-10247
                                                                    CIP

Contents

Acknowledgments

Some individuals are blessed to have supportive academic units that help promote scholarly endeavors. I am one of the fortunate. The Department of Exercise and Sport Science at Pennsylvania State University has provided not only sabbaticals for extended time to do research but also has given me teaching loads that are compatible with scholarly activity. Because of Penn State, I have had the opportunity to do research in more than forty college archives and to search previously uncovered materials. On one sabbatical, I was concluding research at the Harvard University Archives when, on the last day, I discovered a lengthy 440-page diary of a little-known Harvard coach, Bill Reid. I immediately knew it was a treasure and asked the Archives to photocopy the diary so that I could study it further. I want to thank the Harvard University Archives for making this volume possible. Another university has also contributed to this volume. The University of California, Berkeley, Archives contains a William T. Reid, Sr., collection. Bill Reid's father was a president of the school in the 1880s, and the collection helped me to better understand the milieu of the late 1800s in which Bill Reid and athletics came together. Even more important for understanding Bill Reid were the extensive private papers that Thomas Stetson, Reid's grandson, lent to me.

I had the good fortune to receive a grant from the National Historical Publications and Records Commission to be an intern at the Sixteenth Annual Institute for Editing of History Documents in 1987. This two-week institute at the State Historical Society of Wisconsin on the campus of the University of Wisconsin, Madison, gave me the opportunity to think about how this document might be edited for publication. One of the speakers was Sharon Macpherson, an editor of the papers of Andrew Jackson. When discussing the transcription of a document, she said: "Keep the diary in the form it was originally written." I have tried to do this, and the influence of the NHPRC has helped me to keep the original Bill Reid diary almost exactly as it was written.

Professors at a university can learn a great deal from the people in their classes. I have had the opportunity to exchange ideas with students, especially when I have taught a course on the history of athletics in higher education. To the many students who raised questions and challenged assumptions in a seminar setting, I am grateful.

Sport history is fortunate to have university presses as well as commercial presses that are willing to publish quality work in the discipline. The University of Illinois Press in particular is recognized for its series "Sport and Society," which began in 1986 with Melvin Adelman's *A Sporting Time*. Press director and editor-in-chief Richard L. Wentworth has fostered and carried on the series. Sport history has benefited greatly from his efforts, as well as those of Lawrence J. Malley's. Specifically to this volume, I am indebted to Steve Hardy, who told me that this diary is the best document he has read for understanding college sport, and to Randy Roberts, who, as an editor of the series, strongly supported the publishing of the diary. I appreciate the copy editing of Mary Giles, who, as a good editor does, improved the readability of Bill Reid's diary. To my wife and friend Sue Fernald Smith, I thank her again for being first editor.

The Editorial Method

In publishing the diary of William Reid, I have tried to retain Reid's original prose as much as possible while producing a work that would read well. Because Reid wrote well for the most part, only minor editorial changes were required.

Spelling. William Reid's diary included several misspelled words, and because most of these are intelligible, they have not been corrected. The obtrusive *sic* has not been used. When a misspelling would be misleading, it has been corrected with square brackets "[ ]." Thus, Reid's use of "offence" was allowed to stand for "offense," but "indcement" was changed to "ind[u]cement." Misspelled or inconsistently spelled names have been corrected in the index, with cross-references from the erroneous forms, and they are sometimes noted in footnotes.

Grammar and syntax. Reid's grammar and syntax have been allowed to remain in nearly all instances. If a serious ambiguity existed, it has been corrected with square brackets. When a word has been repeated inadvertently, it has been omitted.

Capitalization. Reid's capitalizations generally were not changed. For example, in his use of "Athletic committee," the lack of capitalization of "committee" remains. However, for clarity, his failure to capitalize "balzac" was corrected.

Paragraphing. Reid's use of paragraphing remains. Several multi-page paragraphs were kept in the diary.

Punctuation. Most punctuation marks have been allowed to stand. However, a dash (—) has been used when Reid clearly intended a dash when using a hyphen (-). The use of parentheses, "( )," for parenthetical remarks has replaced Reid's use of slash marks, "/ /." When additional punctuation is needed for clarity, it has been added with square brackets.

Abbreviations and contractions. Reid's use of abbreviations has been allowed to stand (unless there was ambiguity) with the exception of "Penn." for the University of Pennsylvania, and in that case the period has been dropped. Reid's consistent use of "wont" for "won't" has been corrected to include the apostrophe.

Illegible matter. In the rare situation where material is unreadable, suspension points inside brackets "[. . .]" replace the unclear words.

Editorial insertions. Material added by the editor was placed in square brackets. When Reid noted that material was to be found on another page, but it was actually missing, it is noted as "[missing]." Full names of individuals who could be identified have been added in brackets when they are encountered the first time. Thus "Haughton" became "[Percy] Haughton."

Footnote use. Footnotes have been used to identify certain individuals (such as Harvard graduates), place names (such as the Carlisle Indian School in Carlisle, Pennsylvania), obscure terminology (such as football injuries known as "poops"), and miscellaneous references and events.

Introduction

"I don't care how much of a student a fellow cares to be at other times," coach William Reid wrote in his diary four days before the 1905 Harvard-Yale football game, "I don't see how a man can help feeling that hardly anything is more important than to beat Yale." In the first decade of the twentieth century, it was as important for Harvard to beat Yale in football as it was at the close of the century for Alabama to beat Auburn, Oklahoma to beat Texas, or Michigan to beat Ohio State. What had changed was that Harvard and Yale of the Ivy League were no longer major actors, although they had once dominated action. The Big Game had moved westward and southward. Universities perceived the need to gain prestige and bragging rights from football, the dominant social activity. Bill Reid's diary is about Harvard's quest to be number one, only attainable by defeating Yale.

Reid's diary of his year at Harvard is the most revealing document on the nature of big-time football thus far discovered. The account of highly commercialized and professionalized college sport was written during the most important year in the history of college football, 1905–6. That year saw a group of writers rake the muck of big-time football, excoriating it for its brutality and lack of ethics. These muckrakers helped push President Theodore Roosevelt to invite representatives from Harvard (including Reid), Yale, and Princeton to the White House to discuss ways in which to raise the ethical standards in athletics across the country. Roosevelt called Reid to the White House again later in the season. At that second meeting, Roosevelt, a Harvard graduate, asked Reid to explain the action of one of his players, who was banished from a game for slugging an opponent.

Following the 1905 season, several institutions, including Harvard, Columbia, Northwestern, California, and Stanford, banned football. Harvard, however, banned it only provisionally. Through the chicanery of Reid and other friends of Harvard football, the game was saved from the negative vote of the governing board.

The football crisis of 1905 was such that a group of colleges met at the season's end and formed a reform group. The late-December meeting of sixty-eight colleges formed what became known as the National Collegiate Athletic Association. Reid was centrally involved, for he became secretary of the new Football Rules Committee, the pivotal power group when the NCAA was created.

The Reid diary does not discuss the creation of the NCAA or the reform rules that introduced the forward pass. It covers only the period from March 1905, when Reid took over the head coaching position just before spring practice, to late November and Harvard's last game against Yale. Reid wrote of such topics as:

- · Recruiting prep-school athletes,
- · Gaining readmission of former Harvard athletes,
- · Discussions with professors to maintain athletes' eligibilities,
- · Hiring tutors to attempt to keep athletes eligible,
- · Categorizing every Harvard graduate and undergraduate student relative to football potential,
- · Conducting undercover operations to obtain specimens of Yale's superior football equipment,
- · Creating a schedule of games in an attempt to meet Yale both undefeated and in top condition,
- · Attempting to hire game officials who would favor Harvard,
- · Accounting for all athletic injuries by the team physician,
- · Enlisting of a dozen or so coaches, including the payment of one, the country's first black coach, William H. Lewis,
- · Firing the freshman football coach through a well-devised resignation,
- · Discussing football strategy with such luminary football coaches as Glenn "Pop" Warner, Fielding H. Yost, and Amos Alonzo Stagg,
- · Meeting with Walter Camp and others at the behest of Theodore Roosevelt,
- · Creating a ruse letter to forestall Harvard's governing board from banning football,
- · Discussing his own excessive anxiety that brought about loss of weight, lack of sleep, and drinking,
- · Explaining the training rule policy and the various means of disciplining athletes,
- · Exposing the night life and sexual habits of some of the athletes from Harvard and opposing schools,
- · Revealing his methods of deceiving sports writers and offering an opinion on women sports writers,
- · Discussing practice schedules and game plans, and
- · Recreating pep-rally speeches and pregame talks.

Reid, although only twenty-six when he became Harvard's coach in 1905, was highly organized. He attempted to bring about a rational approach to defeating Yale. The entire diary is a testimony to the importance of winning, especially of winning the Yale game. Everything was done with that in mind—even the writing of the diary, which, as Reid said, was done to give advantage to those who would follow him as coach.

William Reid's name is not well-remembered in our sporting heritage, nor even in college football history. Yet his winning percentage during his three years as Harvard coach, 91 percent (thirty wins, three losses, and one tie), was greater than Knute Rockne's 88 percent in thirteen years as head coach at Notre Dame. At one time, however, Bill Reid was thought to be the panacea for Harvard's big-time football woes. A number of supporters believed that Reid might do for Harvard what Walter Camp, the "father of American football," had done for Yale since the 1870s. Reid might have been the Knute Rockne of Harvard two decades before Rockne made football the symbol of the University of Notre Dame. After all, no Harvard coach had ever won twenty straight victories. No other Harvard football coach had ever beaten its chief rival, Yale, as both a player and coach. It was traditional during this period for the leading athletic colleges to engage only their own graduates as coaches.

Bill Reid was a hero in Harvard athletics in both football and baseball. He was probably best known in baseball as an outstanding four-year catcher, being on the winning team against Yale for three of his four years. In football, Reid starred as a sophomore in the Harvard victory over Yale in 1898, when he scored two touchdowns, a feat never before accomplished against a Yale team. The 17-0 triumph was only the second over Yale in the previous eighteen years. Fewer than three years later, upon graduation, Reid was asked to coach the team. He led Harvard to twelve consecutive wins and a season-ending 22-0 victory over Yale. This was the largest score ever achieved against the greatest "jock school" in America for the first half-century of American football. Yale, one must realize, only lost ten games in the quarter-century before its 1901 defeat to Reid's Harvard. Seven of those losses were inflicted by the Princeton Tigers, the second most feared name in college football.

No wonder, then, that Reid was offered the head coach's position in December of 1904. Having been shut out for the third straight time by Yale, Harvard was willing to pay Reid the highest coaching salary in America, $7,000 a year. The hero, it was thought, would return to Harvard and again lead it to glory in its recently constructed stadium, the first steel-reinforced concrete stadium in America. The stage was set for Bill Reid and Harvard and the dynamic year of 1905.

Intercollegiate football had begun thirty-six years before in 1869, when Princeton journeyed to New Brunswick, New Jersey, and played Rutgers. That game, however, might be called a soccer game, for the rules prohibited running with the ball. Soccer, or association football, might have become the dominant game had not Harvard rejected it in favor of its own game of football that involved running with the ball. Harvard adopted rugby football as its favored game after inviting McGill University from Montreal to play two contests in 1874. The first was won by Harvard playing under Harvard rules; the second was a tie using McGill's rugby rules. Yale, which was playing soccer football, wanted to play its social and academic superior from Cambridge and agreed to play rugby, relinquishing soccer in the process. As Harvard and Yale were generally considered the number one and number two leading colleges in America, others began to play rugby football, leaving soccer to be pursued intercollegiately for a later time.[1]

Within two years of Harvard accepting rugby football as its own, football made its mark in elite eastern colleges, and big-time football was born. Harvard, Yale, Princeton, and Columbia formed the student-run Intercollegiate Football Association, and the first championship game was contested on Thanksgiving Day in 1876 between Yale, the victor, and Princeton. Bill Reid was a month old when Princeton won its first championship against Yale in the 1878 Thanksgiving Day game.

Football, by then, was beginning to be transformed from rugby to American football. First, American collegians began to escort the ball carrier and interfere with those attempting to tackle the runner, a violation of rugby rules if the interfering player was in advance of the ball. The result of allowing interference transformed football into a more dangerous game, increasing the need for equipment to protect players from injurious contact. Possibly an even more important transformation was the development of the "scrimmage" from the rugby concept of "scrummage," where a mass of players scrambled for possession of the ball, the "scrum." With the scrimmage came a more clearly defined offense that began each play with a centering (or snap-

---

1. For the early history of college football, see Ronald A. Smith, "From the Burial of Football to the Acceptance of Rugby" and "The Americanization of Rugby Football: Mass Plays, Brutality, and Masculinity," in Smith, *Sports and Freedom: The Rise of Big-Time College Athletics* (New York: Oxford University Press, 1988), 67–98, and Parke H. Davis, *Football: The American Intercollegiate Game* (New York: Charles Scribner's Sons, 1911).

ping back) of the ball. To prevent one team from controlling the ball indefinitely, a system was devised in which a team had to make a number of yards in a set number of snaps (downs) or relinquish the ball. At first it was three downs to make five yards, and, like a gridiron, the field became lined with five-yard markers.

The gridiron game was developing during Bill Reid's youth into a series of mass plays in which a team smashed into the center of the defense to gain the required five yards. An even more dangerous game resulted from an 1887 rule change that allowed tackling runners below their waists. This created a situation in which open-field running was less successful than before. Mass plays reached a climax following the invention of the flying wedge by a Harvard coach in 1892. Lorin Deland developed the flying wedge, adapting to football the military strategy of Napoleon and his first principle on the concentration of force. Football's most ingenious play was first used in the Harvard-Yale game of 1892, when Harvard players formed in two separate groups about twenty-five yards behind the ball. The two groups converged to form a vee, concentrating all their energy at one point of the opponents while the ball was passed over the converging vee to a ball carrier.

The mass-momentum play, as it developed during 1893, was so brutal in nature that it was disallowed the following year. The Rules Committee decided to limit the number of men who could be moving forward at the time the ball was put in play. Nevertheless, as Bill Reid was playing football in his father's preparatory school near San Francisco in the 1890s, football was perceived to be a dangerous and brutal game—and it was. While Reid was becoming a prominent schoolboy athlete at the Belmont School, his father wrote to Walter Camp, head of the football Rules Committee, about his concern for player safety. William Reid, Sr., told Camp that he wished football "might be modified or replaced by one less violent."[2] The question of brutality, however, was not satisfactorily resolved for more than a decade as football moved from one controversy to another.

Football may have had its brutal side, but it was also symbolic of values that Americans held dear. A case in point occurred during the fall of 1897, the year Bill Reid entered Harvard and played on the freshman football team. A University of Georgia football player, Richard Von Gammon, was killed in a game against the University of Virginia. Soon the Georgia legislature passed a bill prohibiting foot-

2. William T. Reid, Sr., Belmont, Calif., to Walter Camp, Yale University, 28 March 1894, Walter Camp Papers, Microfilm Reel 14, Yale University Archives.

ball.[3] Yet, when the mother of the victim deplored the ban and Georgia's governor vetoed the bill, they were reflecting a late-nineteenth-century value stronger than the belief that football was violent. The value was expressed through a belief in the importance of developing virile, manly virtues from the vigorous game of football.

Whether it was from Georgia or from Bill Reid's own Harvard, football became symbolic of not only the manliness of colleges but also of American life. The Harvard-educated Senator Henry Cabot Lodge spoke for the manly game of football at Harvard commencement festivities. "The time given to athletic contests and the injuries incurred on the playing field," he stated in an address to the Harvard class of 1896, "are part of the price which the English-speaking race has paid for being world-conquerors."[4] Even Harvard President Charles W. Eliot, who came to detest football, would write publicly on several occasions that "effeminacy and luxury are even worse evils than brutality."[5]

No one was a greater exponent of the development of manly character than Harvard graduate Theodore Roosevelt at the turn of the century. In the decade before he became president, Roosevelt spoke out for the rough game of football. He said that he "would rather keep the game as it is now, with the brutality, than give it up."[6] Fearing a decline in virility in the emerging urban America, Roosevelt called for the strenuous life, using football as a metaphor: "Hit the line hard: Don't foul and don't shirk, but hit the line hard."[7] To many in Bill Reid's time, the fear of any excess of manliness on the playing field was not nearly as great as the threat of effeminacy in American society. Colleges and universities may have tolerated excesses in football just because college life had for the entire nineteenth century been pictured as effete, impractical, and lacking a strong virile element.[8] If

3. John Hammond Moore, "Football's Ugly Decades, 1893–1913," *Smithsonian Journal of History* 2 (1967): 52–53. At least four other states in 1897 considered banning football: Indiana, Nebraska, Pennsylvania, and Virginia.

4. "Senator Lodge's Speech," *Harvard Graduates' Magazine* 5 (Sept. 1896): 67.

5. Report of the President of Harvard College, 1887–88, 10; 1892–93, 14–15; 1901–2, 4; 1904–5, 46, Harvard University Archives.

6. Theodore Roosevelt, Civil Rights Commission, Washington, D.C., to Walter Camp, Yale University, 11 March 1895, Camp Papers, Box 11, "1895–1906" Folder, Yale University Archives.

7. Theodore Roosevelt, *The Strenuous Life: Essays and Addresses* (New York: Century Co., 1902), 164.

8. See, for instance, Lawrence R. Veysey, *The Emergence of the Modern University* (Chicago: University of Chicago Press, 1965), 178, and Frederick Rudolph, *The American College and University* (New York: Vintage Books, 1962), 317.

they were to prosper and grow, colleges could not appear to lack the manly qualities considered important to the larger American society.

Possibly because football was believed to be the most vigorous of American intercollegiate sports, it became dominant at Harvard and across the country within two decades of its emergence on college campuses. Crowds of forty thousand attended key games in the 1890s. Big-time, commercialized football existed, led by Harvard, Yale, and Princeton. On campuses from Cornell in the East to Chicago in the Midwest and Stanford in the West, the late-nineteenth-century hero was the athlete. As Francis A. Walker, the president of the Massachusetts Institute of Technology, wrote in 1893, no longer was the campus leader noted for "speechmaking, debating, or fine writing"; now acclaim was given to the captain of the crew eight, the baseball nine, and the football eleven.[9]

This was the situation when Bill Reid came to Harvard and participated in his first big game against Yale in 1898. Reid, starting at fullback, scored two touchdowns in the first victory over Yale in nearly a decade. His photograph appeared in the Christmas issue of *Harper's Weekly*, and his aunt wrote to him: "The height of your ambition has been reached. Your prowess has been heralded through the land. Your self-denial and untiring work have received their merited reward."[10] Reid became an instant hero, but his and his father's desire for him to be elected football captain did not materialize.[11] To be a star athlete mattered greatly; to be a superb scholar was of less importance. Shortly after Reid starred in the Yale game during his sophomore year, one of his professors sternly advised that "to keep in good standing in English 22 you must work very regularly henceforth."[12]

Bill Reid's indifference to academics is somewhat surprising. He was neither a weak student nor an outstanding one, but his background would have indicated that he might have been a lover of the scholarly life. His mother, Julia Reed Reid (1845–1918), had graduated from Elmira College after studying Latin and Greek with her father. He was a medical doctor in Jacksonville, Illinois, and had grad-

9. Francis A. Walker, "College Athletics," *Harvard Graduates' Magazine* 2 (Sept. 1893): 3.

10. Hattie Reed, Belmont, Calif., to Bill Reid, Harvard, 20 Dec. 1898, Thomas Stetson Personal Collection. All documents cited hereafter in this chapter are from this collection unless otherwise indicated. *Reed* is the correct spelling.

11. As early as September of Bill Reid's sophomore year, his father wrote to him: "I am inclining more and more to your giving up base-ball—if you are made captain by next year in football." See William T. Reid, Sr., Belmont, Calif., to Bill Reid, Jr., 14 Sept. 1898. Following the victory over Yale, Reid's father stated: "I have no doubt that you would make the best captain." Ibid., 25 Nov. 1898.

12. Barrett Wendell, Harvard professor, to W. T. Reid, Jr., 28 Nov. 1898.

uated from Yale in 1825 and then attended the Berkshire Medical College. Her grandfather had been a Latin scholar, and other ancestors could be traced backed to Governor Bradford and William Brewster of the Plymouth Colony.[13]

Reid's father, William Thomas Reid, Sr. (1842–1922) had been born on a farm near Jacksonville. As a boy he had attended one of the Lincoln-Douglas debates three years before the Civil War. He entered Illinois College but soon enlisted. When he returned from the war, he borrowed money and enrolled at Harvard College, graduating in 1868. He then moved into the field of education, becoming principal of the Newport, Rhode Island, high school. Later he became assistant headmaster of the Boston Latin School, superintendent of the Brookline, Massachusetts, public school, and principal of Boy's High School in San Francisco. He was employed there when William Thomas Reid, Jr., was born in 1878.

The elder Reid was elected president of the University of California, Berkeley, in 1881. He held that position for only four years, and then political pressure from the state forced him to resign. He then founded a preparatory school for boys in Belmont, California, in 1885, which he headed until 1918. The ancestry of William Reid, Sr., could be traced back to Scotland, where James Reid was born in the late 1600s. James, a graduate of the University of Edinburgh, and his wife emigrated to New Hampshire in the early 1720s. Their son, Abraham, fought as a patriot at Bunker Hill in the Revolutionary War before becoming a British Loyalist. One of Abraham's sons, Stephen, moved to a farmstead near Jacksonville, where William Reid, Sr., was born.[14] Education was emphasized on both sides of Bill Reid's family.

Reid's upbringing in Belmont prepared him for athletics and for Harvard College. From an early age, there was evidence that Bill would attend his father's alma mater. He was only ten when his elder sister Julia wrote, "be a good little boy and study hard so that when six or seven years have gone by you will be all ready for Harvard."[15] Three years before, Julia chastised Bill for not being more re-

13. See biographical data in W. T. Reid Papers, vol. 33, "The Cricket" Folder, University of California, Berkeley, Archives, and Aunt Maria Lathrop Reed Thompson, Berkeley, Calif., to Mr. and Mrs. Henry Stetson, Cambridge, Mass., 16 July 1929.

14. W. T. Reid Papers, vol. 3, "Biographical Material" Folder, and "1898–99" Folder, University of California, Berkeley, Archives; also see Stephen H. Reid, West Hempstead, N.Y., to Elizabeth B. Hubert, Greenwich, Conn., 31 Jan. 1951; Elizabeth B. Hubert, Greenwich, Conn., to Bill Reid, Jr., Brookline, Mass., 3 April 1952; Sarah C. Tingle, Eugene, Ore., to Elizabeth B. Hubert, Greenwich, Conn., 24 Nov. 1951; "Memo on Genealogy"; and Julia Reed Reid Bible; *New York Times*, 18 Dec. 1922, 19.

15. Julia F. Reid, Livingston Manner, to Bill Reid, Jr., Belmont, Calif., 12 Aug. 1889.

sponsible to his parents and described how their father had introduced him to sports. "Do you think Papa would have taken the pains to follow the foot-ball practice as carefully as he did," she wrote the seven-year-old, "if he hadn't seen it as an opportunity to bring out and develop certain qualities in you that he wanted to see developed."[16] The game of football eventually became a focus for Bill, who was the captain of the Belmont School's football team as well as its baseball team.

Reid was ready for college in 1897 after traveling east to Harvard the previous year to take examinations in physics, algebra, geometry, French, Greek, and Latin. As a premonition of his future life in athletics, when his anxiety level often reached levels inconsistent with good health, he reported that "after the Greek I was sick to my stomach."[17] His freshman year was not a happy one. He was apparently overwhelmed with pressures both at Harvard and from home to succeed socially. This was difficult to do, for he did not have the same social background as did many of the elite easterners in his class. A classmate remembered that Reid "was chilled and discouraged during his Freshman year by 'eastern exclusiveness' or 'Harvard indifference.'"[18] Yet, he gained much prestige by becoming starting catcher that year on the baseball team.

During his sophomore year, Reid starred in the Yale football game by scoring two touchdowns and helping Harvard defeat Yale, 17-0, for the first time since 1890. Earlier in the season he was not on the first string. His father had lent him some support, having apparently been somewhat of a social outcast himself when he attended Harvard in the 1860s. "I was disappointed not to have had you make the first team," he wrote to Bill that fall, "but not surprised. It turned out just as I told you it was likely to do. It took no great wisdom," he said, "to predict that such considerations would go to Lawrence, Hallowell, & other fellows whose grandfathers & perhaps great-grandfathers were Harvard men."[19] Family pedigree, both Reids agreed, counted for much at Harvard, even on athletic teams.

By his sophomore year, the social elite courted Reid, but he was not receptive to their solicitations. His father advised him to take advantage of social opportunities, knowing that Bill was not prone to do so. "Fellows again and again and again throw their doors open to

16. Julia Reid to Bill Reid, Jr., 3 Dec. 1875.
17. Bill Reid, Jr., Harvard, to Julia Reid, Belmont, Calif., 29 June 1896.
18. Francis C. Ware, Villars sur Ollou, Switzerland, to Christine Reid, Brookline, Mass., 8 Aug. 1902.
19. William Reid, Sr., Belmont, Calif., to Bill Reid, Jr., 23 Oct. 1898.

you, and you don't enter," Bill's father wrote his boy. "It doesn't matter whether you want Lawrence or Hallowell or fellows of their coterie to be your intimate friends or not, when you see that they are going to be the influential men of your class you ought not to reject their overtures to you or treat them with indifference."[20]

Bill's father, who had a strong influence over the first three decades of his son's life, saw the importance of Bill starring in the Yale football game during his sophomore year. A week before that memorable event, his ambitions for Bill's social life were as strong as ever: "To go through Harvard and miss the societies, or the leading ones, is like a woman's going through life without marrying."[21] Following the game, his father described how such fame could affect Bill's social standing. Now, William Reid, Sr., said, "you can choose your friends. You can dictate policy, you can do much to shape college policy & class policy."[22] The success of athletics helped Reid to social success, which meant the possibilities of getting into the best clubs, Alpha Delta Phi, D.K.E., the Institute of 1770, and the Porcellian.

The stress on social distinction may seem rather archaic a century later, but there is no question that it was reality at the time of Bill Reid in such colleges as Harvard, Yale, and Princeton. Reid was somewhat of a paradox. Although he used the club system to his benefit while at Harvard, he also fought the idea of social position ascribed by birth into the eastern families who dominated Harvard life. This was evident when he told his father that John Hallowell would possibly be selected as captain of the football team. "It is an outrage," his father replied, "that a fellow should be given the place with no claim upon it except the prestige of his family & his brothers, and this tendency at Harvard."[23]

Bill's desire to gain distinction through personal performance rather than having it ascribed through heredity was no more clearly shown than before the baseball season of his sophomore year. Reid was upset in February of 1899 that the baseball captain, Percy Haughton (later to became the most famous football coach in Harvard history), had not come to him to discuss the upcoming season and Bill's role in it. Bill had been somewhat miffed by the treatment he had received in baseball the previous year, despite having been the starting catcher in the Yale series. What he wanted his sophomore year was assurance that he would be the starting catcher for the entire year.

20. Ibid., 6 Nov. 1898.
21. Ibid., 16 Nov. 1898.
22. Ibid., 21 Nov. 1898.
23. Ibid., 25 Nov. 1898.

His father criticized Bill for taking the attitude that "if Percy wants me let him come to me and talk matters over" and for "false ambition or pride or vanity." The attitude of "I won't play if I cannot see at the very beginning everything coming my way," his father said, would jeopardize Bill's social position at Harvard.[24] He compared Bill's troubles with his own when he was president of the University of California in the 1880s. When he gave up the presidency, it was a "bitter thing," as was moving to a "less conspicuous place" as founder and headmaster of the Belmont Preparatory School. He thought that Bill should return to baseball without sulking as he had done after his California presidency, even though he had done so with "a good many pangs which I have never before told to any one."[25]

Aspects of Reid's character were being sorely tested—both his opposition to social exclusiveness and his desire to be recognized and break into more prestigious social cliques through his own successes. Haughton and Benjamin Dibblee, the captain of the football team, were concerned enough about the success of their teams to write to Bill's father. They asked for his support, fearing that the elder Reid might withdraw permission for Bill to participate in both sports. While the father was telling his boy to act more responsibly, he was also writing to tell Haughton that if Bill were not treated with respect he might ban his participation.

It was a calculated action, but it worked. Haughton's eight-page letter indicated that some individuals believed that Reid had shown the "worse case of 'Harvard indifference' for a long time" at the same time that he was considered the "best college catcher" among the big-time universities. Haughton was sorry that Bill felt that "I don't want him," but he obviously did. He concluded his letter with the statement that "Bill is needed this spring. He will be practically—yes perfectly—sure of his position."[26]

His position was secured, Reid played, and, of greatest importance, Yale was beaten, but not before an incident in the Princeton game brought Reid a degree of discredit. In a 10-2 defeat, early in the game a Princeton batter interfered with Reid while he was attempting to throw out a runner at second base. Late in the game, with defeat impending, Reid was coming in to score on a hit, and as he did so he ran out of his way to run over the catcher. Reid rationalized that the catcher "on two previous occasions stood in the runner's path, and

24. Ibid., 9 March 1899, 11 March 1899, and 20 March 1899.

25. Ibid., 22 March 1899.

26. Percy D. Haughton, Harvard, to William T. Reid, Sr., Belmont, Calif., 21 March 1899, and Benjamin Dibblee, Harvard, to William T. Reid, Sr., 30 March 1899.

it was high time he was learning that he had no business there."[27] "Muckerish spirit," wrote Caspar Whitney, the leading exponent of amateurism in America, "one of the 'dirtiest' pieces of ball-playing I have seen on a college diamond."[28] Bill's father was mortified that the national press branded Reid a "mucker" and a "dirty player." He wrote to his son: "You don't know how I regret the position you have placed yourself in through interfering with Kafer." He warned Bill that "outside of Harvard you will be seriously blamed and I much fear that your otherwise splendid record is tarnished."[29] Yet, the incident was significantly less important in Bill's life than was the season-ending, best-of-three-games victory that Harvard achieved over Yale. The Harvard baseball conquests over Yale would continue throughout Reid's career.[30]

Reid proceeded into his junior year, emphasizing athletics while doing only passable work academically and searching for the right woman to whom he might eventually become engaged. Having starred in the Yale game the previous year, the fall of 1899 was a frustrating time for Reid. He was hampered both from the standpoint of injuries and from his relationship with captain Ben Dibblee, who did not use him, "shoving him aside" as Reid believed.[31] He strained a tendon in his leg and was used only sparingly, being a substitute in the scoreless tie with Yale.

His mother was probably happy that he played so little, for she believed that Bill should be concentrating on developing higher moral and intellectual qualities. "Your themes demand just as wholesome & healthy body," his mother had written him that year, "as your football." Julia Reid was unusual for her time; she had graduated from college. She constantly reminded Bill that religion and morality were more important in life than athletics. "The spiritual," she said, "I regret to say is left out entirely."[32] At one point, his father agreed that

27. *Philadelphia Press*, 21 May 1899, clipping in William Reid Scrapbook, 1899, Harvard University Archives.

28. Caspar Whitney, "Amateur Sport," *Harper's Weekly*, 20 May 1899, 512.

29. William Reid, Sr., Belmont, Calif., to Bill Reid, Jr., Harvard, 22 May 1899.

30. See Caspar Whitney, "Amateur Sport," *Harper's Weekly*, 15 July 1899, 704, for an account of the game. Whitney praised Reid for his steadying influence and chastised Percy Haughton for two incidents of "muckerish" actions as he captained the team. In four years of participation in the Yale game, Reid batted .233 but made only one error. He captained the team during both his junior and senior years. See John A. Blanchard, ed., *The H Book of Harvard Athletics, 1852–1922* (Cambridge: The Harvard Varsity Club, 1923), 276–78.

31. William T. Reid, Sr., Belmont, Calif., to Bill Reid, Jr., Harvard, 1 Oct. 1900.

32. Julia Reid, Belmont, Calif., to Bill Reid, Jr., Harvard, ca. Jan. 1899.

athletics are "going to cost you the loss of the most valuable thing Harvard has to offer—intellectual & spiritual awakening."[33] Thus both of Reid's parents were concerned that he have a balanced life at Harvard, athletic, social, moral, and intellectual. "The good athlete will not win in life," his father told him, "unless there is something more sound than athletic ability behind it."[34]

Bill, however, had strict personal standards upon which he judged himself and the women he met. He neither drank nor smoked, and there is evidence that his standards of behavior with women were of the highest order. On one occasion he asked his parents whether he would "ever meet a girl who is to have absolute views against drinking."[35] On another, he asked for advice about a young woman who had offered her affections to him. His father's advice was to fight against an unwise engagement although it might gain Bill immediate pleasure: "You have a harder fight in some ways than I had,harder because you are brought more into contact with temptations that are alluring."[36]

In the winter of his junior year, Bill met the young woman who would eventually become his wife. By the fall of 1900, the beginning of Reid's senior year, he had become engaged to Christine Lincoln, the daughter of Albert Lincoln, a successful Boston lawyer. Christine was a nineteen-year-old debutante who chose not to attend college. She lived with her parents just outside Boston in prestigious Brookline and described herself as having "led an easy and useless life, with few if any responsibilities."[37] Christine was strongly attached to her family, which included two younger sisters who were following her into Boston society. She was, according to Bill's father, who liked to judge most things, "a girl beautiful of face, comely of figure, accomplished in manners and attainments—and thoroughly appreciative and womanly."[38] Christine likely embodied all those qualities, but she also acknowledged having "a bad temper and disagreeable disposition" that she had never shown Bill because "no one could be cross

33. William T. Reid, Sr., Belmont, Calif., to Bill Reid, Jr., Harvard, 11 May 1899.

34. Ibid., 21 Nov. 1899.

35. As quoted by his mother, in Julia Reid, Belmont, Calif., to Bill Reid, Harvard, 25 Feb. 1899. See also William T. Reid, Sr., Aguascalientes, Mexico, to Bill Reid, Jr., Harvard, ca. Jan. 1899. A friend had told William Reid that Bill "won't drink, he won't smoke—he won't do anything that interferes with his fine physical development."

36. William T. Reid, Sr., Mexico City, to Bill Reid, Jr., Harvard, 29 Dec. 1899.

37. Christine Lincoln, Berne, Switzerland, to William T. Reid, Sr., Belmont, Calif., 29 Oct. 1900.

38. William T. Reid, Sr., Belmont, Calif., to Bill Reid, Jr., Harvard, 8 Oct. 1900.

with Bill."[39] Bill, who described himself as having an "American eagle nose & elongated Apache face," was not as perfect as Christine viewed him.[40]

Bill made two other important decisions that fall. After much deliberation, and with the blessings of his family, he decided not to play football. There were apparently two reasons for turning down football during his senior year. First, he felt he had not been treated fairly the previous year in being delegated to the position of substitute fullback. Second, he had not fully recovered from a leg injury received in baseball the previous year. Citing the baseball injury, he quietly stepped aside. His father agreed with his decision but knew it to be based primarily upon his being snubbed by the elected leaders of the football team. "Where a man fails to do the right thing he ought to be defeated," his father agreed with Bill. Last year's captain and this year's, "Dibblee and Daly did not do the right thing. Keep out of the eleven [and] let the team pay the penalty."[41] Christine concurred. She wrote from Geneva, Switzerland, "It does seem a pity that men cannot lay aside their dislikes on the field, and realize that they are not individuals only but a team working for the good of the college."[42]

Bill's second decision was to accept his father's offer to become assistant headmaster of the Belmont School after an additional year of study, either at Oxford or by attaining a master's degree from Harvard.[43] The Belmont position would be difficult for two reasons: Christine would be a long way from home, and the job's low pay would make it difficult to support someone used to the ways of well-to-do parents. On both scores the marriage would later be tested.

While Bill decided to give up football, Christine took a seven-month trip to Europe with her family. The official, but unannounced, engagement began with Christine's separation from Bill. This was not particularly unusual, for the well-to-do often tested a potential marriage with a similar separation. She wrote, while en route to England on board the S.S. *New England*, that "our love can stand the test of separation." Yet, almost from the first it was a test for Christine rather than Bill.[44] On the first day of the voyage to Liverpool, Christine

39. Christine Lincoln, Berne, Switzerland, to William T. Reid, Sr., Belmont, Calif., 19 Oct. 1900.

40. Bill Reid, Jr., to Harriet Thompson, Providence, R.I., 9 May 1906.

41. William T. Reid, Sr., Belmont, Calif., to Bill Reid, Jr., Harvard, 8 Oct. 1900 and ca. 2 Oct. 1900.

42. Christine Lincoln, Geneva, Switzerland, to Bill Reid, Jr., Harvard, 12 Oct. 1900.

43. William T. Reid, Sr., Belmont, Calif., to Bill Reid, Jr., Harvard, ca. 2 Oct. 1900.

44. Christine Lincoln to Bill Reid, Jr., Harvard, ca. 12 Sept. 1900. For a discussion

met a young artist whom, she confided in her diary, was "a very interesting fellow."[45] She spent a good deal of time talking with him, and on the second evening, after she told him that she was not engaged, he proposed marriage to her. Christine wrote Bill of the incident, saying that "I like him ever so much . . . but he is not my boy."[46] Meanwhile, Bill's and Christine's correspondence kept their hearts afire. Bill at one point told his fiancée that "It is a big comfort to be decent afterall—even if it does take a struggle. You girls don't realize just what a fellow has to fight against."[47]

At home, Bill struggled and generally succeeded with the social and athletic system at Harvard. Without the participation of Reid, the football season of 1900 succeeded until the final game, when Yale crushed Harvard 28-0. Only once, seventeen years before, had Harvard suffered a more severe defeat. In that one game, after ten straight victories, the season was considered a failure. Reid had escaped the embarrassment. In fact, his star had risen; the newly elected football captain, David Campbell, asked him to be the football coach for 1901 and bring harmony to the team. Bill's father, who intensely disliked the elite who controlled the social and to some extent the athletic life at Harvard, was ecstatic that Bill had been chosen. "It is mighty fine to have you called upon to repair the fortunes of Harvard football," he wrote to his son. "Nothing has come to you in athletics that is such a recognition and such a triumph." Bill was, he said, vindicated in his stand of not playing for Ben Dibblee, who became coach, and captain Charlie Daly.[48]

At nearly the same time, Reid was put up for election for a prestigious marshalship position in the senior class. His competitors for the two marshalships were three football players, Charlie Daly, John Hallowell, and Jim Lawrence. Hallowell and Lawrence were notables from the social set. Reid was neither part of the in group, nor had he

---

of courtship crises, see Karen Lystra, *Searching the Heart: Women, Men, and Romantic Love in Nineteenth-Century America* (New York: Oxford University Press, 1989), 10, 157–58, 190. Lystra observes that "Middle-class courtship usually featured at least one dramatic emotional crisis, precipitated by the nineteenth-century woman as a test of her potential husband's profession of love."

45. Diary of Christine Williams Lincoln, 12 Sept. 1900.

46. Christine Lincoln to Bill Reid, Jr., Harvard, 18 Sept. 1900 and 30 March 1901. Christine eventually told Bill the entire story in a letter from Florence, Italy, six months later.

47. Bill Reid, Jr., Harvard, to Christine Lincoln, Venice, Italy, 19 Dec. 1900.

48. William T. Reid, Sr., Belmont, Calif., to Bill Reid, Jr., Harvard, 13 Dec. 1900. The elder Reid had written on 25 Nov. about Dibblee and Daly: "Confound their petty souls, they got their just desserts. . . . If you had been captain there would have been a different result."

been a football starter since his sophomore year. His father advised before the vote: "Your not having cultivated the Lawrence crowd may defeat you."[49] But it did not hurt him. Lawrence and Reid were elected, respectively, first and second marshals. Reid believed that he had been redeemed socially. "After such a lot of pettiness as entered into this election against me," he wrote his fiancée in Italy, "I feel deeply gratified at having the class stand by me so loyally."[50] After the democratic election, and considering his opposition to elite control of much of Harvard's social life, Reid was ready to bring to Harvard a system of success based upon achievement rather than inheritance.

His personal achievements continued during the spring, socially and athletically. Bill concluded his senior year by being elected into the socially elite Hasty Pudding Club. He also purchased a diamond for Christine after being advised by his father that a one-karat stone was "perhaps a shade small" for someone of Christine's status.[51] When Christine returned from her seven-month European sojourn, Reid was in the midst of captaining the Harvard nine to an 18-2 year. "You musn't let Christine interfere with your first game with Yale," his father had warned.[52] With Reid catching and the future New York Yankee Walter Clarkson pitching, the Crimson swept the Yale series, adding more luster to Reid's career at Harvard by graduation time.

The fall of 1901 saw new challenges for Reid, both athletically and academically. He received a proctorship—a kind of graduate school assistantship—so that he could work on a master of arts degree. There seemed to be no concern that he also was the head coach of the football team. After all, it was common for an alumnus shortly after graduation to be selected coach by the team's captain. Harvard had used graduate coaches since about 1890. While Christine could write on vacation with her family that she could "never think of any man but you," Bill was thinking of picking out the best eleven men for the football team.[53]

The early games of the season went well as usual, with Harvard shutting out eight of the first nine teams it faced. As the University of Pennsylvania game approached, Reid wrote a revealing letter to Christine about his feeling of tension and anxiety—a portent of things to come in his short coaching career: "I am nervous, blue and inca-

49. Ibid., 25 Nov. 1900.

50. Bill Reid, Jr., Harvard, to Christine Lincoln, Venice, Italy, 19 Dec. 1900. The vote was 350 for Lawrence, 346 for Reid, 263 for Daly, and 252 for Hallowell.

51. William T. Reid, Sr., Belmont, Calif., to Bill Reid, Jr., Harvard, 23 April 1901.

52. Ibid., 25 Jan. 1901.

53. Christine Lincoln, Bear Island, to Bill Reid, Jr., Harvard, 24 Sept. 1901.

pable—and it is no fun. . . . I've thoroughly realized how glum I have been, how peevish and irritable, and how sweet, cheerful & comforting you have been. . . . I wish you were here in Philadelphia tonight so that I could love you, kiss you, and hug you—that would ease the strain tremendously—and the grueling that I am undergoing in worry, thought and suspense isn't going to leave much of me behind when its all over."[54] Football coaching affected Reid as it has many other coaches then and since.

Two games later, still undefeated, the Yale team arrived in Cambridge ready to improve on its previous fifteen-game win, three-game loss, and three-game tie record against Harvard in the nineteenth century. Reid, having starred in the most recent Harvard victory in 1898, was in a constant state of agitation, and the crowd of forty thousand that jammed into Soldiers Field did not help his condition. The strain was further exacerbated by a nasty eligibility question that had been festering for several months between Harvard and Yale. Indeed, the question of eligibility had reached a peak the previous spring.

The cases of Edgar Glass and Oliver Cutts in the fall of 1901 were precipitated by the John Spraker incident in track and field when Reid was captaining the Harvard baseball team. Spraker had been taken into Yale's law school without an examination. By Yale's own rules, which barred athletic participation by a student admitted without examination, he would not have been eligible. Yale changed its rules to allow Spraker to participate before the Harvard contest. Harvard challenged Spraker, threatening to break athletic relations between the two schools if he participated.[55] Yale refused to withdraw Spraker, and Yale went on to defeat Harvard as Spraker captured the high jump.

The incident was not forgotten when Harvard discovered that Yale's Edgar Glass was technically ineligible the next fall. Glass had previously attended Syracuse University in 1898, where he had flunked out after his first year. He had, however, stayed around long enough to play in one football game the next fall against Army.[56] Glass then went to Mercersburg Academy in Pennsylvania for two years,

54. Bill Reid, Jr., Philadelphia, to Christine Lincoln, Brookline, Mass., 8 Nov. 1901.

55. Ira N. Hollis, Harvard Athletic Committee chair, to President Charles W. Eliot, Harvard, 23 Jan. 1902, Eliot Papers, Box 143, "Hollis" Folder, Harvard University Archives; *New York Times*, 9 May 1901, 7 and 12 May 1901, 6. Spraker was one of thirteen in his 1903 law class of thirty-nine who did not graduate. See *Alumni Directory of Yale University* (New Haven: Privately printed, 1948).

56. Alfred L. Ripley, Andover, Mass., to Walter Camp, Yale, 10 Nov. 1901, and Harold Stone, Syracuse attorney, to Clive, 13 Dec. 1901, Walter Camp Papers, Box 22, "Cutts" Folder, Yale University Archives.

playing football and doing well academically.[57] At age twenty-two, he entered Yale University and became a starting lineman during his freshman year. Yale's eligibility rule stated that any athlete who had attended another university must be enrolled at Yale for a year before participation. Yale claimed that it had upheld the spirit of the rule, for Glass was not coming directly from another university. Yet, it was technically violating the letter of the rule. After a bitter fight, Captain Charles Gould agreed not to play Glass, the future all-American.

Yale, angered, retaliated by questioning Oliver Cutts, one of Harvard's best linemen. Cutts was twenty-eight, six years older than coach Bill Reid. He had already attended Bates College, playing football there for three years. Following graduation, he taught mathematics and coached football and track at the Haverford College Preparatory School for four years. Cutts then chose to attend the Harvard Law School, and in his second year, the two-hundred-pound tackle decided to play football. Graduate participation in intercollegiate athletics was then a common occurrence. Yale claimed that Cutts had coached for pay at the Haverford Preparatory School. The Harvard Athletic Committee, with Reid attending, took up the question and determined that Cutts had coached football and track but was not paid for those activities. On the day of the Yale game, he was declared eligible.[58] Cutts played outstandingly. Yale lost.

Yale, unused to losing at anything, would not accept the result and dug deeper into Cutts's background after the season. They uncovered a check from Irving Fisher for $15 made out to Oliver Cutts for teaching twenty half-hour lessons in boxing while at Haverford.[59] Harvard apologized but did not offer to forfeit any of its twelve straight victories under the leadership of Bill Reid and captain David Campbell. Reid had escaped undefeated in his first season of coaching football. Several observations of Reid, however, would forecast future athletic involvement at Harvard. One of his players remarked somewhat later, "I tell you, there's no fun playing football under Reid."[60] Reid was a serious coach, but he was also a nervous wreck, and that would haunt him in years to come.

57. William M. Irvine, president, Mercersburg Academy, to Walter Camp, 17 Jan. 1902, Walter Camp Papers, Box 22, "Cutts" Folder, Yale University Archives.

58. Harvard Athletic Committee Minutes, 22 and 23 Nov. 1901, Harvard University Archives.

59. Julian Curtis, secretary of A. G. Spalding & Brothers, New York, to Walter Camp, 10 Dec. 1901, Walter Camp Papers, Box 11, Folder 313, and copy of check from Irving Fisher, 23 May 1899, Walter Camp Papers, Box 22, "Cutts" Folder, Yale University Archives.

60. *Boston Globe*, 24 Feb. 1905, 2.

By spring, Reid had decided to accept his father's offer and become assistant headmaster at the Belmont School in California. First, however, he would help coach the Harvard baseball team, complete his master's degree, get married, and take a half-year honeymoon to Europe. Although his graduate program did not seem to play a dominant part of his life, he did report at one point that he was doing "nothing but books, notes, and study."[61]

Baseball, nevertheless, was the love of his life away from Christine. While coaching the Harvard team in 1902, Reid took the team south to play against the Naval Academy in Annapolis, Maryland. Harvard's starting team included an African American, which was an unusual situation at the turn of the century. The racist Jim Crow policies and attitudes were at their apex in America when W. Clarence Matthews, a graduate of Andover Preparatory School, attended Harvard.[62] As a black, he was an anomaly there and, along with a few other blacks, in college sport. Only a few months before Matthews crossed the Mason-Dixon line to play in the South, the president of the College of William and Mary in Virginia had to appear at a special meeting of his governing board. There he was asked to explain why he would allow his daughter to attend Wellesley College in Massachusetts when the daughter of Booker T. Washington attended the same institution.[63] Matthews met with similar prejudice. "Matthews has created quite a stir down here," Reid wrote to his fiancée. "It certainly is an eye-opener to the Southerners to see a colored man on a team from aristocratic Harvard." Reid believed that if Matthews played, the Naval Academy team would "try to kill him if possible."[64] Matthews was withheld from the game with Navy, but he returned to star in the final game against Yale to win the important series. However, a Yale student later wrote, "Yale, however, has not found it necessary to play professionals such as Cutts—or negroes, in order to win."[65]

With the season over and his degree granted, Reid married the debutante from Brookline, Christine Williams Lincoln, on July 2, 1902.

61. Bill Reid, Jr., Harvard, to Christine Lincoln, 8 June 1902.

62. See, for instance, C. Vance Woodward, *The Strange Career of Jim Crow* (New York: Oxford University Press, 1955), 75, 82, and August Meier and Elliott M. Rudwick, *From Plantation to Ghetto* (New York: Hill and Wang, 1963), 163–64.

63. College of William and Mary Board of Visitors Minutes, 11 Dec. 1901, College of William and Mary.

64. Bill Reid, Jr., Annapolis, to Christine Lincoln, Brookline, Mass., 15 April 1902.

65. Yale student, '08, letter to the Editor, *New York Sun*, 1 Dec. 1905, in George B. Adams Collection, Box 7, Folder 35, Yale University Archives.

They left shortly thereafter for a wedding trip to Europe, but not likely before she became pregnant. It may have happened that first night, for they apparently took the advice of Bill's father to his prospective daughter-in-law when he wrote two months before their wedding that "when you are both strong & fresh & impulsive . . . let the little one come & be welcome at any time."[66] As Bill remembered his first night with Christine, "I love to think of our first night—and I often think of how darling you were to me—to give me all I cared get."[67]

Almost as soon as she knew she was pregnant, Christine wrote from Europe to tell both sets of parents of the coming event. Her closeness to her parents was apparent in her mother's response: "I shall want you and Will with me until after the baby comes."[68] This closeness and the distance of California from the East Coast would eventually lead to problems in the new Reid family. Bill's parents were delighted with the approaching child. In particular, his father looked forward to grandchildren. He wrote jokingly to Christine: "Oh those tantalizing underclothes that you showed me. I warned you of their danger. . . . They simply made the tinder a little more inflammable." And to Bill he added, "This is altogether more serious than coaching a football team isn't it?"[69] It probably was not for Bill.

Parenthood came earlier than expected, and problems were caused by Bill's new $1,200 a year position as assistant headmaster and the fact that Christine lived three thousand miles from her family and friends. The predicted April 1903 arrival date became St. Patrick's Day. William Reid, III, became "Patrick" from that date forward. By that time Bill and Christine had returned from their somewhat shortened honeymoon and taken the train to their new home in Belmont. Unfortunately, they had to live with the elder Reids before their own house could be built. As Christine's father foresaw: "No house is big enough for two families." Christine complained of her mother-in-law's interference, openly resented it, and longed for her former summer home in Cohasset and friends in the East.[70]

While Christine and the baby made trips east to visit family and friends, Bill kept in contact with Harvard and the progress of its ath-

66. William Reid, Sr., Belmont, Calif., to Christine Lincoln, 17 April 1902.

67. Bill Reid, Jr., Belmont, Calif., to Christine Reid, Brookline, Mass., 24 March 1907.

68. Mrs. Albert Lincoln, Brookline, Mass., to Christine Reid, Baden-Baden, Germany, 7 Sept. 1902.

69. William Reid, Sr., Belmont, Calif., to Christine Reid, Interlaken, Switzerland, 14 Sept. 1902.

70. Albert Lincoln, Cohasset, Mass., to Christine Reid, Belmont, Calif., 5 Oct. 1903, and Albert Lincoln, Boston, to Christine Reid, Belmont, Calif., 17 Nov. 1903.

letic teams. In 1903, when the Harvard crew lost for the fourth straight time to Yale, he told his father that he was sure that he could "pick & manage a winning crew" if he were asked to coach it. He reported that Harvard had beaten Yale in baseball again as Matthews "the colored boy—who is so cordially disliked at Yale" hit a triple and a home run.[71] He learned from his sister-in-law, who attended the Carlisle Indian-Harvard football game, of coach "Pop" Warner's famous hidden-ball trick in which the ball was inserted up the back of the jersey of the Carlisle runner. With that play, Carlisle nearly beat Harvard.[72]

Shortly after a defeat by Yale that year, Reid received a letter from Ira Hollis, the former chair of the Harvard Athletic Committee, who wished that Reid had been in Cambridge during the football season to help give the team "a celestial fire of some kind" in the game against Yale.[73] Reid lost no interest in his alma mater even as he helped run his father's school, nor did Harvard lose interest in him. On the same day that one of his old professors and the former head of the Harvard Athletic Committee sent greetings, Dan Hurley, the new football captain, asked Reid if he would coach the 1904 football team.[74] Hurley hoped that the Harvard Athletic Committee would vote to pay Reid $3,000 to coach the team. At the time there was a great controversy at Harvard about whether head coaches should be paid. Many elite alumni believed that sport should be amateur, which meant that the coaches should be amateur. In reality, this meant that former Harvard graduates should do the coaching and do it gratis, as Reid had done in 1901. The Athletic Committee voted no to the Harvard Football Graduate Association's request to pay Reid to coach, squelching any possibility of Reid coming back to Harvard in 1904.[75] Reid likely would have accepted a paid offer, for he set the condition that he would be given "final authority with the captain in deciding disputed points of policy" if he came to Harvard.[76]

The conditions changed later that year following the third straight shutout loss to Yale. Although Harvard might have desired unpaid

71. Bill Reid, Jr., Belmont, Calif., to William Reid, Sr., Lake Tahoe, Calif., 26 June 1903.

72. Louise Lincoln, Brookline, Mass., to Christine Reid, Belmont, Calif., 1 Nov. 1903.

73. Ira N. Hollis, Harvard, to Bill Reid, Jr., Belmont, Calif., 8 Jan. 1904.

74. Daniel J. Hurley, Harvard, to Bill Reid, Jr., Belmont, Calif., 4 Jan. 1904.

75. Harvard Athletic Committee Minutes, 6 Jan. 1904, Harvard University Archives.

76. Bill Reid, Jr., Belmont, Calif., to W. Cameron Forbes, Boston and former Harvard head football coach, 2 Jan. 1904, William T. Reid, Jr., Papers, "1904" Folder, Harvard University Archives.

head coaches, they produced few victories over Yale. Even then, the situation was hypocritical; for several years Harvard had paid $500 a year to an assistant football coach, William Lewis, and the Athletic Committee voted to pay him $1,000 in 1904.[77] There also was plenty of precedent at Harvard for paying head coaches. For a generation, Harvard's crew and baseball coaches had been paid, and those paid to coach baseball had often been major league stars from the Boston Red Stockings.

Bill Reid was ready for the challenge to go east to again coach the Harvard football team and to bring Christine back to her own family. He would easily go East, for Christine spent three months visiting her family during the spring and summer of 1904. After Christine had left for Massachusetts in May, he wrote to her that he "admired the 'stuff' you have shown in putting up with things here." Bill missed her and told her: "This is Sunday afternoon and the bed looks so comfortable. . . . Your being eager for it makes it simply unspeakably delicious to me."[78] Knowing that Christine was "about ready to throw California over—& to live in the East" made it easier to make the move.[79] Believing that her passion lay close to the surface added to his desire to be with her. While at her parents' summer home in Cohasset for a month, she wrote to him, "I cannot tell you how much I am looking to our first night together." She added that "when I get thinking of the delights in store I can hardly wait for the time to come."[80] But going west to be with Bill was to be "a terrible wrench leaving all the family again. . . . I wish I could have my husband and my family too."[81] It would not be long.

Following a 12-0 loss to Yale, Harvard football authorities made overtures to Reid to coach in 1905. He was invited to come East in December to discuss the situation. What Reid wanted was to have supreme authority and an agreement to coach more than one year.[82] Nevertheless, he had Christine and his family to think about. Earlier in the month, their second child, Edith, had been born. To leave his wife in order to check on the football situation nearly tore him apart. "Leaving you was about the hardest thing I've ever done," he wrote

77. Harvard Athletic Committee Minutes, 10 Jan. 1901, 7 May 1902, 21 Dec. 1903, 13 June, 8 October, and 1 Nov. 1904, Harvard University Archives.

78. Bill Reid, Jr., Belmont, Calif., to Christine Reid, Brookline, Mass., 22 May 1904.

79. Ibid., 29 May 1904.

80. Christine Reid, Cohasset, Mass., to Bill Reid, Jr., Belmont, Calif., 28 June 1904.

81. Ibid., 3 July 1904.

82. *Boston Globe*, 22 Dec. 1904, 8.

to Christine, "I feel like a deserter."[83] It was, however, only for about three weeks. The visit east convinced Reid to try again to lead Harvard to success in beating Yale.

This time Bill went east while Christine stayed with the children for a short while in the West. He arrived at Harvard in March 1905, ready to conduct spring football practice. Bill decided then to keep notes, producing a diary that he and future coaches could use to turn out victories over Yale. From a reading of Reid's diary, it would appear that Bill paid no attention to Christine or to his children. Nevertheless, from the letters between Bill and Christine during the few weeks before she arrived from Belmont, it was clear that their love was strong and that their marriage meant much to them. Shortly before Christine left for the East to be with Bill, she wrote: "I want you to know that I love you to the outside, outside limit, and I am only too anxious to have all you can give. You dearie boy!"[84] Bill would find time for that, but football was to be the principal thing in his life until the Yale game was played and Harvard might be victorious again. The stress of the campaign would drop Bill from about 175 pounds to less than 160 pounds. Beating Yale was serious, nerve-racking business.

Reid's diary, more than any other available source, provides an intimate view of turn-of-the-century, intercollegiate athletics. As part of Bill Reid's attempt to produce a winner, the diary becomes a window into both the uplifting and seamy side of big-time football. Reid almost certainly never expected that his diary would become a public document. Later in life, however, he presented it to the Harvard University Archives. It was there, in 1984, while researching the football crisis of 1905–6, that I made what I almost immediately knew was a fortuitous sport discovery. After reading the diary, I saw the value of publishing it in its entirety. I also came to believe that parts of it would make an interesting saga—good enough to be immortalized on film. That, however, is another story.

83. Bill Reid, Jr., on railroad beyond Reno, Nev., to Christine Reid, Belmont, Calif., 27 Dec. 1904.
84. Christine Reid, Belmont, Calif., to Bill Reid, Jr., Brookline, Mass., 2 April 1905.

Coaching Force and Organization, Harvard University, 1905

Head coach:	W. T. Reid, Jr.
End coaches:	Edward Bowditch (all season)
	David Campbell (from Penn game on)
	Frank Hallowell (a few days)
Tackle coaches:	B. G. Waters (all season)
	Malcolm Donald (a few days)
Guard coaches:	W. H. Lewis (all season, in charge)
	A. Marshall (all season)
Center coach:	W. H. Lewis (all season)
	C. Sargent (a few days)
Quarterback coach:	Leo J. Daly (all season)
Back coaches:	J. W. Dunlop (all season)
	W. T. Reid, Jr. (all season)
Defense coach:	W. H. Lewis (all season)
Kicking coach:	R. P. Kernan (all season)
	P. D. Haughton (last week and a half)
Offense committee:	J. W. Dunlop (all season)
	W. H. Lewis (all season)
	W. T. Reid, Jr. (all season)
Regular coaching staff:	W. T. Reid, Jr. (head coach)
	Edward Bowditch (ends)
	B. G. Waters (tackles)
	W. H. Lewis (guards and center)
	Leo J. Daly (quarterbacks)
	J. W. Dunlop (backs)
	R. P. Kernan (kickers)
	R. W. P. Brown (second eleven)
Medical attendance:	Dr. E. H. Nichols

Assistant: Clarence Smith
Trainer: J. W. McMasters
Second eleven coach: R. W. P. Brown
Freshman coach: Ted Meier (later relieved by J. W.
                                   McDonald)
Captain: Dan J. Hurley
Manager: Abe Goodhue
Assistant manager: J. Reynolds
Second assistant: P. E. Dutcher

The Preliminary Season

Inasmuch as the purpose in putting down the information which follows is that of giving to those who succeed me in this work every possible advantage of the experience which I have gained, I am going to make the story of the preliminary season more of a summary than a diary. I have taken notes during the entire spring season with this in view, and what follows is a compact account of what was accomplished. It must be remembered, in going over this work, that what to a reader may seem to be a matter very easily accomplished and in a very short time, took, in reality, a much greater time. This is due chiefly to the fact that it is very difficult to get an enthusiastic response from the various coaches and players in the spring when the actual playing season is so far off; the tendency is to keep putting off the work, with the result that it takes three or four times the length of time really needed to get a thing done. My first recommendation, then, to any coach is that if he has anything which needs to be done in the spring, he should begin on it as early as possible, feeling perfectly certain that he will not get it done any sooner than he had originally planned.

The real preliminary work began before I came east, and had to do in that case chiefly with setting movement on foot to keep the various candidates off probation at the mid-year examinations; the settling of the schedule, and the attempt at getting Harry LaMoyne[1] back to college. Realizing when I was on here in December, and before my

1. The correct spelling is *LeMoyne*. LeMoyne played only in 1903, his freshman year, and received a letter in football at left guard. He did all the punting and averaged more than seventy yards against Army. LeMoyne was also an outstanding swimmer and trackman. He set American swimming records from twenty-five to three hundred yards before entering Harvard. His high school sixteen-pound shotput of 45 feet, 9.5 inches set an American record. He is in the Swimming Hall of Fame in Ft. Lauderdale, Florida. See the *Boston Traveler*, 23 Nov. 1908. Most information on Harvard athletes has been obtained from John A. Blanchard, ed., *The H Book of Harvard Athletics, 1852–1922* (Cambridge: The Harvard Varsity Club, 1923).

appointment, that whoever was to be coach ought to be at work on the scholarship part of the responsibility, I determined to start at it, even though I finally failed to come, in order that whoever might otherwise come should not be put at a great disadvantage. I therefore wrote and telegraphed on to have the records of the various men looked up and reported to me, and the needy men secured satisfactory tutoring. Postal cards were sent out by the management notifying each fellow to get to work and to keep at it. This was no way to go about it, as any fellow who has not gumption enough to do the work for himself is certainly not going to make the effort he should as a result of receiving a circular postal card. What ought to be done, and it is the only effective way, is to call up each individual man for a conference; at this time his standing should be found out also his weaknesses. Then, before he gets out of the office he should be told what to do and then he should be followed up to see that he does it. The circular card warning[,] then [,] which was sent out is entirely unsatisfactory because it is not personal or forceful. I did not find out that this was all that had been done until I reached Boston, supposing from the reports I had that very active measures had been taken, and depending largely upon my own efforts when I reached here. I might add in this connection that when I came on to look over the ground in December I had called a meeting of 35 of the most prominent candidates and told them that their first duty to the football team of next fall was to get their work up. I also told each man what his especial weakness was, having a report in my hand from the office, and asking him whether he was willing to get to work. All of them said they were, and I had a promise from each of them that he would stop cutting [classes], which is one of the worst arguments against a man who is not getting good marks. Most any professor will pass any man in the course who is regular in his attendance who gets in his reports or theses, or whatever else it may be, on time, and who shows anything like a decent interest in his work.

We now come to the matter of the schedule; I insisted on being allowed to settle the matter of schedule as I saw fit, because I felt that in 1904 the schedule was so poorly arranged as to make the proper development of the team almost impossible.

Here is the schedule as it was:

October 1	Williams	at Cambridge
October 5	Bowdoin	at Cambridge
October 8	U. of Maine	at Cambridge
October 12	Bates	at Cambridge

October 15	West Point	at West Point
October 22	Carlisle	at Cambridge
October 29	U. of Pennsylvania	at Cambridge
November 5	Dartmouth	at Cambridge
November 12	Holy Cross	at Cambridge
November 19	Yale	at New Haven

I did not believe in that schedule for these reasons: First, the Penn game came one month only after the very first game was played, this it seems to me was absurd, especially since Penn has been constantly improving in her football and has shown that she is now to be carefully reckoned with.

Second, the Penn game, which is really the next game to Yale in importance, was shelved in order to admit Dartmouth to Penn's position. It seems to me that the order should be Yale, then Penn then anyone else; not Yale then Dartmouth then Penn.

Third, the Penn game came a month before the Yale game, making it absolutely impossible for the team to be in anything like its proper form for Penn and still be of any use against Yale. Yale plays Princeton a week before Harvard, thus enabling her to reach top notch just in time for both games. I should favor this plan too, had we men like Mike Murphy [the Yale trainer] to whom we could feel safe in entrusting the condition of the men. As it is, we have no such man, so that I do not dare as yet to play Penn less than two weeks before we play Yale.

It is my opinion though, that we should arrange the Penn game in the same week as the Yale game as soon as such a thing is possible. Walter Camp, in replying to a criticism b[y] Deland[2] that Yale was taking awful risks in playing Princeton the week before Harvard said—"Talk about risks, why Yale would no more think of attempting to play Princeton two weeks before Harvard than she would fly. To be sure there is some risk in playing Princeton and Harvard in the same week, and yet the risk isn't anything like as Great." It is Yale's policy to develop her team solely for the week of the Harvard and

2. Camp (1859–1925) is often called the father of American football, for he was instrumental as a Yale player on the Football Rules Committee in changing rugby football rules into American football in the early 1880s. See "Walter Camp, Father of American Football," in Ronald A. Smith, *Sports and Freedom: The Rise of Big-Time College Athletics* (New York: Oxford University Press, 1988), 83–88. Lorin F. Deland was an advisor to a number of Harvard football teams and inventor in 1892 of the "flying wedge" formation. In 1896, Deland coauthored *Football*, a book on technique, with Camp of Yale.

Princeton games. The Harvard game is given precedence in Yale minds over the Princeton game, not so much because Yale considers the Harvard team a harder one to beat than Princeton, but rather because she feels that owing to Harvard's greater prominence as a University, there is more credit in winning that game. The Princeton game, then, shows a Yale team at top notch in condition with her offense and defense game practically complete and with the team lacking only in the finesse and experience to be gained from the Princeton game. When the Princeton game is over all that Yale plans to do is to get her men into playing shape again and to touch up all the little imperfections which have come to light.

With the Penn game two weeks ahead it is not possible for the Harvard team to be at top notch and continue so until the Yale game. Therefore, it is necessary for Harvard, if she plays Penn, to present herself for the Penn game in good physical shape, but still far from perfect in offense and defense. Of course in the days of the "Guards back"[3] play it was customary to work up a special defense for the Penn plays, and Penn was, therefore, put two weeks before the Yale game in order that between the Penn and Yale games the team might change from the Penn defense to the Yale defense. Now, however, that Penn has discarded the "guards back" play and has taken up a game very much like that of Harvard and Yale, there is little need of a preliminary period to study up a special defense for Penn and therefore, it seems to me little need of playing Penn two weeks before Yale. Therefore, if it were not a matter of the physical care of the men, I should be in favor of playing Penn a week before Yale.

Fourth, there were only ten games on the schedule. This brought West Point, a hard game, at the end of two weeks and with no semi-hard game as a preparation. It was my idea that we should play some team like Amherst just previous by a week to West Point, thus filling in between the easy and hard games with a moderately hard game. Taken as a whole last year's schedule brought right on top of the earliest preliminary games the hard games with a little breathing space between them, and the Penn and Yale games. With these observances, I submitted the following schedule as the one I should suggest:

Sat., Sept. 30,	Williams	at Cambridge
Wed., Oct. 4,	Bowdoin	
Sat., 7,	Univ. of Me.	

3. The "guards back" formation was evidently invented by Penn's football coach George Woodruff in 1894. It consisted of the two guards lined up behind one of the

Wed.,	11,	Bates	
Sat.,	14,	Amherst	
Wed.,	18,	Wesleyan	
Sat.,	21	West Point	at West Point
Sat.,	28	Brown	at Cambridge
Sat., Nov.	4	Indians[4]	
Sat.,	11	Univ. of Penn	at Philadelphia
Sat.,	18	Dartmouth	at Cambridge
Sat.,	25	Yale	

In this proposed schedule there are twelve games. This would give us a better chance to do what little experimenting we might have to do as a result of my having been out of football for four years, also a chance to get plenty of time on the fundamentals. This could not be done last year because the hard games came so suddenly.

I figure that we cannot possibly weed out our squad down to a good working basis in less than two weeks of trial games and perhaps not even in that time, and therefore I have put down the four first games just as they were last year.

The first change comes in just after these four games. Instead of working in West Point here I propose that we should play some pretty hard game immediately after our four easy games. This would give us one more game for shifting, if we needed it, while [if] we didn't, it would give us a very good game for the first tussle for the first team which we might make a guess at about that time. I put Amherst down for this game. I am not sure but that they may be too strong (which I afterwards found out to be the case). This I should want to find out, but if we could get a good team there and then make the Varsity win the game on its fighting spirit, it would be of great benefit to the mental development of the men; a sort of game that they would have to fight for but which they could win if they did fight.

After Amherst I should put in an easy team on Wednesday, a team that the second [team] could almost beat. Such a team would not make it necessary for us to play all of our best men, if some needed a rest, and yet would give the men a chance to shake a little more together before they tackle West Point the following Saturday.

This gradual working up to the West Point game is warranted I

---

ends, facing the line at right angles. The object was to gain a blocking advantage. Sometimes the guards were lined up in front of one of the half backs. See Tom Perrin, *Football: A College History* (Jefferson: McFarland, 1987), 23.

4. The Carlisle Indian School in Carlisle, Pennsylvania, was where Jim Thorpe would become a star by the end of the decade.

believe by the fact that West Point has beaten Yale twice and tied her once, has beaten Princeton and Penn, and twice all but beaten us. Yale plays them a little later and is thus able to get into a little better form herself—this I think is compensated for in our earlier date by the fact that we, being the first of the big four to play them, are likely to get some advantage from whatever nervousness the Cadets may feel—while after they play one or two other games of the big four they gain strength, confidence and experience.

After the West Point game the midweek games cease. On the first succeeding Saturday I have Brown in parenthesis. What I think we need there is a pretty good team, just such a one as Brown, if she isn't nowadays too strong, a thing I should want to feel sure about before I settled on the date.

Then one week before Penn, and between Penn and Yale, I have Dartmouth also in parenthesis. We want a team there which we can beat 18 or 24 to 0 so that if we need to we can play substitutes in case the legs of any of our men are injured in the Penn game. I question very much whether or not we can stand Dartmouth there, but I want to play her there if possible, and give her a most unmerciful whaling. However, we cannot let our pride get ahead of our judgment, and if Dartmouth seems too strong we will have to cut her out entirely. Certainly we cannot play her just before Penn, nor two weeks before; I would rather make the mistake of playing a too easy game between Penn and Yale than to play a too hard one. In all this I have only the minds of others to guide me in making up my mind as to the strength of our own team, as well as to the strength of our opponents. Having been out of football for three years puts me clear out of the running.

I understand Dartmouth loses eight men next year; if so, it seems though we might put her in at the place I have chosen, but it is worth while talking a good deal about. We don't want to come to the Dartmouth game with a lot of half done up players after the Penn game and find that unless we play our best we will be beaten, and that if we do play our best we are likely to re-injure our men and then lose our game to Yale. That one game in there is vital, and if we cannot feel absolutely sure of Dartmouth then I would rather let her go and play Holy Cross.

To my mind we must have Yale on the 25th of November, Penn on the 11th of November and West Point on the 21st of Oct.; those are the king-pin dates—once they are settled, the others will fall in easily. So much for the work on the schedule before I reached Boston.

I forgot to say in this connection that, anticipating trouble with the schedule, I spent several days when I was east in December getting as much information with regard to Penn, Dartmouth, Yale, West Point and Brown as possible. Just how we finally settled on the schedule will appear a little later.

The other case of very early preliminary work was the starting on my part of efforts to get Harry LaMoyne back to college. From all that I can hear of him he is one of the greatest natural athletes that Harvard has ever had. He is a good kicker, a splendid guard, a good fighter, with good weight, and yet active. He left college because of poor work in his studies, coupled with the remorse which he felt at having two out of three of his room mates die in his freshman year. In my mind it was gross negligence somewhere in allowing him ever to get away. He ought now to be in college, a three year veteran and one of the strongest points on the team. When I first heard about him I determined that as a onetime Harvard man I should try if possible to get him to return, and finally located him on a sheep ranch at Hagerman, Idaho.[5] It was my purpose to stop off and see him on the way East, if he were eligible, and I telegraphed on to find out what his standing was. I got word from [Abe] Goodhue, the Varsity manager, stating that LaMoyne was not eligible and could not return, and so I made no stop-over. Later on I found out that if he were to do a certain amount of work he could return and would be entirely eligible. I mention this simply to show how necessary it is for us to get absolutely dependable men as Managers, and that we should also impress them with the necessity of sparing no pains whatever in getting at the absolute facts in everything they are asked to investigate.

I reached Boston on March 14th, and after I had had breakfast and gotten comfortably unpacked at my headquarters at Brookline, I went over to see Capt. [Dan] Hurley, and later on in the evening to see Dr. [Edward H.] Nichols.[6] As it was getting late in the season, I felt under great pressure in closing up the schedule, and I therefore set about to find all I could about the questionable teams on my proposed schedule. I had quite a long talk with [Edward N.] Robinson, the coach of the Brown team, from whom I received much information as to Dartmouth prospects, and with [Fred E.] Jennings, a former Dartmouth player, and later on a Harvard law school man. Robinson

5. Hagerman is in southern Idaho between Twin Falls and Boise.

6. Nichols acted as team physician, being paid $1,500. He had played four years on the Harvard baseball team (1883–86) and had coached the Harvard baseball team in the early 1900s, being proficient as a drillmaster. He was coach when Reid was the baseball team's captain in 1901. Following the 1905 football season, he coauthored a damning article on football injuries: "The Physical Aspect of American Football," *Boston Medical and Surgical Journal*, 4 Jan. 1906, 1–8.

told me that Dartmouth would lose eight of her last year's team, and that the loss would comprise most of the veterans who had done so much to strengthen the team during the past two seasons. He also told me that so far as Dartmouth was concerned, he did not see where she was going to get the material that would make her anything like as strong as the team she had been having. Jennings told me that Dartmouth was not in the same class with Harvard, and that the Dartmouth successes of the last two years had been due more to the fact that Dartmouth had had for four years the same team, and that it was composed of [. . .] exceptional individual[s]. He said that since Dartmouth beat us in 1903 she had been gradually losing her strength and that in the coming year he looked for her to reach her former position. I had further talks with Joe Pendleton, of Wright and Ditson's office, who does the outfitting for Dartmouth, and he knows pretty much all that is going on up there, and he confirmed in a large measure the statements made by Robinson and Jennings. The one great and uncertain element in all this is the fact that Dartmouth alumni are about as loyal as any body of graduates in the country, and being many of them up country men, are quite ready to violate amateur rules for the sake of seeing Dartmouth strong on the field. This willingness to recruit their teams makes the strength of their team uncertain, and decidedly problematical, although I feel that even if a great many good men go up there, they cannot hope to get in one year a team of experience and thorough training, and therefore we ought to be able to beat them. Then too, it seems to me that the 1903 Dartmouth team which was the strongest one they have ever had, was just about as much a product of [Walter] McCormick, the former Dartmouth coach, who had just left as it was of [H. H. Fred Gorham] Fulsome,[7] who has handled the team since then. It is said that McCormick was especially strong in giving the team fundamental possibilities, but not so strong in giving them final possibilities, and that Fulsome was strong in just the points where McCormick was weak, and that the combination was therefore an exceptionally good one. After verifying the loss of the eight players as reported in the Amherst papers, I took the matter of the Dartmouth game to [William H.] Lewis, [Bertram G.] Waters, and [Malcolm] Donald,[8] and they agreed that under the cir-

7. McCormick was actually Walter McCornack, the coach prior to the individual Reid called Fulsome. Fulsome was actually Fred Gorham Folsom, commonly called H. H. Folsom, who had been a tackle on the 1892 Dartmouth football team. See John H. Bartlett, *Dartmouth Athletics* (Concord: Republican Press Association, 1893), 213.

8. All of these men were former players who helped Reid coach in 1905. Lewis, a lawyer, played for Harvard in 1892 and 1893 as a Law School student after graduat-

cumstances it would be wise to play them. If we can defeat them this next year I question whether it won't be wise to put them away back in the schedule where they will be unable to develop their team, with the sole purpose of beating us, irrespective of what happens to the rest of their schedule. During the last two years they have laid for Harvard neglecting any special attention to Brown or Amherst or her other legitimate rivals. Next year Brown is going to make an even better showing than she did last year, and I think that Dartmouth will therefore have to hold back her development a little bit if she really wants to beat Brown. As I have not seen a Dartmouth team play for four years, much of what I say is in the nature of speculation, but it ought to be pretty safe, since Waters, Lewis and Donald who have seen the games recommend it.

Having settled the Dartmouth game, I set about closing up the Brown date. In doing this I looked up the condition of the Brown team and found that they lose several men, and that there is no great prospect ahead of any new men on the Brown team, like the Dartmouth, and it is likely that Dartmouth will make every effort to get good men all over the country. There is one fact about the canvassing which is being done by the smaller colleges for players, and that is that with so many in the field the best men are pretty certain to be pretty well divided up. I got this information about the Brown team from Dartmouth men and also a good deal from Robinson, the Brown coach, before I had told him that we had any thought of playing Brown, and therefore before he was on his guard. Playing Brown as early as we do will make it practically impossible for Brown to get into her best shape to play us and yet to make as much out of her Dartmouth game as she wants to, and therefore I feel fairly safe in accepting Robinson's statement that Brown will come up to play us expecting more to get good practice and experience out of the game than with any expectation of winning. We finally settled the Brown date after Lewis, Waters and Donald, and many other coaches whom I saw constantly in conference with, agreed to it. That left only two dates to settle, that of Oct. 28th with Wesleyan and that of Oct. 4th with Amherst. We

---

ing from Amherst. He was a center on Walter Camp's all-American team for two years, the first African American to gain all-American recognition, and probably the first African American to coach intercollegiate athletics. Waters was a guard, tackle, and halfback for Harvard (1891–94), an all-American guard and tackle in 1892 and 1894 (while in Law School), and captain in 1893. Donald was a tackle (1895 and 1897–99) and third-team all-American in 1897. He played with Reid in the late 1890s. Most all-American data have been obtained from L. H. Baker, *Football: Facts and Figures* (New York: Farrar & Rinehart, 1945), 145–51.

finally decided to cut out the Wesleyan game entirely, partly because Wesleyan had already closed that date, and partly because we felt some hesitation in arranging a game, easy though it might be, to be played the day before the team would have to leave for West Point. As it is now we have the first three days in the week for shaking the team together and bringing it into a little organization for our West Point game. The Amherst game of Oct. 14 we were rather afraid of. In looking over Amherst's schedule for the past two or three years, we found that they had been putting up a very strong game, and that during the next year they rather expected to have a stronger team than usual. Then besides, Amherst had arranged a game for that date, and wanted an enormous guarantee and other concessions before she would consider a change. We discussed Columbia, Syracuse, Cornell and Penn State College for that date, but felt that they were all of them a little stronger than we wanted, and finally settled on a game with the Springfield Manual Training School, which has been on the Yale schedule for a couple of years now.

It must be remembered that in arranging these dates a good deal of time was lost in writing to one college and another finding what dates they had and comparing them with our open dates, in the matter of arranging guarantees and in settling other questions which always come up. We only got our Brown game after paying Amherst a considerable guarantee for releasing Brown from a date.

The schedule as it now stands, then, is:

Sat. Sept.	30	Williams	at Cambridge
Wed. Oct.	4	Bowdoin	
Sat.	7	Univ. of Me.	
Wed.	11	Bates	
Sat.	14	Spg. Manual Tr. School	
Sat.	21	West Pt.	at West Pt.
Sat.	28	Brown	at Cambridge
Sat. Nov.	4	Indians	
Sat.	11	Penn	at Philadelphia
Sat.	18	Dartmouth	at Cambridge
Sat.	25	Yale	at Cambridge.

That gives us four easy games in which to sift over our material, then a fairly hard game in which to try out the best material, then three good hard games in which to weld it together before the first of our big games, then what ought to be a good stiff g[a]me between the Penn and Yale games, where we shall meet pretty nearly the Yale style of game, and finally Yale; eleven games in all, with the Yale game a week later than last year, thus preventing the crowding of our harder games on to the earlier preliminary ones.

Taking up now the question of LeMoyne again, I went to extreme pains to get him back. I went five or six times to see his parents in Brookline, had a talk with them and found everybody but the father exceedingly anxious that Harry should return. The father was quite ready to have him return if he would actually get down to work, but determined that after having fizzled once in the high school, and once at Harvard, he was not prepared to throw away any more money needlessly. One of the daughters had been sick, it seems, and her hospital bills had been very heavy, and the other daughter was on the point of being married, so that, as Mr. LeMoyne put it, the extraordinary expenses of that particular occasion had left him as dry as a sucked lemon. After one or two days consideration, Mr. LeMoyne said that if Harry were willing to go back and really get to work, he would give him means to go through, provided some arrangement could be made to carry him through that part of the year between March and the beginning of college during which time he would have to do some tutoring in order to regain his class. I therefore set about trying to make some arrangement that would make this possible. I got a complete statement of LeMoyne's case from the Scientific school, and accepted a room from Leavitt and Pierce's agents for the Little's Block, for the time mentioned. It so happened that when I first came on and before I knew what the status of the LeMoyne matter was, Leavitt & Pierce had offered me a room which they had not rented, and which was simply vacant, to do with whatever I might wish.

When the matter of getting a room for LeMoyne came up it occurred to me that I might use that room, and Leavitt & Pierce assented. Then I went to Nolen, the tutor, and he promised me to tutor LeMoyne through his staff of men, and in every way to do what he could to help put him through. That left only food and transportation to be secured. Herbert White[9] volunteered to get a pass, and tried to, but failed. Mr. Strecker, however, of the Commercial Advertising Co. of Boston, Al Ayer's employer, got it arranged.

Then I got several prospective jobs for LeMoyne whereby he could earn his food. Having done this I communicated with LeMoyne by

9. White was one of Reid's closest advisors. According to Reid, he graduated from Harvard in 1893, although there is no evidence of that in the *"Index of Graduates," Quinquennial Catalogue of the Officers and Graduates of Harvard University, 1836–1910* (Cambridge: Published by the University, 1910), 145.

telegraph but failed to get him, then I got into communication with Charley LeMoyne, his brother. Negotiations went on very slowly and finally I got Herbert White and a number of other men to write also. It happened that just at this time the sheep were being rounded up for shearing and that a most busy time was on. To get Harry away from the work required the permission of the head of the firm for which he was working, Mr. Dan Dewey. I was able to see Mr. Dewey, and he telegraphed at once to LeMoyne stating that he might come on, and that he would be glad if he did come. From all of these communications I got no response, and so I finally arranged with a Mr. F. W. Williams, a storekeeper in the town of Hagerman, Idaho, to take the letters and messages to Harry on horse back. This he did, but there was still no response. Meanwhile I got several of Harry's old friends to write him a round robin letter from Cambridge. I also got the Chicago Harvard Club to write him a letter and finally during the April vacation I got one of Harry's friends to go and see him. After all this I have never heard one single word from LeMoyne acknowledging anything. If I had not known that he had received the letters I should doubt as to whether anything had ever reached him, but under the circumstances I do not see what excuse he has for acting in such a discourteous way. Up to date, and this is Aug. 2, I have heard nothing from him nor has anyone else, with the possible exception of his family, who are at present in Canada. I therefore feel that the whole affair has turned out to be something of a wild goose chase. Harry LeMoyne apparently likes the ranch work very much and I understand that he and his brother are attempting to buy out the Company, so that I don't believe we shall ever again have LeMoyne in college. I was extremely sorry to have to give him up, and did not do so until I had exhausted every means in my power to bring him around.

The matter of following men up in their studies has been one of the most trying tasks that I have had during the whole time. Why it is that men who are big enough to go to college have not interest, energy and sense enough to do their work, I don't understand, but it is perfectly true that unless one keeps everlastingly after them there is very little possibility of having them pass through their examinations. I have had to do more police duty this spring than anyone would have considered possible, and only because it was absolutely necessary. It seems as though the present generation of possible athletes is way behind that of a year or two ago in the way in which it takes hold. I went to several men at odd times, whose work was in poor shape, and asked them if they did not think they had better tutor, and then whether they could afford it. In every case they answered yes, to both questions, and I immediately asked them what there was that would hinder them from seeing a tutor now, and have either accompanied the men at once to a tutor to see if possible that the matter went through, or else have written out a statement on the back of a postal card addressed, and dated so that the man himself might mail it just as soon as the arrangements were completed. Keeping tap of all these little matters has been almost distracting at times.

Just as soon as I came on I made out a list of men who according to common report were supposed to be good players and had their records looked up and a statement made to me, and I arranged that every man should do something special in getting himself ready for the April hour examinations. Nor was the work wholly along mental lines. One man named Preston Upham who weighed about 225 lbs. had a good head, was fast, and when he wanted to be, entirely able, had on several occasions gotten into a great trouble with the office, and had been once expelled, but later readmitted. This fellow was considered one of the best men on the squad, and all of the football men said that he must be kept somehow. I didn't feel much confidence in the fellow from what I could learn of his private life, but it has been my policy to try and get every man possible eligible, and then to sort them over and throw them out when I got them on the field. So I set out to retain Upham. I went to see his father and mother, and talked the matter over with them. I appealed to Upham on every ground I could think of and at times he showed signs of getting to work, but the work never lasted long. He cut, went in town continually, and stayed in for three or four nights at a time, on occasions signing himself off as sick, got into street rows, into automobile scrapes, and bad repute in money matters, into gambling, and other forms of trouble. He did not hesitate to lie and seemed to have absolutely no filial or moral sense.[10] After a time I telephoned him on those dates when themes were due, but finally gave it up because he was always out. I went to see personally all of his instructors, and talked with them, and they were all of them ready to give him every show. Most of them acknowledged that when he wanted to he was able to lead his class in most any subject. All complained of his cutting and of his sleeping in the class. One Professor said that if it had been anyone else he would have put him out of the class, but that he always took a seat well off to the side where his sleeping disturbed nobody, and from

10. A popular New York play at this time, George Ade's *The College Widow,* satirized college athletics and student values. When one of the play's characters, Flora Wiggins, states "Don't never have nothing to do with no students," she could well have had in mind a character such as Preston Upham. See the *Boston Globe,* 27 Aug. 1905, 25.

whence, when he awoke he occasionally gave a pretty good recitation. I wrote out a schedule of his work and together we planned out a period of study for each subject. He kept this up for a day or two, and then dropped back into his old state. I went to and talked with all of his friends among the boys, to try and get them to lend a hand in bringing him about. Some of them said they would, and others didn't take any interest, with the result that their influence amounted to nothing. As an example of his deceitfulness, the following story might be told. His father and mother, who were indulgent with him to an extreme, and who catered to his whims in order to try and get some permanent interest developed in him in some particular thing, gave him a check for $20.00 for the purpose of buying a set of Balzac, which the boy said he wanted very much, and which he could get second hand from a fellow out in Cambridge. He took the check, got the fellow in Cambridge to endorse it, and spent the money. At about two o'clock on the night of which all this happened, he rang his people up and asked them whether the books had come. This was only an example of his deception. His father, unwilling to trust him to work out in C[a]mbridge, and because the college refused to allow him to stay out in Cambridge at any rate for a certain time, in a room, had insisted that the boy live at home. He gave the boy enough money each day to get his noon meal and pay his carfare. Instead of going home the boy gambled a good deal, and being very successful at cards he won considerable money. With this money he would go in town and stay. With the father's permission I tried to use the home living question as a sort of lever and told the boy that if he would agree not to cut at all during the two weeks just preceeding the April hour examinations, and would do his work, I would recommend to his father that he be allowed to room in Cambridge instead of staying at home. The pledge which he signed was as follows,— "It is understood that I, Preston Upham, hereby agrees not to cut for any reason for a period of two weeks, and that I will also prepare every lesson in that time, giving to each study not less than one hour of real preparation. If I do this it is agreed that Mr. Reid will recommend to my father that I be allowed to room in Cambridge, this to take effect from April 1st. Signed, Preston Upham, W. T. Reid, Jr." He kept this pledge just about three days, and everything was as badly off as before. Feeling that animal passion was at the bottom of much of the trouble, I tried to get Upham to do some regular gymnastic work every day, and agreed to get him over there regularly. This, too, went by the board after a short trial. The fellow seemed to lack all idea of responsibility or sense of decency, and all interest in things except loud women. I consulted a couple of doctors to see if he could not be relieved in some way from this, but found it was impossible. As the examinations approached I got one of Upham's class mates to ask Upham if he would not like to come and work with him, arranging privately with the fellow to pay him for his tutoring, all of this with Mr. Upham's permission, of course. For about a week Upham took hold of the work in good shape. The fellow, whose name is Ryan, went after Upham just before the recitations took place, and accompanied him[,] accompanying him personally to them. This went all right so long as Ryan could find Upham, but later on when Upham began to stay away, the thing fell through. When spring practice was on I got Upham out all I could, but that was very irregularly. It will perhaps seem as though there was no possibility of use in trying to work further with this man, and that is the way it seemed to me, but I felt that football was about the only thing that I knew of that would help him over his passions, and about the only thing in college for which he really cared. Last season he was out regularly playing on the second with no possibility of making the first, through his college standing, out simply because he liked the game. I rather hoped that if I could get him eligible, he would not only come out regularly as he had done on the second, but might perhaps be forced to do his work on pain of being dropped from the squad, and so I kept on. In the middle of all this work, Upham got into a row in town and knocked out three policemen. By lively work among the newspaper men, several of us managed to keep the affair out of the papers, and probably prevented an expulsion. I had many talks with Dean [Byron] Hurlbut[11] and other men of the faculty about him, and Dean Hurlbut had some talks with the boy himself, but all to no purpose, until finally the faculty passed a vote that Upham be allowed to t[a]ke his final examinations on condition that he should return to college next year. On his final examinations he failed of promotion by one C, and his father has put him to work out in Kansas City with a telegraph linesmans' gang. I understand that he is doing pretty well there, but after my experience, he will have to do mighty well before I shall take much stock in him. It seems to me that the parents in this case are largely to blame. The boy has been threatened with all sorts of things, and nothing has every actually taken place, through the pleadings of his mother and sister. The boy has taken advantage of this, and gradually the father

11. Hurlbut was dean of Harvard College. Previously he had received a master of arts degree from Harvard in 1888 and became a professor of English. See *Quinquennial Catalogue*, 290–91.

has lost what little hold he had. I have given this fellow's case in some considerable detail in order to show how much time one can spend on such a fellow if there is sufficient reason for it.

Another man with whom I had considerable trouble was a fellow named Talbot. He played guard on the freshman team last Fall, and weighed something over 200 lbs., and besides this he was a good kicker. This fellow had very low marks on his mid-years, and so was put on probation; and I went after him at once. I had him in the office a number of times and talked with him. I kept track of this work at the office too, so that I knew he did not cut and that he had tutors in his subjects, the best tutors to be had, from the time I arrived until the final examinations. At that time he failed in every single course, which would seem to indicate a lack of capability, for no man of even ordinary ability can possibly fail to get through Harvard if he attends his lectures regularly and does a little work with some thinking.

Capt. Hurley seemed to be on the edge in his work, but he took hold in first rate style. When the final examinations came off, he failed of his degree by a full C, and is now at work in the summer school. He seems to be finding his work extremely hard, and I am considerably worried for fear that he won't get through. I expect to put a good deal of time in with him this week getting ready for his examinations next Monday. If Hurley doesn't get through, it will be because he has not the brains, for he has done no cutting whatever, and has studied hard and faithfully. He began tutoring two or three days ago with Nolen.

Bartol Parker, who was taken on to the varsity squad from last year's freshman team, failed of promotion by a half of one C. He also is at work in the summer school. I worked personally with him during the spring, and saw that he had tutoring. His whole trouble seems to be with his makeup, which is rather a lazy one. How it is that these fellows are willing to let their work slide, and then have to spend half their summer making it up, I can't see.

There is little use in going into further detail individually. It should suffice to say that I saw and arranged with personally forty men who were weak.

In order to get myself back into the game again, having been out of it for four years, and in order to get some of the coaches interested, I had a number of meetings at the B. A. A. [Boston Athletic Club] where we had dinners and talks. These dinners were given through the courtesy of Herbert White, who has been one of the greatest helpers I have had. He is always ready to do what he can to keep things moving, and to go to whatever trouble is necessary to do so. The meetings were by position, and the first one, which was a meeting of the guards, came on April 4. At this meeting Waters, Lewis, Hurley, [George] Bouve[12] and I were present. We talked over the qualifications which we should like to see in a good guard, and talked over especially the question of the way in which the guards should play both in relation to their tackles and to their centre. Lewis has for some time been teaching the guards to get down with both hands on the ground, and to charge forward as soon as the ball is put in play. The objections to this way of playing, as given by the other coaches, is that the men are too anchored, and are not therefore able to cover as much ground either on defensive or offensive as they ought to. This in turn has reacted on the tackles playing further out, since they have been compelled to be doubly active in order to cover a portion of the ground which the guards left uncovered. We talked over this matter, and then took off our coats and did some experimenting with positions, and although we came to no conclusion, yet I think every one carried away with him the main point in dispute, and the opinions of the various ones present as to that point. Another thing that the meeting did was to get men into harmony with each other, and to show what men are probably going to take the greatest interest in the work this Fall.

On April 6th, we had another dinner at the same place, this time for the ends, at which meeting were present F[rank] W. Hallowell, [Edward] Bowditch, [Norman W.] Cabot,[13] Hurley, and a stenographer. The latter I had come in because in the previous meeting there was considerable which I would have liked to have had taken down, but which I could get down myself only in brief. Much the same ground with regard to ends was covered which was covered at the other meetings. We were all agreed that there were certain qualities which an end must have, which the ends last year did not have. Among them are speed, shiftiness, and judgment. Again, it was unanimously agreed that our ends for the past year played altogether too far out on their tackles, thereby allowing many plays to pass between them and tackle, for short gains which, if the end had played closer,

12. This is presumably George W. Bouvé, a two-time letter-winning guard on the Harvard football team in 1896 and 1897, and a third-team member of Walter Camp's all-American team in 1897. Camp began his all-American selections in 1889.

13. Hallowell was a four-year letterman end on the 1889–92 Harvard teams and a Walter Camp all-American in 1890. Bowditch also won four letters as an end from 1900 to 1903, including being a second-team all-American in 1901 and an all-American in 1902. Cabot won four letters as an end from 1894 to 1897, gaining all-American status in 1895 and 1896.

might have been prevented. This was especially true of [Clarence] Randall. Playing out as far as he did, our end was frequently able to get a runner, but not before he had made gain enough to ensure the keeping of the ball. The matter of how to get around the blocking of the ends, as Pennsylvania played it last year, was also taken up, and it was agreed that two things ought to be done to prevent it. First, the ends should be given practice early in the season in getting down the field with men blocking them; and second, we should adopt a quick kick as a means of allowing our ends to get away promptly and cleanly. We looked over the list of varsity squad of last year with a view to picking out any good men for next season, but found almost none. Frank Hallowell suggested that we ought to go to the hockey team for such men, inasmuch as hockey, and for that matter tennis, require many qualities which an end needs also. This meeting was very satisfactory indeed, one of the most satisfactory of all.

On April 7th I had a similar meeting for the backs. Hurley, [Henry] Shoelkopf, [John] Dunlop[14] and I were present. [Edgar] Wrightington[15] was asked but could not come. We talked over the question of starts, whether it was wise to start with both hands on the ground or only one, or just how, and we decided that each man should be allowed to start in his own way provided he did not take any backward steps, and provided he did not get off slowly. In case a man is unable to start with a method of his own we should suggest one or two ways from which he could be taught to pick the one best suited to him. We discussed the ways of catching the kick in the back field, and the stuff in most of the men who will be back with us next year. This discussion was extremely valuable to me, and it gave me some insight into the characters of many of the squad, whom I am trying to know as thoroughly as possible before next Fall; and I might say here that I am meeting and talking with members of the squad as often and under as many different circumstances as possible.

On April 12th we had another meeting: This time of the tackle coaches. [Bertram G.] Waters, [Malcolm] Donald, J[ames] Lawrence,[16] Hurley, and I were present. This was one of the most valuable meetings of all. Immediately after our supper we took off our coats and worked over the question of the distance the tackles shall play from their guards, and what their special function should be in meeting

14. *Schollkopf* is the correct spelling for the Harvard fullback and letter-winner in 1903; Dunlop was a Harvard back and letter-winner (1893–96).

15. Wrightington was a Harvard back and letter-winner (1893–96), as well as captain in 1896.

16. Lawrence was a tackle (1899–1900) and a second-team all-American in 1900.

the heavy mass play of the present. After the meeting was about over, and the concensus of opinion established, Waters dictated a careful statement of what had been decided upon, to be considered by the guards. Here again we talked over all the possible material, and discussed the possible effect of likely changes in the rules on tackle play. The question of the relationship between the rush line backs and the tackles was also taken up.

On April 20th I had a dinner for the past head coaches of recent years. Waters, [John W.] Farley, [John S.] Cranston,[17] Wrightington, Hurley and I were present, and we discussed principally the question of changes in the rules. Bob Wrenn,[18] our representative on the rules committee,[19] wanted instructions, and so I tried to get a working basis from these men. We talked over all the various changes which have been proposed and decided that we should like to see several things go through. In fact the first was, we were agreed that the present close formation game allows of great possibilities for holding and other unfair tactics in the line. Last year Yale held abominably in our game, and profited very considerably by the practice. As we don't propose to coach the Harvard team to any such practice, we thought that the best way to even things up would be to try to open up the game. It was very clearly brought out by the meeting that in order to open the game the offense and defense should both be moved further back from the rush line. If either one or the other is moved without a corresponding move on the part of the other, it is practically impossible to accomplish anything, for if the defense is moved back and the offense allowed to play where it chooses, it will be played close and will be enabled to get in its blow before the defense could get to the spot attacked. If, on the other hand, the offense were moved back and the defense were allowed to stay up near the line, it would be impossible for the offense to reach the line before the defense of the opposing team had concentrated at the point of attack. Therefore it seemed wise to us to recommend that both the offense and defense should be put back at least three and one half yards be-

17. Farley was a Harvard letter-winner at end in 1898; Cranston was a center and guard and letter-winner (1888–90), an all-American in 1889 and 1890.

18. Wrenn was the Harvard quarterback and letter-winner in 1894. He also played tennis and baseball for Harvard.

19. The seven-member, self-perpetuating Rules Committee was comprised of men from the University of Chicago (Amos Alonzo Stagg), Cornell (Louis M. Dennis), Harvard (Bob Wrenn), the U.S. Naval Academy (Paul Dashiell), Penn (John C. Bell), Princeton (John B. Fine), and Yale (Walter Camp). A unanimous vote was necessary for any legislation to pass. Camp, who had been on the committee since the 1870s, was its dominant figure.

hind the line. In consideration of this limitation in distance, both the offense and defense should be left entirely free in the matter of the number of men to be used and their positions. Various other questions were taken up, and Waters agreed to write individual letters, copies of which appear on the opposite page [missing], with a view to getting their cooperation. As will be seen later, when the question of the meeting of the rules committee is taken up, our work availed us little, as the committee is practically powerless against the vote of one man. One of the chief points of value in this meeting was the fact that we all had a chance to think over what our tactics would probably be in case certain changes were made.

On May 19th we had the last dinner of the series, for guards and tackles again. At this dinner were Jim Lawrence, Bert Waters, Lewis, Donald, Bouve, Hurley and myself. The question of playing the guards a little more apart from the centre and tackles was taken up, but Lewis maintained that the old style of defense with the guards in pretty close was, in his mind, much better than the proposed change to more of the Yale style. At present this matter is still unsettled, but I propose to settle it once for all in a few days. Meanwhile I have given Lewis a copy of Waters' ideas on the way the tackles should be played, to which all the tackle coaches and the other guards agree. I think the chances are that it will go through.

Spring Practice

The Spring practice this year was exceedingly valuable to me for several reasons. In the first place, since I have been away for four years, and did not know the men, it gave me a chance to meet them and work with them and look them over; also a chance to get out a number of coaches, and to see from their work out there just how valuable they would be in the Fall, and also a chance to look over the kickers in college to see on what men to spend the time next Fall; and still again a chance to get out and try out new men whose weight, age and experience would seem to make them possible candidates, in order to see where they would probably play. It is generally felt by some of the coaches, I think, that spring practice is a good time to try out plays and formations, but I do not think it true. In the first place no formation can be tried out by men who are not in good physical condition, and are not out regularly, and who have not had scrimmage work enough to make the test real. Again, it is very difficult to get two full elevens out, and if it were not, there is every likelihood, in having scrimmages before the men were in good shape, that some of the best men would be injured.

After the experience of this year, it seems very clear to me that the chief value of spring practice lies in the opportunity for getting acquainted with your men well, and for starting men who are wholly green in a position, or in kicking, for instance, in such a way as to put them some little way ahead by Fall. It also should enable a coach to find out whether it is any use spending any time at all on certain men. Of course the better a coach knows his men, the less spring practice he would need unless it were for the sake of keeping busy certain fellows who need exercise but who without it are likely to run wild.

We called the men out on April 5th, having a meeting on the evening before. A great many men came to the meeting, but a disappointingly small number turned out for actual work, in fact only 16 men came out. It was raining and that of course accounted for the poor showing to some extent. It is of course very hard to get up any enthusiasm in football so early in the year, but it is not too much to expect of any man who wants to make a kicker of himself or who is really anxious to make the team, and is not a candidate for some other varsity team, to come out regularly for this work. Our squad increased during the next two or three days until we had 40 men out. The work consisted in a short dumb bell exercise, careful instruction in falling on the ball, in kicking, catching, running ends down the field without tackling, and some little breaking through work for the line men. By dint of great effort I succeeded in getting out [Robert P.] Kernan[20] to coach the kickers, Bowditch to work with the ends, and on occasion, [Roger A.] Derby, Waters, Lewis and Donald[21] to work with the line men. We required the men to be prompt and to do faithfully what they were told to do, and generally had a good response although our attendance was pretty ragged, in fact disappointingly so.

Don Nichols, who has done some kicking for the varsity in the last couple of years, and who is a most erratic performer, in that he is just as likely to kick 10 yards as 50, came out for a day or two, and then stopped in order to play a substitute position on the second varsity nine. This lack of interest on Nichols part when his own poor playing has at times actually affected our chances in the Yale game, makes me question very seriously whether he has the right stuff in him or not. I very much doubt it. Kicking is something which no man who does not take a vital interest in his own progress can ever hope to excel in, and here is a man with the build for a kicker who has let his chance of de-

20. Kernan was a Harvard halfback and letter-winner (1901–2), an all-American in 1901, and captain in 1902.
21. Derby was a Harvard tackle and letter-winner (1903–4).

veloping himself go in order to take part in some other sport which has less work in it. What is true of Nichols' kicking is also true of his defensive work, which is very poor; and I think it is more than likely that he will turn out to be a man much like [Eliot T.] Putnam[22] was,—brilliant at times but too erratic to be dependable.

I tried to get [Karl F.] Brill and [Bartol] Parker and [Charles G.] Osborn[23] out to do some work. Parker came out a few times, but was behind in his work, and I finally allowed him to withdraw entirely.

Osborne is a big, bright Englishman, weighing about 195 pounds and with just the build for a first rate tackle. He was the second best goal tender in the association [soccer] game in England last year, and would have been the first man there this year if he were not going back to Harvard. He is an "A" man in his studies and has a splendid head. One of his greatest handicaps is the fact that he was brought up under the English system of athletics.[24] How this has interfered with his progress I will now make plain. Osborne played last year a part of the time at fullback, and has great possibilities as a kicker. This next year we are going to need tackles and so I wanted to get him out and see if we could not make a tackle of him. He said he could not come out except on certain days, owing to the fact that he was playing on the association football team and also on the cricket team. I tried to show him that his responsibility was chiefly with the football team since the college cares very little for cricket or association football, and I tried also to make plain to him that he should get in all the time possible on his tackle work and on his kicking. What I said had little effect. Finally, however, he promised to come out as soon as the association game was over and work on his kicking. When that time came, however, he entered a tennis tournament and finally

22. Reid is probably referring to Eliot Putnam, a halfback on the 1901 team, which Reid coached, and on the 1902 team.

23. Brill lettered in football from 1904 to 1905, Parker from 1904 to 1907, and Osborne in 1906. Osborne, a former Oxford University soccer player, helped introduce association football to Harvard in 1904. Along with a Canadian, Beaton Squires (a football letterman from 1903 to 1905); a Swiss, Gordon Means; and A. Brooks, who was also English, Harvard students began playing soccer in the fall of 1904. By the next spring, intercollegiate soccer was introduced on American campuses when Haverford and Harvard played the first game.

24. The upper-class, amateur system in England to which Reid refers would suggest that people be good in a number of sports yet not devote themselves to any one to the exclusion of others—thus producing well-rounded individuals who play sports for the fun of participation. The more open social class system in America developed a different model, one that emphasized excellence, specialization, and a professional spirit, not an amateur spirit. See Ronald A. Smith, "Amateur College Sport: An Untenable Concept in a Free and Open Society," in *Sports and Freedom*, 165–74.

in one way and another, failed to do anything. Now it is a question whether we could make a tackle out of him even though he turns out to be fit for it, in the little time that we shall have during the Fall, and while we are experimenting with him, some one else will be handicapped in like measure. I am going to tell him when he comes back just what the situation is and unless he responds at once, and I think he will, I shall put him on to the second team and keep him there until I am sure that he means business.

Brill didn't seem to make good last Fall, the coaches seeming to think that he had babied a good deal, and so I wanted him out especially to study his nature and to develop his kicking, which had been good at Exeter. He claimed that his feet were very sore, and that he was behind in his work and needed all his time to make money enough to get through. The result was that I got nothing from him. A letter which I wrote him a little later, a copy of which will be found further on in the book, will indicate that action I finally took with regard to him. These three men are typical examples of the way which most of the varsity players of last year took hold. I could get nothing out of [Dillwyn P.] Starr,[25] who seems probably to be the most likely man for quarter back, and I got very little out of most of the other men, with the possible exception of [Frederic H.] White and [Richard E.] Sperry,[26] who came out pretty well. The regular spring practice ended on April 28. From that date until May 26th we had none but kickers out. By petition to the athletic committee I got some cups awarded for place kicking, drop kicking, punting, and goal kicking. The notice of the conditions for winning the cups appears here.

KICKING CONTEST, Friday, May 26th

On Friday, May 26, a kicking contest will be held on Soldiers Field. Cups will be awarded for punting, placing kicking, drop kicking, and goal kicking.

The winners in the various events will be chosen by a board of coaches on the basis of form, speed, accuracy and distance. To compete in this contest a man must be eligible for University eleven, and must have reported on the field of practice no less than three times each week between now and the date of the contest. There will be coaches on the field every day to assist candidates. It is hoped that a large number of men will come out.

25. Starr was a Harvard quarterback and letter-winner from 1904 to 1907.
26. White and Sperry were Harvard letter-winners only in 1904.

When the kicking contest was about to take place, I looked up the list of men who had been out regularly three times a week, and found that no one would qualify under these conditions. Rather than give up the contest altogether, we allowed every man who had been out a certain number of times to try, and in order to get out certain other men who had not been out for practice, we had a sort of open competition. At the date of the contest Percy Haughton and Bob Kernan,[27] and I judged the punting, Will Burnett judged the place kicking, and Leo Daly and Karl Marshall[28] the goal kicking and drop kicking. A high wind was blowing, and so the records, which are given on the opposite page [but are missing], were hardly satisfactory. The scheme for having an open contest proved to be a good one, and we turned up several unexpectedly strong men. From this kicking work I made a list of all the kickers in college, which list I give on the opposite page [missing]. During the preparation for the kicking contest, Kernan and I gave our special attention to the kickers, and devoted to each man whatever time was necessary in order to help him to an improvement in any special weakness, so that each man who was out regularly really accomplished some special thing. Not being satisfied with the kickers that were out there, I looked around for others, and finally found a man who I thought ought to be able to kick, over on the ball field. His name is [Hatherly] Foster,[29] and from his build I feel sure that he will make a kicker, and his nature is just the right kind also. He set to work with a will, and worked most of the spring, and has also done some considerable work this summer. I have been down to Soldiers Field with him half a dozen times at intervals, and can see distinctly the progress he is making. Before long I shall get Percy Haughton out in order to check up what I have done. Another year I would suggest having the spring practice begin earlier and end earlier, unless in the case of some few special men. Of course this year while we were canvassing the college, I had any man whose card looked well report to me on the field, so that I might look him over

27. Haughton, a Harvard tackle and fullback and a letter-winner (1896–98), was a second-team all-American in 1898. Kernan was a halfback (1901–2), attaining all-American status in 1901. Kernan and Haughton were the kicking coaches during the 1905 fall season. Haughton became the acclaimed Harvard coach from 1908 to 1917, when his teams generally beat Yale, the first time that Harvard ever dominated Yale in football. His 5-2-2 record against Yale and 5-1 record against Princeton were unsurpassed in Harvard history.

28. Burnett was a Harvard center and guard letter-winner (1898–1900) and a third-team all-American in 1899; Daly was a letter-winner in 1902; and Marshall was a quarterback letter-winner (1901–3).

29. Foster was a Harvard halfback letter-winner (1905–6) and captain in 1906.

and see whether it were worth while calling him out for the varsity squad in the Fall. I let those men who came out regularly for two weeks, and about whom I had made up my mind go as soon as I had made up my mind, and then tried to keep the squad going with the new recruits.

Mr. [William F.] Garcelon[30] of the track team came over once or twice and suggested several exercises for football men, which made agreeable changes in the routine. He had men line up on the line, each with a ball in his hand, and facing others, man for man, about 30 yards distant. At the word "go" the men with the balls started off and passed the ball to the man opposite, who then rushed back in an endeavor to cross the starting line first. Another exercise was to line up 8 or 10 men with an interval of about 3 yards between them. Then a man was given the ball and was made to run in and out among these men as fast as he could go. This was good practice for the larger men attempting to get control of their bodies. Then a row of footballs was placed upon the ground about 15 yards from a row of men, and with plenty of interval between them. At the word "go" the men ran at the balls, fell on them and rushed on across a finish line some distance further. These and various like exercises afforded some amusement with the work. I had several times during the spring practice to make appeals to the college, through the Crimson, for more interest, one of these notices follows—

SPRING FOOTBALL.

Thus far the response to the call for candidates for next season's University eleven has been exceedingly disappointing. Less than 40 men have reported for work, and many of these ceased coming out after the first Week. When it is remembered that the great majority of football players now in the University are unknown to the present head coach, it will be readily seen what a handicap he will be forced to work under this fall unless he is in some way able to meet the men this spring and to see them at work. It is not expected that men who are occupied in the major sports should report, but it is certainly reasonable for the football management to expect other men to come out in numbers. It is hoped that this appeal will make any further call unnecessary.

D. J. Hurley
W. T. Reid, Jr.

30. Garcelon was a Harvard track letter-winner (1893–94). He became the graduate treasurer for Harvard athletics by 1908, a position held earlier by Herbert White, Reid's close advisor, beginning in 1894.

In order to get as much as possible of the detail work done before next Fall, I decided to try and settle upon the officials for next season at once. I was greatly handicapped in trying to get this done because of the fact that no list of possible officials has ever been kept. I therefore print on the opposite page [missing] a list of officials for 1901–1904, and the present season. In choosing officials for this present year, it has been our policy to try out as many men as we safely can in order to get a good permanent working for following years. There are therefore several new names on the list. By unanimous agreement of the coaches we have decided to replace [Paul] Dashiell[31] as umpire in the Harvard-Yale game. Dashiell is a very pleasant man indeed, in fact he is almost too pleasant. He umpires the games partly because he likes to, but generally because of the money in them, or at any rate that would seem to be the way he feels about it. Yale seems to have him just about where she wants him, and he has allowed Yale to do about as she pleased in her games. Yale has therefore been very enthusiastic about Dashiell. We have absolutely refused to have him, and have suggested [Bill] Edwards.[32] Yale, as usual, is dallying along about the matter, and trying to delay things so long that it will be necessary to have Dashiell, but they will find this time that they are up against it. Dashiell will not umpire the game this year if there is no game. We have cut out all of the Pennsylvania men from our list, as we do no[t] wish Penn to get as close to our players as they could as officials. We have put Dashiell in as an official in the Dartmouth game in order to let him down easily, and at the same time to see whether he will keep his eyes open any better against any other team than Yale. In my opinion Dashiell is pretty much of a has been, and it is time we changed permanently for the better.

When I first came on this spring there were three things which I had in mind to accomplish at once. First, to get every possible man in college in such shape as regards his work as to make sure that he would be eligible. Second, to canvass the University thoroughly and get out every possible man who can play, whether he has had experience or not, who seems likely to be good stuff. Third, to get the coaching department thoroughly settled and organized before the work begins. The canvass proved to be a work of about three and one half months for ten men, although I believe that if men of proper en-

---

31. Dashiell actually became the Harvard-Yale umpire in 1905, and a great controversy, the Burr-Quill incident, arose.

32. Edwards, a 225-pound guard on Princeton's football team, was its captain in 1898 and a second-team all-American in 1899. See Jay Dunn, *The Tigers of Princeton: Old Nassau Football* (Huntsville: Strode Publishers, 1977), 71–72.

ergy had gone at it they could have done it all in a month. It took me alone less than one and one half months to do it when I was captain of the ball nine. I first had a long talk with Henry Thompson, the manager of the Union,[33] concerning the methods which he had employed in canvassing the college for Union membership, and he made several very good suggestions to me. First of all we put cards, one of which appears on the opposite page [missing], at every seat in Randall Hall, and likewise in Memorial. We then had the managers circulate about the dining hall asking men to fill them out, and at the doors collecting them. In this way we gathered about 1500 cards. Cards were left at all the eating clubs and societies, and permission was granted whereby cards were left at each man's place in the Freshman course of English A, which is a prescribed course. Then we called meetings of each of the classes and collected cards wherever possible then. We sent in bundles of cards to men appointed to see that they were filled out in the various graduate schools. Here was where we had our first real trouble. Of course among the undergraduates there was a certain amount of nonsense handed in, but among the graduate students the amount was very annoying, from the law school in particular. This was due, of course, to the fact that the law school comprises men from Universities all over the country who are not at all interested in our work here, and who tried to make whatever fun out of it they could. We got permission from the office to have men at the places of registration after the April recess. The President of each class together with a couple of managers, was at each place of registration, and the scheme worked pretty well. Return postal cards were sent out in quantity, the managers went around on bicycles and made personal calls, and at the end wrote personal letters to some men in order to get answers. A card was received from every man in the University, and several men were discovered in attendance of whom the college authorities had no record. 4200 cards came in altogether. I sorted these over personally with Captain Hurley, and we put aside the cards of such men as, from physical qualifications and other evidence, showed football possibilities, whether of experience or not. There were about 200 of these all told. We have had three copies of these cards made, and have them arranged in the form of a card catalogue. In one drawer is an alphabetical list of the whole lot,

33. The Harvard Union was constructed in 1901, the first student union in America. It included a restaurant, meeting rooms, library, and ten overnight rooms for guests. It was an attempt to ameliorate the social disintegration occurring as universities grew rapidly in enrollment. Athletics, obviously, were used to create social integration and esprit de corps.

so that any coach may find any man so long as he knows his name. In the second drawer is a similar list arranged according to positions, so that an end coach, for instance, can locate at once all men who are trying for end; and in a third drawer is yet another list arranged according to weight, from 130 lbs. up, the variance in graduation being ten lbs. For instance, the first section in the catalog will be from 130 to 140 lbs., the second from 140 to 150, so that a coach can get at any desired weight irrespective of previous experience or position.

This list will make it possible for us at any time to get at a man in case we are short of material, and will prevent the escape of such a man as [Frank] Schoenfuss, who last year, would probably have made a first rate guard had he been gotten out early enough, and who has been in college for the past three years. It is very difficult to get at heavy men at any time during the season unless you know them and can get around and see them personally. It is my hope that by going over the list carefully next year we can at the end of the year in preparation for next season make out a list of 70 men, we will say, which we are absolutely sure contains every man of any football possibilities in the University. It will mean doing a considerable amount of trying out this Fall, but it ought to be done without interfering with the rational progress of the varsity, and when it is done, it ought not to need repeating. Then, if the freshman team is only properly handled, no further canvass of the college need ever be necessary. The canvass has served one or two other purposes, also. It has served to show to the University that we are dead in earnest, and that in case any man who can play does not come out, it will not be our fault. What is more important than either of these two considerations, it will show clearly that every possible chance of letting in the slightest tendency to favoritism[34] is obviated, because for every man in the University to feel that statistics have been gotten from him with regard to football, a like card having been received from every one else, makes all feel that everything possible is being done.

As we were in need of a varsity second assistant manager, we had 14 men present themselves as candidates from the freshman class. These men were set to work on the canvass and in other ways doing things which showed what they were made of. The test was a long and severe one, and we certainly got the best man. The matter of selecting the managers most carefully ought to be made a special point

34. Reid, from the time he was an undergraduate, attempted to rid social class favoritism from Harvard, both in social clubs and in athletics. See, for instance, Bill Reid, Jr., Harvard, to Christine Lincoln, Venice, Italy, 16 Dec. 1900, Thomas Stetson Personal Collection.

of as recent years our football teams have been abominably managed. It seems this year as though no way whatever appears to avoid dismissing Vanderbilt from position as first assistant. This seems necessary because he shows almost no interest in things be[y]ond that of getting done what he is asked to do so that he can get away. The result is that he volunteers nothing, anticipates nothing, and only half does what he is told to do. Inasmuch as it has been customary for the first assistant manager to become varsity manager the next year, I feel as though it were fairer to Vanderbilt to dispose of him now than to get along with him during the strenuous season which is about to begin and then tell him at the end of the year that he cannot be manager. Following custom this year, the second assistant manager was chosen from the freshman class. I very much doubt the wisdom of this policy. I do not think that a freshman is well enough developed at that period to make it certain that any choice is a wise one. I should incline to favor choosing a man from the Sophomore or Junior class. To be sure, such a man would not have the experience by the time he became varsity manager that the freshman would have, but I don't think that that figures as strongly as the fact that an older man of greater ability and interest in the work can pick up enough in a very short time to do the work very creditably. The manager of one of the varsity football teams should be always on the lookout to see whether he cannot foresee some worry or annoyance to the coaches or Captain, and head it off without waiting to be told, and he should do without fail whatever he is told, so that whoever gives the order need have nothing further on his mind. Time after time this spring I have asked that something be done and later found out that it was not done, thereby causing me to keep on my mind a quantity of detail which was very worrying, and which ought not to have been necessary.

The question of getting a new trainer came up for consideration and I talked it over pretty thoroughly with Dr. [Edward] Nichols, Waters, Lewis, Prof. [Archibold C.] Coolidge of the Athletic Committee, Donald, and Wrightington. Some of the men, Wrightington especially, believe that [J. W.] McMaster is getting old and so is on the lookout to keep his position to such an extent that he is very slow about really expressing his opinion. He is, they say, rather acquiescent in whatever the coaches suggest than ready to initiate himself. As McMaster's term expired this year, the matter had to be settled for two years more. After considerable discussion I decided that we had better hang on to him a year or two longer. I feel this way about it; there is no question but that McMaster is not better than a first rate man of secondary capacity. He is surely not thoroughly up to date, and does not look after certain details of the work unless the coach constantly calls attention to it. [. . .][35] On the other hand, coming in to this work new, with little or no experience for four years, and with many of the conditions considerably changed, I feel that it is decidedly risky to undertake so serious a change as would be involved in getting another trainer. There was too much work to do this Spring in order to get things into running order to allow of the necessary time being given to a proper choice if we were willing to make a change. That this feeling was a wise one is thoroughly proven by the experience which [Walter] Camp of Yale has had in replacing Mike Murphy. Mr. Camp has been all over the West seeing men and talking with them, and now after almost three months of investigation is still without his man. Another point is the fact that the athletic committee, after having accepted the great expense to which I have been put in coming on, is not ready to pay what they would have to pay for a really first class trainer. On the other hand, I have worked in baseball and football with McMaster and understand him pretty thoroughly. I believe that if it be insisted that he give frequent expressions of his opinion, he will do so. At any rate he did so in 1901. Furthermore, McMaster knows every man on the squad. He knows what men were injured last year, what they have done in other branches of athletics, where to get rubbers,[36] where to go for men to do all the petty jobs about the field, what food can best be gotten in Cambridge, what is to be avoided in dealing with the outfitters and other men, and in general is quite familiar with the place. For these reasons, then, in the main, McMaster has been signed for two years more. Meanwhile we shall be on the lookout for a first rate man in case the Athletic Committee feels willing to consider a possible change.

On the opposite page I have put down a list of the men whom Camp has considered, so that when the matter comes up finally there will be some names to start with.

POSSIBLE TRAINERS

- - - - - - - - -

Keene Fitzpatrick, of Michigan University.
Mike Sweeney, of the Hill School,

35. The following nonsensical sentence was removed: "He is not up to date about expresses it."
36. Rubbers were individuals who could give athletes rubdowns.

John F. Moakley, of Cornell.
Al Copeland, who coached the Yale Track Team in 1899.
J. F. Nellingan, the Amherst track coach.
John Boweler, the Dartmouth coach.
Stave Farrell, of Bowdoin.
Otto Monahan, of the Hotchkiss School.
"Pooch" Donovan, the Worcester Academy coach.
Sydney Coe and Jack Doughan, both New Haven men who have
    had to do with Yale's Track Team for several years.

- -

Since we shall need all the time possible in the Fall to sort out our
candidates, it seemed wise to have the practice begin as early as possible. I therefore went before the Athletic Committee and asked permission to begin practice on Sept. 9th. They were unwilling to allow this
on the ground that it was too near to summer practice,[37] but finally did
allow me to have the men report back on Sept. 12th, which is the date
set. The Committee also refused to allow me to take ten or twelve men
irrespective of position but chosen for their spirit only, up to Penob-
scot Bay [Maine] at a Summer cottage which Herbert White owns.
White very generously offered to stand the expense of a dozen men
for ten days stay with a view to working up a spirit of harmony and
team work just as Cam Forbes did at Naushon [Massachusetts] in '98,
but the Athletic Committee would not hear of it for the summer practice reason. For the same reason I had to decline a like invitation to a
summer camp on Lake Ossipee [New Hampshire]. I think that the athletic committee was entirely right in refusing permission even though
I had no idea of running through any plays or anything of the sort. I
merely intended to get the men together and to have a good out of door
time of it before the season opened at Cambridge.

In 1901 I started a scheme of getting out a set of papers on each position, dealing with the particular things which the coaches in this position wanted to have their pupils get hold of. Those that were printed
then have been in use ever since. Though they were rather incomplete,

37. Football practice during the summers had begun possibly as early as the 1880s,
but was certainly in existence in the early 1890s. In 1894, for instance, Harvard trained
at Newcastle and Sorrento [Maine?]; Yale at Travers Island, New York; Princeton at
Gould Island (near Newport, R.I.); and Penn at Cape May, New Jersey. The Harvard
Athletic Committee opposed this practice in 1895. See Harvard Athletic Committee
Minutes, 25 Feb. 1895, Harvard University Archives. Harvard was soon joined by Yale
and Princeton, but not Penn, in abandoning summer football practice. See Agnes Rep-
plier, *J. William White, M.D.* (Boston: Houghton Mifflin, 1919), 75.

so this spring I set out to try and finish the set up, and to bring those that are at present in existence up to date. I got Waters to write a first rate article on the tackle position. It deals with the tackle from every point of view, and ought to be a most valuable help to the tackle coaches this Fall. On the quarter back position I got Charlie Daly[38] to write an article for us. He spent some considerable time on it, and he and I put on our suits and had a photographer take a number of pictures to be used as illustrations. Then Leo Daly, who is to have charge of the quarterbacks, also wrote a short article so that with the text book work on quarter back and these articles, we are pretty well off. The end position was revised by Frank Hallowell, Jack Hallowell, Peter Bowditch, Norman Cabot and Farley. Dave Campbell[39] had promised to write me a good article on end[s] in the near future. We have a first rate article on the Yale system of defense, written by Charlie Daly with diagrams, and I have collected into one article everything bearing on generalship that I could get hold of. Lewis has rewritten his article on centre rush. With the help of Schoelkopf, Capt. Hurley, Dunlop, Wrightington and I rewrote and simplified an article on the play of tackles as well as an article on the position of full back. Edgar Wrightington, Dunlop and I revised the old papers on the play of the rush line backs, largely a defensive article. Percy Haughton and Bob Kernan together revised Haughton's article on kicking and the three of us posed thirty or forty times for pictures as illustrations. As a further help in this illustrative work I had the mutoscope and biograph Company of New York, which takes pictures for Keith's biograph, send us on a special operator. This man took 1200 pictures of Haughton, Kernan and me in the act of kicking. Being very rapid, the pictures show every phase of kicking, and inasmuch as pictures were then in profile as well as face to, we got very complete results. Certain of these biograph pictures will be reproduced in the kicking article written by Haughton, and the rest I shall have framed so as to be able to take any kicker in and show them to him, that he may see wherein his faults lie. The pictures all told cost about $75.00, but I think they are wholly worth it, and they are permanent.

It takes but a very few words to tell about these various articles,

38. Daly was a Harvard quarterback and letter-winner (1898–1900), achieving all-American status in 1898 and 1899 and becoming captain and second-team all-American in 1900. He then went to the U.S. Military Academy, where he continued to play, becoming all-American in 1901 and third-team all-American in 1902. This was the same Daly for whom Reid refused to play in 1900 because he felt that he had been treated poorly the previous year.

39. Campbell was a Harvard letter-winner (1899–1901) and was all-American each year at end.

and it may sound as though it required very little work to get them, but it took me four and a half months to get them all done. I was constantly put off and put off, for one reason and another. Even after I had the rough proof of most of the articles I had to wait for a proof from the printer and then had to correct that proof, return it and then recorrect it. The illustrations made it necessary to arrange for a photographer on days when I could get both Kernan and Haughton out. Sometimes one would come and not the other. Then I would have to begin all over again. Then if a given picture was not satisfactory, we had to try it over again; and so on indefinitely. It seemed as though we should never get them done. The article by Lewis on the guards will complete the various positions. This article is a little late because we were afraid that the changes in the rules might affect the guards more especially.

Having determined that there have been altogether too many coaches out on the field, and having decided that this next Fall any man who is to coach must be out regularly, and then only when I want him, I thought it best to notify the football fraternity in general of that fact, so that there might be just as little friction as possible when the season opened. First [of] all I therefore got a list made out of all the old football players as well as the names of many prominent men interested in football or in other ways connected with it, and I sent them the letter which appears on the opposite page [missing]. I received several answers to this circular, all of which were in favor of the plan. I can't help whether the plan is favored or not: we certainly cannot get along with everybody on the field, and everybody talking, and I would rather make a good many mistakes and yet have things go along in the same groove than to make none but skip all over. The list to whom this circular was sent was gathered in every way I could possible manage it, and is pretty fairly complete. It should be pretty handy hereafter. A copy of it appears on the opposite page [missing].

I think that a little account of my experience with the rules committee will be rather interesting and instructive to anyone who has never had anything to do with that phase of football. In the first place the meeting of the committee was postponed four or five times for various reasons. Finally it was called on the night before the morning on which Dashiell, the Chairman, had to go abroad with the American Tennis team. In other words, it was very evident that whatever was done must be accomplished in one night, and that the chances were that those who had called the meeting were not aching to have much of anything done. The members of the committee present were Paul Dashiell, Chairman, Walter Camp of Yale, [John C.] Bell of

Pennsylvania, [John B.] Fine of Princeton, [Amos Alonzo] Stagg of Chicago, [Louis M.] Dennis of Cornell, and myself for Harvard. The meeting was called to order at 8 o'clock and from then until midnight the question of minor changes was taken up and discussed. Several good changes were made in that way. At midnight there was a short adjournment in the nature of a recess and then we went into session on the matter of opening up the game. Preliminary to this, a unanimous vote was passed that it would be a good thing for the game if it were opened up somewhat. Then a discussion was opened as to the best way of accomplishing this. Camp stated that he was not in favor of making any change which would limit either the offense or defense, and that he was pretty well satisfied with things as they are. Bell of Penn said little except to motion for adjournment continually. Our suggestion that the game be opened up by putting the offense and defense each back received more consideration than any other proposition, but Camp, Stagg and Bell would not hear of it, and inasmuch as the vote must be unanimous in order to have anything pass, nothing went through. Camp proposed increasing the distance to be gained to 10 yards, but no one was willing to consider that for a moment. I believe now, as I think of it, that that is really a good scheme, for where the distance is so great, it will be more difficult to keep possession of the ball, and therefore possession of the ball will be of less importance than it is now, because it will change hands oftener. That in turn will be likely to cause people to be willing to take bigger risks in open play for the sake of making bigger gains. It would probably need some few limitations, but I think I should almost be willing to see it tried, although Yale, with Camp's inventiveness, would very likely take the lead for a year, owing to our inability to develop plays on our own. I shall not attempt to go into the various suggestions that were made for changing the rules, since they will be found on the opposite page [missing] where I shall put them for future reference. At half past three in the morning, we adjourned with practically nothing done.

Before going down to the rules meeting I had quite a talk with President Eliot regarding the course he thought it wise for me to take, and he agreed with me when I said that I did not see that there was any course for me inasmuch as I could do nothing but bar anybody elses progress without making any myself. For these reasons it seems to me that the Rules Committee is a dead letter and ought to be abolished at once. At present it is merely a tool of Camp's. The members of the Committee ought to be elected by their University instead of being guests, and they should have the power of carrying a thing through on majority vote instead of being at the mercy of any one man's vote. I brought the matter up before the Athletic Committee on its first meeting after my return, but nothing was done about it. It seemed best to lay it on the table until the Fall.

It seemed advisable to get the coaching staff for next Fall settled about as soon as possible, so, in conference with Waters, Lewis, Hurley and others, we finally decided on the following men: For centres and guards, Lewis and Bouve; for tackles, Waters, Leo Daly; for half backs, Dunlop and Wrightington; for kickers; Kernan and Haughton; and for full backs, Schoelkopf and myself. Waters and Lewis need no comment. Bowditch at end was appointed in Cabot's place for these reasons,— first, of all Cabot said that he would be unable to give as much time to the work as heretofore; second we are trying to establish a permanent system here and Bowditch, who is liked and respected by the men, ought to be a first rate coach. He took hold well in spring practice, and being in the law school is right at hand. I have set on foot a movement in Boston whereby Kernan and Bowditch shall each be employed in Boston rather than in their homes in New York, in order to keep them within e[a]sy call of Soldiers Field. Neither of the men graduates for two years yet, but if they are going to stay here they should be beginning to shape their minds that way so that they won't be looking out for work in New York. Helping Bowditch as advisers will be Cabot, Frank Hallowell, and any other men whom Bowditch would like to have out, but Bowditch will be responsible for the position, and will do most of the work.

Leo Daly at quarter back was appointed after I had carefully gone over the list of possible men. Bob Wrenn has just got married and has gone off for his honeymoon abroad. He will not be back in time to do much active work when we need him, and besides that, he will live in New York. Then too, he is on the New York Stock Exchange. I tried hard to get him to change places with his brother on the Boston Stock Exchange through the football season, but it seems that it is against the rules of the stock exchanges to allow any such practice, so that Bob Wrenn was an utter impossibility. Dudley Dean,[40] owing to his father's recent death, finds it necessary to be gone West during the month of September, which is when I shall have to have the

---

40. Dean was a Harvard quarterback and letter-winner (1888–90) and had made all-American in 1890. Dean had played baseball at Harvard (1889–1891) and had also traveled with Albert G. Spalding's world professional baseball tour in 1889–90, when he was paid 4 pounds a week plus expenses. The tour went to such places as England, Italy, Egypt, and Australia. See Notarized Document in Walter Camp Papers, Box 2 Folder 46, and Box 20, Folder 564, Yale University Archives.

most careful work done on the field. I tried to get this trip put off, but Dean says that it is imperative that he should go because the interests of his mother and sister and wife demand it. I tried hard to get Charlie Daly and went up to West Point to see him on two occasions. On the first occasion I found that my getting him would depend largely on what Daly's standing was at graduation. Looking that up, I found that with the standing that he had, he would probably be assigned to infantry work, which meant either Panama or the Philippines.[41] It turns out that it was Panama. Hoping even then that there might be some way of getting Daly, I wrote to President Roosevelt and asked him if there was any possibility of Daly's being assigned to any of the forts in Boston Harbor. He wrote back that he hardly felt warranted in interfering with the War Department. As [William Howard] Taft, the head of the War Department, is a Yale man and off in the Philippines, it was impossible to get any word to him before Daly received his commission. [William L.], Garrison[42] could not spare the time regularly from his work, and besides is so set in most of his opinions that he has caused some little friction on previous occasions, which it will hardly do to have next fall. Leo Daly has once coached the freshman football team, he has played a year or two on the varsity base ball team, and but for a bad leg would have played regularly in Marshall's place on the varsity in 1901. He is a good fighter, a good thinker, and a hard worker. The only condition that he made upon accepting the place was that he should be allowed to give all the time to it that he wanted. I wish that most of the other coaches were interested enough to do the same thing.

I forgot to say that after some talk, Capt. Hurley and I decided to give Reggie Brown[43] charge of the second eleven again. He did it last year, and was very highly thought of by the members of the squad, so much so that they presented him with a souvenir of some kind. Knowing the men as thoroughly as he does, and having done the work one year, he will give to it a much increased effectiveness. I regard this position as a very important one, since I intend this year to

---

41. When Daly graduated, after earlier graduating from Harvard, there was a good chance that he would be commissioned to duty in the Philippines or in Panama. The Philippines had been under U.S. military control since the islands were acquired from Spain following the Spanish-American War in 1898. The Panama Canal Zone was acquired in 1903 following the American-aided Panamanian revolt against Colombia, which had previously controlled Panama.

42. Garrison was a Harvard quarterback and letter-winner in 1897.

43. Brown was a Harvard fullback and letter-winner (1895–96).

have the second eleven trained in fundamentals and otherwise just as carefully as the varsity men; and the same is true of the freshman team, for which I have as yet not been able to settle upon a coach. I want a man who knows a certain amount of football, and who, above all, will do as he is told, and who commands the confidence of the college. I shall expect the freshman coach this Fall to be responsible for the work that his candidates do in their studies, as I am convinced that the first half year's work in a freshman's career decides as to whether he is going to get through the year or not. Almost every freshman that I have looked up who has failed at the end of the year has had a very poor record at the first hour examination or at the Mid Years. The trouble is that in changing from school to college the men are unable to make themselves do the studying which masters have seen that they did do when at school. The result has been that the work has been neglected until it was too late to do it. The freshmen this Fall must be made to do their work from the start.

Kernan will have special charge of the kicking, because I could not depend on Haughton's getting out regularly. I hope that he can come out often to confer with Kernan because he is a valuable man, but Kernan will have the bulk of the work to do, and I believe him to be fully capable.

Dr. Nichols will be medical adviser for the eleven, and is going to be a mighty valuable man there. Already he has made a quantity of first rate suggestions. Among other things, he has consulted Dr. Pfaff, of the Harvard Medical school, on the matter of diet, on which we are not at present as well up as we ought to be. Then he has suggested a clean towel for each man every day, and the necessity of washing out the jerseys every so often in order to keep them reasonably clean.

I believe that this complement of men, with any other men out from time to time, will make a harmonious company. In case any other man wishes to come out and see the practice at any time, he will be entirely welcome, but, as my circular letter said, will be given a pad and pencil and be asked to take notes. The pads and pencils are all ready now. I have been to see personally every man that had anything to do with the coaching of the Harvard team during the past twenty years, and know pretty much what men can give me the most valuable points on certain features of the game this fall. I shall not give a list of the coaches I have seen, since such a list would comprise sixty or seventy men.

In order to settle on the method to be taught men of catching punts,

I arranged a meeting on Soldiers Field, Carl Marshall, George Gray, Charlie Brewer[44] being invited, besides Hurley and myself. At that meeting, to which Brewer failed to come, we each of us expressed our opinions as to how the ball should be caught, illustrated our ideas by actually catching, and then concluded that except for one or two slight features we were all agreed. The main difference that came up was one emphasized by Geo. Gray, where he wants the ball caught almost below the stomach and against the upper part of the legs, using one of the legs as one side of the basket formed by the body, the arms and the hands. This meeting was a very successful one, since the discussion brought something definite to have in mind for the backs next Fall. We shall take the backs and have them catch thrown balls first, and then kicks, thus gradually building up confidence and safety. I am bound that the team this Fall shall be thoroughly drilled in these respects. Charlie Daly, in the discussion I had with him about catching, argued that the ball should be caught more up on the chest, but after trying it for some little time, acknowledged that it was largely a personal matter with him and not a safe thing to teach anyone else.

As soon as the changes in the football rules had been worded, so that it was evident that none of them affected the play at all, we sent around to each of the coaches the circular which appears on the opposite page [missing]. Aside from one or two very general suggestions, we got nothing out of it, and I hardly think the experiment worth while repeating, except perhaps, to show outsiders that things are moving.

In order to get everything possible bearing on football at hand, I got together the notes and books of all the previous coaches, all the literature that I could pick up, also. I shall get all of this at my fingers' ends this summer, so as to be thoroughly up on it this fall.

Immediately after the card catalog was finished, I took around a complete list of all the men on it to the following coaches: Donald, Waters, Lewis, Bowditch, Farley, Brown, Wrightington, Leo Daly, Bob Kernan, and got each to check off the list such men as he should like to see come back, whether they were candidates for his position or not. In this way they checked off, all told, 278 men. After that was done, I had a list printed off of them all, and had it taken around to the office, where Mr. Cram gave us the standing of the various men.

44. Gray was a Harvard halfback and letter-winner (1892–93); Brewer was a fullback and halfback and won letters from 1892 to 1895, being an all-American in 1892, 1893, and 1895. He was the ball carrier of the first flying wedge play, invented in 1892.

74 men are for various reasons ineligible, either because they were dropped or graduated or were sent away or left college on their own accord, or were sick, or for other reasons. It is gratifying to find that only one man who was out on last year's varsity squad has thus far failed to qualify. This speaks pretty well for the police work we have done this spring. The one man who failed was Upham, who was sent away not because of inability to do his work but on moral grounds. That leaves me with about 204 men to call back. Of that number I don't suppose more than 150, if that many, will show up for the first day o[f] practice, but I shall be glad if everyone of them appears. In the two weeks just previous to the opening of college we ought to be able to look over these men in such a way as to be sure of their playing ability. In this way we ought to be ready for the greater outflow when college opens, at the same time relieving ourselves of the bulk which came out early. By taking the varsity squad as though it were the only squad out there and giving it all the work we think it wise for it to have, it will be possible to handle the balance in the odd moments without in any way interfering with the development of the eleven. I shall throw into one squad at once the 50 best men of the lot, and give them special attention. The rest of the time we shall give to the remainder of the squad, passing men into the squad of fifty as fast as they show capability. I firmly believe that the material should be carefully sorted at the beginning of the season, and that every man who has a show should be carried from the start of the season on, in order that he may be in shape at any time during the season when it may be necessary to call up him. Heretofore we have frequently left men untouched because at the moment we didn't want them. Then someone has been injured and we needed them badly, but could not get them into shape in time to have them render us any great service.

In order to get the heads of the various departments to thinking about football, and to get their minds pretty clear on their positions, I sent around a letter asking each man to hand in a list of the qualifications, physical, mental and moral, which he would like to have in his man if he were able to pick him himself. In addition to this I asked for a list of the fundamentals which they planned to teach their men. After some considerable nagging, I got these out of the coaches, and I think they will turn out to be valuable. To my mind one of the criticisms to be made on our coaching in recent years has been the fact that in picking a quarterback, for instance, the tendency has been to go on to the field and choose at once the man with the best technique, forgetting that the technique of the position is the easiest thing to acquire, while the head work and freedom from injury are too very necessary qualities which cannot be given. By having the coaches write out the special qualifications which they would like to have in their men, I think they will be led to go a little deeper into the qualifications of the candidates next Fall, instead of deciding too early on a man and then finding out too late in the season that he lacks one or two of the most essential qualities of such a player. Taking last season for an example, the quarterback coaches took Hugh Kernan and Steve Noyes as being first class quarter back material, and played them as varsity men the greater part of the season. Toward the end of the season Noyes was continually getting hurt, Kernan was overworked and nervous, Noyes was not equal to the generalship, and things were in a bad way. In that crisis, the coaches turned to the freshman team and picked up Starr, who, two weeks before the Yale game began work with the varsity, and proved to be a better man than either of the other two.

Similarly with regard to the ends [Clarence] Randall had not the making of an end in him, and it was useless to try to play him there; nor was it wise to play [Oliver] Filley there when he could only practice a limited length of time on certain days of the week. To my mind, these unfortunate mistakes might have been partially at least, obviated if the coaches at the beginning of the season had made up their minds to look carefully through their candidates even if a certain man looked at first sight to be the right man. At any rate that is the basis upon which we shall work this next Fall.

The signals which the team has been using for the past four or five years have been very crude and inadequate, so I determined to see if we could not improve on them this year. To that end I collected all the suggestions and information I possibly could with regard to them from books and individuals, and then tried to arrange with [Lorin F.] Deland[45] to help me put them together. Deland has exceptional inventive ability and has given much thought to this particular part of football. At first Mr. Deland was entirely unwilling to take any part in football at all, but after much urging on my part he consented to give me some time. From that time on I tried in vain for two months to arrange for a meeting with him. I telephoned him at least forty times; wrote him four letters; went to his office and his home seven

45. Deland was neither a Harvard graduate nor a football player. He was, though, a Boston businessman who found great satisfaction in adapting military strategy to football as well as to business. In *Imagination in Business* (New York: Harper & Brothers, 1909), he used a military metaphor that could be applied to athletics: "Business is intellectual warfare, a battle of wits—in which one does not repulse solid shot with blank cartridges" (19).

or eight times; and did everything I could to get hold of him, but without avail. Finally I located him while he was off for his vacation at Kennebunkport, Me. After some considerable correspondence I went up there for three days, and we worked out from my suggestions six or seven different sets, copies of which I give on the opposite page [missing] for future reference. I don't feel wholly satisfied with what we have yet, but think that we can work out something first class before we are through with it. I believe that the system of signals where the plays are numbered is the kind to have, but it is a very difficult matter to do this until your plays are finally picked out, which may not be until late in the season. It is therefore pretty hard to find out just how to get around this point. We want signals which shall be simple, clear, easily given, with single digits, and unintelligible to the opponents. Some of our signals heretofore have been altogether too complicated for serviceable use. It is well to keep in mind in these matters the axiom of Cam Forbes: "It is better for you to know your signals and for your opponents to know them than for neither of you to know them."[46]

During the spring I made a point of trying to find out what fellows had been injured last Fall, and whether they were well over such injuries. I found that many of them were not, and that by Fall they would be very little better off than they were at that time; so I made arrangements with Dr. Nichols to examine these men, and to put them in as good shape as possible.

[Karl F.] Brill, it seems, had some enormous corns on the bottom of his feet which made walking painful to him and which needed constant attention. Dr. Nichols gave him a certain kind of shoe to wear, and at this writing Brill's feet are all right. [Roger] Derby, the captain of the freshman team, last fall had a bad knee, and we also looked that over. [James] Montgomery had another knee, and we had a steel brace made for him. Another valuable case was that of Bartol Parker, candidate for centre, who seemed to weigh more than his ankles could support, with the result, that one of them was weakened from straining. He was put through a course of massage and bandages, and this summer he says his ankle is all right. Another man, not of any known ability, by the name of Fultz, had a very bad broken down arch. He claimed that he had been to several doctors about it but that they had been unable to do much for him and that he should probably not be

46. William Cameron Forbes was a Harvard letter-winner in crew in 1891. He became Harvard's football coach in 1897 and attempted to put Harvard football on a more scientific basis, which included a new system of starting signals.

able to play. Dr. Nichols had a special shoe made for him with plates, and one thing and another, and if there is any chance that Fultz may play, it will be due to this treatment. Upham, who will not be a candidate because of dismissal from the University, had a fractured arm a year or two ago which was rather weak, and which we wanted to get toughened up for this Fall. With a leather armlet and wrestling he had that up so that had he been allowed to come back he would have been in very fair shape. I regard this looking after injuries during the spring as being most important, because an injury only half looked after is very easily renewed, especially in the beginning of the season when the men are soft.

One of the most valuable things that we did during the whole spring was to investigate thoroughly the matter of football clothing, in which Harvard is pretty much behind the other leading colleges. Brine, the outfitter in Cambridge, has probably done just exactly what he has been ordered to do, and done it pretty faithfully, but he has not kept up with the progress in general. He wanted me at once to promise to give him the order for our suits, but I held him off and gave him something of a scare, which will, I think, tend to put him more on his metal this next year. Of course it is a great deal better to have the outfitter here at Cambridge where he is on tap at any hour of the day than to send to such a firm as Spalding of N. Y. and have to wait sometime for the orders to be filled. I made up my mind to find out all that I could about the clothing of all the colleges at hand. Somewhat by accident I got hold of a felt shoulder pad such as Yale has been using customarily and with this as a basis I worked out the Yale clothing pretty thoroughly. On the occasion of the Yale-Georgetown game this Spring, in baseball, I went down to New Haven to take notes on the Yale team for the varsity nine. Reaching there as I did three hours before the game I spent the time in nosing about New Haven. I finally found a store run by Doc Hull who was at one time a Yale trainer and who from his talk seemed to be rather out of humor with the Yale methods, presumably because he had been displaced. At first he was not disposed to give me much information that amounted to anything, but by using all the little points I had been able to pick up with regard to Yale clothing I seemed to convince him that I knew pretty much about it, and when I told him that I had written to Murphy[47] about his ankle brace and one or two other things, which was true, he gave me much information that I was glad to get. He was a little behind in some of the clothing, but told me of the three

47. He is referring to Mike Murphy, the Yale trainer.

places where Yale gets most of her stuff. In the first place Spalding Bros. of N. Y. for general material; and a man name J. Stroehle, living at 1077 Chapel St., New Haven, just a little bit above the New Haven House, where a crude sign of a Yale football player, probably Bliss, indicates his shop; and a man named Schneider, also on Chapel St. above Park I think, at any rate some three or four blocks above Stroehle, and on the left hand side. It turned out that Stroehle and Schneider made a great many things to order for Yale, especially shoes, head gear, shoulder pads, elbow pads, knee pads, and any special harness which any particular occasion might demand. Stroehle was on the lookout for business and exceedingly glad to have me come in. After some considerable talk he showed me samples of everything he had as well as the orders which he had had from Yale for next year, and those that he filled this year. I will begin with the shoes and tell what I learned. The entire Yale Varsity have their shoes made to order, the order being given during the Spring term so that the shoes are on hand by the time the men return to college. The line men have, of course, especially heavy shoes, and the backs pretty fairly heavy ones too. Each man has usually two pairs of shoes during the season. These shoes [S]troehle makes for them out of good leather, first class workmanship and good fit, for $8. a pair. These shoes are supplied with the Murphy steel ankle brace which every man on the team is required to wear. It is customary for them to wear very few ankle supports such as we have used, and they don't seem to have suffered any in an increased number of sprained ankles. The Yale cleats are somewhat different from ours, being more in number and a little differently arranged, altogether more flexible and better looking, to my mind, than ours. In rainy weather, to keep the men from slipping, one especially long cleat is placed in the middle of the sole of the shoe, about two inches from the toe, just behind the first natural cleat that occurs there. This is taken on and off according to the weather.

In the matter of shin guards, Yale uses very few, and puts them on only when an injury needs protection. They are seldom worn by custom. It seems to be customary to slip a small shin guard down inside the stocking which may be shifted or removed at any time without much difficulty.

For knee pads Yale has something which is, to my mind, distinctly ahead of what we have been accustomed to have, and in getting these pads Yale has made one step forward in the theory of football padding. Instead of having pads in the knees of the trousers, Yale's pads are all on the body of the player, so that there is no possibility of a shifting of the pad or exposure of any portion of the knee. The pad which they wear consisted this last year of a square piece of flexible felt about three quarters of an inch thick, and varying in size from eight inches by six or seven, to greater or less dimensions according to the size of the individual. Across the lower surface of this felt about an inch up from the bottom a leather strap is sown with a buckle. This strap is meant to go around the calf of the leg just above the calf and just below the knee-joint. One of these pads, when made, looks something like the half of a cylinder and protects the knee in front and from the two sides. To prevent binding of the knee by this pad there is a strap above the knee, so that when a man stands straight up the pad comes up along the surface of the leg some little distance above the knee. When the knee is bent, the upper part of the pad keeps the direction of the lower half of the leg and is therefore at right angles with the upper part of the leg. This stiffness, however, wears off very soon with use, so that the knee pad becomes pretty well moulded to the knee and is not at all bulky. It is the custom of the Yale people to get this felt in large strips, then to cut out pieces for each individual according to the size wanted. A pair of pads can be made up in this way within ten or fifteen minutes.

This next year Yale seems to be planning something of an improvement over this felt style, although I am not wholly convinced that it will be an improvement. Stroehle showed me some of the models which he had made, and while they fit the knee beautifully, and are much less bulky, I doubt very much whether they are as comfortable to the knee as the plain felt squares. This new style of pad has a leather outside moulded to fit the knee and reminded one of the old Roman armor for the knee. The interior of the leather is lined with a thin layer of felt. Trying on one of these pads in practice, it seemed to me that my knee received a much severer jolt from a tumble with one of these pads on than with one of the plain felt ones. I suppose this is due to the fact that the leather exterior to the new pad rather prevents the give in the felt lining which the felt alone allows. However, we shall try to have a few of them worn and see how they go. Stroehle certainly has great skill in modelling and his models are all that could be desired in their line. I have an idea that by cutting out a circlet of the leather outside which is over the knee cap, the knee cap will have the soft protection which the plain felt pads afford. We shall try this out anyhow, and I hope to get something good out of it. With these pads on there is, of course, no pad except in special cases in the knees of the men's trousers. Yale orders her trousers without any padding in them at all. The men wear these felt pads on the knees and no one would realize from a casual glance that they did not have pads in their trousers.

The hip pads are smaller than those which we wear, but are fitted to each man so that very little extra pad has to be carried. The thigh guards are rattan which Yale wears protect more of the thigh than ours do, and for that reason are probably a little better. The Yale jerseys are of course blue in color, and they do not have to struggle against the running of the color as we do. Nevertheless, the different men on the team wear under shirts with quarter sleeves under their jerseys. This undershirt can be washed and lasts a season, each man having two. In consultation with Dr. Nichols, we have decided to have the men here wear undershirts. There will be two advantages in doing this. In the first place, increased cleanliness; in the second place it will be possible on hot days for the men to run through their signals in these undershirts, thereby avoiding the sweating out process which jerseys would force. I expect that we shall save the men a good deal in this way. Yale's elbow pads are markedly smaller than ours, and are different in two other respects. First, they are of hair, which makes them light and cool, and second; the hair is covered with leather. Still again, the sleeve of the jersey is tight, so that this smaller pad does not have a chance to shift on the arm. Our pads heretofore have been so large as to almost encircle the arm. They have, to be sure, afforded protection, but have been very clumsy and unnecessarily large and hot. When one comes to think of it, we almost never have any bad elbows due to falling on them. They are usually twists or sprains, which no pad can stop. I had Schneider of Yale make me up a set of these hair pads on my jersey, and I have worn them now in eight baseball games which I have played this summer, and so successful have they proven that in all the sliding which I have done on some very rough diamonds, I have not received a single scratch. Schneider called my attention to the fact that the bulk of the pad should be above the elbow, as the tendency of the jersey sleeve seems to be to work down rather than up. To prevent the horse hair from working through on to the arm, a lining is used which in my case has been very effective.

For shoulder pads, Yale is away ahead of us. Acting on the principle which I spoke of some little while ago, that of placing the pads on the body rather than in the clothes, Yale had adopted a felt pad for the shoulder. This pad is cut to order like all the others, and is enclosed in a piece of cheese cloth for a covering. Pads are cut for each shoulder, fitting close to the neck on either side and running out over the point of the shoulder. The pads are then laid on the shoulders and elastics are put on to keep them on. Two elastics in front hold the shoulder pads of the right and left shoulders together at top and bottom. A similar pair in the back hold them there, while an elastic loop running under each arm pit holds them down over the shoulder. After a man has put on his undershirt, he slips these pads, which are thus fastened together, over his head like a yoke, and slips his arms through the elastics at the shoulder. Over this he puts his jersey. There are then no outside pads in the ordinary Yale suit. In case a man gets an extra bruise of any kind, and needs something more than the felt, he is given it, and any man who has had a bad shoulder in one year is given an extra pad at the start of the next year to prevent recurrence. Of course these felt pads may be of any thickness and may be made into any shape to cover any special deformity. Aside from the lack of padding which such a scheme seems to give, and which will take away the babied look which our men recently have had from overpadding, the men will actually be better padded.

As to head gear Yale men use at the beginning of the season some made to order out of hair and canvas, which are no where near as hot or bulky as those to be bought, and which have in their crown a hair pad to protect the top of the head on the inside.

Before I left New Haven I got together a sample of all these things, some $40. worth, and brought them home with me. I forgot to say that to protect their men from "Poops"[48] Yale used card board strapped onto the leg with elastic in place of the ruled out aluminums. This card board seems to me to be pretty poor stuff and when it gets moist flattens out. It is the only part of the Yale pad which I think we can probably improve on. Besides these pads I got a number of special pads for special things; steel and leather supports for the wrists, felt and leather protections for the ribs, sole leather shoulder protections, sole leather knee protections and various other pads of which we have samples but which it is very difficult to describe.

Yale had her clothing department so arranged that in case a man got hurt, we will say today, a special pad would be on hand for him covering the injured spot tomorrow, thus preventing him from getting hurt a second time in the old place, and allowing him to play much earlier than he could have done with us. In other words, Yale's system of padding is a much more flexible one than ours: a pad for an injury, no matter where it is, until it gets well,—that seems to be their theory. In looking over a Spalding order of Yale, which I shall take up later, I saw an item of some two or three dozen leather wrist-

---

48. "Poops" were likely deep bruises of the leg muscles, often resulting from being kicked. This might today be called a hematoma, a swelling filled with blood.

lets. As we have seldom used many of them I was rather puzzled for a time to see what Yale should need of so many. It finally occurred to me that in all probability the men are required to wear them during the fundamental work of the early part of the season when, in charging, breaking through and opening up holes, the man's wrists are put to a very severe strain without very much of a toughening process. These wristlets then are worn to tide the men over this beginning period and are gradually left off as the men's wrists become more and more used to the strain.

Before Spring was over I made two or three more trips to New Haven, and satisfied myself that I had pretty nearly all the ideas that I could get, and a sample of everything on hand. I had Mr. Brine go down to New Haven also and see these men, in order to give him a clear idea of what I wanted and what there was. I think that it opened Mr. Brine's eyes considerably to find out what a lot there was that he didn't know about.

Having talked the matter over with Dr. Nichols and Hurley and the graduate manager, we decided to give Stroehle an order for the shoes of most of our prominent varsity men for next Fall. Accordingly, a couple of days before class day, Stroehle came up from New Haven and measured the following men,—Brill, Parker, Starr, Hall, Osborne, Reynolds, Montgomery, Squires, Hurley, Grant, F. H. White, Leary, Nichols, J. D., Appolonio, and Boyer. I had a few other names down, but unfortunately had to go without them, as the men were scattered and hard to get at.

Feeling dissatisfied with the Yale protection for "poop" I determined to investigate that matter as carefully as I could. I had some correspondence with [Glenn "Pop"] Warner,[49] the old Carlisle and the present Cornell coach with regard to the fibre protection which he claims has been absolutely satisfactory, and which I believe [Fielding H.] Yost[50] of Michigan has been using. I got Mr. Warner to send me down a set of thigh pads as well as a set of shoulder pads of the same

49. Warner (1871–1954) played football at Cornell University. He coached at Georgia, Cornell, the Carlisle Indian School, Pittsburgh, Stanford, and Temple. In forty-four years of coaching, his record was 312 wins, 104 losses, and 32 ties. He developed the single- and double-wing formations and was innovative in developing equipment. A good source for well-known football figures is David L. Porter, ed., *Biographical Dictionary of American Sports: Football* (Westport: Greenwood Press, 1987).

50. Yost (1871–1946) received a bachelor of laws degree from the University of West Virginia, where he was a tackle on the football team. He soon went into coaching at Ohio Wesleyan, Nebraska, Kansas, and Stanford before gaining fame at the University of Michigan. His coaching record showed 196 wins, 36 loses, and 12 ties, with ten championships in fourteen years in the Big 10.

material. They are certainly a great deal stiffer and tougher than the Yale pasteboard pad, and perhaps a little heavier, though I think altogether more satisfactory. Unfortunately the pair I had were too long for me and interfered somewhat with my knees, but I have ordered Brine to get a number of them on hand so that we may use them if we find it wise. A frequent objection to theses fibre pads is that when they are wet they straighten out. Warner claims to overcome this by careful varnishing and shellac[k]ing of the fibre after it has been moulded and thus making it water proof. I guess that it can be kept in shape if it is properly handled. The fibre can be had of a firm in Philadelphia, a firm which makes a practice of cutting it out in the flat surface to patterns, and sending on the pads in the flat. Warner takes them then and soaks them in warm water and moulds them to each individual man. They are encased in cheese cloth and strapped to the leg with broad elastics, through which the leg slips, they being put on somewhat in the style of a stocking. Another suggestion which Warner made was the use of "interlaced curled hair" as padding for the shoulder and perhaps the knees. This hair comes in big squares six feet on a side and is quite thick, black, and very coarse. Warner says that they have been entirely satisfactory for him, but I don't believe it is as good as Yale felt for several reasons. First, the hair is extremely coarse and rather stiff; and second, it cannot be worn as a knee pad fastened to the body, since the hair will not mould to the leg as the felt will. I have some of it on hand as a sample in the sample room, which I have fitted out so that it may be considered by any other coach, if necessary. One other thing Warner suggested of which I have a sample, and that is a combination thigh, knee and shin guard, all in one piece, but with joints which make it work pretty well and freely. This pad is to be used, of course, only in very exceptional cases, and seems worth while having on hand. It is surprisingly elastic for such a cumbersome looking arrangement. Other than the "poop" and combination guards which I have just spoken of, I got very little from Warner that was of service. I finally concluded that in case a man got a "poop", we should have him wear aluminums, at any rate in practice, being careful to have them well padded to prevent injury to the other players. Dashiell will allow such pads in a game if they are protected, because I saw him on this point. That will make it possible for us to wear them in the Dartmouth and Pennsylvania games, if it were so desired, since I have arranged it so that he shall be the official in those games. This will perhaps make it possible for us to get through those two games without getting too much battered up.

When I was at New York at the meeting of the rules committee, I got hold of Stagg,[51] the old Yale player, and coach of Chicago, and talked with him from half past three in the morning, when the meeting broke up, until quarter of six, on the question of clothing and signals. The signal part I shall leave for that particular province, but the clothing I shall mention now. Stagg uses sponges put into the men's stockings for knee pads, and has found them thoroughly successful, owing to the great amount of resilience in the porous sponge. He says that if the stockings are pretty fairly tight there is no danger that the sponge will shift, and that the sponge is not only light, but fairly cool. To prevent injury in falling on the ball, Stagg practices a pretty good scheme, but when I suggested it to McMaster, he said it had been proven bad in his experience owing to the fact that the sand kept getting in the men's eyes.[52]

I went up to Exeter in the Spring, to see the Exeter-Princeton game and get points for the [base]ball nine on the Princeton team. While up there I renewed my acquaintance with Jim Robinson, the trainer of the Princeton team, and with Hildebrand, the old Princeton football player and coach. I had a very friendly talk with them on the matter of clothing, and found that they wear substantially what Yale does, and find it entirely satisfactory. They do not, however, wear the pasteboard "poop" protectors. I had intended to go down to Princeton when I was in New York at the meeting of the rules committee, but found that the Princeton team, together with all the men that I wanted to see down there, were up in New York to play Yale in the final game of the baseball series. I may yet, however, bring about a more thorough investigation of Princeton pads. At the Harvard-Princeton game in Cambridge I tried to get Jim Robinson to look over the pads with me, but found it impossible owing to the great jealousy between McMaster and Robinson, and the latter's absolute unwillingness to place himself at a disadvantage to McMaster such as he felt he would be placing himself in if he understood to advise me with regard to padding, which McMaster considers a part of his work, a part however, in which he has amounted to very little. Then, too, the loss of the game to Harvard

---

51. Amos Alonzo Stagg (1862–1965) was hired by the University of Chicago in 1892, the first football coach to have a standing academic appointment in a university. He coached at Chicago until 1933, when he was forced to retire at seventy years of age. He continued to coach at the College of the Pacific, Susquehanna College, and finally retired as kicking coach at Stockton Junior College at age ninety-eight. His winning record of 314 wins (181 loses and 35 ties) remained the standard until surpassed by Paul "Bear" Bryant's in 1982.

52. Reid likely is referring to the idea of using a sand pit when practicing falling on the ball as one way to prevent injuries.

made Robinson and the other Princeton men so down in the mouth that they were unwilling to do much discussing.

I had a long talk with E. W. Robinson, the coach of the Brown eleven, on the matter of padding, and found that he uses considerable of the Cornell outfitting, which of course left me very little to gain from him. I found out, however, that at Exeter, where they had previously worn red jerseys, they had changed the jersey to a green in order to get around the running of the red color, which has been so serious a handicap to us. In case the present undershirt plan does not prove successful this year, it seems to me that it would not be bad to consider a change from red to green at Harvard, with the possible exception of the arm from the elbow down, where the red effect might still be kept. It is, of course, undesirable to change our color in any way, but we had better do so, if necessary, than to have three or four cases of blood poisoning occur each year owing to the fact that the die has gotten into cuts or bruises. I thought of having our jerseys lined under the arms and around the neck with linen or chamois, but on trying it found that after a while the linen wrinkles up and causes the neck and arm pits to become irritated and raw.

I have yet to have a long talk with Yost, the Michigan coach, on football, and I am rather hoping that I may find out a few things with regard to Western clothing which may prove valuable. If I do[,] note of it will appear later on.

When I went to see Daly at West Point, I talked over with him carefully the clothing West Point uses, and found that it differed from that which we have usually had very little, namely, pads in the jerseys and trousers, the old leather ankle supports, etc. etc.

After having discussed the matter of clothing with everybody who was willing to discuss it, and after getting all the information I could from the various other colleges, and after some considerable experiment on the part of Brine and myself, I had a suit made up which embodied all the improvements which I felt we ought to make, and wore it for about two weeks tumbling around on Soldiers Field. Two difficulties developed. First, the fibre thigh guards slipped down on my thighs and interfered somewhat with my knees; and second, the space in the knees of my trousers was not sufficiently large to give my felt knee pads sufficient play, so we had to have my trousers enlarged. Otherwise everything went very satisfactorily, and with Hurley's consent we have told Brine to prepare for such an outfit.

I forgot to say that Yale uses quantities of electric tape, adhesive plaster, and surgeon's plaster in binding up sprains and bruises.

On one of the occasions when I was in New York, I went down to the Spalding Brothers and looked over their goods and got a number of samples of things a little different from what I had seen previously, among them a set of light moleskin trousers which I have observed some of the Yale men have occasionally worn, just why I have never been able to make out. The chief value, however, of my visit was the fact that I got a duplicate of the order which Yale had placed with Spalding for next year, and which with some supplement and additions I have ordered Brine to duplicate with this preparation, I confidently expect that we shall put a team on the field this Fall not only better clothed than any previous Harvard team, but as well clothed as any in the country.

In order to try and help the kicking along, I made a hard leather tongue made to my instep, which gave considerable good surface on the instep for a blow. This at first seemed a fairly good scheme, but after using it a few times, I found that it impeded to a certain degree my running, and that every time I kicked a ball there was something of a reaction against my ankle, which seemed to deprive me of a certain amount of the blow. Another scheme was that of having three ribbons of leather about the size of a shoe lace put across the front part of my kicking shoe, from about the big toe to a point just beyond the little toe toward the heel. These ribs were put on with a view to affording the kicker a little more friction in getting off spirals. After trying them for about two weeks time I concluded that I was just as well off without them, and after talking the matter over with Haughton and Kernan, concluded to give up any further attempts along the same line.

After college closed I had about thirty five foot balls sent around to different men for summer use. In order to get some real effort out of these men, all of whom ought to be doing something in their kicking, I wrote each man an individual letter telling him not only what he had to do for kicking, and general conditioning, but also telling him of any criticism which I had heard expressed concerning him, or anything else that in any way affected his chances. In one or two cases, the letters were pretty severe, but were wholly merited and entirely fair, if they were pretty blunt and unfeeling. On the opposite side will be found a number of these letters including the strongest, with one or two replies I received showing how they were taken. I planned that by writing to the men in this way they would clearly see that I am vitally interested in the work, and that my whole object is to get the most effective results from the whole squad, and that I am willing to go to any amount of pains to do it, but that I expect to be met half way. I have not said in any of these letters that in case a man does not come back on time he will be put at the second training table and kept there for some considerable time, until we feel pretty certain of his spirit, but I have in every case made it sufficiently plain how important it is to be back, so that no individual can say that he did not have fair warning.

[One letter and reply are included.]

22 July 1905

Mr. Bartol Parker
South Lancaster, Mass.

Dear Parker:

I am much disturbed and greatly disappointed over your seeming failure to show a satisfactory interest in the coming football season, and I am especially disturbed because, when I first came East, I had you in mind as one of the most promising and capable center candidates on the squad. Gradually, however, and much against my will I have been forced to place something of a question mark after your name.

You were a disappointment in the way in which you failed to respond to the spirit of the spring practice and now in the summer you are showing like signs of failure to recognize your responsibility. Every time I have seen you you have been smoking and in company with a number of fellows who didn't seem any more serious than you.

Meanwhile you are getting fatter and fatter and slower and slower, and the time when you might be passing and kicking the ball is slipping by. At this rate the fall will find you out of the running, for the other candidates are not acting so.

We are going to have a center this year who will fight, who will take a lively interest in his position, who is able to move enough to get about the field and make tackles, who can pass accurately and consistently and who will hang on like grim death. No such work as was had last year will be tolerated, and if the regular centers cannot afford the goods we will take someone else and teach him. Previous Varsity records won't count for anything unless backed up with the "goods".

You are in the summer school and your first duty is to get your work done, the second to do a little football work. The work in the school is hard, I know, but you can and ought to spend an hour a day at some recreation. Let it be passing and kicking a football and falling on it, four or five times a week, and something else, such as tennis or handball, or the others.

Now, all this is said in a friendly spirit, and I do not want you take offence at it, but I do want you to wake up. You are of a slow going, lazy disposition, and it is greatly to your benefit that you should correct these faults before they interfere with your life work, whatever it is to be. This is the age of "hustle" and hustle you must, if you expect to be anyone or to get anywhere.

Now, "get together" and "at it;" if you want help Captain Hurley or I will be only too glad to give it. Cut down the smoking, as fast as you can, and do wrist work in the gymnasium; that will strengthen those wrists for passing.

We have been licked about enough and we want to see you with your coat off, "after them" with us.

> Sincerely,
> [William Reid, Jr.]

> Lancaster, Mass.

Dear Mr. Reid:

You seem to have sized me up quite carefully and perhaps accurately. I wonder whether this is the reputation given me by last year's coaches or by your own observation. Since Summer School began I have been living at home, living a healthy and, I should say, fairly strenuous life; passing the ball nearly every day and running some, has been the foot-ball part of my exercise. Sometime ago I asked you what special things you wanted me to do; you said that you would write me. Mr. Reid, if you think you can bully me into playing and working hard, you are mistaken, but I am more than ready to do my damdest to lick Yale, however hard I have to work. I hope you will believe this in spite of the conclusions you have come to as to my character. At least, believe it till the season opens. I may not feel as strongly later, but I have only just read your letter.

> [Signed] Bartol Parker.

I think I mentioned, some way back, that just before the final examinations were on, I went around to see the various professors of shaky men. In order to show what a task this was, I present on the other side of the page a copy of the names of the men I went to see, with their addresses [see below], showing what an enormous amount of ground I had to cover. I believe that this was a good scheme, although it did take up an enormous amount of time, almost two weeks solid, but I also think that I should have begun earlier, for I found that it is a custom of many of the instructors to go off for their vacations as soon as the examination period begins, and to return only in time to give their own special examination and take off the books. Sometimes I think that seeing an instructor in this way and explaining to him that such and such a man is pretty slow in his work but entirely earnest, or whatever the case may be, one is likely to gain for the fellow whatever slight margin may be possible, and at any rate to gain special consideration in the correction of his work. This prevents carelessness of assistants in dashing off an approximate mark which they hate to change afterwards, where with a little more care they could very easily and conscientiously give the man a little higher mark. I might say in this connection that next year if I am still here, I do not propose to have to do anything like so much police work as I have done this spring, since we shall keep the men up to their work from the start of the season in an endeavor to prevent anybody from getting so far behind, with the possible exception of a few cases, as to make it necessary to give them such special care. By the end of this season we ought to be able to pick out the fifty or sixty most promising players in college and follow them through the winter safely.

Jones, H. S., 111 Hammond, Prince. Engl.

Ogg, F. A., 65 Hammond, Hist., 1a, Orr, Parker.

Clarke, D. A., Assistant, Conant, 29. Gov. 1. Talbot, Orr, Prince, Boyer.

Whitten, A. F., 128 Ellery St., G.S. Talbot, Fr. 2c.

Daggett, S., 342 Harvard St., Orr, Ec. 1.

Ayres, H. M., Drayton 2. Eng. a. Orr Starr.

Pahlow, E. W., Fairfax 7, Hist. 1a. Talbot, Starr, White.

Goodale, G. D., 5 Berkley St., White (Bot. Drawing) Pierce, Bot.1, Pell.

Fuller, H., Claverly 16. Eng. a. Lincoln; Eng. a. Parker, Pell, C.C.

Potter, M. A., 191 Commonwealth Ave., Boston. Hurley, Pierce, Fr.2c.

Weiner, L., Ayer. Slavic 4. Hurley (O.K.) Parker, Pierce

George, J. A., 51 Trowbridge St., Gov. 1, White, Starr, Reynolds.

Hall, T., 102 Mt. Auburn St., Eng. 28, Parker, Orr, Boyer.

Sturtevant, A. M., Divinity 16. Germ.a, Talbot, Germ. 1c, McDonald.

Fryer, C. E., 9 Francis Ave., Derby, Hist. 1a.

Babbitt, I., 6 Kirkland Rd., Fr. White.

Muenter, E., 63 Oxford, Ger. White.

Kennedy, F. L., 5 Mercer Circle. Eng. 3a. C. E. Lincoln.

Palache, C., 6 Buckingham Pl. Harrison (d) Mineralogy 2.
Parker, C. P., 1075 Mass. Ave., Lat. Reynolds.
Underwood, C. M., Perkins 13. Italian 1, Reynolds. A. or B.
Wright, C. W., Perk. 49, Ec. 1, Corbett, C.
Munroe, W. B., Dana 37, Gov. 17. Corbett, C.
Chase, G. H., Grays 24, Fine Arts 3, Corbett C. Pierce, C.
Usher, R. G., Asst. Perk. 35. Hist. 10. Corbett C. Pierce.
Farabee, W. C., 75 Garfield St., Am. 1, Corbett, D Plus; Pell.
Maynadier, G. H., 49 Hawthorne St., Eng. 7b, Corbett D-E, Pell.
Castle, W. B., 243 Beacon St., Boston. Eng. a. Barney.
Howland, Perkins, 34, Ec. 1 c. C. C. Pell.
Marcon, 42 Garden St., Fr. 2c. Boyer and Ball.
Briggs, 3 Ellsworth Park. Ger. a. Boyer.
Brigham, 12 Reservoir St., Hist. 1a. Boyer, Ball.
Nutter. Eng. a. 50 Beacon St., Boston. Eng. a. G. Ball.
Copeland, Hollis 15, Eng. a. J. F. McDonald.
Fritzell, 11 Summer St., Eng. 1d. J. F. McDonald.
C. L. Jackson, Holworthy 11, Chan. 1, McDonald.
Smyth, H. L., 9 Buckingham, Harrison (Min. 1 D Plus.)
Custis, Holyoke 7, Ec. 9b Harrison.
Sawyer, C. R., Boylston 10, Lincoln, Baring.
Wells, Dean's Office, Derby, Eng. F. Boyer.
Pierce, French 2c. Geology 4d. Talbot, Music, Slavic 4.
Goodale, 5 Berkley, Botany
Parker.
    French, 2c. Whethan 128
    Ger. A. Sturtevant, D. E.
    Gov. 1, Clark, E.
    Hist 1A. Pahlow.

When I first came on this spring and found out that while Yale and Princeton and Dartmouth and perhaps Cornell had been having on their teams regularly a goodly number of Andover and Exeter men, and that Harvard in six or eight years had not had a quarter as many as Yale or Princeton had had in any one given year, I determined to try and see if something could not be done to even up this average. Consequently I set about the forming of a Harvard Club at both Andover and Exeter, in the endeavor to create interest up there, which would rather taboo the thing, and so we simply let the club part of it rest. We got busy, however, in other respects, and made some progress. The little Harvard-Andover club which did exist up there and which never amounted to much, joined with the Harvard club of the town of Andover, made up of graduates of Harvard who live there, and bought a first class set of pictures of Harvard to put into the building at Andover where already Yale, Princeton, Pennsylvania, Dartmouth, Amherst, Cornell and the University of California have long been hung. The pictures which we sent up will be the finest up there, and will take up more space than any others, so that perhaps we are not so badly off in that respect, after all.

The biggest thing that happened up there this year, though, was the appointment of Bart Hayes as coach of the baseball nine. He took it and turned out a winning team, much to the joy of the Andover boys. To help along in the work of Wallis Rand,[53] Dr. Nichols and I went up occasionally and helped in coaching. In all our work there no mention was made to a single man about coming to Harvard unless the man himself voluntarily gave the information. We simply went up there to coach, and came away. The result was that after a most muckerly exhibition on the part of Yale's Varsity nine at Andover, the sentiment of the school became quite friendly to Harvard. Then the baseball management invited the Andover nine to Cambridge to see the Harvard-Princeton game, and then had them as guests at the Union for supper. Besides this, members of the Harvard Andover club frequently went to Andover, more frequently than heretofore, in order to keep matters moving, I had a long talk with Principal Stearns of Andover, and he will be very glad to welcome something of an Harvard invasion, because, as he says, the school already has a reputation of being a Yale school, somewhat to the disadvantage of the school from the standpoint of parents intending to send their boys to Harvard, who fear that if they are sent to Andover they will not receive the same treatment as those fellows there who are going to Yale. From the conversation I had with him, it seems that Harvard gets from Andover most of the students and literary fellow[s], Yale the better type of athletes, and Princeton the very poorest type of athletes and men, Princeton frequently taking men out of the lower classes in Andover as specials or graduate students, and then playing them on their teams only to lose them at the end of one year, through inability to keep up. We made something of a similar effort at Exeter, although we had no baseball coach there, since they had a hired coach. Pictures have been sent up there and the varsity baseball team tried to arrange a game with the Exeter boys, but was

53. Hayes was a Harvard baseball pitcher and letter-winner in 1898, a team on which Reid caught as a freshman. Wallis Rand was likely Waldron H. Rand, a Harvard baseball outfielder and letter-winner (1895–98) and captain in 1898.

unable to owing to the overbearing manner of the Exeter Manager, which caused some little feeling and misunderstanding. Graduates of Exeter with whom we worked were Mr. Burr, of Parkinson & Burr, Mr. Gleason, a lawyer in Boston, and Maurice Connor, commonly known as Roger Connor, who has had to do with the track teams at Exeter, and who is regarded most affectionately there. In addition to these Cranston should be mentioned. I do not much believe that Harvard will feel any great benefit from anything we have done yet, but I believe that we have started a feeling up there, especially at Andover, which may bear some fruit in the future. At Exeter Hart and Mac-Faydon, the two most promising men, who have been intending, of their own accord, to come to Harvard, will probably be bought out by Princeton or Pennsylvania, and thereby be lost to us, although they are legitimately our men. They will probably drop out just as [Jim] Cooney and [James] Hogan[54] did, through inducements which we cannot and will not offer.

I had several opportunities to explain the football situation at Cambridge, and in other ways to keep us before the schools and public, and I took advantage of most of them. Among other things, I spoke before the Association of Harvard Graduates, of Boston, before the Newark Harvard club, wrote a little statement for the Buffalo Harvard Club, spoke for the Milton Academy boys, Stone School, Noble & Greenoughs, and the Fay school. Then I wrote articles for the Harvard Graduate's Magazine, the Harvard Monthly, the newspapers, the Crimson, Illustrated Evening News, and one of the periodicals published by Stanford University in California. These articles together with the talks rather helped to make plain to people what we are trying to do here in putting our athletics on to a more permanent basis, and why in many cases we have failed in the past. Perhaps all this may lead to less severe criticism such as has often been the lot of Harvard teams of the past.

I shall now devote a paragraph to a number of small details which it is impossible to handle in more than a brief way, and which have really no especial connection with anything that I have previously said. The Hotchkiss school tried to get a game with our Freshman team, which we wanted very much to let them have, and which we were unable to give them because the athletic committee would not let our Freshman take another trip away from home; also because we did not really want any more hard games for the team, and because

---

54. Cooney became a Princeton football great, as did Hogan at Yale in the early 1900s.

our schedule had been already closed before the offer was made. The Hotchkiss graduates who are in college were very enthusiastic about the matter and said that if it were a matter of expense they would be willing to subscribe half the expense which either team should be put to in making the trip, and it seemed to me if possible next year to arrange this game, it should be done. During the winter, in order to keep some of the football men in shape, Hurley had [the] squad for dumbbell work, chest weights, and wrestling. The one difficulty of such a squad is that at that time of the year the men are not very enthusiastic about football, and don't respond very regularly, which helps along a spirit of do as you please, instead of the prompt discipline under which the men are expected to play in the Fall. In my opinion it is simply a question of allowing the men to come whenever they can and getting out of them whatever work you can, without making it too much of a matter of necessity with them. On the other hand, they do not want to feel that they don't have to come at all. We have arranged with the college office so that this Fall when the Freshman class enters, we can have men at the registration rooms to see that the freshmen fill out the blank cards for the football canvas. This is the first time that the college has ever allowed anything of the kind, and I feel pretty good over it. [Dan] Hurley, [Bartol] Parker, [Harold] Barney, and Carl Lincoln have had to go to the summer school in order to get courses enough off to make them eligible for the Fall. Hurley and Parker are taking work in Cambridge, while the other two men have been up to the Harvard Engineering Camp at Squam Lake. I find that the summer courses at college are extremely hard, and that anyone who takes them must expect to have to work right along. I have kept watch of Parker and Hurley in attendance, and have asked them every now and then how they are getting along. They told me all right. When I went to see their instructors I found out that in one course which they are both taking, they have had no examination or test of any kind, and that their one mark will be on the final examination. I asked Parker some questions which were calculated to test the knowledge he had of the course, and I found him extremely weak in it, and therefore insisted that he tutor with Nolen, and later that he work with a man named Smith, who was an assistant in the course last year, and who is a very good man. I turned in and spent a week taking notes on some of the outside reading of the course to help along, and had Parker down at my house in Cohasset over Sunday, during which time I went over the entire course with him, having him recite to me from a topical list which I had and about which I knew enough to tell whether he knew his course well enough for passing. Wherever he showed weakness we stopped at once and read up. The examination comes now in a few days and I am rather on edge about the result. If Parker does not pass, he will not be eligible, but if he fails to pass it will simply be because he has made an absolute ass of himself. If it were not for the fact that I were so vitally involved in the thing, I should feel very much inclined not to say anything more about it, but to let him rip, which is what he deserves. As it is, I shall keep at him at top speed up to the last minute. One of Hurley's courses is in mathematics, in which he is doing only very average work. I tried to get him to tutor with Mr. Hill, who published Wentworth and Hill's Geometry with Mr. Wentworth, but Mr. Hill was too busy, and so we accepted a man whom Prof. Huntington recommended. Neither Hurley nor Parker seem to show anything like the interest in their work that I feel in it myself, except perhaps Hurley, and he does not seem to realize what his neglect to get a tutor a little earlier, may cost him. I mention all this to make it clear to any one else that the summer school must not be considered as a joke, and that any man who takes the courses there must be followed up from start to finish, and be tutored all the time if necessary, if he is at all slow, in order to get him through. A man cannot loaf in that work. From all I can hear, the men at the summer camp are doing better. I have had a number of letters from various schools and colleges asking that I recommend some coach for them. I have had almost no man whom I could recommend, and some good chances have passed by. Andover wanted a coach, Tulane Univ., Dorchester H.S., and a University in Indiana. Next year I shall ask the squad, if I think of it before the men leave, whether there are any of them who care to do that sort of work, so that I may have a list to draw from. What is more, I am going to notify the schools that on one evening in each week I shall be at some room where I shall be glad to talk over football problems with anyone representing any of the schools in order to try and be of service to the school systems here, for which we are able to do very little. I spent some considerable time this spring figuring out a plan for the position of the men on receiving kick off. I consulted the picture of the Yale team, as it lined up to receive kick off from one of our games, and after consultation with Lewis and Waters, got a pretty satisfactory formation, I think, although I shall want to try it out early this Fall. In order to get reliable information concerning Pennsylvania next year, I have arranged with Clothier, an end a year or two ago, who lives in Philadelphia, to send me such information as he is able to pick up. He has already notified me of several rather important moves which are contemplated at Philadelphia, and has also told me several things about individual men on the team which may be very valuable. I have learned that last Fall many of the men on the squad, feeling that the question of their weight was a pretty vital one, handed in false weights to the managers on many occasions. Of course that was mighty poor spirit on the part of the men, and I hope won't be manifested this year, but I shall see to it that the manager checks off each man's weight by seeing him when he gets on to the scales. I am considering whether it will be wise to allow the coaches to smoke on the field, whether actually coaching or not, or whether to limit it to the side lines. I feel pretty clear that we should not allow it on the part of any coach who is actually doing coaching, but that we shall allow it on the side lines, or at any coaches' meeting afterward. As Deland is a man who has keen powers of observation, and can get a great deal out of seeing a team play, I tried to arrange so that he should referee the West Point game this Fall, but owing to a change in the personnel of the coaching staff up there, and the danger of having Yale feel that West Point was acting rather under handed in the matter, I had to give it up, much as I hated to, Charlie Daly felt that he could not ask it in any way, and Mr. Deland no longer knows any of the men up there well enough to propose it himself. Of course a proposition of that kind coming from me is wholly out of the question. It will not prevent us, however, from seeing Yale play that game from the side lines. In order to find out what exercises are best for helping guard candidates along, I wrote a letter to Bill Burden[55] in New York, a[s]king him for ideas. He told me that during the summer he used always to run half a mile every day at top speed; that on occasions he ran three quarters, but always made it a point to go faster and faster the longer he was at it. He also spoke of boxing hard with a good man for fifteen or thirty minutes each day. If, says he, a man begins to feel run down, he must reduce the amount of his work until he feels tip top. In the matter of swimming, he says that the men should not stay in too long, as too long immersion in any kind of water is bad. This he had learned from his own experience, being a very excellent swimmer. He also recommends tennis. It is interesting to compare this with what Dr. Nichols thinks, which is as follows. He says that we put men through a pretty severe course of training under extreme strain during a fairly short length of time, and that we therefore do not wish them to be too much trained down when they come back. He suggests such games as tennis, squash ball, hand ball, or anything which necessitates quickness and agility. The

55. Burden was a Harvard football letter-winner (1898–99).

kickers, of course, he says, should do kicking practice and get themselves into as good form that way as they possibly can, the danger
being overdoing. I went in to call on "Slugger" Mason, to see if he
would give me anything of value concerning the Dartmouth team,
or its game, but he was extremely surly and showed no disposition
to give anything unless he were paid for it. Inasmuch as I would be
willing to pay not to have him around, I did not press the matter, and
let it go. After his row with the coaches out here sometime ago, it is
pretty evident that he has no interest in Harvard beyond what he can
get out of it to personal advantage. Among the men whom I had in
mind for freshman coach are the following,— [Walter S.] Sugden,
C[arl B.] Marshall, [Raymond H.] Overson, [Andrew] Marshall, [Fran-
cis L.] Burnett,[56] and one or two others whom I have since found were
not available. It will be well, I think, for coaches to see to it that at
the time the first copy of their record is made, two or three other copies are also made. In this way, although the first copy takes a little
longer time, the time and expense of making separate copies thereafter, is obviated. In this particular case I am having three copies made
including the original. I tried to see if I could not get [Oliver S.] Cutts[57]
to do some coaching this Fall, and finally located him out in Washington or Oregon, where he is in law, and is coaching one of the University teams out there to help along. I think it would be a very good
scheme if it could be arranged in some way or other to get him to
work in Boston, for he is by all odds the best tackle coach of the
younger fellows that we have, and could be used to great advantage
as a field coach where Donald and Waters acted as advisory coaches
and gave directions. I had quite a long talk with Wrightington over
his season[58] and feel that a great many things he told me are going to
be very valuable and will prevent a repetition of some parts of the
policy which later proved to be a mistake. I have talked a good deal
with Billy Sullivan, city editor of the Boston Globe, and a Harvard
man, and find him to be a very sound advisor and a man to go to

56. Snyder was a Harvard football letter-winner in 1902, C. Marshall from 1901 to
1903, Overson in 1904, A. Marshall from 1902 to 1903, and Burnett from 1898 to 1900.
57. Cutts was a Harvard tackle and letter-winner in 1901 and an all-American in
1901, under the coaching of Reid. He was involved in an amateur-professional controversy, playing, even though he was a professional, against Yale and helping to win a
rare victory over Yale. Yale had been forced to drop Edgar Glass before the game for
also being a professional. The Cutts-Glass affair was one of the continual rancorous
conflicts between Harvard and Yale, beginning with athletic encounters during the
1860s.
58. Edgar Wrightington coached the 1904 Harvard football team, losing to Penn and
Yale.

when in critical positions. It was his suggestion that one of the first things to do in organizing the coaches for next fall was to try and gather around me the football brains which were available. I think this a very wise suggestion, and believe that it will prevent me from having too much second rate coaching around. It is certainly true that many of the players last year resented the coaching of [Arthur L.] Devens[59] and others who like him never actually made a position on the Varsity and never had the possibilities of being really first call themselves. Of course, it is not necessary to have been successful as a player, but it is necessary that if a coach was not a successful player, he should have exceptional football knowledge to offset it, which was not the case with some of the outsiders last Fall. A letter from W[alter] T. Harrison[60] on page [no page number] of this book will show how at least one man on the squad felt about it, and why he felt as he did. [Letter follows.]

Camp Kahkon, Chesuncook,
via North East Carry, Maine
August 2, 1905

Mr. W. T. Reid, Jr.

Dear Sir:

Your letter has given me a good chance to explain my apparent lack of interest and to say some things which I never said to anyone else. Before I say them I want you to understand that I have no ill feeling toward you but simply know nothing about what methods you use in coaching a team.

During my Junior year—the only year in which adverse criticism could have come up, I started the last week of practice with a boil on my neck which spread all over my chest and lasted until after Christmas—; Parkinson had a boil on his leg which lasted a month or two longer. It seems to me that this tells somewhat of a story when I had never had boils before or since that. It certainly was someone else beside myself who was to blame. And you should know how a man is when he is overtrained.

A second point is that I object to having men such as Waters and Lewis stand behind the line and whether justly or unjustly call me a "Son of a ———." This sort of language does not make me work any harder or drive me any faster, nor, as I think, can

<hr>

59. Devens was a Harvard football letter-winner in 1900.

60. Harrison was a Harvard football letter-winner only in 1902, but he did not graduate until 1906.

it do aught but bring a feeling of personal resentment in the mind of any self-respecting person. A third point is that I do not enjoy asking some of the minor coaches such as Devens and Motley, who have been in the habit of being on the field about every day, to show me about some point or other and have them turn away without giving any information. Perhaps these men do help the team, but they should be impartial in their advice.

A fourth point—and this is the only case of "pull" or discrimination which has ever been plain to me—is Derby's case. In the fall of 1903 he appeared about two weeks before the Yale game and without much ado he was tried on the 1st. Now I have seen Lewis send Bob Bleakie to the side lines from the 2nd as soon as Derby went in because Bleakie used to put it all over Derby. Last fall I was not connected with the squad, so I could only watch this case from the outside and so have nothing to say. You may perhaps think that I am "sour" or something of the sort. I am just one of the sort who sits back and keeps quiet hoping that for the good of Harvard athletics someone will take hold and use his own judgment and change these things.

The Randall case of last fall was a climax of the sort of feeling which had grown on him from watching four years of college athletics.

The so-called "Rank and Fil[e]" of Harvard believe in you and I think they are willing to go to defeat with you, if they must, but they expect you to make reforms in the coaching and cast out the "deadwood" and the men who are not up to date, from the staff.

Another point which you should know is that Vanderbilt your assistant manager makes a practice of "cutting" men on the street whom he has known through football. This, I think, tends to bring bad feeling and so should be stopped.

I have purposely made this letter very frank and I am willing to stand up for anything I have said if you feel like using it.

> Yours sincerely,
> [Signed] Walter T. Harrison.

The geometry is coming along quite well. W. T. H.

On one occasion after I had made something of a talk, Parkinson, who, it will be remembered, had a pretty serious time with a sore on his leg and who was severely criticised for his poor passing and play in the Yale game, came up to me and asked if he might make one or two comments on the past year, in a perfectly friendly manner. I told him that I was only too glad to have him. He said that he thought that the coaches colored the accounts of the practice, and cursed out players almost too much for the best results. He said that if the coaches felt that a man was not doing his work, even though the man himself might be doing the best he could, they were likely to put rather scathing criticisms of him in all the papers, and in every way to make it uncomfortable for him. Parkinson said that in his case those notices were very discouraging to him when he felt that he was doing everything that he possibly could to overcome his faults, and some days felt that he had made distinct progress, only to find in the accounts of the practice more abuse than before. He commented on the fact that in the accounts of the Yale practice, if a man plays well, there is a brief comment on that fact, and if he plays poorly there is also one; that a man could feel that the comments on him were quite just, and in most cases quite accurate. With us he says the accounts so misrepresent things that it ma[k]es a fellow feel almost ashamed to go among his friends when he feels that they have probably read what was said about him. Further than that Parkinson said that he knew that if he had been treated a little differently, more could have been gotten out of him, but that when a man felt that he was unjustly treated, it was almost impossible for him, no matter how good his spirit, to rise absolutely above such a state of things and even improve on his work. His plea was that individuals should be treated as individuals, and not be dealt with as a squad. I think there is a good deal in what Parkinson had to say here, and it simply makes me feel surer than before that the policy I had already determined upon for next Fall will be altogether the wisest. If I do not wish a thing to be known, I shall give no account of it, but simply ignore it, while whatever account I do give will be entirely true, though perhaps lacking in some of the fuller details. I think that it is about time that we got along without constantly lieing about our practice, especially when it can be easily avoided. Another change along these same lines will be the cutting out of any side line coaching whatever. When I was on here before we did some of it, and my reasons for it are given in my other book. My reasons for changing are simply that side line coaching is against the rules, and is therefore unsportsmanlike. Word came to me in rather an indirect fashion that in line with the present very common plan of importing players to strengthen a team, the Carlisle Indian school was seeking to recruit its strength with four or five Indians from the Sherman Indian school in California. The report was that this was due largely to a change in the commandant of the post, the man in charge now having determined to raise the Carlisle Athletic standard higher than it had ever been before. Wishing to find out just what the situation was, I wrote to Mr. Thompson, the Supt. of the school, and told him frankly what had come to my notice. He wrote back and told me that it was a Government rule that there should be so many Indians enrolled and that at certain times they graduated or lost so many men that it became necessary to solicit in order to keep the school up to its proper standard. He said that inasmuch as the Government paid the expenses of the Indians from start to finish, there was no matter of ind[u]cement concerned, simply the offering a man the change from one school to another, where he might perhaps have greater advantage. He said that it was quite possible that some football men had come from California, but that they had come not as a result of special representations to them from the school. I feel, in spite of what Mr. Thompson said, that there is something a little crooked in the affair, and shall watch with great interest to see what kind of a team they have. I have tried for some time to make up the committee on offense, which I hope to get some work out of, and finally chose as the men whom I should like to have on it the following,— Deland, Lewis, Haughton, Wrightington, Reggie Brown, C. D. Daly. Of these men Lewis will serve I know; Daly will serve as long as he will be in this neighborhood; Deland will serve so long as he doesn't have to come to all the meetings; Haughton and Wrightington and Brown I have not yet seen, though I don't anticipate any trouble in that matter. The one difficulty with an offense committee is that as a general rule it never gets to work until the last minute, and therefore it deliberates in a pretty hurried fashion. At Waters' suggestion I propose to remedy this trouble by setting a date on which the committee on offense is to dissolve, whether they have accomplished anything or not. This, I hope, will bring out before that time, with some little pressure, the ideas upon which our offense will ultimately be based. I then expect to take those ideas and work them over carefully with Lewis, in their relation to the Yale defense, and after having made out a set of formations and plays, will call a meeting of the committee and submit them for discussion. Then I propose to take those plays and in the light of the discussion, reorganize them in the most effective way; while I have been up in Cambridge this summer, I have occasionally arranged to do some kicking with Foster and Brill, in order to keep them moving in their personal work in the proper lines. Foster has shown marked improvement, Brill some, but the latter has been rather slow. I believe that whenever we have not a kicker, and where hereafter a coach can get the time, since there will not be anything like as much preliminary work to do again as there was this year, he ought to put a good deal of time during the summer on the best of the kickers, so that by Fall they shall have mastered most of the elementary principles and be ready for speed, height, and accuracy, which, of course come last in the kicking program. When I first came on, I found that F. K. Leatherbee, who had been on the Freshman team during the year previous, looked to the coaches to be one of the most promising end candidates that we have. On hunting him up, I found that he had just left college and gone into business. I immediately went in to see him with a hope of being able to persuade him to come back before he had missed so much work as to make it impossible. I had a very good talk with him in which he told me he did not like study, had had a good business offer which he did like, and had therefore withdrawn from college to accept it. I brought what pressure I could to bear on him, but to no purpose, so I was forced to lose a good man. On the opposite page [missing] will be found a list of the best kickers whom the spring practice developed. This list may come in handy to some later coach as a means of following up some men who may stop playing without the coach's knowing that they had ever played. I expect that we shall find other men during the early part of the Fall, but this present list seems to be pretty complete up to date. I spoke earlier in the book of an investigation I made concerning the probable strength of some of the teams which we consider as possible competitors. Here are some of the figures which I got. The Dartmouth team of 1904 should lose next year Patterson, a half back, who has played four years, Vaughn, a half back, who has also played four years, Nibbs, the full back, who has played four years, Melville, quarter back, who is a senior, Clough, a guard, and Gilman, the other guard, both of whom have played four years, Lillard, an end, and senior, and Keady, a tackle, also a senior. If this list is correct, Dartmouth will have only three of her last year's team back at the beginning of next Fall, losing in her line some of the strongest men she has had. It was a result of finding this out that caused us to place Dartmouth where we did put her. I heard of several men whom Dartmouth was trying to get from Exeter and some of the other schools, but cannot tell enough about it to know how strong they will be. A good man to go to for information of this kind is Joe Pendleton, of Wright & Ditson's, who outfits many of these smaller colleges and who knows pretty well what is going on. West Point, according to a statement which Daly gave me, is to lose Doe and Graves, her tackler, Hammond, T. and end, Tipton, centre, and one guard, thus leaving only an end and one guard of their entire line. Although of course

West Point will have a strong team, we felt that the loss of so many men ought to enable us to hold them off at the early date on which we play them, even though we are unable to beat them. Brown, according to their coach, loses Coulter, the center, Winslow, left guard, Webb, right tackle, Swin, left end, and Savage, full back. Besides these loses, it seems likely that Brown will have one or two others due to the fact that several of her men who are also baseball players, have signified their intention of playing professional ball this summer, thus rendering themselves ineligible. Pennsylvania we shall have to play anyhow, and the only difference that her possible team might make would be that of shifting the Penn game a week later than we had it. This I didn't do because, as I said before, I don't feel that our training is of sufficient strength to make sure of getting the team into condition where it can stand Pennsylvania and Yale in one week. Pennsylvania's known losses include Smith, their full back, Piekar[sk]i, a guard, and Butkiewitz, a tackle. Lamson, a tackle, has, I believe, already played four years, including a couple which he played in Colorado, and which Pennsylvania will, I think, try to forget, but which we shall, if there is any truth in the report, bring to their attention. Drake, who played left end last year, is reported also to have played his limit. It is certainly said that he has played now five years. Just how these cases will come out I cannot say at present but we shall join with Cornell in making it as uncomfortable for Pennsylvania in her ringer practice as we possibly can. Cornell considers her Pennsylvania game as her biggest game. Last year she protested a couple of the Penn men, whereupon Penn threatened to break off relations. Since Cornell is dependent on Pennsylvania for her only big game, she kept quiet and Pennsylvania did as she pleased. This year I have arranged with Warner, the Cornell coach, so that he will give me whatever information he gets, which I shall at once bring to Pennsylvania's attention as of our own discovery, thereby accomplishing for Cornell what she cannot accomplish for herself, and at the same time serving our own interests. I determined this Spring to see if we could not have somebody look after the drop kicking for the whole year, from the start. It has been frequently the case that a Harvard team has found itself within Yale's 25 yd. line on a third down with three yards to go, an admirable place for a drop kick. We have almost never had drop kickers in recent years, and I don't see why we should not get a moderately good one this year if we start about it early. Such a man could at least make Yale feel mighty uneasy under such conditions, for there is no telling when such a man might make a successful try. Accordingly I looked around for drop kicking coaches. I

saw Frank Mason,[61] who was, I believe, a very successful drop kicker of former times, and had quite a talk with him. He seemed to know
a good deal about it, but spoke about the possibility of teaching a man
to drop kick on the run, and a few other such impossible things under the present game, and so I gave up all idea of having him out
except perhaps as a casual observer something during the year. I went
also to see Marshall, who was successful in 1901 in a drop kick from
the 43 yd. line, and he is a good example of the kind of man I want
for this year. In 1901 Marshall got off only that one kick during the
whole season, partly because we didn't begin work with him until
very late, and partly because he was not given very many chances to
make kicks. I talked over Carl's ideas and found them pretty much
as I expected to, and in entire accord with those of Leo Daly, who was
Marshall's substitute that year, and who as a substitute kicker kicked
two or three goals that same year. Inasmuch as Leo Daly is to be the
quarterback coach, I had it in mind to combine if possible in him the
drop kicking coach so as to save having any extra or special men out
there for that purpose. I want to avoid having too many coaches on
the field and this is one way by which I hope to bring that about. I
also had a talk with Joshua Crane[62] and I found that, as he explained
it to me, his ideas are about the same as those of Marshall and Daly.
I therefore decided to have Daly in charge of most of that work,
helped occasionally by any of these other men that he may choose to
have out. Daly's size up of the drop kicking technique was pretty
good, I thought, and ran about as follows,—The kicker wants to stand
at whatever distance behind the line is settled upon, to stand in an
easy relaxed position, with arms extended but with them no higher
than his waist, since in a drop kick, as compared with a punt, the ball
is dropped clear to the ground instead of being kicked before it strikes
the ground, it therefore being wise to receive the ball as comfortably
near the ground as possible. Immediately the ball is received it should
be so adjusted that the longest axis of the ball is vertical to the ground,
or with a little slant forward or backward. The matter of the slant is
largely a matter for the individual himself to settle. The further the
kick has to go, the further from the body the ball should be dropped;
the shorter the kick, the nearer the body, with different variations in
the slant of the ball as may seem necessary. As to the way in which
the ball is held in the hands, the question of whether one hand shall
be across the front with the other across the back, or whether there

61. Mason was a Harvard football letter-winner (1882–84).
62. Crane was a Harvard track letter-winner in 1890.

shall be one hand on either side, is wholly a matter for the individual. In dropping the ball, it should be held as near the ground as possible without so cramping the body as to make the kick difficult. Of course the nearer the ground the ball is placed, the less chance there is for inaccuracy in its fall. Previous to the kick the kicker should draw a line on the ground indicating the direction in which his kick is to go, for when the kick is made, the eyes of the kicker must be on the ball and his foot rather than on the goal. Immediately on receiving the ball, the kicker faces so that the pendulum swing of the leg shall follow in the direction of this line. The leg must be swung with perfect directness and free from any side swing or twitch. The blow should be a sharp one made by a quick click of the leg as it straightens out, and should be carried through much as a drive in golf. This general outline will serve to show what most of these coaches felt was the wisest plan. I put it down in this brief form as a possible reference. In reading over the rules, which I am getting down thoroughly, I notice that in the quarter back kick, the ball doesn't have to go ten yards. I had not realized this before, and it relieves me a great deal in the matter of the quarter back kick, which I think is a strong play. I had quite a talk with Al Ristine, who played on the team in 1901 and who is now coaching the University of Iowa team. I learned nothing whatever about the actual coaching of the men but he gave me several very good ideas with regard to training and conditioning of the men which he got from his trainer, who, he says, is an excellent man. The man's name is J. P. Watson, Ames, Ia. Ristine says that Watson has his men do a great deal of walking during the early part of the season, and thereby strengthens their ankles before he has them take up sprinting starts and the other more violent exercises. This seems to me to be a pretty good point, since many men are hardly ready for the abrupt strain on their ankles when they first come back from their vacations, unless, indeed, they have been doing a good deal of running or have been playing some active game such as tennis. I remember that in 1901, one or two men got fairly sore ankles through the early starts, and I shall look into this matter pretty thoroughly this Fall. I shall also find out at once what fellows have weak ankles of any kind and shall probably put them in a squad by themselves to be given special work. Ristine says that like Yost, Watson does not allow the men to fall on the ball much in the early part of the season, for fear of injury. This, I think, is rather unnecessary, since falling on the ball is an extremely valuable exercise as a toughner, and if properly supervised can result in very little danger. I shall put every man, next Fall, through a course of falling on the ball, in order to be sure that every man out there knows how. Those that don't know how I shall take off by themselves in a special squad and teach them slowly, so as to avoid the likelihood of severe injury in attempting at once to fall on the ball before the men have a clear idea of the method. Watson doesn't allow the men to take any soft water baths, but instead has each man sponge himself off with a bucket of salt water. Ristine says that this salt water toughens up the skin of the men in a remarkable fashion, and seems to save much skinning up of the men. Dr. Nichols is a little skeptical as to whether the water really does this or whether it is the nature of the men they have there, but says that it will do no harm at any rate to have the men shower under salt water baths provided, of course, they are not allowed to stay there too long. The special things Ristine says Watson is most valuable about is in removing "poops" and in treating water on the knee. Ristine says that in one or two cases they had "poops" which Ristine thought would put a man absolutely out of the game but which Watson handled so well that the men were out playing within a week. Here is the impression of the treatment which I was able to get from Ristine, and which in case we have any bad cases of "poops", I shall ask the doctors to look into very carefully, perhaps in conference with Watson. In the case of "poops" the 1st thing that they do is to wet two or three bath towels which are put around the injured spot. On top of these towels comes a hot water bottle, then over that a dry wrung out towel on top. This combination, Ristine says causes a great deal of steam on the leg and keeps it steamed just as we have done by the constant application of hot cloths. If for no other reason than that it will save some considerable time in this very respect the suggestion is a good one. After the leg has had a most thorough steaming of this kind, Ristine says that Watson manipulates the man's leg with his hands, seeming almost to lift the muscles up, and Ristine says that in this way, although the first part of the work is painful, to a certain extent, the clot of blood becomes carried away and the man's recovery gradually facilitated and extremely thorough. Dr. Nichols in commenting on this scheme says that broken tissue such as in the case with a "poop" cannot remend inside of, I think he said, fourteen days. Watson's treatment of water on the knee consists of placing a dry sponge over the injured knee and then bandaging that sponge tight to the knee. He then wets the sponge with salt water and as the sponge expands thereby puts a constant pressure on the knee. The sponge seems to flatten the knee cap down and forces the water off. As practiced at Iowa such a bandage is kept on three or four days. As I said before, I don't know just how these various things will work out, but they are at any rate worth trying since they deal with the most serious injuries which we have on the field. With this I shall close this paragraph of incidental comment.

During the spring just passed, I have had my attention called to a great number of possible football men who would like to come to Harvard or who have not had any thought of coming to Harvard but whom somebody else would like to see come. Inasmuch as every coach is bound to have something of the same experience that I have had in the matter, I shall give a little account of it as well as a statement of what the whole thing seems to be worth. To begin with, I had a letter from Charlie Bull,[63] from London, concerning a very prominent football player in Arizona who had kicked a great many drop kicks in the games there, and whom Bull said must be, judging from reports, an exceptional man. Bull wanted me to write him and see if I could not get him to come. I talked the matter over with Prof. Coolidge, acting Chairman of the Athletic committee, and he felt that it would be altogether unwise for me to write directly to Wolf, which is the man's name, since being in an official position out here, such a letter would seem like a matter of college policy, but he said that if I could get any graduate or other Harvard man to take an interest in him, there was no objection, provided only that whatever was done was entirely within our eligibility rules. I therefore wrote Dave Goodrich[64] who was out in Arizona, and got Mr. Sullivan of the [Boston] Globe to write to the boy direct. In answer nothing was received in either case, so that apparently the matter has passed off. A man name Laurie wrote on from Chicago asking if there was any way by which athletic ability could in any way be exchanged for a means of getting through Harvard. I wrote and told him that there was not, but that if he would see Ayers Boal,[65] the secretary of the Chicago Harvard Club he could find out exactly the condition of affairs. I sent Boal Laurie's letter and Boal wrote to Laurie, but received no reply. These two men are good types of this kind of man. They want to go through college without doing much of any work, and are willing to go to whatever college will offer them such a chance in exchange for athletic ability. The moment it becomes plain to them that Harvard does not offer such opportunities, all communication ceases and presumably the man goes elsewhere. It seems probably, therefore, that while it is worth while to answer any such communications as these, it is

63. Bull was a Harvard crew letter-winner (1896–97).
64. Goodrich was a Harvard crew letter-winner (1896-97).
65. Boal was a Harvard football letter-winner (1897–98).

probably never going to be productive of anything material to us. A man named Draper, who weighs 190 odd lbs. and played tackle on the Springfield Manual Training School, last year, wanted to come to Cambridge to go to the Medical school. Captain Hurley and a graduate or two took the matter up with him, but found that the man was probably unwilling to try to come, since no one is admitted to the Medical school without a college degree which he has not got and which it would take him four years to get. This man will probably turn up at Dartmouth or one of the other colleges where the entrance conditions are very lax, and the course poor. This shows how the strictness of our examination record and graduate school work cuts down the percentage of men who would like to come to us. Contrast this situation at all with Dartmouth, where men can get in without examination at all, and it is very easy to see how Dartmouth can persuade a man to come up there who really wants to come to Cambridge, by showing him how much easier it is at Dartmouth than at Cambridge. One of the graduates wrote me a letter telling me that a Judge Fitz of Chelsea had a son who had been intending to come to Harvard, and who was a good football player, but that owing to representations from Amherst or one of the other fresh water colleges,[66] he was planning to go there. I immediately wrote to Judge Fitz and asked him whether his son were coming on to Harvard or going elsewhere, but received no reply. As I did not wish to seem to be trying to induce Fitz to change his mind again, I let the matter rest there. The names of Robinson and Sargent were sent to me as being those of good football players of Hebron Academy in Maine, I think. These men had in no way indicated that they were planning to come to Harvard or cared anything about it, and so we had no communication with them whatever, except I believe that one of the football men who knew them and who lives up there, undertook to see them and find out what their plans were. Nothing came of it. During the track meet here in the early spring, Trainer Jim Robinson, of Princeton, made a trip to Boston and pretty thoroughly canvassed the athletic material of the schools in this neighborhood, and offered two manual training school boys who had been planning to come to Harvard almost "anything they wished" if they would go to Princeton. They could play both football and baseball, and one of them was good at

66. The term *fresh water college* meant a college not on the Atlantic Coast. The term may have been used first in a derogatory manner during the 1870s when referring to such upstart crews as the Massachusetts Aggies (University of Massachusetts) and Cornell, which defeated favored Harvard and Yale, the established and elite institutions near the ocean.

track, also. Hearing of this I asked the boys to call on me at the athletic office, which they did. I asked them if what I had heard was true, and they said it was. I then told them that I was not going to try in any way to change their minds or to urge them to come to Harvard, but that I should advise them to choose their college with reference to their life work, and stick to it through thick and thin, even if the college which they thought would fit them best did not seem as rosy in opportunities as some others. I further said that I should advise them to look Harvard over pretty carefully before they went elsewhere and to consider also whether if they accepted a bribery offer from Princeton, they would afterward feel as proud of a Princeton diploma as they would of any other college diploma squarely earned, and gained by work wholly above board. I advised them to go to Princeton if they felt they could get what they wanted there, and under no condition to accept any offer of assistance that was not wholly right. Without my asking it, both these men, Kennedy Parks and Win Adams, said that they felt that Princeton was not the place for them. They said nothing, however, about coming to Cambridge, and I didn't press them for any expression of their choice. I didn't care especially whether they came to us or not, but I wanted to take that occasion to hit Princeton's proselyting scheme in the head, and I think that I did so, at any rate for the time being. This practice of trainers going about and making offers of this kind is habitual with Pennsylvania, Princeton, Brown, Dartmouth, and is also done at Yale as far as Mike Murphy can do so without raising a rumpus. The name of a man Duffy was sent me as being a first class guard of the English High School. He was thought to be favoring Princeton, and perhaps to be going there. I could find no one that knew him, but after conversation which I heard in the front vestibule of one of the electric cars when on my way to Cambridge, and which I later substantiated, I feel that it makes little difference whether he tries to come or not. These two school boys whom I heard were standing on the front of this car just to one side of me, and one of them said to the other,— "Where is Duffy going to college?" "Princeton, I think," the other replied. "Why doesn't he go to Harvard?" said the first. "To Harvard!" answered the other with some considerable incredulity, "Do you suppose Duffy could ever get into Harvard? Why he could not pass the examinations in ten years." This I believe is true of him, although I should not be at all surprised to see him get into Princeton, which seems to have room for all the athletes whose scholarly work is such that they are not able to stay in Princeton for more than one year. In looking up the list of men in the law school who might be possible candidates for the team, I ran across the name of [Matthew W.] Bullock, a colored man who has played heretofore in Dartmouth.[67] I asked him into the office to find out whether he was eligible and found that he had played four years. Knowing that he had a brother at Andover, I asked him where his brother was going to college and he said he was going to Dartmouth. I asked him then how it was that he preferred Dartmouth, and he said that it was because he thought his brother would have a better show there than he would have here. I merely commented that Dartmouth was apparently a pretty good college for a man to work his way through, and the conversation ended. I find now that this small inquiry changed the older Bullock's mind so that he had his brother, who weighs 190 lbs., and plays full back, change over to Harvard, and that the brother has taken the Harvard entrance examinations.[68] It is rumored that he has failed them, and it may be the case, and I think most likely from what Mr. Stearns of Andover told me about him. Mr. Stearns said that Bullock was not bright and that whatever chance he had of passing in his examinations had been spoiled through the swelled head which he had as the result of the importunities of Maine, the Dartmouth captain of next year, and other Dartmouth players, that he go to Dartmouth. I believe that Mr. Stearns' size up will be clearly borne out when the examination results are in. A man named Church, of Washington, D. C., came in to see me one day to talk about football, and stated that he was going to enter the freshman class this next year. He told me that he had been offered the presidency of a freshman eating club[69] at Princeton and that they had been doing everything they could to get him to go there, but that he had told them from the first that he was going to Harvard and that he had made up his mind to do so. This is

67. Bullock played end for Dartmouth from 1901 to 1903. He was the recipient of racist action when Dartmouth visited Princeton in 1903. The Dartmouth team was refused entry into the Princeton Inn, and the Princeton football team picked out Bullock to be put out of the game with brutal play. The incident ended his playing career at Dartmouth. He became the first black head football coach at a predominately white college when, in 1904, he coached the Massachusetts Agricultural College to a 5-2-1 season. See President Tucker to William H. Ward, 7 Nov. 1903, Pres. Tucker Papers, No. 1, "Athletics I–Z," Dartmouth College Archives, and Jack Berryman and John Loy, "Matthew Bullock the First College Black Football Coach," *Black Sports* 2 (Feb. 1973): 18–19.

68. Bullock never lettered in football for Harvard.

69. An eating club was the usual method of boarding at a number of colleges. The presidency of an eating club was often a sinecure for an incoming athlete, as it provided free board and the prominent athlete would attract others to eat at the private eating club, a profitable arrangement for both athlete and club owner.

one of the few cases where a man has shown gumption enough to decide for himself, irrespective of offers of any kind, what college he wants to attend. Something of a similar case was that of Colton, full back on the Dorchester H. S. team last year, reputed to be a very fine player and track man. He had been preparing to go to Technology,[70] but wasted some athletic work too, and decided to come to Cambridge when he heard that the Harvard football system was likely to be altered. I had no communication with him whatever in the initiative, his father writing to me and his mother also, several times. When I found that he was really thinking of coming I asked him over and took him around to the Scientific School office to see about changing his Technology credits to his balance in the Scientific school. This was done, and the boy has passed enough examinations for admittance already, with several honors, and plans to take one or two anticipatory subjects this Fall. I think he is of the right type, and I consider him one of the most valuable new men in reputation that we seem likely to get. At [A]ndover my attention was called to three men, Lanigan, the pitcher of the school team up there, Thompson, a guard and captain of last year's team, and Brown, an end on the football team, and a supposedly good catcher. I said nothing to Lanigan about coming, but as I said before, went up and helped Bart Hayes on two occasions in coaching, and got Dr. Nichols to go up there. We showed Lanigan such special attention as a pitcher would need, and did what we could in that indirect way to help along. He is no football man, but might make a baseball pitcher. Brown I met on one occasion up there, more out of curiosity than anything else. Al Eyre knew Brown and his brother very well, and undertook to persuade Brown to come down here, Brown having stated that he wanted to come to Harvard rather than go to Yale, but that he felt as though it would be very difficult matter to get any work at Harvard such as would help him to work his way through. Apparently Eyre's connection with Brown was rather secret, for Brown continued to state that he was going to Yale, while he had quietly made arrangements with Mr. Love, of the Scientific school, to transfer his Yale credits when he took his Yale examinations, to Harvard. Eyre claimed that Andover is such a Yale school and so unfair toward Harvard that the moment a man gives out that he is coming to Harvard he is pretty much tabooed, and that if it had become known that Brown was planning to come to Harvard when he took his Yale examinations, the Yale professors would have failed him in them. The absurdity of any such condition of af-

70. He probably is referring to the Massachusetts Institute of Technology in Cambridge.

fairs needs no comment. Brown took his examinations at New Haven and failed most of them. Just what will happen now, I don't know. Brown is Eyre's friend, and I am leaving the whole thing to Eyre. Thompson the guard, is a Yale man by birth, living in Waterbury, Conn., a big, strong and promising player and a man that we could use here very effectively. Eyre had him down here once or twice and tried to imbue him with a desire to come to Cambridge, but staying on the fence for some time he finally settled permanently on Yale ground. This was exactly what I had expected, and I was not at all surprised. Here again Eyre seemed to want to talk about the matter in whispers for fear of some rank injustice to Thompson, owing to any inclinations he might have to come to Harvard. This is the only case of secret service in the whole spring work.

A man named Irish wrote me a letter with regard to a 190 lb. man named Tappin, who has always been planning to come to Harvard, but whom Amherst men are working hard for. Mr. Irish wanted me to write Tappin, but I refused as I did in the case of the Arizona boy. I offered, however, in case Mr. Irish would bring Tappin over here and introduce me to him, to show him about the place and do anything I could to give him a thorough insight into Harvard, and I sent to Mr. Irish copies of the recent Harvard examinations, for Tappin to consult in preparing himself for entrance. Tappin is a good scholar, from what I can hear, a fellow of splendid physique, very hard and strong, and not afraid of work. He impresses me as being one of the best of the men to come to my notice. As he has all along intended to come to Harvard, and is only now laboring under the influence of Amherst men, I feel as though we had a legitimate right to make something of a fight for him. The main difficulty with the thing at present is that he is so far from the centre of things, being well away from the R. R., at home camp, that he is almost inaccessible. Two other men came to my attention, a man named Horr, and a man named Pike, each of them big scrawny guard material. These men want to get into Harvard and work their way through. The working their way through could be easily arranged, but the getting in was beyond them owing to their lack of mental ability, so that we may look for them in Pennsylvania, or some of the other ringer colleges. I have, of course, heard of many other men, but these are types to show the general run. As will be seen, we are not likely to get in a single man as a result of any representations which we have made, and the men who would like to come and can't are men who, if they did come here, would have great difficulty in maintaining their standard and who might be too stupid to be of any service. Most of them are hardly a type that

will go to make a thoroughly representative Harvard team. When I
first came on this spring, I felt that we ought to devote more time to
the schools, and to men of this type, but I feel now that the really safe
basis on which to work is to have no communication with men who
do not communicate with us, to take such men as enter the University
of their own accord, in spite of offers from elsewhere, and to do
more than this, we begin to approach the line of illegitimate proselyting, and it is very difficult to lay down a safe boundary between
what is legitimate and what is illegitimate in this way. To my mind,
what I did in the endeavor to get LeMoyne back here was not wholly legitimate, as I look back on it now, even though everything I did
was sanctioned by the athletic committee. Where a man gets tutoring for nothing, and other privileges, which come only from someone's patriotic willingness to contribute something to the success of
the teams, I can hardly feel as though he were really on his own feet.
If we cannot compete successfully on this basis it seems to me that
we ought to force our competitors to adopt the same point of view
or else choose new ones. I don't believe in attempting to compete on
even terms with a team which in all its make up shows trickery, de-
ceit and a studied willingness to beat out any rule if such a thing is
possible. Another thing which occurs to me in thinking over this matter, is the fact that most of the men who want to get through easily,
are men who have not brains enough, and therefore ambition enough,
to do thorough enough work, if they did come, to maintain themselves. This has caused me to wonder whether a proposed eligibility
rule which "Life" advanced in one of its editorials is not after all the
best that we are likely to find. "Life" proposes that no man shall be
eligible for a team who cannot show and account for a bank account
on his entrance sufficient to cover his tuition for the first year. This,
to be sure, would be an injustice to some men, but I believe with some
modifications it could be a basis for successful legislation. I base this
opinion on the fact that in every case that has been in dispute, of recent years, the man has been unable to see his way through college
and has accepted some shady way of getting it for nothing in return
for his athletic ability. Take, for instance, the case of [Oliver] Cutts,
who, I think, however, was absolutely honorable in everything he did,
the case of [James] Hogan, [James L.] Cooney of Princeton, [Andy]
Smith of Pennsylvania,[71] and, were the various cases to be looked

71. All three were Walter Camp all-Americans, Hogan from 1902 to 1905; Cooney
in 1904 and 1906; and Smith in 1904. Smith became an acclaimed coach at Penn, Pur-
due, and especially California, compiling an overall record of 115-33-11.

over, many other men of the same type. All these men had to work their way through, and were therefore subject to the commercialism which has developed in relation to athletics, and which has for its basis the inability of any man to provide for his own education. The English idea of an amateur I believe is synonymous with the idea of a gentleman, a man who does not have to labor, especially at college, with his hands. In other words, a man who is in possession of a bank account. Now, while we cannot draw any such line as that here, we ought to be able to make some line which is based on a man's purse, which would stop the practice of this commercialism. It might do to make any man who has not money enough which he can account for legitimately in his possession to get through college, ineligible for any team during the first year of his attendance at the college. That would give the college authorities a good chance to find out what the man's motives were, and would enable them to feel certain that the money which he had already in his possession was legitimately earned. Whether these suggestions will be of any service to the athletic committee I do not know, but I shall propose them for discussion, since unless the buying up of players is stopped, athletics are going to enter upon a thoroughly decadent period.

I shall now take up, in closing, the cases of eight fellows with whom I have had a great deal to do in connection with football, and which will give a very clear idea of the amount of following up and constant effort which I have had to devote myself to in order to keep these men up to standard. First, the case of W[alter] T. Harrison.[72] Harrison was a fellow who had been dropped now I think for two or three successive years, and who only had an opportunity to play football for the part of one year of his residence here. He is a big fellow and from what the coaches and players say, he has put up a very good game at full back. He has impressed me as being very lazy in nature, and is lacking in ambition in many ways. However, as the last year's full back leaves this year, and we shall need a good man, I made up my mind to try to get him eligible. I called him up and asked him about his work, when he told me that he should probably not be back next year, although he had not yet his degree. He said that he should like to come back, but that he did not feel willing to ask his parents to send him any longer, for he had done so poorly. This statement in itself seemed to indicate some promise, but I rather thought that if the fellow felt that way toward his parents, he might have put a little harder work on his studies while he was at them, and thus spared

72. Harrison won a football letter in 1902 but not in 1905.

his parents any such feeling. I found out that he would return if his folks would let him, and that he had a brother in Boston who was older than he and was doing well. So I went in to see [him] and frankly talked the situation over with him. He agreed to do all that he could to get his parents' permission to have his brother return and finally he accomplished it. Harrison should get his degree by the coming Christmas, and will be eligible under certain conditions this Fall. I took him over to the office of the Scientific School two or three times, and we looked up his record and found out just what he would have to accomplish in order to make himself eligible. In the first place it was necessary that he should pass off all the courses that he took this spring and with fair grades. I therefore called him up every now and then to see whether he was doing his work and how things were going, and whether he needed a tutor. He got through the term in fairly good shape. On going over his record finally with Mr. Love of the Scientific school, I found that he had been dropped for the last two years owing to failure to pass off entrance conditions in solid Geometry. This condition he had tried to remove on three successive years, but without success, and he was therefore unable to be promoted into the senior class, and unable to get his degree, since all entrance conditions must be removed before the degree is awarded. Furthermore his failure to be promoted caused him to be put on probation, complicating the matter in some considerable measure. All he needed, then, at the end of the spring term, was to pass off this entrance condition in Geometry. I tried to get him to enter the Summer school and get it off in this way, but he did not want to go to the Summer school because he wanted to get off to the sea shore. When the Summer school is a perfectly certain way of removing the condition, and when after three years of trial in his own haphazard fashion he had failed to pass the examination, it would seem that any fellow who was dead in earnest would gladly take the chance of the Summer school. Instead of that he did not stay but went off to Maine. Previous to his going he wanted to petition the faculty to take him off probation, and wrote out a petition to that effect. It was worded in such a way as to be a demand rather than a request, and so he asked me to rewrite it for him. I did so, and the administrative board, as I told him it would do, said that they would postpone taking action on his petition until after the September examination, when he was expected to pass off his condition in Geometry. Two or three weeks passed of the vacation without his accomplishing anything, and finally I wrote him a very strong letter which appears on the opposite page [missing]. Some of the suggestions he makes there are very good, and the spirit of it is pretty fair. I question very much whether he is going to show ambition and energy enough to fill the position of full back acceptable, but that remains to be seen. He says in his letter that he is getting along very well in his Geometry. I hope it is true, and hope that he gets off, but do not feel that he has awakened to the responsibility of making sure of getting that off, as would have been evidenced by his staying here and doing the work. To be sure, he claims that the entrance examinations in Solid Geometry are easier than the Summer School. That may be true, but no man who really works can fail to do the work of anyone of the summer school courses with ease, so that Harrison's unwillingness to do the summer work would seem to be a matter of laziness. It will be interesting to see how near my prediction in regard to him comes true this Fall. I suspect that he will hardly be better than a substitute. In Harrison's case, as in the case of almost all the other men whom I shall mention here, it seems to be a question of putting a collar around the neck of the players and leading them about instead of having them willing and unable to follow without leading, and even to go ahead and do a few things by themselves. The utter helplessness of these big fellows is disgustingly ludicrous.

The second case is that of F[rederic] H. White,[73] who last year played guard in the Yale game. This fellow, when I first came on, was in very poor shape physically, and from the standpoint of his studies. It hardly seemed as though he was going to be able to get through by any chance. By getting hold of him early, however, and actually taking him around in person to different tutors, I got him to work, and I will say that once he had gotten to work, he stuck pretty faithfully at it, and to my surprise secured his promotion. White's family affairs have had a great deal to do with his work. In the first place his mother is dead, and his father has been suing him constantly for a portion of the money left him by his mother. All through last year White averaged one law suit a month against him by his father. These lawsuits together with the interruption which attendance in court caused in his studies, occupied White and kept him in quite an uneasy state of mind, and I think there is something to be said for his lack of accomplishment. Just this vacation White, who was doing some work in the summer school, got wind of the fact that his father was contemplating still another suit which would make trouble for him in October, and so, after consultation with Mr. Love of the Scientific School, White decided to finish up only a part of his summer

73. White lettered in 1904, but did not do so in 1905.

work and then to go off where his father could find no trace of him. This he did, and for two days I had a most lively time trying to avoid the father, who followed me all over Cambridge to Soldiers Field, to the depot, and everywhere, in the endeavor to get his son's address from me. I managed to escape. White weighs about 230 lbs. and more, and has an immense stomach. I worked for some time with him this spring after the summer school began endeavoring to have him get himself into some kind of shape, since last year he was too bulky and logy to move. I wrote him a letter giving him certain instructions which I explained to him verbally when I saw him, as to how to re-duce this weight. He moved along without doing these things, and without paying much attention to my suggestions, and so I finally wrote him the letter which appears on the opposite page [missing]. It was pretty severe, I know, but I had tried everything else, and there was nothing else to do but to let loose. He came up to the athletic office apparently on the run, and hatless, and explained that he meant to get to work. I told him that he had been telling me for the last month that he meant to get to work and had not done anything, and that it was time he did. This seems to have awakened him somewhat, and sin[c]e that time he has been doing his work faithfully. It is a pe-culiar thing to me that any fellow who has seen for himself under what great disadvantage he is working, owing to his excessive amount of flesh, and who has never played on a winning team, should not make up his mind that things are going to be different, and then set out with a definite purpose to get himself into tiptop shape for the new campaign. White is, I believe, a very faithful worker on the field, but how different from Bill Burden,[74] who used every day of the entire summer to run from half to three quarters of a mile, to do boxing, swimming, wrestling and dumbbell work in order to get him-self into the best condition for the Fall work. We don't seem to have any such men nowadays.

We now come to the case of [Karl F.] Brill. Brill weighs about 215 lbs. out of condition, and should weigh a little over 200 lbs. in his best condition. He is powerful, and at Exeter, where he was captain of the team, did some splendid kicking as well as first class tackle work. He came down here by choice in spite of offers from the other colleges, and was undertaken to work his way through in the hardest kind of way. He has done work over in Randall hall as a waiter, he has chopped wood, beaten carpets, acted as an automobile agent, and done odd jobs wherever they presented themselves. He had some Zech blood in him

---

74. Burden was a Harvard football letter-winner (1898–99).

and gives the impression of being a mulatto. He is also of a rather dreamy nature and has a good many rather queer ideas. At Exeter he was usually on the side lines a good deal even though captain of the team, and seemed to play largely without much headwork, continuing the same policy down here. For some reason or other, his work here has not amounted to what it ought to, and so I have taken a great interest in him ever since I came, in the endeavor to find out just how to handle him. In the first place, as I have already mentioned, I had him go to the doctor about the corns in the bottoms of his feet. Then I tried to get him out for spring practice, but without much success, he pleading off on the ground that he had to work to support himself, and needed what time he could spare for study, and besides had bad feet. Inasmuch as his work was not very well up, I didn't press the matter, but he came out later and threw the hammer, which was just as violent as anything I had wished to have him do, so that if he had really cared to do the football work he could probably have found time. He got through his final examination all right, and was looking around for a [j]ob for the summer. By speaking with Mr. Thompson of the appointments office, and the head guide of the college yard, I arranged to have him one of the college guides, even though his examination was not a first class one. This was the job he especially wanted, since it gave him an opportunity to do a certain amount of studying in the summer. Then, in order that he might have recreation I got special permission for him and a special key so that he could use the Newell Boat Club at about 5 o'clock in the morning. And here I might say that previous to all this Herbert White had gotten him the agency in automobile tires and had given him a list of men from whom he could probably get orders for the tires if he would go and see them. Brill did not follow up this list as he should have, and lost two or three hundred dollars as a result. For this White was justly very much annoyed, and gave Brill a sound talking to.

This summer, just as Brill seemed to be getting along all right, he suddenly dropped completely from view and we could find no trace of him. I had the Newell Boat Club looked over to see whether there was any boat missing, had Brill's locker looked into to see if he could possibly have gone in swimming and drowned, had a notice put in the paper stating that there was a letter for him in the office, went to the post office to find out whether he had changed his address, wrote up to his father at Exeter, went to his place of residence in Cambridge, and in fact did everything I possibly could to locate him. The only trace I could find was that given me by the head postman, who had seem him on a car on his way in town a couple of days after he disappeared. One week exactly after he had gone Brill appeared. He came into my office and told me the following story. He said that for several summers three or four fellows who lived in New York and who were in no way connected with Harvard, had invited him to go sailing with them and that each year he had been unable to go. This year they had renewed their request, and he had told them that he could not possibly get away owing to his work. They then invited him to go for a short sail on a Sunday morning, promising him to return him to Cambridge in time to begin work at 6 o'clock that night, at Randall hall. Accordingly they set sail. Brill claimed that he had no knowledge of where they went or what they were planning. However that may be, late in the afternoon Brill suggested that it was about time to put about, whereupon his hosts smiled and said they would go on just a little further. This excuse was continually offered until Brill finally began to suspect that something was wrong. At last when he had made it clear how serious it was for him to be away, they agreed to put him on the first steamer or [v]essel which they should meet that was on its way back to Massachusetts. Having sailed off on Sunday no vessel was met until the following Tuesday, when a collier for Portsmouth, N. H., hove in sight. Brill was transferred to this collier, which did not reach Portsmouth until the following Saturday night. From there Brill managed in some way to earn money enough to pay his way back on a midnight train, arriving in Cambridge early Sunday morning.

When I asked Brill how hard he had told those fellows that he should be back, he said that that was where he had been weak, that he had not urged it with sufficient strength. Then I asked him why immediately when he got back he had not hunted up his employers to tell them why he had not been on hand, he having waited until Monday before reporting to them. He said that he was tired and didn't know where to find them. I talked the whole matter over with Mr. Thompson and Dean Hurlbut, and decided to accept Brill's story. I urged on the head guide of the yard that Brill be dismissed from the guide force as a lesson to him, and this was done. Brill, however, got back his old position at Randall. After the matter had cooled down for a day or two, I called Brill in and gave him a pretty straight talk, at which he broke down. Several days later, on seeing no disposition on his part to get at the kicking of the [f]ootball, which I had told him was a part of his duty, I wrote him a letter which appears on the opposite page, and which was again very severe. [Letter follows.]

July 21, 1905

Mr. Karl Brill
469 Broadway
Cambridge, Mass.

Dear Brill:

At the close of last year's football season there was much criticism of a number of individuals composing the Harvard team, and you came in for your share of the criticism. Some said that you had avoided work by complaining of injuries which weren't so serious as was at the time supposed; some said that you didn't have the fight and others that if you had it, you'd never shown it. Now, I didn't see any of the games and therefore do not know anything of the circumstances, and am unwilling to make up my mind on indirect evidence, but this I do know; there is a big question mark after your name in the minds of most people, and a question mark which you simply must absolutely obliterate. If you don't, as I told you the other day, you are going to add an almost insurmountable handicap to those under which you are at present working. With your big body and splendid physique you have enormous possibilities, if you will only command that body.

At Exeter, too, you weren't in the play as much as a captain should be, and it was felt. By your actions last year, the feeling was fanned, until now your work is stiffer than it need have been.

In tune with all this, has come your lack of response to the call for kickers this spring. Coming here with a reputation from Exeter as a kicker, and with the Varsity in bad need of a punter, it would seem to be "up to" every kicker in college to come out and work. I sent for you and you came out three or four times but complained of your feet and of your work. Later on you threw the hammer which certainly took as much time and effort as the kicking would have done, and only recently you have been rowing early in the morning, showing that you can get the time for what you really want to do. It will not do to say that there is no one to work with, for if you cannot find anyone, at least you can kick by yourself, as I have done several times this summer. Long kicks are not necessary and the side of the baseball cage affords a good place to kick at, and also makes chasing the ball unnecessary.

I am sure I don't know what is the matter with the present Harvard undergraduate, but certainly the athletics are way behind those of the past five years, the athletes lacking in energy, determination and fight. The attitude at present seems to be one of lordly indifference, a sort of well "I'd like to make the team if it's convenient" attitude.

Now such an attitude as that won't do, this fall, and I want to make it plain from the start. The eleven men who make that team are going to be earnest workers, interested, fighters all of them, and anxious to do all they can to restore our athletic reputation. I want every man "out" who feels that way, and I don't want out the others, no matter how large, how powerful or how experienced. Football is a game dependent on team work, and team work in turn is dependent upon subordination of the individual to the team and for the team, and this subordination must be made with all the heart and spirit that the candidate possesses.

Many of us have taken a lively interest in your possibilities and all of us have gone out of our way to help you along. We were all put to great trouble when you last disappeared trying to find out where you had gone and in making what apologies we could until we too became disgusted.

All this, Brill, is written in a thoroughly friendly manner, and with a view to putting the situation clearly and plainly before you. I want you to mull over it and see if you can't make up your mind to get down to hearty, enthusiastic work. It won't be enough for you to do only what you are told; you will need to think all the time and add something on your own hook, and all of this in the most cheerful, hearty spirit you can command.

It was claimed last year that you could go through any line, but that you went through blindly, and therefore ineffectually. This year I want you to go through in an intelligent way. You will be wisely coached and will be expected to do promptly and without question whatever you are told.

Take the ball, then, and get at your kicking. Be careful not to work over half an hour at first. Come around to me any day and I will show you what to work on, especially, so that you may work intelligently.

Don't allow yourself to get glum or discouraged and remember that Hurley and I stand ready at all times to give you a lift. I have adopted as my working motto—"Do it now" and I find it very effective. Perhaps you might find it of value in meeting your obligations. I have gained much through it, I know.

Sincerely,
[William Reid, Jr.]

Brill came promptly around to see me about it, and since then, which was almost six weeks ago, his conduct has been unexceptional. The Superintendent at Randall tells me that he has been as regular as clock work over there, the Newell Boat Club man says that he has exercised very regularly down there, and I know that he has been doing his kicking. Further than that, I have been down there and kicked with him on some occasions. From time to time I have also been over to see him and find out whether he was getting proper food and good sleep, and have asked him down to see me at Cohasset, where I hope he will be able to have a little rest and give me a still better opportunity to study him. He seems now, August 14, to be in splendid condition, and weighs about 205 lbs. I feel quite hopeful that he may really be of great value to us this year.

Now the case of Squires. Squires played guard last year, is a big man, and a Nova Scotian. He, like Brill, has worked his way through college, and is a thoroughly respectable and decent fellow, although he is perhaps a little thick headed. He had odd jobs much as Brill has had. It seems that last year he was a conductor on one of the electric lines to Revere Beach. On one of his trips a drunken man got onto a car ahead of his and had to be put off, it requiring the conductor and motorman of the car ahead with the motorman of Squire's car, to make the ejection. Later the man got on to Squires' car and refused to pay his fare. Squires said to the man,—"I want your fare." The man said, "Well, young fellow, you can wait until I am ready to pay it." Squires said, "I want it now," whereupon the other said, "You can't have it", whereupon Squires said, "If you don't give it to me I shall put you off," to which the other replied, "Let's see you." At this Squires grabbed the man by the nape of the neck and the lower part of both trousers, lifted him up and threw him off bodily, back down on the ground, a most risky thing to do, but illustrative of Squires' strength and seeming purpose. This matter resulted in a suit against the Company, which, however, came to nothing. Squires was, however, dismissed from the service of the Company with the simple remark, "You are too strong for us; come back next year." An interesting sequel to this electric car experience, one which has no bearing on football, has just come to light. In the game with the Univ. of Maine last year, Squires wore a nose guard and perhaps a head gear, and his opponent pretty nearly the same equipment. At about the middle of the game both men unmasked, and Squires found opposite him the motorman who had driven his car on the Revere line. The game from that [point] on waxed fierce around the tackle position.

Squires has been able to do his college work in passable shape, and has, like Brill, been helped by Herbert White, who got him a job as mate on a yacht. This summer Squires was after a job and sent to the appointment office to get one. None turned up for sometime, but finally one appeared down in Cohasset, near where I live. I immediately thought of Squires and started to get hold of him. I rode around to his house two or three times and found no one in. I wrote a letter to him at his house and had no response. I asked his friends where he was, and they did not know. The appointment office did not know. I finally located him through the post office where I found that he was down in Everett. I was greatly annoyed at his going off and leaving no address or story of a change in his plans for those who were trying to get him a position. This was particularly annoying in this case because three good jobs came up at one time, none of which were available at the time we finally located him. Having sent for him, he came up and realized in a rather irresponsible way how careless he had been. Meanwhile the position at Cohasset had been filled, but filled unsatisfactorily, and the man there wanted another man for the place. Meanwhile I had written Squires the letter which appears on the opposite page [missing], and which hit him pretty hard. As soon as this place was open again I sent for Squires, rang the man up on the telephone and put Squires in communication with him. On the same day another job came up which Squires wanted to look into and therefore held off the one at Cohasset until he could make a choice. He agreed in case he chose the other job to notify the Cohasset man about it so that he might not be left in the lurch. Squires did not appear at Cohasset and so I presumed that everything had been squared up. Exactly one week later Squires called me up on the telephone and asked me if I would please notify the Cohasset man that he was not coming. This second slip after the first one clearly indicated that the main point which I had made in my letter about Squires' irresponsibility, was absolutely just, a thing which he reluctantly admitted over the telephone. Just what is going to come of Squires this Fall I cannot tell, as these peculiar actions on his part make his standing rather uncertain.

The next case is that of Parker, a freshman of last year, and supposed to be a very promising candidate for centre rush. He weighs about 220 lbs. and came from Milton academy with great ability in place kicking. Last Fall he only had a chance to play a little, but during that time played himself completely out, putting apparently, his whole soul into the work. Unfortunately he was played at guard, for a while, a position for which he is in no way fitted physically. At the end of last year he was dropped, so this year I have followed him along very carefully to see that he kept up. For this same reason I did not require him out for Spring practice, although I did not think that his work would have suffered if he had come out. Sometime before the final examinations took place, I got him to work, doing special tutoring, and tried to make sure that he would get through. He passed off enough so that he lacked only half a "C" for promotion, and so I told him that he would have to go to Summer school. This he did. The Summer school lasts just about eight weeks, and the work in some of the courses in the college year, are about the same as those taken up at the Summer school, except that the work is much more concentrated. Parker took a course known as Fine Arts 3, and I had him tell me whether he was cutting or not and how his work was getting on. He told me that he was not doing much cutting, and I told him I wanted that little bit stopped, and he was in pretty good shape. A week and a half before the examination took place I undertook to quiz him on the course and found that he knew practically nothing about it at all, that I knew more about it after five years out of college than he did after having just taken the course. I went once to the head of the course, Mr. Chase, and asked him how Parker was doing, and he said that it all would depend on the final examination, but that Parker had been cutting more than he ought to. I had Parker explain to Mr. Chase that three of the four cuts he had taken were unavoidable, being due to failure of the train service between South Lancaster, where Parker has been spending the summer, and Boston, and that therefore there had been only one deliberate cut. I then got Mr. K. K. Smith, at Mr. Chase's suggestion, to tutor Parker right along, and I told Mr. Smith that he simply had got to get Parker through. To help out I got Mr. Nolen to work on Parker, and I did a certain amount of the outside reading in the most careful way, taking Parker down to my home at Cohasset, where we put in eight good hours. I felt very much disappointed over Parker's lack of get-up in going after this course. Here is a man who has already failed of promotion once, who apparently has a good chance for the team, who has taken the course at the Summer School, who must pass that course in order to be eligible and to be promoted, and who yet shows an absolute lack of responsibility in doing the work. Had I not gotten a tutor for Parker there is no telling how he would have come out, and I shall not know until tomorrow now, though I think the chances are in his favor. If I hadn't looked after his tutoring myself he would never have done any, and his course would have been a dismal failure. I blame myself in great measure for not having kept closer tabs on him from the start whereby I could probably have spread the work out more and have made the final work much less severe and more certain. I strongly advoc[at]e that in any case where men have to go to the Summer School hereafter, the coach follow the man from start to finish, and see that he not only attends his course regularly, but that he does whatever reading there is, and takes careful notes. Most of the Summer courses will pass any man who shows an earnest attempt at doing his work, but they are very severe on men who cut, since the Summer School is composed of teachers and students who are here for a purpose, and whose absolutely clean record as far as cuts are concerned, shows up in marked contrast to the tendency of undergraduates taking Summer courses to cut, even ever so little. In addition to this, it is mighty important that the coach should be sure that the men don't elect too stiff courses, because the easiest courses in the Summer School are harder than the medium courses in the regular work.

Now the case of Spear. Spear was a student here some two or three years ago who was ineligible to play owing to conditions or something of that kind. Just as he was getting into a condition where he could play, he was offered a position in a mine in Arizona, and accepted it. He weighs about 190 pounds and is a man not afraid of work and very active. He played football at Worcester Academy and did very well. This year he gave up the job there and has been about Boston with nothing special to do. One of the fellows suggested that he come back to college, and brought him round to see me. After talking with him, I found out that he was quite ready to consider coming back if he could in some way raise enough money to do so. He said that his father was very anxious to have him come back but that he could not afford to give him any help. It then developed that Spear has a claim for something over $500 against Joshua Crane[75] of Boston, on some mine trouble in the Arizona matter. Spear said that if I could get Crane to settle up this debt, he would return. I will see Crane tomorrow and try to make a note of what I am able to accomplish. This Spear case is a good illustration of the sort of outside work

75. Crane is likely a Harvard graduate of 1890 and a letter-winner in football in the same year.

a coach may find it necessary to do, and which has no bearing whatever upon the actual field work, but which may be very important.

The last case is that of [John] Cunniff.[76] Cunniff has been a candidate for centre for a year [or] two, and last year was put on probation, besides having broken his wrist, so that he was unable to play. He is in peculiar position in that he is doing a certain amount of business in Boston at the same time that he is attending the University. His business causes him to make a great number of cuts, although standing high in his classes. Unwilling to allow Cunniff to cut so much with the faculty's taking notice of it, he has been kept on probation most of last year, even though, as I say, his marks were As, Bs, and Cs. I think I have arranged matters so that the faculty will allow him to play this Fall, and I don't know but that he may prove to be a very valuable man. He is Irish, but one of the tamest Irishmen that I have ever seen. I wrote him a letter a copy of which appears on the opposite page [missing] in which I urged him to do a certain amount of preparatory work. His reply, which follows [missing], was a good one, especially his last remark as to the lack of fight which he had displayed.

These examples which I have given are among the more prominent ones with which I have had to deal, although there have been hundreds of cases like them only without quite so much detail. If Parker gets through his Fine Arts examination, and Hurley passes all right, I shall feel that I have done this Spring every single thing which I could possibly do to contribute to a thorough season this Fall, and no matter how the works turns out then I shall have nothing which I omitted in the Spring with which to upbraid myself. Once again let me say that I don't believe too much importance can be attached to the Spring work, and that any man who expects to make things go right in the Fall must go into it heart and soul.

76. Cunniff was a Harvard football letter-winner in 1904, according to Blanchard, ed., *The H Book of Harvard Athletics*, 598.

Daily Season Record from September 13 through November 25

Wednesday, September 13, 1905

Morning:

Practice did not begin until the afternoon. I spent most of the morning in talking with Capt. Hurley and McMaster [the trainer] about things and in getting ready for work. On my way out to Cambridge I stopped in town and had a discussion with [William H.] Lewis on the manner of snapping the ball back, and he is coming out if possible in the afternoon to take a glance at the men.

Afternoon:

The weather to-day was fine and cool, just suited to foot ball work. When the squad was called together at 2 o'clock we found that 50 men were on hand, a rather disappointing showing in view of the urging which we have done to get the men out on time. Those who came, however, were mostly all old Varsity men and that was a little gratifying. One-fifth of the men exactly were "H" men and almost all men who had been on the squad last year. This was in spite of the fact that I sent out 201 notices at both before practice began and followed it up with a secondary notice a week before the men were expected to report. As soon as the men were dressed I called them up stairs and made them quite a long talk on what we are going to try to do and the way in which we are going to try to do it. I said in brief something like this:

"Before practice begins this season, I want to have a pretty fair understanding with you fellows as to what we are going to try to do and how we are going to try to do it. Most of you have heard in one way or another that I am very strict and disciplinary and many of you are wondering how you are going to get along with me. No man will have the slightest difficulty with me so long as he pitches in in the right way and does his work as he is told, but I shall aim to make it as uncomfortable as possible for any man who shows intentions to shirk or to fail of a response.

There are several points which I want to make absolutely sure from the first. First of all we are going to try to find the very best football players in the University and make a team out of them. In the second place, class, family or society standing will have nothing whatever to do with the choice. We shall do our best to get the strongest team in the University. Some of you are down here with the idea of trying for a certain position. Now we shall try as far as possible to accommodate those men, but in case we find it wise to make a change we shall make it, and expect the player to do his best in his new position, feeling assured that in case he cannot after a wholehearted attempt to play it make a success of it, he will be given a try elsewhere if he shows the right stuff. We are not playing for ourselves or for an "H" or to make the team, but to try to drag the University on to its feet, just having passed through the most disasterous Athletic year that Harvard has ever known: beaten [by Yale] in baseball, football, tennis, track and crew, and in fact everything that really counts.

Last year the discipline was in some cases lax, a thing that is not going to happen this year. It was reported to me that several of the players last year faked their weights in order to retain their position on the team. I call this absolute dishonorable, selfish and mean, and shall regard any such action this year as severely as I would a man who had broken training, and will put him off the squad. If a man cannot take the welfare of the University to heart he is not the man to try for the team.

There seems also to have been some breaking of training last year, which must also stop. When a man is told to do a thing he must do it, and that must end it, and in case any man breaks the training rules, he will be put off the squad without a moment[']s hesitation whether he is the best player on it or not, or whether he has ten associates or none. We will not have a man on the team this year who breaks training.

In order to keep up the relationship between the coaches and players I am going to ask as we did in 1901 that the players speak to the coaches as Mr. So and So or coach So and So, and never Tom, Dick or Harry. This is not said with a view to creating arist[oc]racy among the coaches but merely to make everyone feel that he is just as near being intimate with a coach as anyone [el]se.

There is to be no grumbling whatever. In case anything does not go right, I shall always be ready to talk the matter over, but remember that any man who talks in criticism among his fellows is not doing what is best for the best interests of the squad. If there is anything to be grumbled about, grumble to me and be manly. Every man must be frank and open or there will be friction, and with friction it is impossible to accomplish anything.

The work this year is going to be hard, and to do it and make the team, each man will have to make some sacrifices and undergo some inconvenience. If you do not feel like making these sacrifices or like giving the time, do not come out, but if you do, come out and stick to it."

I supplemented those remarks by a few others, and then had the men go through a five minute dumbbell drill, after which they were taken out onto the field and divided into squads after Yost's idea. All the centres and quarterbacks were put together, while all the rest of the squad acted as halfbacks. The guards, tackles and ends acting and backs just as the regular backs. I spent a great deal of time showing the men how to hold the ball for buck plays, and explained that it might be held with the long axis vertically up and down, being clasped to the body with two hands and arms, so as to hold it solid. The other way with the long axis parallel to the ground and where the ball is put into a pocket formed by a man's stomach flatways to his body and grasped with both arms and both hands. This work was plan[n]ed to give the men plenty of wind and to increase their speed. By working one of the faster halves with one of the slower linemen, I made the linemen feel that they must move more speedy, and this got them to put more effort into the work. I insisted that the quarterbacks try to put the ball for the buck plays in just the spot where the man wanted it, neither too far out nor too far in or too high or too low, but just right, there being sometimes as many as six backs to a side, twelve in all to a squad. I had each man as he got the ball yell "bullseye" in case the quarterback put the ball where it belonged. I made a point of having the men keep their arms in close to the body, so as to prevent insecure handling of the ball as well as to prevent the quarterback from being interferred with. After putting the men through this sort of work about half an hour I sent part of the squad in, keeping out however, the centres and punters. I had for kickers Foster, Lincoln, Leonard, Hanley, Lockwood, Hall and Wendell. We held a practice on the Freshman team end, and shall continue to hold it there for about two weeks. We had the field roped off so as to keep the inquisitive spectators away. There were a good many on hand to watch, and I raised the question as to whether another year it would not be well to keep the gates of soldiers field closed, and thus limit sightseers, as they are likely to make remarks and be frequently in the way. After the practice was over we had the men weigh themselves and give the weights and positions to the managers, and to write down also what previous injuries any of them had ever had, where and how long. We gave to these men for whom shoes were ordered last spring each a pair of shoes, and told him to wear them tomorrow morning at practice.

When everything was done for the afternoon, Capt. Hurley, Coach Lewis and I talked the situation over for a few minutes, then Capt. Hurley went down to Cohassat with me where we worked in the evening in plan[n]ing out the work for tomorrow.

Thursday, September 14, 1905

Morning:

According to my plan of yesterday I limited the practice this morning to just one-half hour. We had splendid weather for the work. Before the men had their dumb bell work I gave them a considerable talk on fundamentals, and showed the linemen some squatting exercises which I expect them to take, and the reasons for them. I cut out the starts this morning, because I found that the men were not able to take them safely, and I was sort of afraid of making more legs sore. I had the usual work in running all of the men through signals and centre plays in squads comprising of centre, quarterback and two halves. I made a special emphasis on getting the ball right and hanging on to it. In order to make th[e] work approximate a regular play, I had the quarterback yell the signals, which, although they meant nothing to the men, yet they had a chance to hear the q.b. speak and get accustomed to his voice. This bothered some of the men quite a bit, because they were a little bit upset by the sound, and some of them forgot about keeping their hands close to their bodies after they received the ball. There were forty-five men out altogether.

The papers this morning were all very enthusiastic about the work, and I have plan[n]ed to talk to the newspaper men in a day or two or perhaps this afternoon, in order to get this matter straightened out.

After some considerable signal running and some squad practice for the line, I took those men who are trying to do place kicking and gave them quite a talk about it. I did not allow any kicking, since the talk lasted quite a while, but I explained the necessity of absolute team work between the man holding the ball and the kicker, and for careful work in aiming the ball, putting it down and then watching it while it is being kicked. The morning work was pretty light, and I think it ought to be.

Afternoon:

I had all of the punters up by the Union between 2. and 3.15 o'clock to-day, where I gave them a long talk on punting, going over the various punts and trying to explain each one carefully. I told the men that one of the things that must be done to make kicks successful is to get them off quickly enough so as they won't be blocked. I showed them that the speed that is necessary to do this cannot be acquired all at once and must be the result of learning first how to think slowly and then quickening up after one once knows how. I then took up the idea of kicking step by step, much as follows:

The very first principle in kicking is to get the proper distance back from the centre and get it every time so that the centre may be accustomed to the distance which he is expected to pass the ball back and also the height to which the man in the back field waits to receive it. Of course, if the kicker stands at different distances the passes are bound to be irregular. The next thing is the position of the man's feet and arms. I explained that the man's arms should be extended over towards the centre only when the fullback is ready to have the ball passe[d] back. Many fullbacks get their arms out before they have got their distance, just as it should be, and then by a motion of their fingers indicate to the centre that it is time for the pass to be made. The difficulty of this plan is of course, that the other side will start when the fullback moves his fingers and will thereby give a great advantage in getting through on kicks. I explained that the fullback should get his distance first, and then when he is ready to have the ball passed back put his hands out about waist high and stand there with his arms out that way until the centre passes the ball, he doing it at the first opportunity. In this way the other side cannot tell whether the ball is going back when they expect it or not and yet the kicker is ready for it. I explained that the kicker should not have his arms out stifly, since by doing so is likely to fight the ball, but should rather have his arms comfortably limber so as to give a little as the ball strikes the hands. The man's weight should of course be more on the foot which he does not expect to step forward or backward with as the case may be. The body of the kicker should feel pretty limber and not be in a strained condition. A kicker should have a limber body, which cannot be gotten by keeping his muscles stiff. He should catch the ball in his hands and as far as possible handle it at almost arms distance from his body rather than draw it in to his body, then push it out again, by doing which he must lose time. What is more he should handle the ball after he has received it by turning it with his hands wrist rather than by tossing it into position, where for a small portion of the time a little wind or some atmospheric condition may swing it as it drops so that it will not drop true on the kickers foot. This is something to be tried for by the kicker, but not to be worked on so that the kicker loses his confidence in handling the ball. It is really a matter of secondary importance. It is important, however, that the ball should be placed with its longest axis horizontally to the ground, so that it may be hit by the foot in such a way as to cause the ball to travel on its longest axis, which is, of course, in keeping with the rule of physics. The steps that the kick takes should be limited to as few as possible, and if it is possible only one step after receiving the ball, involving thereby perhaps a very short step made with the foot with which the ball is kicked just previous to the one step with the other foot, following which the kick is made. This step has many times been ruled out by our kicking coaches, and I think it is a mistake since it is natural to everyone, the coaches themselves included, to do it, and to my mind no man can kick without it. It is alright to make the step, short, but to tell the man not to make it at all for the purpose of making it as short as possible is a mistake, for the more intelligent try to get along without it and therefore throw themselves in such disorder that they are unable to kick at all. The two ways of standing are to stand with both feet nearly on the ground, and in case the kicker is a right footed one with his weight on his right foot and then as the ball reaches the kicker have him step back seven or eight inches with his left foot and then take a short step of about six inches with the right foot following this up with a full step on his left foot, at the end of which step the kick takes place, or standing with the left leg behind the right leg receiving the ball in that position, stepping forward then with the left leg and then kicking with the right. It is my judgment that no man's footwork should be bothered in the slightest so long as he is getting his kicks off in anything like a respectful length of time. When a coach un[d]ertakes to trifle with a man's footing he will do more damage in most cases than good.

To get back now to the time just after the kicker has got the ball and got its longest axis horizontal with the ground, the next point is how to drop the ball so that it will be far enough out so as to hit on the right portion of the foot. This is something every kicker must decide pretty largely upon himself. The ball must be dropped in the same way everytime. It must fall in the same way and have the same relation to the foot. The ball should strike the foot at the point just below the ankle and between the ankle joint and the point where the toes join the foot. There is a hump at that spot on which every kick should hit. After the kicker swings his leg for the kick he should straighten out his toes as horizontally as possible in order to expose the spot on his foot on which he wants the ball to hit so that the ball will not be in danger of hitting his foot in two or three different places, as would be the case where the toes were turned up. Some men in swinging their leg are inclined to get a little side swing to their blow, which the coaches are likely to try to cut out. This to my mind is always a mistake, since in my own particular case I never could kick if I could not do that, and more kickers have been spoiled by trying to make them do things which are not natural to them than by any other way. Let the man swing his leg as he chooses so long as his kicks travel good. It is a mistaken idea in kicking that the man's leg should be swung stiff as it hits the ball. Such a blow lacks the springy quality of the golf drive and has not the carry through, which is so effective. Instead, the leg should be kept limber, and just as the ball is about to be struck a quick knee snap should wield the blow. It will often be found that an easy blow of this kind will easily send the ball further than one of the harder blows which ought to, according to one's feelings, carry the ball further. All of these points need to be looked after in getting the kicker into shape, and the problem for the coach is, where he can make alterations that will help the kicker without hurting his effectiveness. In kicking behind the line, much practice as possible should be given. The men must watch the ball as they kick it, and not the man coming through. After all of these details are pretty well straightened out the kicker may begin to quicken up and try for distance, height and position.

Having gone over these points carefully with the men, and some others which I have doubtless omitted, I took them into my office where I went over with them some of the pictures which I had taken in the spring, and showed them what was going on into the picture. I expect this work to lead the kickers to do some intelligent kicking of their own. As Kernan said in a letter to me, "No kicker that you have got to coach the last three weeks of the season is going to be worth anything to you", and I agree with him.

The squad as usual reported at 4 o'clock, and I found there a number of men who ran with their feet so nearly in a straight line that it is impossible for them to do successful turning. McMasters is going to take those men and show them how to run. I had each man on the squad run in front of McMasters to see which of them had got to be corrected. Lewis came out this afternoon and took the linemen and gave them some drilling, and Waters came out quite late as did Daly. Lewis and Waters, to my great delight settled in harmony the question as to how the guards and tackles should play this year. This almost made me feel like cheering as I left the field, as since Lewis and Waters were able to agree it would mean that portion of the coaching would go along smoothly, otherwise it would mean that one or the other would be doing what he did not believe in, which would be very ineffective. Daly was out too late to do any coaching, but helped one or two men in a little drop kicking. I ran the men through practice in squads as before. One squad contained [Waldo] Pierce centre, [Bartol] Parker q.b., [Frederic] White and [Somers] Fraser h.bs. I had a lot of punting and some kick offs with two easy starts and then four quick ones. I sent most of the men in after the hours work. I instructed the men in falling on the ball, and where they failed to do so three times in succession, I sent them in. Dr. Nichols and Farley, Lewis, and [John L.] Motley[1] came out, but I did not allow any of these coaches to talk to the men, but asked them to look on.

Before the squad came on to the field [John] Cunniff, White, [Harold] Barney and Parker came down and did some hammer work[2] which McMasters laid out. The ends ran down the field under the kicks, two-thirds of the team watching the man catching the ball instead of the ball, which means that everytime a back in the back field misjudged a kick the ends were very much upset by their failure to get into proper position of approach. Motley came on the field smoking, and as I hold that no coach should come onto the field smoking where the men are, I asked him to discontinue.

I sent off sixty-one telegrams for more men, and went down to the Adams House to dine with Dr. Nichols before going to Cohasset. We talked over things in general but the medical end of it in particular, and shall have more equipment in the way of antisceptics, etc., than we have ever had before.

Friday, September 15, 1905

Morning:

Capt. Hurley and I left Cohasset on the 8-02 train, coming immediately out to Cambridge. Immediately on our arrival we walked over to the college office and saw Dean Hurlbut about the question of get-

---

1. Motley was a Harvard football letter-winner in 1902.
2. Hammer work may have been some exercise using the weight found in the track and field event, the hammer throw.

ting Parker off probation. He said that he would see Parker and give him instructions about making a position. From the college office we went over to the Bursar's office in order to ask that the foot ball men be allowed to live in their college rooms, even though the college buildings are not supposed to open until next Monday. Several of the men had asked for the privilege but had been refused. By asking him to allow us this privilege and offering in every way to carry out any agreement which we might make with him, he finally allowed the men to go into their rooms on two conditions: In the first place, on condition that they do not go into any other boy's rooms and in the second place, on condition that they do not attempt to move into their rooms unless they had furniture already there. This was wholly reasonable and we accepted it gladly. The understanding is that next year it may not be allowed, and that this year is only done as a special favor and on trial. Realizing this we cautioned the men to keep strictly to the rules so that we might have the same privileges next year. We find that many of the men are living out of town and going back and forth continually, and this being the case, we are put to some considerable expense and considerable inconvenience. I think, therefore, that it would be a good scheme next year, in case the college does not choose to open its rooms, to try and arrange with some private boarding house for accommodations for the men at a trifling expense, until more permanent quarters can be obtained.

On my way down I ran across my cousin, Oscar Taylor, who has been sent on here by the foot ball men of the University of California to study the Harvard system. He is going to have access to most of the coaching squads and to get what he can to take out to California with him.

At the field we had dumb bell work at 10:30 and [Karl] Brill was the only man late. He had gone in town it seems and gotten out just too late for that work. I took him severely to task for it and do not believe it will occur again. After Brill's experience of last year, I decided to allow no leeway to him another time in the matter of excuses so that there may be no possible slipping through our fingers. I have now got a small block of excuse blanks about 2" x 3" on which I write out an excuse for a man every time he is absent or is to be absent, the Manager holding every man late whenever he does not present an excuse blank.

Before the men went on the field, I spoke of taking particular care of the bruises and urged each man to get to work at once to correct any special weaknesses which he himself knows he has, as well as the coach, and not to wait until the coach came around and told him to do something. I ordered Cunniff, Hurley, [Hatherly] Foster, [John] Wendell, Parker, Peirce, and [Fisher] Nesmith to report to the field at 2 o'clock this afternoon in order to, myself, see that they are properly clothed. I have asked McMaster to be on hand so as to show him what I wanted so that he might take that work himself and get it off my hands.

Having trotted the men around the field and having given the whole squad several starts, in which I allowed them to get off easy in order to prevent strains, I had Cunniff and [William] Quigley kick off while the rest of the men divided into two squads ran down on the kicks. I was careful that the men on the kick offs did not get off side, that they ran as hard as they could, and that they were around when the runner got the ball. I had every runner yell out the name of the man who would have caught him if they had been tackling, which made the men very keen in their efforts. The kickoffs were not very satisfactory, and I was able to out kick any of the men on the squad.

Following these starts, I had the men divide up into squads of four each, center, quarter back, and a heavy man with a quick man, and had the quarter back say which one of the men would take the ball and rattle off a number of signals, which meant nothing and which had nothing to do with the time in which the ball came back, simply to get the backs accustomed to hearing the signals and the quarter backs to give them with proper sharpness and vim. I found that the giving of signals distracted some of the men so that they forgot how to take the ball as they ran. This was what I expected and I told the men of it and by the end of the work they had gotten pretty well over it.

Remembering from 1901 what a hard time the backs had in getting one hand under the ball so as to prevent its falling through their arms, I still kept the backs at work catching with one hand, emphasizing the necessity of keeping the hand well under the ball. It is awkward work and many of the backs were not very successful, but it is teaching them more than ever to give properly with the ball as it hits the body, which is exactly what I want. I found that I had to watch the men very carefully on this to prevent them from trying to pin the ball to their bodies from the outside as it fell, instead of having one hand beneath the ball where they could easily swing it in to the pocket which I have told them to form with their stomach. I did not allow them to use the other hand at all.

After the catching work, [R. J.] Leonard and Cunniff kicked some goals with Hurley and [H.] Kempner holding the ball.

The next thing we did was to set the line men to work walking around the field close to the ground, with their knees bent low, in order to make the line men more flexible and able to move strongly about in that position. It seemed to take them in the knees and thighs and I did not give them much of it, although they all seemed to think it a most valuable exercise. I showed them how the weight of one's body, and the most effective part of it, lies between the chest and the knees, and that the nearer one can get that part to the ground the stronger will be his position, and with the legs spread wide apart the greater the chance of shifting the weight to some other position where it will be more useful and more effective.

After this work, I had some of the other men kick off down the field to a squad composed of some of the heavy men, in order to get them accustomed to getting in front of the ball and catching kick-offs.

To prevent any accident to the backs practicing catching in the back field, I made a rule that only the one man who fumbled a kick should go after it. Until I made this rule, I was constantly afraid that two of my best backs would be bumping into each other, owing to the lack of condition in either one of them. Before I sent the men in, I had them roll around on the ground on their backs preparatory to the first bit of falling on the ball which we shall have and which will come tomorrow morning. This made the practice pretty long and I had only time to dress and get up from the field to dine with Prof. White[3] at the Colonial club. I dined with him in order to talk over the eligibility of a man named Armstrong, who played for two years on a college team while still attending a public school, and who then played three years on the college team afterwards. Mr. White said there would be no question but that he would be ineligible, as he had played really five years of college foot ball, even though the college had really no right to allow him to represent them while he was in school. That makes another big line man.

The next question I took up was that of protesting to Penn against their wholesale importation of players. Mr. White agreed that Penn is all wrong, and also that it is putting ourselves to a great disadvantage to undertake to play them on even terms, when they have such great advantage over us. It finally seemed to be the wisest thing to notify Penn after the first meeting of the Athletic committee, that Harvard will not consider herself bound to play Penn next year, and that we wish the same freedom with regard to arrangement of our Penn schedule as we have with that of the other colleges. While this

3. This likely was Horatio S. White, chair of the Harvard Athletic Committee from 1903 to 1907.

will not be giving any reasons, Penn will understand very clearly what is meant, and I rather expect that it may make some slight difference in her actions this fall. Capt. Hurley has seen a letter or so which one of the Penn coaches has written to a man named Draper asking to go to Penn. The man has gone. I also took up with Prof. White the question of remuneration for Lewis, which has been left unsettled.[4]

Afternoon:

I found that I was the one to arrange with Coach Lewis in regard to his remuneration, and I shall take the matter up again in a few days. There is a man named McLeod just here from the [Massachusetts] Institute of Technology who is trying for the team. He was admitted here by the Scientific school on probation until Christmas, which would make him ineligible. I went around to the Scientific office to find out whether on probation in this case meant on probation in the sense that it is usually used in, or whether it referred more to the question of being a matter of trial. Mr. Love was not in the office so I talked with the Secretary, who told me the man was on probation in the real sense, but suggested that the boy petition to be admitted on trial until Christmas instead. McLeod seems to be a good man and I hope he may work out all right. I saw Mr. K. K. Smith, who did so much work during the summer to get Hurley and Parker through in their studies, and I thanked him as heartily as I knew how for his splendid efforts. After making these arrangements, I went down to the field at 3 o'clock in order to dress properly several men whom I had ordered to be there for that purpose. I started out with the men stripped and gradually clothed them in the most thorough fashion, those men who had stockings with holes in the feet were given new stockings, those who had been measured for shoes last spring were given their shoes, those who were not measured were given shoes with the Murphy ankle brace in. Next, we had each man get a cotton under shirt with quarter sleeves to prevent the red of the jerseys from getting into cuts and scratches and to enable us to wash the jerseys at stated intervals. After this I fitted each man out with felt pads and straps about which I spoke in my account of clothing for Spring practice, taking care that the pads were big enough to go well around each man's knees. Then I fitted each man out with the felt shoulder pads, taking

4. Beginning in 1901, Lewis had been paid $500 a year for several years to assist in coaching Harvard football; the amount was raised to $1,000 in 1904. See Harvard Athletic Committee Minutes, 10 Jan. 1901, 7 May 1902, 27 Dec. 1903, and 8 Oct. 1904, Harvard University Archives.

care to see that they fitted well around the neck and shoulder, and covered the outside point of the top of the shoulder. Such men as had bad shoulders last year I allowed to wear leather pads on the outside of their jerseys, but the other men will have none. Every man was provided with a jersey without pads except for pads on the elbows, which were fitted to each man after his jersey was on. I took care that the jersey arms were pretty tight to prevent these hair pads from shifting. In case any men liked his own trousers better, I allowed him to wear them, provided he took the old pads out, and in case the new pads were too bulky and bound his knee, had his trousers widened at the knee to accommodate the new pad. I had hair pads put on each man's hip to his order. I had McMaster on hand watching me so as to get him acquainted with what I want.

At the roll call at 4 o'clock Brill was late, having stayed in town on an errand just long enough to miss the dumb bell work. I told him that there were to be no more absences on his part and he took it in good shape and I do not believe we shall have future trouble on that score. I had every man who was absent report to me and explain his absence, so as to show the squad that I was coaching on the score of promptness. After the dumb bell drill, we took the men out on to the field and had [Nathan] Hall, Foster, [Phillip] Lockwood and Wendell kick while the ends ran down under the direction of [James] Montgomery. I gave the ends a certain amount of instruction and the backs also, in catching kicks, the handling of a bouncing ball and the way in which an end should look for it. All the backs were made to continue catching with one hand in order to get into the habit of having one hand under the ball. Some of the men were taking hold of that idea pretty well, and I saw Hall catch a full fledged punt in one hand while holding two foot balls under his other arm. I had the whole squad take four starts for speed and then sent the line men, from tackle to tackle, to Coach Lewis, who gave the men careful work with the charging machine,[5] the work being very light indeed. Daly took the centers and quarter backs for a little time and helped with drop kicking. Lewis' observation of [Beaton] Squires and Brill seemed to be pretty good. He said that they were both powerful slow moving and slow thinking machines. They are going to need much waking up both mentally and physically.

I forgot to say that at 3 o'clock McMaster had several of the heavy men down swinging a big mallet and driving blows first with one hand and then the other at some stumps which he has out near the

---

5. This probably would be called a blocking sled today.

stadium. His work is to take down the men's weight and to build them up in strength. I am asking the squad before each practice what men have diarrhea so as not to put men through a stiff course of work in such a condition. I am also seeing that the men look after the skin which has been rubbed off from their ankles and which ought not to be the case, if they get over the first week or two with the skin unbroken. I kept the men at work for exactly one hour and then sent them in, remaining myself to have a talk with the newspaper men and to ask them not to take quite such a rosy view of the situation. I showed them how we were fixed for material in general and think that I can convince them that the situation is not so bright as they might think. I took the 8:13 train to Cohasset pretty well tired out. The thing that worried me most was the fact that Capt. Hurley strained his leg, but I had the consolation of knowing that I had given every warning that I could prevent any such trouble. We shall lay him off until he is entirely well so as to make sure that we do not injure him permanently.

Saturday, September 16, 1905

Morning:

This is the day I gave the men only one [s]ession, but made it quite long. I started out with the view of having the men go through an examination on what they have had this week, but found that I could not begin to get through it thoroughly. We were out altogether for 2 1-4 hours. Forty-five men reported. The weather was very drizzly. [John] Reynolds, a half-back on last year's freshmen team has had to stop playing because of his knees which he hurt last year. I gave the men a talk on falling on the ball as it lies still on the ground, illustrating to them by doing so myself. I showed how as a man approaches the ball he must begin to turn his body so that his shoulder will be almost at right angles when it hits the ground and the track in which he is running. This prevents the shoulder from getting the blow and causes the man to hit on the round of his back where he cannot hurt himself. I line the men up in two squads, and gave them all five or six starts. I gave the q. bs. work in passing the ball to the backs. I took special care in seeing that every man received the ball as he ought to. I had the backs do some catching to see how well they had that, and had some kick offs, and after carefully going over the falling on the ball with the whole squad, and throwing into a squad by themselves the men who did not know how, I sent the men in.

After my talk with the newspapers reporters yesterday, all the reports this morning were changed greatly, and everything as it should be. I was very glad of it, because we have not the first-class material this year, and I do not want anybody to misjudge.

I had a talk with Dr. Nichols in the afternoon, and afterward went to Cohasset.

Sunday, September 17, 1905

Feeling that Leo Daly, who is to have charge of the quarter backs, was not perhaps quite at ease on the afternoons when he has come out, I invited him down to Cohasset to talk over the work, and that of the quarterback in particular. He was with me from 2:00 o'clock until 6:00 and we had a most profitable discussion. After going over a great many points with him individually and emphasizing the necessity for making allowance for the individuality each player in assigning him to a certain position in receiving the ball and in doing anything else pertaining to the position, I took him over to Dudley Dean's house, not far away, where we went over the entire question of quarter back play in every phase.

In the first place we took up the question of how the center should pass the ball back and how the quarter-back should stand. We decided that we should, as much as possible, allow the quarter back to stand in the easiest position possible for him to get the ball away in, and then expect the center to accustom himself to whatever style of pass was necessary in order to make the quarterback's position most effective. I showed both Leo Daly and Dudley Dean the two different ways of passing the ball back which we have had in mind this year. The first one is the old last year's style of putting the fingers over the farther end of the ball and by a short quick wrist snap propel the ball back to the quarterback's hands. The second one was the one which Yost uses in Michigan, and consists in taking the ball at about its middle point and standing it up with lacing up and the farther point away from the body and rising to an angle of about forty degrees from the ground. In discussing the first method, we found this great criticism; that is, that there must be a distinct change in the way in which the ball is held in passing for kicks as distinguished from the way it is held in passing for runs. In Yost's method the ball is held exactly the same way for each and does not, therefore, allow the opponent to surmise just what is going to happen. Then, in our old way of last year it is pretty difficult to snap the ball back any great distance, the result being that the quarter back had to reach way down under the center in order to get his hands near enough to receive the ball, a position which made it hard for the quarter back to get away quickly from. I passed the ball back to Daly both ways to show Dean what we meant, and then we had him try to receive some. He agreed with us that if possible we should use the Yost method. Another great advantage to the Yost method is that in passing for kicks there is no necessity for lifting the ball off the ground as there was in the old last year's method of picking it up, and which in many cases ended in the center's passing the ball over his fullback's head. As far as the quarterback's were concerned, then, it was pretty well agreed that the Yost method would be the best if practical.

Figuring that, in connection with safety, the quarter back should get his hands as near the ball as possible in receiving it, so long as his starting was not interfered with, we concluded to instruct the quarter back to get just as near the ball as he possibly could and yet get away his quickest. As to the position of the quarterback's feet, whether both feet should be on a line or whether one or the other should be back, we decided to leave it largely to the quarterback's own judgment. One cannot successfully compel a foot ball player to handle himself in any one particular space of ground by trying to tell him just where to put his feet. The individual, with proper guidance, should have considerable freedom on this point. One thing we agreed on also in this connection was the fact that the quarterback should try to have his hands exactly in the same place in the air every time so that the center might pass with some considerable confidence. Then as regards the position of the hands: After a long discussion with Charlie Daly in which he took up the[,] what he calls[,] three-cup system, we were all agreed that the ball should always be caught in the hands and that no plan should be taught whereby the ball should be caught either in the fore-arms or against the body, as Daly has described in his article on the "Play of the Quarter Back" which is printed in a little red pamphlet. Having decided, then, that the ball should be caught and handled always in the hands, the question came up as to how the hands should be placed. It was pretty clearly agreed, after some discussion, that one hand (whichever the quarter back felt the most natural about) should be held under the probable flight of the ball and that the ball should hit that hand first, that the other one should then be clasped over the ball and the pass begun. This sounds, as written, as though there were two very distinct motions to it, but such is not the case, as the ball is almost received at the same instant with both hands. We decided to begin the quarter back work with nothing but constant drill on receiving the ball from the center, and secondly, getting it to the runner; in other words, making sure of the first stage of the transmission between the center and the backs before hurrying on to the next stage. In 1901 I remember that we were constantly having fumbles between the center and the quarter backs because the quarter backs were too much hurried in getting the ball to their backs and in trying to look in the direction that they were about to make their pass before they really had the ball in their hands. The result was that very frequently the ball would hit the ends of the quarter back's fingers and drop, or that in beginning to turn to pass the ball he would change the position of his hands so that it would be impossible for the center to pass it with any accuracy, the hands being so variable. To overcome this it was very clear to me that at the start the centers and quarters should practice handling the ball between themselves, and second, that they should try to pass it to another man after they have gotten it well. The quarter backs are to be coached to criticise the passes of their centers, doing so in a pleasant fashion with a view to getting the co-operation of the centers in getting the ball back absolutely the same every time. In other words, while criticising each other in their detail work, the center and quarter must at all times be in absolutely good humor with one another. There should be no ill feeling whatever over the criticisms that either one or the other may make. The quarter of course must not fight the ball with his hands, but must give with it.

The next point that we took up was the question as to whether the quarter back should stand as did the Penn quarter back last year—at arms length from the center and almost erect save for a little squat in the knees, or whether he should get down pretty much as the Yale quarters and our quarters have done. The disadvantages of the Penn style, though it is also practiced by Yost of Michigan, seemed to be, first; that the center has to pass the ball farther for the quarter back is so much in view during all the passing that it is practically impossible for him to conceal the ball very well, and in the second place; that the quarter back is so far from his line that it is impossible to start the offense quite so near the line. When one considers that Yale's defensive backs have been placed almost on the rush line it must be clear that no offense can well hope to cope with it so long as it is started so far from the line as to give Yale's backs and line a good chance to see what is going to happen before it happens. That was the weakness of the Penn guards-back play.[6] On the other hand, the position might perhaps be a little stronger for any man who was planning a

---

6. Using guards and other linemen in the backfield to gain blocking advantages was legal until after the 1905 season, when the number of players required to be on the line of scrimmage was increased to six, and the seventh forward, if playing behind the line, had to position himself outside the end. See Parke H. Davis, *Football: The American Intercollegiate Game* (New York: Charles Scribner's Sons, 1911), 113.

quarter back run, since it was perhaps easier to get off for the circling run which the quarter back had to make from that position than from a position a little nearer the line. Be that as it may, in our system and in the Yale system it is a good deal harder to see who has the ball—the offense hits the line quite a little quicker and with just as much force, and there is much greater possibility of deception. On that basis we decided to hold to the Harvard and Yale style. I shall watch Penn carefully this year to see what other advantage there is in her way so that next year we may profit by any advantage, if there is one. [We] thus decided approximately on the pass, on the position of the quarterback's feet, on his proximity to the center, and on the proper precedent of the different stages in perfecting the quarter back play.

We then took up the question of the actual passes. First, the pass for a play between guard and center on either side. Here we had some little argument. In the Harvard and Yale style it has been the custom of the quarter back to pivot toward the man with the ball on the foot nearest him, swinging the farther foot so that when the ball is delivered to the back the two feet will come almost on the same line. The method employed by Yost was to pivot on the farther foot drawing the nearer foot back so that it is behind the other foot and almost in the same line with it.

The criticism that Yost makes on our style of play is that in not swinging back the foot nearest the runner we are likely to leave an obstacle in his path over which the runner is likely to trip, while by swinging the foot nearest the runner in the rear of the other foot any possibility of tripping the runner is eliminated. It seemed to all of us, however, that there were three or four reasons why the Harvard & Yale system is better than the Yost system. In the first place, on any offence the rush line is expected to advance a foot or so the moment the ball is put in play; that being the case the forward step in the Harvard system will bring the quarter back a little bit forward in the extra space that is now given him at the same time that it throws his weight on the forward foot, which places him in a splendid position to follow the runner on through the line. On the other ha[nd], in the Yost method the man is forced to step back in the opposite direction from which the runner is coming and also away from the play, making a little longer pass necessary and making it, since in the Yost method the weight must be on the backward foot, a little harder for the quarter back to regain his balance and help the runner out. In addition to this, the stepping back from the advancing rush line loses the advance which the rush line has made, at any rate to a small extent. In the light of those arguments we decided to adopt the Harvard and Yale idea.

Daly was not at first in favor of having the quarter back run on into the line of play with the man, since when he played and for the last two or three years our quarter back has been coached to stay out of the play. I maintain, however, that if the quarter back stays out of the play we are making the play with just ten men instead of eleven, whereas the quarter back can be of the greatest service to his runner by running with him holding him up and preventing the opposing rush line back from twisting his runner to one side or the other if he has made a good game. In 1901 when we played the tandem style[7] of game the Yale backs got hold of the forward man and twisted him to one side for the simple reason that there were no opponents on either side of him to hold him in place. This argument convinced Daly that the quarter back should then go into the play, and as Dean was already agreed that matter was settled. We decided in connection with this point to have the quarter back wear shin guards a portion of the time to prevent him from getting his shins badly cut up by his runner.

In passing the ball for any buck play[8] we decided to tell the quarter back to be sure and put the ball to the back in exactly the right spot every time, and either vertically or horizontally as the runner found easiest.

We then took up the pass for the half back dives on their own side of the line. Formerly it was the custom to toss the ball into mid air in front of the on coming back and to expect him to catch it and take it on into the line. As will readily be seen, this was a very risky proceeding and many a fumble was caused by a too high or a too low, a too hard or too slow pass. To prevent this erraticness we decided to adopt the method which Charlie Daly has suggested, namely, to all but hand the ball to the back. This is accomplished by having the quarter back pivot on the foot nearest the runner until his back is to the rush line and he is facing the runner. This will bring the foot farthest from the runner a great stride toward the runner so that in most cases the quarter back will have only a very short pass to make on the end. In case the quarter back has to go forward on one knee, it will be allowable, since in a play at such a distance from him the quarter back cannot possibly get into the play along with his back and can only hope to assist by pushing in the rear of the play. In this play, as in all the others in which the quarter back is called upon to make the pass, the quarter should take such a position in relation to his piv-

7. The tandem style of play was made popular in 1893 by the Princeton captain Phil King, who placed the ends and the backs in a straight line behind the tackles. See Davis, *Football*, 97, 397.

8. Buck plays were aimed at the interior of the line in which the backs often crossed, giving misdirection to the defense.

ot foot and the other one as shall make for the least possible friction[,] in making the turn. For instance, if a pass were to be made at the left of the line, the quarter should see that his left foot turns pretty well out in that direction in order to anticipate as far as possible the pivot work. Were he to turn his toes in the friction caused by his cleats as he pivoted would be such as to slow him up and possibly even cause an injury to his ankle. This rule for anticipating the position of one's foot should be drilled in every quarter back until he has practically no difficulty whatever in getting instantly into that position best suited for his work. As Charlie Daly says, the other team very seldom has a chance to watch the quarter back so closely as to know where the plays are going, and if they did they would be fooled so often that it would hardly pay them to continue. I believe that this point is one of the great factors of good foot work in the quarter back position and which will make a great point of it this year.

The next point that we took up was that of the pass for an end play, where we had also quite a discussion. Presuming that the run was around the right half back to the left, it was [William] Garrison's idea for the quarter back to receive the ball and to start toward the end with it. On the run he was to change the ball to the hand nearest the runner and then make a sort of side-wise motion with the palm of his hand toward the runner and throw the ball almost shoulder high. This idea we tore all to pieces on several grounds. In the first place we all agreed that no runner is ever going, as he should go and as hard as he ought to go until he has the ball in his possession, therefore, that the quarter back should do as little running with the ball in his possession as possible. In Garrison's method the quarter back had to run with the ball in his possession, since he could not change it from both hands to the nearest hand to the runner without carrying it a little distance. This pass slowed up the backs a great deal, and at the same time was exceedingly inaccurate because the quarter back's body was not facing the direction in which the pass was to be made, but the pass was rather made in an entirely different direction. It being very difficult to catch[,] the speed of the runner was light so as to get the ball where it belonged. This method we discarded.

We then considered the method of having the quarter back receive the ball and start to run passing the ball to the back with his arm farthest from the back, necessitating in this case a pass across his own body. We discarded this pass also, although we considered it a surer one than the first plan, because it is a very difficult thing to pass a ball on the run across in front of ones own body so that it will come just right for the opposing back. Instead we determined to have the quarter back pivot on the foot farthest away from the runner, as he stands in his position, and bring the foot nearest the runner so that, as in the pass for straight bucks between the tackle and guard hole, the quarter back is turned to his own line and is facing his back, who, meanwhile, has left his position and is coming nearer every moment. In this case the quarter back of course finds himself facing his man, quite near to him, and ready to start running in the same direction that he is taking, and at the same time in a position where he can pass the ball to his back straight ahead and with both hands. While the back is standing ready to make his pass we decided that the ball, at any rate during the first of the season, should be held pretty close to the quarterback's stomach for safety and that the pass should be made with both hands toward the farther hip of the runner. By passing at the farther hip of the runner the ball will of course have to be thrown a little ahead of the runner, which will tend to increase his speed in the endeavor to reach it instead of, as in the case where the ball was thrown at his nearer hip, causing him to slow up for fear that the ball would get by behind him. In all these passes the quarter is to try to make his back work for the ball. The pass, then, for end plays should be made as quickly as possible, and the end should then find himself well back from his line and in a splendid position for leading the interference.

I forgot to say, in connection with the buck plays, that it is Charlie Daly's idea on all buck plays to crouch in passing the ball and to lean up against one or the other of the three center men as the pass is made. It seemed to us that while in case your line were absolutely certain of never being in the slightest moved backwards, that they might so do and mix up the pass, whereas, in case the quarter back delivered the ball with a little interval between himself and the line, there is less likelihood of any pass being spoiled by the interference of one of his own line men.

The other pass that we considered was that of plays around tackle from his place in the line. I have decided to use this play in the beginning of the season in order to quicken up the line men and give them a little practice in carrying the ball before putting them at the head of a tandem and driving them into heavy smashing plays. In these plays we decided that the quarter should face toward the tackle and should put the ball into the tackle's stomach with his farthest hand, bringing his nearer hand around the tackle to support him as he makes the whirl from his position to the point of attack. The question as to how far back the tackle should run will depend a great deal on the ability of the tackle to get away.

We finished up the discussion by taking up the method by which a quarter back should hold the ball for goal kicks or place kicks. After some considerable discussion we decided to have the quarter back lie at full length on the ground with his weight on both of his elbows.[9] The side in relation to the kicker on which the quarter should lie depending wholly upon the kicking leg of the kicker. We decided that the lower point of the ball should in most cases be held between the middle and fore fingers of the hand nearest the kicker, while the ring finger and little finger were curled up, the thumb being used to assist in turning the ball. The middle and fore finger should be spread far enough apart so that the lower point of the ball will project beyond them, which will enable the holder to have the point of the ball touch the ground without having the fingers touch, in which case the fingers can be withdrawn without moving the ball in the slightest laterally. The farther hand should be placed at the top of the ball and should be manipulated with the thumb, fore finger and middle finger. They should be placed at the top of the ball on the side nearer the kicker, never on the side between the kicker and the direction in which he is to kick the ball. This is a fault that many holders have, which is likely to embarrass the kicker and possibly spoil an important goal. Of course the quarter back should clear a place for the kick to take place on so as not to have any chance for failure owning to the catching of a man's cleats in the ground. We decided to insist that the nearer hand of the man holding the ball to the kicker should be at the bottom, because in case the farther hand is at the bottom, the nearer hand from the fingers to the elbow will be more or less in the way of the kicker's leg. Another point in not having the nearer hand at the top of the ball and up from the ground is that in case the holder of the ball has been doing some pretty serious running he is hardly likely to be able to keep his free arm steady enough to prevent motion in the ball, which in turn will make the kicker nervous and unsteady.

After this discussion I walked to the station with Daly and urged him to talk with all the quarter back coaches he could possibly get hold of and to get opinions from them on all subjects at the same time that he took charge of the quarter backs himself. I tried to show him how to go to work with a man to get them to respond with enthusiasm, and how to ask his men questions such that they would be made to work out much of their position for themselves, thereby believing in it more than they would if someone else had simply told them di-

9. Lying down while holding extra points was a common practice. The team trying the extra point had no rush from the defense until after the extra point holder touched the ball to the ground. Thus he did not have to be in a position to catch the ball, only to hold it, and lying was a natural position to hold for the extra point.

rectly what to do without showing them the why and wherefor and the wisdom of it. I explained to Daly that a good many people are going to wonder whether he has the ability to do the work, and that he has simply got to get in and make things good. He is living in Boston, and if he is properly handled this year, ought to make a most invaluable man to us from now on, as he is a hard worker, a good fighter, and is possessed of good common sense.

After dinner in the evening, I planned out the work of tomorrow partially, leaving the rest of it to do tomorrow on my way up on the train.

I feel as though the quarter back question was about 150% more settled now than I have been able to feel for some time.

Monday, September 18, 1905

Morning:

I left Cohasset on the 8:02 train and came right out to Cambridge, spending my time enroute in completing the plan of the day's work. Immediately on my arrival at Cambridge I dictated a considerable letter to Yost of Michigan concerning his method of snapping the ball back to the quarter back. When I was visiting him he told me he would be very glad to do anything he could to help us out, and so I asked him if he would mind sending on some pictures of his center and quarter at work, illustrating the various stages of the pass. After this I went immediately to the field to get dressed. Down there I learned that [Charles] Osborne, a 198 lb. full back which we had counted on this year, had got typhoid fever and will be unable to play. This is pretty hard luck, but probably means that we have simply got to make a full back out of [William] Hanley.

The dumb bell drill was of five minutes duration as usual, and was lead by Montgomery. We deemed it wise to have Capt. Hurley rest further on his leg. Immediately after the dumb bell work I called for all of the men who have bowel trouble, two or three, and those who have slight strains, and instructed them not to do any starting or running during the day's practice. I then gave orders to the squad to turn their shoes all in to the shoemaker after the afternoon practice in order that he might cut down the cleats from three thicknesses of leather to two. This was done of course to make the men gradually accustomed to standing on wabbly shoes and as a protection against possible twists and wrenches. In giving this order I asked the men what they thought the reason was; some said that it would be likely to hurt the players in the scrimmage work, which follows pretty soon, if the cleats were shorter, others said that if the cleats were long they would drive up into the bottom of the shoes, others thought it would help the speed. I firmly believe that the way to get intelligent cooperation from the team is to show them clearly what you are driving at, the reasons for adopting the course which you have adopted, and the way in which that course ought to be persued. In that case there is no reason why each man should not be a good judge of his own welfare. The more we can make the men this year reason things out, the more things they can do, the less drudgery it will be for them, and the more intelligent will they play. I found out about men who had strained themselves and there seemed to be two main reasons for it, one of which at least, can be avoided. In the first place; some of the men have done a great amount of hard swimming during the summer and are a little bit muscle bound. Quick starts for such men as these seem invariably to produce a crick in the thigh muscles. The other class of fellows seem to be those what have gotten themselves into hard condition already and whose muscles, much like the muscle bound men, are very much affected by quick starts. I think it would be well next year to see to it that the men do not swim so much as to injure themselves to any great extent in this way, and to take other precautions which the doctor may advise against such possibilities.

I was very much pleased to find a man named [David] Boyd, who was out about 170 lbs. now and has been teaching in a school for a couple of years, now returning to the law school. He is 25 years old and shows a great advance over his previous work due largely to his maturity. I expect him to do some good work behind the line.

I find that I cannot get the time to superintend personally the clothing of the men who are on the squad, and have asked McMaster to look after that for me. I have had him on hand while I dressed two or three of the men and have shown him what I wanted done. After the men are dressed I shall go around and see how things fit and make whatever alterations I feel are necessary. The squad to-day which McMaster had to look after was made up of the most promising players whom I have not already looked after, and were clothed during the period from 2 to 4 o'clock. To-day has been a very muggy and sultry one and we therefore cut down the practice from what it would have been otherwise, it being clearly evident that on such days practice should not be so long. I had a big bundle of blankets taken down to the field in order to throw them over the men whom I could not keep active enough to keep warm. This proves to be a very wise scheme. I also had the rope which surrounds the playing field let down so that there might be no necessity of the players jumping the rope and spraining their ankles. I also took care that the men who lead the squad out lead them over such a portion of the field that there were no sticks or irregularities in the ground over which the men in the third and fourth ranks of the squad could fall over owing to their inability to see where they were going caused by the men ahead of them. I do not intend to lose any man this year on the squad through any trifling carelessness which I might have fore seen.

Immediately after the dumb bell work and the little talk which I gave the men we trotted the squad out onto the field, and once around it in order to get them stretched out a little. After they had completed the run I had them line up on the five yard line in the middle of the field in two squads in order to run down on several kick offs which I had the various place kickers on the squad get off. Parker having loose bowels did no kicking and Cunniff probably did the best work. I let the kickers kick several times easily so as to accustom their legs to the blow, and had each of the squads in turn take three or four very easy starts so as to get their legs accustomed to that strain. In spite of all this care three men on the squad, none of them very promising material, received slight strains in their legs, upon which we sent them immediately to be bathed off in hot water. A strain of this kind handled immediately cannot be serious, whereas even a mornings play on such a strain would be likely to lay the man up for some considerable time. I have decided, in view of this experience, to cut out the starts which we have been having in the morning and make the work pretty light and limbering, leaving the starts and other heavy work until the afternoon. In going down on the field I cautioned the men to run hard and to collect around the man with the ball, and I was careful to pick out those who lacked any special censure. Everyone this year must travel. I placed three of the varsity backs to receive the kick offs and cautioned them to take into consideration the wind, the probable distance of the kick, and, in case of a bouncing ball not to try to handle it until it came well into their arms. I kicked off several times and made several bouncing kicks so that the backs had to catch the ball with almost the entire squad around them. This will give them good practice in nerve. Having noticed that most of the backs are having pretty heavy work and have been working hard, I decided in conference with McMaster, to lay the following men off tomorrow morning: Wendell, Foster, [Dillwyn] Starr, Nesmith and [Carl] Lincoln. After the kick off starts I separated the men into three squads. On squad one I put all the men who show any promise of varsity form and took them in charge myself. First I had them fall on the ball as it lay on the ground, each one the side that he most liked and emphasized getting the shoulder and body well around the ball and leaving the feet so that the body was very near the ground as it approached the ball, thus saving severe jars to the hips, and at the same time enabling them to get as low as possible, thereby preventing an opponent from getting the ball away from us by being lower. Then I had them fall on the other shoulder and simply cautioned them not to try to do it hard until they felt sure. Every time I found a man who hesitated I put him on a squad off to one side to practice it alone and by themselves, which squad I took hold myself individually. After I had finished my work with the first squad, the men having gotten the idea of falling on the ball in a stationary position in pretty good shape, I started ro[l]ling the ball away from them and having them fall on it on both shoulders. They got this very well, but I did not deem it advisable to give them any more for the present, though I expect to have some tomorrow morning. Squad two was made up of the men on the squad about whom I have not yet been able to make up my mind. Some of the men are certainly not Varsity material; others have a very slight possibility. This squad I put in charge of Foster and Hurley in falling on the ball and later took them myself. I told Foster & Hurley to vary the work of falling on the ball with a little work in catching in order to prevent the work from becoming too much of a drudgery. Squad three was composed of those men who did not know how to fall on the ball properly, and whom I wanted to instruct personally. Such men were those who fell hard on one hip, who grated hard along on the ground, who fell too perpendicularly on the ball instead of approaching it in a dive fashion, who did not get their shoulders far enough around to prevent injury, who were not as familiar with the work on one side as on the other. After the falling on the ball was completed I had the line men walk around the field with their squatting exercise; with their knees close to the ground and their legs spread well apart, enabling them to change direction quickly and also to keep the trunk of the body as near the ground as possible, where it would be the hardest to upset. This work for the line men lasted only for a short while.

Following this I divided the men into squads of a center, quarter back and two halves. The halves were in each case a heavy man with a light one with a good fast back. I put as many of these squads to work as I had centers and then had the remainder of the quarter backs hand the ball to lines of the rest of the squad for practice in receiving the ball for bucks. Seeing several of the squads resting pretty frequently, I called those squads together and said something like this to them: "Now fellows you know why you are divided up this way and what we are trying to accomplish. You know that it is common sense work for your benefit and for the benefit of the team. Now I cannot watch everybody on this team and so I am expecting you fellows to get hold of the work and make it good without any police work on my part. When you are winded you may rest, but don't loaf, and as long as you play play hard." The men responded splendidly to my appeal and I felt no longer any concern as to the work these men were doing. After these squads had done a good deal of this running work we sent them on a slow jog around the field and then sent them in. Cunniff, however, kicked a few goals with Capt. Hurley holding for him.

I forgot to say that in speaking to the squad before they went off the field I asked them how many had read the rules and not a single man raised his hand, whereupon I gave them a rather severe criticism with a view to setting the men to work thinking. This matter of the rules must be insisted upon and the men who are on the team are going to know the rules from head to foot. I have enough rule books down at the field so that each man may have one so that there is no excuse for any man's ignorance.

It occurred to me this morning that the time to have Varsity possibilities of the Freshman class is to have them when the fall practice first begins. In this way a great deal of time can be spent in studying up the men while at the same time they are not being played in any of the minor games, and being made ineligible, for that one year from a four year's standpoint. Next year the men from the preparatory schools that we call on must be discovered before hand and be called back here the very first of the year. Such a scheme will give the kicking coaches a splendid opportunity to teach a freshman kicker some of the fundamental positions and put him that much ahead in Freshman drill.

The Father of the big guard[,] [Frederic] White[,] telephoned me when I got up from the field after the practice and made one statement which is certainly true and which it will do well for us to keep in mind. It was this: He said that down at Yale the coaches always got the men into their permanent positions as soon as possible and stopped changing the men about at the earliest possible moment, so that each man had the longest possible time in his own position. Mr. White said that he thought that last year there had been too much changing of the men about too late in the season, and I think he is absolutely sound in making this statement. We shall try and not make the same mistake this year, although we must of course do some considerable experimenting at the early period of the game.

I have told Brine's man to see to it that the names of each man is put on to his clothing so that there may not be any mix-up in that matter.

Immediately after the practice was over I went about among the men urging them not to stay under the showers any longer than was absolutely necessary to get the dirt off, explaining that hot water is weakening and, too, it prevents the skin from getting tough. I urged them, also not to get any more water on their ankles than possible, because it softens the skin and makes the ankles much more likely to become skinned. Then I sent around to where the men were dressing to make sure that any man who was sick or strained was properly attended to. Afterwards I came up to the University Cafe for lunch. The University Cafe is where the foot ball men are eating until the training table starts on the coming Thursday. A man named Schmidt runs it and he is not over cleanly in his work. We decided to have the men go there, however, rather than to the Dunster Cafe because it is more quiet there and there is not the odor of food which is so prevalent at the Dunster and the publicity is not quite so great. The meal which I had was very fair, but the table cloth was rather spotted up and things were not especially attractively served. Another year I think a great improvement may be made in this respect by choosing a better place and looking after it more in detail.

Afternoon:

Right after lunch I sent Capt. Hurley over to the Gym. to superintend the taking of the strength test[10] by the players. In a general talk in the morning I warned them not to undertake records, showing how their muscles were not ready for such strains and ordering the men

---

10. Dr. Dudley A. Sargent began strength tests at Harvard in the 1880s to determine which sports were appropriate for individual students based upon their strength. By 1890, the test was required for athletic participation. If a certain level of strength, based upon what Sargent thought necessary for a specific sport, were not attained, a student would not be allowed to participate. Sargent said that the 1905 football team was the poorest he ever tested, indicating that Reid was successful in having his players do only what was necessary to pass the Sargent test. The test was not scientific, for no one knew what strength was needed for particular sports, nor, in fact, if a certain level of strength were needed to prevent injuries. The test called for strength tests of the back, legs, upper arms, and grip as well as lung capacity. The greatest strength was required of members of the crew and football teams; the second greatest of members of baseball and track and field teams; and the third greatest of members of cricket, lacrosse, and tennis teams, with a strength ratio of 7:6:5 of the three groups. See D. A. Sargent, J. W. Seaver, and Watson L. Savage, "Intercollegiate Strength Tests," *American Physical Education Review* 31 (Dec. 1897): 216–20, and the *Boston Globe*, 23 Sept. 1905, 8.

to simply do enough to get through on. For fear that some men might forget himself and try more I sent Hurley over to superintend it all and we got through about 15 men without any strains, although two of the men, one of them a Freshman, did not get enough to pass. That will not amount to anything as both of the men can pass it on a second try and one of them was a Freshman and didn't realize how much he would have to do.

I went down to the field, where I met Mr. Rowell, Caterer of the Union, to talk over the question of opening up the training table on the coming Thursday, and the arrangements to be followed out in so doing. The question of having colored waiters came up and Capt. Hurley and I both decided that we did not care to have them. One reason was that the Union does not pay enough to get first class colored ones and second class ones are abominable, so we said we must have white help. We insisted that there must be at least one servant to every eight men in the room; that they must have their finger nails clean, aprons clean, and their whole make up neat. Then I specified that I wanted the windows open before the men went is so as to get the food odors out of the room, and I wanted the windows kept washed and the floors clean. I also said we wanted good clean table clothes, clean napkins, folded in different ways to show the men that things were being made as presentable as possible for them, some flowers on the table to give a sort of lively appearance, that the food should be served properly, that it should be piping hot, and that it should not be brought on in trays in such a way that one man's plate is to be smeared with potatoe or other food from some other man's plate. In other words, I specified that they must be just as particular as they possibly could at that table, so that the men may feel that they are going to have an attractive table, good food, and that everything is clean. From my standpoint, nothing is quite so tiresome as going to the table and finding the food is cold, cloth is spotted up and things slowly served. When one considers that a foot ball player is likely to come in pretty well tired out, it will easily be seen what a mental rest it is to have things cleanly. Mr. Rowell said that everything I asked for was entirely reasonable and that he would see that we got it. That will make it all right if he looks after these points—if he does not, I shall remind him.

Immediately after this we had dumb bell work, although ever since lunch the men were being clothed and their pads, etc. put into shape by Mr. McMaster. Inasmuch as Lewis was to put the line men through their first scrimmage work this afternoon we had each man, from tackle to tackle, put on a leather wristlet in order to help prevent strains or sprains to the wrists owing to the sudden wrenches brought about by such active exercise. We have regularly heretofore had a sprained wrist or something of that kind happen, and it is my plan to wear these until the men have become accustomed to the work and their wrists settled for it.

When we got down on the field, I took the kickers and had them kick down the field to backs who worked in pairs and had the ends running down on the kicks, but no tackling. During the practice we had the first injury for the season that amounts to anything, when [George] Ball, one of the ends, had an elbow thrown out of joint through a plain foot ball accident. I hope he will be well soon. After we had had a good deal of kicking and catching work and the ends and backs had a good deal, I lined the men up and had them each take a ball to show that they could carry it for a buck play, then I sent them down the field and into the building, the men who had any trouble with their legs did not do any running however. Mike Farley and [John] L. Motley[11] were both out and volunteered some very good information on the ends. I did not allow any coaching by them and I asked Motley not to smoke on the field.

A man named [Morton] Newhall, to whom I sent a telegram calling him back some time ago, sent word to me that he was off for two weeks vacation and would be along in a week and a half, whereupon I had the manager send him a telegram saying that if his vacation was all that was keeping him from coming he could report at once or not at all. He replied that he would be here tomorrow morning. Any fellow who is called back early who has not interest enough to come back, particularly when there is such a good chance for quarter backs as there is this year, has not the right spirit about him, and I intended to find out whether Newhall was or was not worth anything.

While the kicking and catching and end work was going on Leo Daly had the centers and quarters working on the pass and the stepping work, and Lewis had the line men. It being a very muggy afternoon, we limited the practice to shorter time than usual. After the main work was over, I spent considerable time looking after Lockwood and Hanley, trying to give them some special help in their weaknesses.

I forgot to mention that [Reginald] Brown[12] came out to look over the material. I gave him very little to do until he should see what I

11. Motley was a 1902 letter-winner in football. Mike Farley might be John Farley, a football letter-winner in 1898.

12. Brown was a Harvard football letter-winner in 1895 and 1896.

had been attempting to do. I am very much disappointed that [Edward] Bowditch and [Bob] Kernan are not at hand, as I have to do a great deal of individual coaching which I ought not to have to put the time on, and which I can hardly spare the time for with so many other duties.

After the practic[e] was over, Lewis and Hurley, Dr. Nichols and I had something of a talk on the Freshman coach proposition. The three possible men are C[arl] Marshall, [Walter] Sugden, and Ted Meier.[13] The question as to which would be the best came up. Dr. Nichols wanted to know which man showed the greater likelihood of continuing at the work and there didn't seem to be any choice in the matter. Then the question of C. Marshall coming back and forth from Boston every day and living in the same town with the men came up. That was a pretty vital one, and then, for some reason or other, Carl seems to have lost his hold on the undergraduates out here, which would make his appointment seem doubtful on the ground of public opinion. The objection to Meier was that he lacks enthusiasm and is very quiet, while the man we want is a man who will get the Freshmen enthused and working hard, and who will show interest in them. Sugdon has had some considerable experience at Tech., where he coached last year, he is a very good natured fellow, quite enthusiastic and in earnest. The question is whether he wouldn't be, perhaps, the best man. It seemed to be the opinion that the choice would lie between Sugden and Meier, and just which one we didn't come to any decision about. I intend this year that the Freshman coach shall come out with the Varsity squad until the Freshman squad is called out so as to learn all the fundamentals which we are teaching the Varsity in order to give the same instruction to the Freshmen. Then I shall expect to plan out a good deal of the work which the Freshmen are called upon to do with a view not necessarily to beating Yale, but with a view to turning on to the Varsity squad next year a number of well trained, carefully conditioned men. This year the Freshman team of last year has contributed very little to our Varsity squad, since almost no men on last year's Freshman squad got through the season without some serious injury.

Lewis, Hurley and I had dinner at the University Cafe and then came over to the office at the Union where we worked out carefully the assignments for several of the plays from the first formation, which we propose to give the team within a day or so. We wrote them out and argued them over in great detail, and just as soon as we have revised

13. Sugden was a football letter-winner in 1901; Meier in 1903.

them carefully, I shall have copies of the detail made up to be pasted on the opposite leaves of this book. I think we got better detail than ever before and do not see why our first formation work should not be quite successful from the start. I spent the night in Cambridge.

Tuesday, September 19, 1905

Morning:

The first thing I did this morning was to dictate some matters, which lasted from 8 until 9:45. Just before I was ready to go down to the field Bowditch, who is to coach our ends, came in to go down with me. I want to make this a point for next year right now, and that is, that no coach will be appointed to do the work next year who will not agree to be here ready by the beginning of practice by the team so as to give them careful fundamental work in his particular department. I have had to do some little work with the ends, with the kickers, with the backs, and in fact with the whole squad so that I have not been able to give as much time to the general policy of the work as I should like to.

When I got down to the Locker Building I found three or four more men out and we started them off on dumb bell work, telling those, however, who had strained legs not to do any of the leg exercises. The reason of this must be plain. While this work was going on Capt. Hurley and Parker were out on the field kicking goals, Hurley lying on a blanket with his sweater on to protect himself from the constant drizzle that persistently fell, and before the squad went on to the field I called for those men who had bowel trouble or injuries of any kind to see McMaster and get themselves in shape. Then I gave the squad a short talk on the ways in which the ball has been fallen on up to date, and the ways in which the ball is to be held for a buck. After this review I added falling on the ball when it is rolling to right and left and catching the ball with both hands as well as the way to hold the ball for a run around the end.

In all my talk on this method of falling on the ball I laid great emphasis on the necessity of keeping the ball in one's possession and the necessity of holding the ball properly. I told the men that we were trying to have them learn to hold the ball properly and safely no matter what the circumstances and so that they need give no attention whatever to that detail of the work. I told them of the two ways for holding the ball for a run around the end, one where the ball is held pretty well down on the hip with a view to making out of the projection of the hip as a pocket against which to hold the ball, and the other, where the ball is held higher up and more free from the body. I asked the men why the first method was not satisfactory and got several replies. One of them said that the body did not have much freedom of motion when the ball was held there as in the second case, which was quite true. Others suggested that in falling the men would fall on their hips which likewise would be rather dangerous and make the ball hard to catch, and still another felt that the ball was too low down on the body to enable the arm to get proper pressure to hold it well. After showing them the weaknesses of the system, I showed them the way of taking the forward point of the ball at nearly the palm of the hand and with the arm hugging the ball tightly to the side while the rear point of the ball sticks under the arm in such a way that the longer axis of the ball is almost horizontal to the ground. This latter point is very important since if the axis of the ball is turned up too much it is very easy for the ball to be punched out from behind, while if it is pointed down too much, it is easy to punch the ball out from the front. I spoke also of making the clasp on the ball absolutely secure and vice like so that after once getting it into place there is no possibility whatever of loosening ones hold of it if he is thinking how his best way is to get by any particular opponent, who may be in the way. Following up this talk, I asked several questions on the rules, which the men were unable to answer, and so I gave them two or three questions to be prepared to answer tomorrow morning. Among them were these: "If on a punt the ball is kicked across the side line, whose ball is it?" "If one of the opponents beyond the side line tries to catch a ball across the side line and fumbles it, if one of our men were to fall on it, would it belong to him instead of to the opponent?" Again, "if a man standing near a side line were to attempt to catch a ball and were to fumble it so that it rolled out-side and one of our men fell on it, whose ball would it be?" Then I asked also whether "if a ball bounced in front of a half back so that the ball were bouncing perpendicularly and not laterally, if our end were to bat the ball toward the opponent's goal, an opposing back had the right to pick it up and run with it—whether batting the ball thus was a foul or not, and whether, also, in case one of our men batted the ball and then fell on it himself, he was entitled to the ball." I told them to be prepared to answer these questions in the light of the rule which says that "no man shall bat the ball toward the opponent's goal" and the rule that says "play shall cease only when the referee blows his whistle or some other official calls time." This will probably afford a very interesting discussion tomorrow morning. I also asked the men whether the ball was put in play by a scrimmage at the first of the game or not. Most of them said it was not, where-upon I asked them how it was that an official might put a team back five yards in case they started ahead of the ball on the kick off. I explained this point to them telling them that the definition of a scrimmage was the putting of the ball to play either by kicking it forward or snapping it back, since at the kick off if the ball is kicked off it is a scrimmage. After this talk, and the inquiring after bruises and sore feet, we took the squad out on to the field.

It is very evident to me now that one of the most important things at the very first of the season, perhaps in the first two or three days, is to do nothing but to see that the men are properly clothed, and especially that their shoes are comfortable. Any man can easily get his feet in very bad shape in three days by wearing shoes that are to[o] small or too large or which are in other ways uncomfortable, and since a player's whole action must be on his feet, it is obvious that the sooner the feet are gotten into the best condition possible the better. I think we should have all the men's shoes made to order the summer previous so that when they come back in the fall they may have something to put on that fits them. It is a very gratifying thing to know that not a single man of those who had their shoes made by Stroehle of New Haven has had a corn, a blister or a bruise of any kind come to his feet. The difficulty has invariably come from the ready made shoes furnished by Brine. With a view to getting these shoes properly done, I am going to tell Shamrock, the shoemaker of the foot ball squad, to make a couple pairs this fall to order, in which case if they are satisfactory, we shall be willing to let him do the work next year rather than the New Haven man. It is something of a disadvantage to have the shoes made in a town two or three hundred miles off, when with a little effort they might just as well be made in our own town.

When the squad went on to the field we jogged them around once at a slow pace telling the men to breath through their noses and lift their feet. Then I took the best men out there and had each man fall on the ball in the different methods which we had thus far, namely; with the ball lying still on the ground, each man fell on it first to the right, then to the left; then I rolled the ball away from the men and had them fall on it both ways. After some considerable work on this line, during which time Capt. Hurley had the poorer men on the squad (my policy being to take charge myself of the best material out there so that it may get every possible benefit of the coaching, and then to take secondary charge of the remainder of the squad). When I had finished showing my squad about falling on the ball, I took

Hurley's squad and had him superintend the different men on my squad as they tried to place the ball properly in their arms for the end running. After some considerable work of this kind, during which time I was taking Hurley's squad and showing them about falling on the ball, I lined the men on my first squad up and had them rehearse receiving the ball from the quarter back for a buck play. It being a very wet day, and uncomfortable, I said to the squad when they first went out, "now this is a wet day and it will give us good practice on handling the ball safely. It may not be comfortable, but we cannot be sure but that the Yale game will come on a day just like this, and we must be ready for it. It may not be pleasant, but we must all grit our teeth and eat mud if we have to." There was no shirking by anyone.

While I was working with the squad which Hurley had had, I saw Brill miss a ball and it rolled off to one side. O'Brien, the Freshman, started after it, when, much to everybody's surprise, Brill, who had already started for the ball, yelled out "get out of there" and dove for the ball, recovering it in handsome shape. Brill seems to be waking up and I believe that by getting the other members of the squad to make friends with him and be as much comrades as possible, he will reach possibilities this year which he has never yet ever approached. After this work we sent the men in, they having been out just about three quarters of an hour of easy work. I kept out, however, Hanley to do some kicking in order to get time to coach him individually on his step and the way of going about directing it. He took hold very well and succeeded in mastering one or two small points.

Although Bowditch was out on the field he did little coaching, preferring simply to watch the men and learn their names preparatory to seeing them work this afternoon. I then had luncheon, after which I did a certain amount of dictation. Right after luncheon Capt. Hurley went over to the Gym. to see that no men strained themselves in the continuance of the strength test, which will go on in the same fashion for several days and of which I shall take no further notice, except to see that somebody is there to prevent such strains as happened to Brill last year, who without any preliminary work, undertook to make a record, with the result that he strained his leg badly.

Afternoon:

Right after lunch I dictated an account of the previous day's work until practice time. When I went down to the field there was still a drizzling rain, and the grass was very wet. On this account I did not allow the kickers to kick as much as usual for fear of hurting their legs with the extra heavy balls. Capt. Hurley and Parker came down to the field early in order to kick goals. After the dumb bell work was over the squad was trotted around the field as usual, and then I had Lockwood, Foster, and Hanley punt, while the ends under the direction of Bowditch ran down on the kicks. Reggie Brown, who is to coach the Second, was out, as he will be regularly from now on, and relieved me greatly by taking charge of a number of the poorer men, so that I had that off my mind, and I felt that they were getting something of a show. I had the best men out there falling on the ball a few times, and they took hold in good style. When Coach Lewis appeared I turned over the linemen to him for the breaking through and blocking work, while Bowditch after he had given his ends considerable work running down on kicks, took them into the house and gave them a talk on running down on kicks. This was a very valuable talk as was proved during the practice this morning.

I am convinced that we have been making the practice a little too heavy and too long, and we shall aim to cut it down. With all of the work the men have been about two or three hours on the field each. day, although, of course, a good deal of the work was very simple and without much effort. Leo Daly was out and he started in on his quarter-backs with great care, and has got them pretty well ahead of the men we have had in other years.

Several matters came up for discussion this afternoon, and I was able to dictate only a short time. In the first place there is a rule which makes it impossible for a man to eat at the training table until he has paid all his training table bills.[14] I found out that Brill and [Beaton] Squires were both owing, and must look to their getting funds for this purpose. Just how it is to work out I cannot say.

The photographers have been very persistent about the field, and I have asked them not to take any pictures with formations or of dive

---

14. The concept behind the training table was that better food would help create winning teams. Training tables began during the 1860s in colleges that had crew. Harvard created its football training table in 1882. By 1893, the Harvard Athletic Committee voted to collect cash deposits or bonds from each player to cover the cost of the training table, because previously a number of athletes had not paid their part (the usual cost of board at Harvard) of training table costs. Herbert H. White, Reid's advisor in 1905, had been hired in 1893 as the general financial manager of athletics, and it was part of his duty to collect training table costs. By 1905, problems arose again in collecting board costs, and the Athletic Committee required all athletes to file a bond for usual board costs. See John A. Blanchard, ed., *The H Book of Harvard Athletics, 1852–1922* (Cambridge: The Harvard Varsity Club, 1923), 382, and James Barr Ames, chair of the Athletic Committee, to President and Fellows, 9 Jan. 1893, Charles W. Eliot Papers, Box 264, Folder "1893, Jan–Apr," Harvard University Archives; and Harvard Athletic Committee Minutes, 5 April 1905, Harvard University Archives.

work of any kind in blocking through. I have agreed with them to give them an opportunity to get individual pictures of any of the men on the squad that they want if they will give me a list. After my experience o[f] trying to sandbag the newspapers wherein I got very much the worse two or three years ago, I came to the conclusion, as one of the coaches expressed it, that it is much better to butter a newspaper than to try to beat it.

The food at Schmidts is very poor indeed, and I believe that it has been wholly responsible for the diarrhea, which has been quite common on the squad. There is, of course, always a certain amount of this, and it does no great harm, but on the other hand there is no necessity of having any more of it than possible. Schmidt has recently served up some stewed peaches that were old and tough, and which must have been made from some peaches bought at very low price. I think that it will be extremely wise next year to arrange for the men's meals some where else, and to go to some little pains about it, so as to save ourselves in this matter all we can.

As a matter of curiosity I weighed myself so as to see at the end of the season how my weight holds up. On the first day I weighed 164 lbs., my weight this afternoon was 160 lbs. If I go on loosing at this rate my voice even will not be left by the end of the big games, however, I am eating and sleeping regularly and enjoy the work very much.

Before the squad went onto the field to-day I gave them a considerable talk on one or two things. In the first place the matter of the newspapers. I advised each man on the squad to let the football stories in the newspapers entirely alone, telling them that the papers were not strong in their accounts at all, and that if any man was playing well or was not playing well he would soon find it out from more authorit[at]ive sources. I further told them that frequently a newspaper would speak of a man as having played a splendid game because he made a long run, when as a matter of fact, he had played a very poor game and the run was a result rather of not following the interference as instructed than as a result of doing as he should do. I called attention to the fact that some of the kickers are critized as being slow. I said to the squad that they were told to be slow at this time of the year and I do not wish them to try to be fast. In this way I thought that I rather took the bloom off of the newspapers as I intended to do.

I then went over the signals and gave the assignments on end runs to the men, asking a number of questions in the meanwhile. The assignments of the play are given on the opposite page [missing], and I shall not go into the details here. After going on to the field we had work falling on the ball, and then lined up the teams and had them work through the end runs, then trot through them, making the men take their assignments and explaining to them why they needed to be in the different places.

[Charles] Blair, who is being tried out for an end, missed signals once or twice, and was very slow, which may determine in the end whether he is able to do the work there or not, as I believe that the men must be quick witted and very active in that position.

We then had the usual practice in kicking and catching work, in which Coach Lewis and Marshall took quite a prominent part, while Dick Lawrence[15] looked on and Motley stood by Bowditch and looked on to see what the ends were doing. Daly took the quarter backs and gave them more good work.

The Coaches at the end of the practice were told that the men were very slow and inactive, and we decided that they needed a rest, so we decided to lay them off tomorrow morning.

Bowditch brought me an outline of his plays of the ends, and they were very good.

Before the practice was over, I found that [Frederic] White, the guard, was entirely able to kick goals, and kick them well with only one step, and from now on I shall try to develop him along these lines. He kicks in the surest possible way, and I was exceedingly pleased with it.

Wednesday, September 20, 1905

Morning:

I left Cohasset at 8:02 this morning and came out to Cambridge at once. There I found that Boyd, who had said that he could not afford to come in and out from one of the suburban towns and pay for his meals also, had been straightened out by [Francis] Goodhue so that he is now rooming with one of the other fellows and does not have to travel back and forth.

The weather was muggy and so we decided to make the work very light. I found, also, that a good many of the men had pretty sore feet, due apparently to either the thinness of the soles of their shoes, or to the fact that the morning's and afternoon's practices had been pretty long and the men had been subjected to bruising processes on the bottom of their feet, due to their being on their cleats so long. This being the case we determined to make the morning work lighter here-

---

15. Lawrence won a Harvard football letter in 1901.

after and perhaps to cut it out altogether some day this week. It would be well for succeeding coaches to look out for this sort of sore foot trouble, since some of the men have developed very sensitive corns with some puffs at times, even with the careful way in which we have handled them. I gave the men a long talk before they went down on the field, including a few minutes discussion of the rules and a very brief outline of the Yale system of defence,[16] showing how certain plays cannot work against the Yale Defence and how others can. I also gave several examples of cases where very serious results had happened through the inability of a man to tell just what he should do at a given instant through ignorance of the rules. I told them the story about Brewster of Cornell, who lost the Princeton-Cornell game by catching a punt on his own one yard line and then deliberately turning around and touching it behind his own goal line, thinking all the time that he was only making a touch back. I showed the men also how it was necessary to think all the time in order to outwit the other fellows if possible, and by their brains overcome physical disadvantages. The talk was pretty general and too long, but I had the undivided attention of the entire squad during the whole time. Taking the men onto the field, I took the most promising men on the squad and had each man fall on the ball six times; once on each shoulder with the ball rolling parallel with them. Then I gave them practice in holding the ball for a buck and for an end run. I forgot to say that before the men came out of the house I gave them a set of signals which we shall start off with this year, and which I expect to work in permanently. I spent considerable time coaching Foster and Leonard on their feet. Foster seems to have good form now except in dropping the ball from his hands to his feet, when it is very likely to turn in the air. He is also likely to drop the ball too far out. Leonard is likely to drop the ball too far on the outside of his foot so that it goes off to one side every now and then. He also does not get quite enough height to the ball. By throwing the ball too far from his body, Foster was getting very poor results for two particular reasons: In the first place the ball fell so far from his body that he was wholly unable to reach it unless he had his leg out straight so that when he hit the ball he was unable to get any snap into his blow, with the consequence that the ball travelled very poorly. Then, too, he was unable to get any height at all. The ball must be kept fairly near the body in order

16. Although this was only the beginning of the second week of practice, Reid was already getting the team ready for the one truly important game, Yale, the last game of the season.

that the knee snap may be secured. This is a valuable point to keep in mind in coaching the kickers. While Foster and Leonard were kicking, I had Nesmith and Kempner catching. These two men have been catching with their arms cramped too close to their body instead of pretty free, with the result that the ball frequently hit them on the body before they were able to get their hands on it. I had Nesmith keep his arms away from his body and he quickly grasped the idea and in a very few kicks seemed to have the new principle pretty well in mind. Kempner's greatest trouble seems to be in judging the ball. Those that he judges properly [he] catches high; those that he misjudges he fumbles badly. It should be kept in mind in coaching catchers that the ball must be caught with the arms and hands with the body as a back ground, and not with the body with the hands and arms as a back ground. The hands and arms are capable of giving with the catch, while it is very difficult to give an elasticity to the body. I had one or two men doing some work in drop kicks and goals also.

Afternoon:

I had luncheon at the University Cafe, which was a[s] sloppy as ever and discussed with McMaster the question of getting Peirce and [Patrick] Grant so that they are able to run properly. Peirce runs stiff legged, as does Grant, and it seems as though neither of them could hope to get down the field fast under these conditions, or if they do, whether they would be able ever to successfully change direction going so. McMaster was very much put out because I suggested getting [James G.] Lathrop[17] over to work on these men. I hardly realized for the moment how very sensitive all professional trainers are over any subdivision of their work among other men. It is universally true that trainers are exceedingly jealous of one another and it is altogether wise not to stir up any trouble in this way. When I found that McMaster had some feeling about it I consented to his taking the two men and told him to hand them back to me able to run. If he does not I shall call in Lathrop anyhow, expecting, of course at the same time, to have an issue with McMaster as to who is to decide whether anyone else is to come in to do special work of that kind— he or I. I shall allow no argument whatever in this matter, even though it ends in getting another trainer. However, I do not see that in case I am at all tactful how there is any necessity of having any clash.

Immediately after lunch I was called on by a man named Tappin,

17. Lathrop was hired in 1885 to coach the track team. He remained at Harvard until 1900, when John Graham, track coach of the Boston Athletic Association, replaced him. Graham resigned in 1905, and Lathrop served again until 1909. See Blanchard, *The H Book of Harvard Athletics*, 472.

who was to come here and about whom I wrote something in the story of the preliminary season. I took him over to the Scientific school office and to the College office to find out how it would be best for him to enter,—It seeming best that he should enter as a special in the Scientific school. Then I took him to Mr. Thompson of the Appointment Department and got him something to do, as Tappin is in need of funds. While I was doing this Capt. Hurley was at the Gymnasium superintending the strength test. Immediately after I was through with Tappin I dictated the assignments for the ordinary plays of the first scrimmage where the full back bucks on either side of the line and where two halfbacks run around the opposing end.

When the squad was together in the afternoon I gave them the assignments on the two fullback bucks with careful detail as to the cross blocking and so forth, which linemen have to do in order to cover the contingencies arising from the playing of the opposing lineman. The assignments were as Coach Lewis, Captain Hurley and I decided on last night.

It is extremely wise to have the strength test early as we are having it this year, because men are always lame after it, and as matters now stand they will be all over their lameness before we have any scrimmage. On the other hand the strength test ought not to come before the men have been out at least a week, in order to get them in proper condition to stand it. Before taking the squad on to the field we read off the list of those who are to go to the training table to start with—There were ten of them: Captain Hurley, Foster, Wendell, Nesmith, Starr, White, Cunniff, Parker, Squires, Brill.

When we went on the field the men jogged around it once, and then I lined up two teams without any special attempt at making a Varsity pick out of them, and had every man walk into his position and show in each case just what his particular duties were. I formed another eleven in the same fashion, and would have formed a third had there been anything like enough linemen to fill out. As it was, even by changing the ends and backs off I was unable to get more than half the squad into the practice. After walking through the plays I had the men trot through them and then let them run through them. They got the signals very readily, and we did not have one case of mistake on signals all afternoon. We substituted new quarters for those that were in once or twice, new backs and new ends. The men took hold with tremendous snap and the plays looked very powerful. There was almost no fumbling during the entire signal practice, showing that the fundamental work so far has begun to tell.

We found that there were two or three things which needed looking after in order that the plays should go off properly. In the first place, the quarter back must be careful in helping the runner through the line, not to block off the backs who are behind trying to push. The tendency of the quarter backs was to run into the line in too broadside a fashion, thereby to interfere with the playing more than to help it. We got this to working better as the plays went on. Then, we had trouble in getting the tackle and guard on the far side not to push. According to the assignments the guard was to be the first man to get there, the tackle the second, but we found that it was probably wiser to have the tackle go in first and the guard second, although it would be very difficult for either of them to get in until the play has hit the line owing to the very sharp circle on which they have to travel.

The mosquitos were very thick on the field and we found that the best way to protect ourselves from them was to wrap newspaper around our legs, which seemed to taste poorly to them or else they were too tough for them to bite through.

I am seeing to it that every man in all the line plays sets to work to do his trick and to do it instantly and with all his might—I will have no loafers around.

After the signal practice, I sent the line men from tackle to tackle to Coach Lewis, the ends to Coach Bowditch, the quarter backs to Coach Daly, while I took the kickers myself. I had those men who had not done any kicking in the morning, take their work in the afternoon, there being Brill, Hanley, [Rudolph] Gring, and [Phillip] Lockwood; besides these men, Cunniff had some goals and one or two men did some drop kicking. I divided the backs into pairs and had them catch, and did some little coaching of them in the back field. The day was very hazy and Wendell, who had already told me that his eyes troubled him on certain days, informed me that there was trouble with them do-day and that he was having difficulty in judging the kicks. That being the case, I questioned the two backs as to what they had better do about it, and finally got out of them the point that Wendell, then, should play in the position where he would be the least likely to get the ball. As Brill was kicking at that time and most of his kicks were going pretty well off to the right, this worked in very well. I found the backs also playing too close together so that each one could, without difficulty, overlap the other's territory, thereby leaving a great amount of space on each outside uncovered. I corrected that and then put one back a little nearer the kicker than the other so that he could take the kicks and so that his companion behind him would be far enough back to take the long ones. I gave the backs practice in catching long kicks, high kicks, low kicks, kicks to the right and to the left, and kicks which fell short and bounced very uncertainly along the ground. I coached the men to take a bouncing ball only when it could be gotten well into their hands, not to reach for them, also to back each other up where the ball was coming down the field at a pretty good rate and was likely to take a deceptive bounce, at most any moment. I also had each back coach his partner as to whether he was far enough back to get a certain kick or whether he was too near. I also insisted that each back should try to help his companion to overcome any fault in catching which the other had; such a fault would consist in catching the ball too high up on the chest, or in not having the arms out far enough, or in not starting quickly enough toward the general position in which the ball was most likely to fall. This work was taken hold of with great vim by the backs and they got it pretty well.

I watched Daly working with his quarter backs and urged him to put his whole attention for the present on receiving the ball from the center and on having his men take the proper steps with their feet without paying any special attention as yet to the runner, as in all foot ball work it seems to me that the matter of the foot work of the men is the first thing to dispose of, since as long as one's mind is occupied in directing one's feet, one cannot use his mind for anything else.

Bowditch spent his entire time showing his ends how to start down on kicks and how to keep on the outside of the runner, showing that it is unsafe to watch the opposing back with a view to determining where the ball is coming down, since the opposing back may be very slow in judging the ball and therefore be some distance from the ball, thereby drawing the end in when he ought really to be further out. I believe that Bowditch has instructed his ends to run down the field as hard as they can for about 10-yards, then if they hear the ball kicked to glance at once to see where it has gone, then to size up where the ball is likely to hit and to run full speed for that spot keeping on the outside. In time the men should be able to decide instantly where the ball will land and then have nothing to do but get down the field quickly and slow up in time to get the runner. The ends have had nothing whatever said to them about using their hands to get at the catcher, and Bowditch is extremely wise in not giving that to them, because it is very necessary that the men learn one lesson at a time in order that they may get it thoroughly and that there may not be so much given them at once so that there will be nothing new for them to learn which they haven't already heard about thereby causing them to get tired of the work. If the men are kept learning something all the time, and have something new added to that something just as soon as they know it, there is less danger of monotony and more certainty of thoroughness. The more I think of the situation, the more I feel that we should begin with the most thorough drilling of the fundamentals, taken up very slowly and mastered, meanwhile depending in our games upon our general strength to get through. I believe that thoroughness in the details will pay well in the end.

After dinner, Coach Lewis, Capt. Hurley and I went to work on some more plays of the first formation and stayed with it until after 10 o'clock when Hurley went to bed and I went to Craigie Hall to sleep. I found that Peirce was to sleep in the same set of rooms that I was and was quite surprised to have him come in at five or six minutes past eleven when the instructions were that he should be in bed promptly at eleven. I gave him a very severe talking to and sent him at once to bed. I do not wish to be over severe if I can help it, but I intend that the training rules shall be carried out absolutely.

Thursday, September 21, 1905

Morning:

I did a good deal of thinking last night after I went to bed over the question of whether it would be wise for us to give the line men on the offense any particular assignments which included cross blocking. Last night I argued it with Coach Lewis and he was strongly in favor of doing it, stating that our teams had always been backward in that sort of work. I took hold of Camp's book on foot ball and after reading it over carefully for about the 20th time I concluded that we were wrong in giving the men anything but the most elementary line work. As Mr. Camp says in his book—there should be no inter-dependence of the line men at first, for if there is each line man will not give to each play his full effort since he will be expecting under certain conditions, assistance from one of his teammates which will make his work very much easier and put him much less to the test, whereas if no inter-dependence is allowed and each man has to handle his own men no matter where he is, each individual in the line will have to exert himself to the utmost in order to do the work, which two men ought really to do, and will do later on. Having the men attempt this work will, at any rate, force the line men to cover more ground, to learn to get into stronger positions at some distance away, and to use their heads to overcome a special strong position of an opponent. Having thought of this during the night, I concluded that there could be no argument on the matter and so I decided to stop all cross blocking for the present and to require each man to do his own work. I talked this over carefully with Capt. Hurley when I saw him and he agreed with me. I fully believe that by making this change

I have avoided one of the most serious mistakes which it would be possible for me to make at this time of the year and I am absolutely sure of it. I fully believe that when I tell Coach Lewis of my decision that he will, after thinking it over a little, agree with me heartily, as I am sure Coach Waters does already.

After having breakfast I read over a very cheaky letter from [John] Owsley,[18] the head coach of the Yale Varsity eleven, concerning our refusal to accept [Paul] Dashiell[19] as an official. Owsley remarked that Yale had found recently that both Harvard and Princeton were constantly wanting to change officials after being beaten and that so far as he could see Harvard had had no cause to cry. It was rather surprising to get such a statement as this from the Yale Coach, and we are questioning now whether to slap back while the mud is still wet or to wait a few days until it dries and then brush it off. I think we shall probably wait and see if we cannot keep our balance a little better than our opponents have done.

I gave the plays which Lewis, Hurley and I worked out last night to the stenographer to copy, and then found in my mail a fine letter from [Crawford] Blagden,[20] the old tackle. He says that he has been planning a hunting trip some time in October, but that in case we are able to use him he would be glad to give it up and come and play on the second against the Varsity, or do anything else he can to help out. That is just the kind of stuff that we want, and I shall write him a hearty letter at once.

I sent word to the editor of the Boston Herald that I should be unwilling to write anything, except possibly a criticism of the Penn and Yale games, and then went on down to the field and made a short talk to the squad before the dumb bell work, giving them the formation for a kick, asking a couple of questions on the distinction between the touch back and safety, and explaining to them that we did not want any more cross blocking, but that each man should take the man opposing him instead.

I had the Manager make out a list of the unexcused absences and had the men report to me to explain them. All but one were regularly excused. I cautioned the men about not taking off the pads that I

18. Owsley had played fullback for Yale on a 1903 winning team against Harvard.

19. Dashiell taught chemistry at the U.S. Naval Academy in Annapolis, was a member of the self-perpetuating Football Rules Committee, and probably was the best known football official in America. He had previously officiated the Harvard-Yale game at which Harvard had been held scoreless.

20. Blagden was a Harvard football letter-winner in 1901 and a second-team Walter Camp all-American at tackle. The 1901 team, coached by William Reid, was the last one to beat Yale.

had given them because they happened to be clumsy or for any other reason. This is something that should be insisted on from the first, since it frequently happens that men will take off their pads without saying anything about it, and that the coach will not find out about it until the man is brought in hurt. I found out from [Dan] Knowlton's[21] brother, who is in college, that he will be back in the law school this year, and I shall start at once to get permission from his parents to let him play. His brother says that he has been sick for some time and probably won't be able to play anyway, but it won't do any harm to try. I told the men that from now on they would be expected to be in their rooms at half past ten promptly, and that any man who was not in their rooms then would be liable to dismission from the squad for breaking training. I also told the squad that each man must consider that he is not only trying for the Harvard team, but that he is also trying for the same position on every team that Harvard is to play, that every one of the colleges which we are to play there is a man who is trying to beat him out, and who is working every day to that end, therefore, said I, each man must set out to master each lesson at once in order to be a little better than his competitor. I stated also that the men must not try for the team to get their "H's" or to make the team simply, but in order to fight for the University, that no man who was out simply for an "H" or for a place on the team was the kind of man we were looking for, that each man should strive to make his position the strongest that it has ever been. I emphasized the fact that Penn and the other colleges, many of them, are buying up material and that it must this year be a case of making patriotic though perhaps slightly inferior material to do more than mercenary though superior material can do, this difference to be brought about by the spirit with which the men enter into their work.

The men were trotted around the field once as usual, then I lined up two teams and rehearsed for a few minutes the matter of affording protection for the kickers. This was good practice for the men and brought out several interesting points. I insisted that the center men from tackle to tackle block the men toward the inside and under no conditions to spread out the line. I put the defensive backs five yards behind the line with two men in front of the kicker toward the side of the foot with which he kicks. I showed these men that they must not take a position where they would best cover the spot in which the kicker was to stand at the start, but rather at a spot which would protect the particular spot at which the kicker was planning to get

---

21. Dan Knowlton became the starting left end and acting captain in the Harvard-Yale game that ended the season.

his kick off. I called the attention of the squad to the fact that this spot would vary with different kickers, and that protection must be given accordingly. I made it clear also, that the men who protect the kicker should not usually advance to meet on coming men, unless they advanced together, since in case either one man advances and the other does not, an interval will be left between them through which an opponent might go and block the kick. I told the backs to stand low, with their feet pretty fairly spread apart and their weight ready to shift in any particular direction. If with any individual kicker they found that they were too close to the kicker's foot as he kicked, they were to stand a little closer to the rush line to prevent it. I instructed the catcher not to hold his hands up for the pass until he had looked over the line and made sure that he was properly protected, then to lift his hands and expect the ball any time thereafter. The quarter back in this defensive scheme stands to the left of the line of pass in order not to subject himself to the heavy defensive work. I further showed that the backs on the defense must not stand too close together because of the ease with which opponents could probably get around, and I also called attention to the necessity for watching carefully to see who was the first man through the opposing line and where he was running.

After these explanations, I took the best men on the squad and gave them practice in falling on the ball, after which McMaster ordered the men in, it being a very warm morning and therefore very ennovating.[22] I had planned to have considerable kicking done but gave that up. One very agreeable surprise came to me in the shape of finding out that White, the big guard, can without doubt, be made into a very reliable goal kicker. I held 6 or 8 kicks for him and he got them all over nicely. In addition he takes only the one step which makes his kicking very secure. I then went up for my luncheon at the Union. I found the waiters in dress suits with a clean table cloth on the table and 3 attractive vases of flowers and the food hot and well cooked. I was greatly pleased at the situation and Capt. Hurley says the men have all remarked on it also.

Afternoon:

After the practice and after I had seen the men run through the assignments which we had given them on the different plays, especially the linemen[,] I had misgivings as to whether we had not given the linemen too much that approached team work, and I began to be very much afraid that the men would not get thoroughly grounded

22. Probably means enervating.

in the fundamentals of their positions, and so just as soon as practice was over I took it up with Lewis and Brown. These two men differed entirely in their opinions, Brown thinking as I did and Lewis thinking the other way around. My point was that if, for instance, the opposing guard plays in such a position that our guard has rather a hard time to handle him, it is an excellent chance for our guard to stretch himself and make the most of his instruction in blocking so that his individual play should be brought to its highest standard. Instead of that, I argued that where one lineman helped the other, as our assignment, dictated, the other man would come to expect help and not exert himself quite so much. On the other hand if no matter where the man plays, our man had to get after him, it would make our man a little more original and dependent in his methods. I was fearful lest the men would let their individual work slip to do the more easy team work, which I considered these assignments to involve. I talked it over all the way up from the field and at the table where the coaches sat. I did not have a chance to finish out the discussion then, because I was very much tired out and wanted to go home for a good night's sleep. Dr. Nichols went in on the car with me, and after talking over the situation came to the conclusion that Lewis was right.

On my way down to Cohasset I went over all the books on football that we have with a view to finding out what the different other men thought about it, and I came to the conclusion that I was pretty well justified in my position. My feeling was one that we ought to have those assignments later on, but Lewis shook that argument by saying that we did not stick to this formation for a very long time and by the time that we were ready to give these assignments the men would not be able to get them before they would have to be learning something else. Meanwhile, in getting the assignments they would be learning a considerable of the rudiments of the game, at the same time that they were given the more individual work before the line-up. Lewis' argument was so strong and yet the point was so vital that I determined to think the matter over carefully before calling off the double assignment and make everything a simple assignment. I felt as though the question of doing this was almost a vital one and should be mighty carefully thought over before anything further was done.

Friday, September 22, 1905

Morning:

I took the 8:02 train from Cohasset this morning and spent some considerable time on the train reading up the various books concerning the question that had so puzzled me last night. As we were to have no practice this morning I stopped in town to see Waters to talk over the matter in mind, but found him out and also Lewis, and so I came on out to Cambridge where I saw Professor White in regard to [Somers] Fraser. Fraser played centre rush on the second team all last year, and was not hurt and never had the slightest trouble. This year in taking the strength test Dr. Sargent was not satisfied with his heart action and refused to pass him. The question is whether Dr. Sargent or Dr. Nichols has the jurisdiction. Professor White has taken the matter under advisement and will let me know. I had from Professor White a copy of the letter concerning Lewis' services and found that I was given authority to engage him so long as I did not offer him more than $1500 and so long as it was understood that he (Lewis) was to receive nothing further from any source whatever. I told Professor White that I thought Lewis was worth every cent of the allowance and that I would like to offer it to him without any haggling, to which Professor White assented, so that on the first opportunity now I shall make the arrangements with Mr. Lewis.

There was a man out last year named Palmer who tried for the position of end who weighs quite a bit, but whose father told him he could not play this year owing to a condition or two which the boy had not removed. In order to get this boy out I telephoned to his father who was very nice about it and said he would come out in the afternoon to see me. Later on the boy appeared and told me that his father was not coming out and that he (the boy) had permission to play on two conditions; first, that he should be given a chance to show what he was worth in the first three weeks, so that in case he did not make good he could stop playing and go back to his work. This I agreed to. The boy seems to be a great talker and is not thought a great deal of by the other coaches. I had told members of the squad that I would talk with them over their prospects for individual play during the morning, so I had a considerable talk with Boyd on his kicking. He took hold of it very intelligently, and I hope will do something at it.

Then I telephoned to Waters, and arranged to meet him in town. I went in and went over the question of line play in the first assignments, and he practically agreed with Lewis, except that perhaps he put a little more emphasis on the necessity for blocking and blocking along in the line. His point was that it was the duty of the lineman in the neighborhood of the spot at which his play was being directed to hold the ground of the rush line until the play hit, so that there might be no possibility of an opponent getting at the play behind the line. He pointed out that in case any one member of the rush line in the neighborhood of the play advanced out of the line that he immediately left an interval between him and the man on either side of him through which an opponent might get at the play. He did not believe that any lineman ought to leave his line position to get at the play until the play was almost in the line and the play properly protected from the flank, but firmly believed that the men should be taught the assignments from the start. This being the case I felt very much relieved, and almost felt that the matter was much cleared up. I had a horror of not grounding the men well in linework and it was not until Waters made two points, which I shall give in a moment that I came to see that in reality individual work was being furthered, although there was perhaps a slight basis left for the team work. Waters said each man on the rush line must consider two things. First he must remember that his individual position in blocking is dependent solely upon the space he has to protect. In the second place, if the individual has decided what space he must protect his next consideration is how to go into his man properly when he gets up against him. In other words, each individual must decide for himself how much and how long his blocking must be, then what man he is to take and then what method he is going to use in taking him. I therefore decided without any hesitation whatever to allow the men their assignments, but to make clear the fact that the men must not leave the rush line until the play has gotten far enough along so that it cannot be stopped from the flank. I discussed also with Waters the question of the freshman coach, and he rather advised Sugden[,] of Sugden, Marshall and Meier[,] on the ground that Sugden has more enthusiasm, has done some little coaching before and is not retiring as is Meier. I had a telegram sent to Sugden asking him if he would consider taking it, and had an answer later on that he hardly thought he would have time. I shall see however, as soon as he reaches Cambridge if I cannot make him change his mind. I also asked Waters to consider whether he thought it wise for us to try to change to the Yale style of defence or how much we should change towards it, since upon that question are depending a great measure the kinds of ends which Bowditch will be on the lookout for. I also asked Waters to be considering whether Brill has speed and head enough to play tackle successfully, if so we must concentrate all our attention to making him play a heavy game, and the same with Squires. If not, Brill must be given a try somewhere on the line further in. Lewis says, that he does not want all the riffraff in the centre and that we must not expect him to make a silver purse out of a sow's ear, to which I responded that in this case he was not getting the ear of the sow, but perhaps the whole one.

Afternoon:

I had luncheon in Boston, and then came out to Cambridge. I was exceedingly glad that we had not had practice in the morning, for the day was a very warm one, and would have taken a great deal out of the men.

When I reached Cambridge Captain Hurley brought in [William] Quigley from the squad, and told me that Quigley was pretty nearly certain that he could prove that [Andrew] Draper, who had gone to Penn was payed to play football. If such is the case we shall keep the information and use it. Nothing whatever has been said to anyone about it, so that I hope everything will run along alright. One of the Assistant Professors on the Fine Arts courses volunteered a very nice piece of help in suggesting that any man who needed "C's" in certain courses should see his instructor and ask him that the instructor keep him posted as to whether he was doing "C" work, and to tell the instructor also that he meant to attend regularly to his work and do his part. I think this will be a mighty valuable suggestion and I shall make use of it just as soon as college opens.

Goodhue met me on the way down to the field and told me that the track man had asked permission to practice on Soldiers field during football practice. I am a little bit doubtful about it because I do not wish the football men to have to be dodging track men or take any chances of being spiked. What is more, I do not wish any track team spectators hanging around and seeing things which I prefer that no one should see. It seemed wise probably that an agreement with the track men whereby they may use the track for a certain period of the afternoon be made, because we ought if possible to help the other branch of the sport along and be willing to make a slight allowance for that reason.

When I got down to the field I made the men a talk showing the necessity for blocking along in the rush line and explaining to them what is likely to be taking place behind the line and what they must be protecting their backs from. I also asked one or two questions on the rules. Then I went over very carefully the assignments of the plays that we have had thus far very carefully [drawn up], illustrating some of the assignments by having men stand up on the floor and by showing the squad how these assignments should be taken and how not. I found that several men had gotten pretty well banged up in the work which Lewis had been giving them in blocking and breaking through, and it occurred to me that we had at once better fit the men out with aluminum or with fibre thigh protectors in order that the men might get the experience in blocking and breaking through without the bruises which would prevent them from playing further. I have an idea that Yale uses something of this kind to start with, and I think it is a very good plan. Therefore on Monday afternoon the linemen will be provided with aluminums ready for the first scrimmage.

We have now arranged to have the men's undershirts and stockings washed twice a week, on Wednesday and Saturday. The men's jock straps are to be steamed once a week, and any other article of clothing that cannot be successfully cleaned will have some such attention. It is particularly necessary at the beginning of the season to see that the itch or any other skin infection does not get started among the players. I found one man who apparently had something of the kind, and sent him into a specialist who pronounces it simply a rash, which amounted to nothing. Thus far this year we have had no boils and no infections of any kind. I want to try and keep that up. I am going to make out now a schedule of the weaknesses which each man on the Varsity squad has thus far developed, and give each man a list of those weaknesses in order that he may go about correcting them in a perfectly sensible manner. I believe that if we do this for the backs and kickers, ends and linemen that in another week's time we ought to have made great progress toward eradicating these points. Men who are weak in certain points should be able to work intelligently to correct their faults.

As soon as the men came out on to the field I took into my squad all of the ends who have thus far shown any ability and gave them practice falling on the ball at right angles with the direction in which they are coming. Immediately after that I trotted them all over to the dummies[23] and turned them over to coach Lewis for coaching in tackling. The only tackle that was given the men for the afternoon was a simple head on left tackle. In making this tackle we made the following points with the men. In the first place the tackle must be made at a point somewhere between a man[']s knees and his waist. If a man tackles below the knees the runner is very likely to get free from the tackler or be pulled free by some other player, while if the man tackles above the waist his legs are left free and he is able to drag the tackler on over the play. To illustrate this I had one of the smaller men on the squad grab me around the waist and then I told him to throw

23. Tackling dummies were evidently an invention of Chicago's Amos Alonzo Stagg in 1889. See L. H. Baker, *Football: Facts and Figures* (New York: Farrar and Rinehart, 1945), 592, and Amos A. Stagg and Wesley W. Stout, *Touchdown!* (New York: Longmans, Green, 1927), 109. Stagg used a rolled-up mattress made into the size of a man's body, suspended it from the gymnasium's roof, and used a mattress underneath to help prevent injuries.

me if he could. I walked around the spot where the dummy was and was able to keep my feet and drag him around which I pleased for almost a minute, when he finally had sense enough to trip and upset me. The illustration was pretty successful and I think the men will realize that a tackle must be made between the waist and knees. The next point I took up was to ask the men why it was that we wanted to tackle across the knees or just above them, and finally drew out the answer that if you could stop the motion of the man's body at his knees that any motion he could make above or below his knees would enable him in moving away. That the mere fact that his knees were pinned together would make him very unsteady and easily upset. As the man approaches the man he is to tackle he should aim to get his head on one side or the other of the man he is after and get the face of the opponent across the back part of his own shoulder, thereby saving his collar bone and the top of this shoulder from liability to injury. Many of the men kept their shoulders down but kept their head up instead of putting their head down to[o] and thereby kept their collar bones up after a ta[ckl]e and very much exposed, besides being in no position to lift a man because their backs were too straight. We warned the men not to stick their heads into the body of their opponent but to use the opponent[']s body to break his own fall. The man should approach the runner cat[c]hing him just above the knees, wrapping his arms tightly around him, hitting him with the back part of the shoulder with his head to one side or the other of the runner, and at the time the tackle is made should both lift the runner and push backwards so as to topple him backwards. As the opponent falls his legs should be between the legs of the tackle, thereby giving a good place to hug the legs of the opponent in towards the tackler, which when combined with the forward momentum of the tackler makes it so much easier to throw the upper part of the man tackled backwards. We explained that it was not a dive tackle because a man did not leave his feet. We found that many of the men would misjudge the dummy as it came head on and not get down low enough to it soon enough and that was one reason why many of them caught the dummy away up on their chest instead of on their shoulders. I called attention to the fact that the man who was tackled was not borne back several steps but was dropped more nearly in his tracks except that he also went backwards. To enable men to get their shoulders down low enough I suggested to them that one foot be left a little in rear of the other one, a scheme which would allow the tackle[']s body to be pretty near the ground as he approached but cautioned them in doing this to bring the other leg up so as to be able to throw the opponent[']s legs between his own. I found one or two of the men with a tendency to spreading their legs out too far and therefore being unsteady on their feet. The men took hold very well, and although the tackling was pretty crude nevertheless it showed thought and there was some improvement on the second round. Much of it was due to the questions I asked the squad about each man who tackled poorly. I did not put much emphasis on tackling too viciously, because, as before, I said that my idea this year was to urge no man to any speedy work which he does not yet know how to do slowly.

To protect the men from injury in falling on the ball I had the ground well cut up, with a mixture of sand to prevent it from being muddy on rainy days, and then had the whole thing covered over with a good thick covering of grass clippings from the different fields. Care must be taken in the tackling that the dummy can be released hard enough so as to help break the runner's fall a little bit, and it should be remembered that this regulation is a very simple matter, by adjusting the spring which holds the dummy up.

Immediately after the tackling I took squads A & B,[24] which were made up as follows, and ran them through the signals,—

Squad A

Center	White
Left Guard	McFadden
Right Guard	Peirce
Left Tackle	Brill
Right Tackle	Squires
Left End	Blair
Right End	O'Brien
Quarterback	Starr
Full back	Hanley
Left H. B.	Foster
Right H. B.	Wendell

Squad B

Center	Cunniff
Guards	Brown & McLeod
Tackles	Montgomery & Carr

24. Surprisingly, of the twenty-two players noted on the A and B squads, only Squires, Brill, Starr, Wendell, and Foster of the A squad and Carr of the B squad started in the Yale game concluding the season.

Ends	Hall & Grant
Quarter Back	Quigley
Full Back	Lockwood
Left Half	Nesmith
Right Half	Lincoln

We ran them through the signals and then made changes,—As full backs, we played Boyd, Dearborn, Schohl, and as half backs, Gring, Leonard, and one or two other less promising men. I gave Fultz a chance at tackle and put Parker for a time at guard. Bowditch sent in four or five other ends, and then I divided the squad into sections sending the line men to Lewis, keeping three or four kickers myself, the ends to Bowditch, and the quarter backs to Daly. In this way we kept them going the rest of the afternoon. The men with strained legs or poops, of which were only two, simply stood around and watched. Brown had charge of the poorer element, of which there are now about 20 or 30 all told. I dropped one man off the squad because he is exceedingly clumsy and takes up so much time that it is out of the question to teach him anything this year and this is his last year. At the end of his work with the end men, Bowditch took the ends into the Locker building and showed them how to stand for starts down the field and for other work that he had planned out for them.

I had a little talk with [Oliver] Filley[25] over a man named [Robert] Guild, who was out for end last year, but who is not out this year because he intends to row. Filley says he is a good man for rowing, so I do not believe I shall try to press him to service. Lewis told me at the end of the day that he did not know whether Parker would make a guard or not, as he seems to be rather fragile. I think this is likely to be the most serious criticism with Parker, and hope that he will not prove so badly off as we fear. I also had a talk with the news paper men again in order to get them to describe the practice in a general way instead of in such an explicit fashion as they have been doing. They have been giving every little detail of the work, and have been making it very evident to everyone everywhere what we are trying for. I told them also that Dr. Sargent had said of the foot ball men who had taken the strength tests that this year's was the poorest crowd he had ever had taking the test. I did not tell them, however, the reason was because we did not allow any man to try in any way for a record.

25. Filley was a Harvard crew letter-winner (1903–6) and won a letter in football in 1904.

The big scale plan of the field has come, and is a splendid piece of work. I believe that it will be of the greatest possible service to us in illustrating plays and in discussing the rules.

After supper Lewis, Brown, Capt. Hurley and I worked over the simple plays of the first formation until 11 o'clock and added in that time only one to the number we already had. We propose to have the team know pretty well by next Saturday, when the first game is played, the two full back bucks on either side, also the two half back dives on either side of the line, the two end runs, the two cross buck plays and the tackle around tackle plays, besides the formation to receive the kick off in an ordinary kick formation.

Saturday, September 23, 1905

Morning:

I dictated this morning until it was time to go down to practice. Down there I went over the present training rules, which are that a man shall eat nothing between meals and shall be in his room at 10:30 promptly every night, and that the men shall, of course, not smoke or drink or dissipate in any way. I have given the team permission to go to the theatre tonight, but not to have supper afterwards. I do this to relieve the monotony of the past week, which has been pretty heavy. I expect to have morning practice next Monday again, but shall cease having it altogether just as soon as we have scrimmages in the afternoon, which I expect will begin on Tuesday.

After jogging the squad around the field to get them limbered up, we lined the men up in a long line and McMaster and I stood off to one side while one after another of the men ran. I did this in order to find out what men knew how to run and what did not, in order to see how to go to work to get them to running. Four or five of the men we found will need special attention.

In order to get rid of the newspaper men who have been in the way, I agreed with one of the photographers to send over to him any men whose pictures he wanted so that the matter might be finished up at once and so at intervals during the practice I sent over to a photographer who was near 30 or 40 men. This simplified the newspaper matter very decidedly and prevents, also, a great deal of friction.

I took a squad of 50 odd men, the best that we have, and gave them work in falling on the ball, criticising each man individually and carefully. I gave them work in receiving the ball for a buck, and work in placing the ball properly under their arms for an end run. This latter point, of holding the ball properly for an end run is one on which I shall dwell with much care during the season, as I think the ball is more often poorly held in this fashion than in any other way. I showed the men that if they tilted the point of the ball, which should be under their arm, up too far and a man should hit it from behind and a little but upward, the ball will snap out of the hollow of the arm very readily, while in case the ball is held with the point under the arm tilted slightly downward, a man hitting it from the front and downward will knock it out. I showed the men that if the ball is held under the arm with just enough of an upward tilt to it to secure one end of it in the hollow of the arm, that the opponent would only have an opportunity to hit the very end of the ball, in which case the blow would immediately react on the hand which is resting around the forward end of the ball, so that there would be very little danger of dropping the ball. I showed them that the arm on the side which the ball is held hugged the ball close to the side so as to prevent it from slipping off the side of the body. I also showed them how important it was not to swing the arm holding the ball back and forth as they ran, and how, instead, it was important to keep the arm pretty still so that the ball would not be shifting position along the man's side as his arm moved back and forth. Many fumbles come from not knowing how to hold the ball properly—more than from any other cause, that is when the runner fumbles after he has already gotten the ball in his own possession. Another important reason for careful attention to this detail is that in case a runner cannot put the ball under his arm instantaneously he will have to carry it in his hands unadjusted for some considerable distance, during which time, in case he is tackled, he is almost certain to drop the ball. At the same time, the man can run as fast as he ought to if he has his mind on putting the ball away properly. The ball should be received and placed instantly so that the runner may divert his entire attention to getting off, and to devising a method for passing his interferers. After this work, I took the squad over to the tackling dummy and gave them each two or three tackles, then I brought them back and ran squad A & B through the signals, and then sent the men in. The one thing that I left out which I hoped to do was to get in some kicking. I did have White, Cunniff and Brill kicking goals, but that was all. The practice was very long and it was two o'clock when I had my lunch. After lunch I dictated a portion of this account, and cleaned up also, a portion of my very backward correspondence.

I met Coach Owsley of Yale at the Touraine with Capt. Hurley at 6:45 this evening to talk over the question of officials. Capt. Hurley and I agreed to agree to nothing, but simply to find out Yale's position and then make a decision accordingly. We propose to have a satisfactory man this year and no amount of urging or bluff or anything else on Yale's part can change our minds on Dashiell.

Monday, September 25, 1905

Morning:

Immediately after reaching Boston from Cohasset I came out to Cambridge, where I had a talk with [Francis] Burr, an Andover freshman who weighs something like 200 lbs. He seemed a little backward about coming out, and I told him that some people had reported that he lacked the stuff of a football player but that I thought he had it and hoped to see him show up. He will be out this afternoon. I saw Parker, and he says his leg is troubling him somewhat, so I had a talk with Dr. Nichols, who says that Parker's leg bones are too small for a man of his weight, and for that reason Parker will probably be fragile. We are to have a special brace made for him, and hope to be able to use him a part of the time at least.

I saw Dan Knowlton's brother, and [he] says that Dan will return to Cambridge this year but will not be able to play because he is planning to take the Law school course in two years. We have got to have Knowlton, and if necessary I shall take a trip to Marion where Knowlton's parent are, and endeavor to get their permission.

I went down to the field at about 10 o'clock, and gave the men a caution about care in taking the strength test and care of straining bad legs. Then I gave out the assignments for the Half back run through his own side. Then had the dumb bell work, and then jogged the whole squad around the field. Following this I gave Cunniff, Brill and White practice in kicking goals. Following this I took the linemen and ends over to the tackling dummy, giving the ends to Bowditch and taking the linemen myself. We had nothing but straight left tackle, and the men took hold of it well. I then took out squad "A" for signal practice, changing the ends and backs when I had put the first combination through signals a few times. Then I took squad "B" and put them through signals and started them off. Squad "C", which comprised of all of the other men out, Captain Hurley took hold of, and gave them practice in receiving the ball and in coaching. I had Brill, and Foster do some punting and Starr, Wendell, Lincoln and Nesmith caught. After this I sent the whole squad in with the exception of Newhall, [Laurence] Rumsey, Burr and [Herbert] Miller. Newhall seems to me to show every promise of being a first-rate quarterback and handles himself well. Rumsey is too small and lacks ginger.

Miller is a new man out, who said in a letter he could kick about 50 to 60 yards. I found he could kick only very fair, and probably won't amount to much this year. Burr, who I set to kicking, turned out to be the surprise of the day. In punting he had no difficulty in outkicking everybody on the field with punts of tremendous height and distance, which he got off with either foot. He took one too many steps, but I found it possible to reduce him to only one step, and did so on the spot without hindering his work in anyway. He is certainly the most natural kicker we have ever had here, and with a little polishing up he will have very little to do except keep his form. After he had made a few kicks I sent everybody in.

After lunch I got off some work with Goodhue, and had a call from one of my old class mates, and then went down to the field. Immediately after the dumb bell work I took the squad out to the field, and jogged them around once, and then put the squad which I have usually taken in charge through a course in falling on the ball. I had the ball roll to the right and left of the men once around, and coached each man individually in case he was doing poorly. Then I lined the men up and rolled the ball anywhere it happened, calling to any man on the squad to take it. This kept the whole squad always ready and prevented the work from being too monotonous. I sometimes called the same man twice in succession, so that no man could feel that he was safe. The men did the work very well. To my gratification Bob Kernan turned up, and after a short talk with him he decided to do no coaching of the kickers until he had seen them perform. Immediately after the work in falling on the ball I took the squad over to the dummy, where Mr. Lewis gave them the first practice of dive tackling. They got hold of it pretty well. The work was brought to a close by the breaking down of the dummy. I turned over to Reggie Brown and Captain Hurley the poorer men on the squad, and then ran squad "A" and "B" through signals, making numerous changes in the line-up. I told squad "B" to consider the second number on the list given by the quarterback as the significant one, so that in the game which we expect to have tomorrow the men will have a good chance to get off their plays without having squad "A" know where they are coming. I put squad "B" to work running through signals. When after several changes in the men I sent the linemen from tackle to tackle to Coach[e]s Lewis, Waters and Marshall, while the ends reported to Bowditch, and the kickers to Kernan and I, while the backs paired off catching the kicks.

John Dunlop was out for the first time, and just looked on in order to get the ideas which we have been trying to get into the men.

There was rather a gentle protest on the part of the coaches that the half backs be not allowed to start with their hands on the ground in order to force the men to balance themselves rather on the balls of their feet. I think this is rather a good scheme and with the exception of Capt. Hurley, it will probably be allowed. In getting forward on the hands the men are likely, particularly on both hands, to get their weight too far forward and be unable to get off their end runs successfully.

Coaches Lewis, Waters and Marshall put the line men through a pretty long piece of making holes and breaking through and the men were quite tired after it. Brill began soldiering again as a result of a crack on his calf of his leg, and Waters was rightfully very much disgusted with him. If Brill is going to do this we shall take him off and put him on the Second and keep him there until he gets over it. I will not tolerate that in him this year. He is being given every show and must either make good or get out. I would rather have Montgomery, a far smaller man, in there than Brill, when I feel sure that Montgomery is doing his best all the time, and when I know that the team places absolute confidence in him as a fighter and a worker. Squires seemed pretty "dead" during the work. After consultation with Mc-Master and Dr. Nichols I told the men on the main squad that they need not report for morning practice tomorrow. Squires has got to be coached to see that he does not get overdone.

Kernan and I stood behind the kickers as they came up in succession and watched them kick, criticising each man to one another. We decided that Burr was by far the best kicker on the field and needs very little coaching and none at all for two or three days, until we know exactly what he needs, if he needs anything. Leonard we also decided was kicking well, also Nat Hall, Foster pretty well, then Wendell, and lastly Hanley, [Leo] Leary and Lockwood. The backs caught pretty well and I had them make several "fair catches" in order to accustom themselves to this point of the play. The ends ran down under the direction of Bowditch meanwhile, and have certainly improved greatly. O'Brien seemed to me to be the best end stuff that we have. He is a Roxbury Latin school man whom I mentioned in the report of Spring work. He is very strong, a good fighter, intelligent and quick.

After the practice, Lewis, Dr. Nichols and Regy Brown took dinner with me at the training table and we discussed the question of Burr's playing. Lewis wants Burr very much and there is a question of whether Burr, having had typhoid fever about a year ago, is strong enough to stand the strain. If he is, and his father will let him, we want to play him. I told Burr to see his family Doctor and his father and find out what they thought about it and to let me know in the morning.

After supper Brown, Lewis, Hurley and I worked out the assignments for the tackle run around the opposite tackle, the position for receiving the kick off, and the position for kicking off. After we had done this, we went over a list of Brown's squad with him to see what men were worth keeping and what were not. He thinks that there are only one or two men that he wants to drop, and I am entirely willing. At about 10:30 we broke up and went to bed.

Tuesday, September 26, 1905

Morning:

Right after breakfast I had a long talk with Kernan on the way in which I have been coaching the kickers and on various points in the kicking policy which I want followed. I took it from start to finish and I think Bob and I agree on everything essential. He is not going to change anything about a man's style without speaking to me, as I am fearful of spoiling some good kicker because of attempting to make him do things which are not natural to him and which handicap more than help him. For instance, we are going to let Leonard drop the ball onto his foot about as he chooses. We are not plan[n]ing to shift Burr very much either, since we can remember Butterworth and Brook[26] in their best days held the ball close to the ground as Burr does, and made a splendid success of it. We are going to try not to have another catastrophe such as happened to us in the LeMoyne case, where by attempting to improve an already good kicker we succeeded only in making him worse and in the end l[o]sing him entirely. We decided that the only thing to be done to help Hall along was to work on his getting the ball onto his foot at an angle suitable enough to give it sufficient height, while with Foster we decided that it was wise to work slowly for the present on his dropping the ball in proper fashion onto his foot.

Ted Meier, who is to coach the freshmen this fall appeared in Cambridge this morning, and I had a long talk to him explaining to him that I consider the coaching of freshman team a most important matter and one that he will have to think over and give his time to. I gave

26. Reid may be referring to Frank Butterworth, the Yale fullback from 1892 to 1894, and William A. Brooks, the Harvard football captain of 1886 and later Harvard football coach in 1894.

up having Sugden because I received a telegram from him stating that he would be unable to do it and because Meier is likely to be around here next year and is likely to get more time for it since he will not be in attendance at college but will be able to put the whole of every afternoon at it. I told him that I should hold him responsible for the scholarship standing of the men and should hold him responsible for his Yale game in only one thing, and that was that he should send into the Yale game a team thoroughly drilled in the fundamentals, conditioned and padded and good fighters all of them. I told him that I did not wish him to drop any men from the Freshman squad without seeing me and I should wish to have the Freshman kickers coached by the Varsity coach so as to help along in getting the Freshman kickers ready for next year. We are going to have first rate material for a freshman team, and properly handled ought to yield us some first-class varsity material next year. I told Meier that I would like to have him out for practice from now until the Freshman squad is called out in order that he may see and get clearly in mind what we are trying to do and how we are trying to do it.

Having excused from morning practice almost all of the men who are going to do any lineup work this afternoon, I took out the remainder and gave them a sort of test on end proficiency in falling on the ball and in holding it for bucks and end runs. This latter fundamental proved to be the hardest thing of all since no two men can carry the ball in exactly the same place, owing to the fact that their fore arms, wrists and hands vary in length, which in turn forces them to hold the ball at a little different angle in order to get a sufficient grasp on it. The men were very awkward in getting the ball into position quickly, which is another important point, as it is very dangerous work to carry the ball any great distance while it is still in an unsafe position. This I consider a very important fundamental and one upon which we cannot spend too much time in our attempts to erradicate the frightful fumbling which has occurred. I went over the details of holding the ball very carefully, and told the men they must try to protect themselves from a blow from any direction and particularly from such a direction as the one in which there is no hand, arm or body to repel it.

After this slight preliminary work I sent the men in, but stayed out a while longer with Meier and went carefully into the details of falling onto the ball and handling it. I had lunch at about 12:30 and dictated from then or nearly then until about 1:30.

I propose now to raise a question with the coaches as to whether or not to start off Saturday with the best team that we think we have and to begin practising that team alone right away, or whether to keep two squads going up until the Friday before the game and then put the best we have together. I am inclined to think that after to-day we had better for the time being put the first team together and keep it at it for Saturday, being ready to make substitutions from what is left at anytime. As many of the men out on the field now may or may not be eligible to play Saturday, I shall give the manager a long list of men this afternoon or tomorrow to submit to the faculty and Athletic Committee for approval. I do not want to come to the Saturday game and find that we are lacking enough men to play a fifteen and ten minute half without tiring the men.

Afternoon:

This afternoon the squad reported at 4 o'clock as usual and I looked over the padding of the men whom I decided to line up so as to be sure each man was well protected. Then I told the squad I did not wish any man to go out without the protection which had been provided for him unless of course, he first spoke to me.

As soon as we got the men onto the field I turned over the most unpromising men to Bowditch who took them for some tackling at the dummy, whil[e] the squads A & B went through signal practice in preparation for the work. We divided the men into two squads as follows:

Squad A.

Left end, Blair; left tackle, Brill; center, White; right guard, Peirce; right tackle, Squires; right end O'Brien; quarter back, Starr; left h[a]lf back, Wendell; right half back, Foster, full back, Hanley.

Squad B.

Left end, Blagden; left tackle, Montgomery; center, Cunniff; right guard, McLeod; right tackle, Fultz; right end, Hall; quarter back, Quigley; left half back, Lincoln, full back, Lockwood.

First of all I was careful to walk the men through their plays and to see that each man understood pretty well what his particular work was to be, and I had some line men stand up in front of the squad with which I was drilling so that the line men had also a chance to indicate what their assignments were. After we had done this, I took a cord which was exactly 3-½ yards long and measured out the distance for the backs, telling the full back that in case he did not get his distance every time I was going to take him out and put somebody else in. I then followed both A & B up and down the field a couple of times going through the signals, and then lined them up for ten minutes of actual playing, it being divided into two 5 minute halves. During the line up I had only two changes made, in that Leary and Grant played the second half on squad B. Squad A received the kick off and carried the ball some little distance, when they fumbled and the second squad got the ball. Squad B was unable to make any distance and Lockwood kicked. This work was very full of life, the men playing very hard and the work was fierce. After some little time Lincoln got around the end and scored on the first. This was due largely to the fact that our rush line backs were playing too close to the line and were easily boxed.

Immediately after the line up I put through two more teams in signal practice and with Dunlo[p] coached them on the way to get at the play. This work over, I sent the line men to coach Lewis and turned the kickers over to Kernan, while the other backs caught the kicks. After more considerable running down on kicks and considerable work in the back field, we sent the men in for the day. No one one was hurt and the work was hard, which was very gratifying to us.

Wednesday, September 27, 1905

Morning:

I was thinking over a number of the points that ought to be kept in mind in connection with the game with Williams on Saturday and I have come to the conclusion that we should be very careful not to play anybody who does not seem pretty certain of doing something or not doing something. I have been arguing very strongly as to whether O'Brien the Freshman end should be played or not, since he is going to be a Varsity man before he gets through anyway, and in case he is unable to make it this year, we would probably lose him for one year's playing later on.[27] I therefore thought the matter over carefully and we shall not play him unless the coaches feel pretty nearly dead sure that he will make good, and the same with everybody else that we play. These smaller games do not give anybody practice enough but what in case we are in doubt about a man, we

27. Because Harvard athletes had four years of varsity eligibility, what Reid was thinking of doing was "red shirting" O'Brien his freshman year to preserve the four years of eligibility for later. As it turned out, O'Brien never was a letter man. In 1906, Harvard, Yale, and Princeton agreed to limiting eligibility to three years and no graduate participation as part of college athletic reform.

can learn full as much about a player in our own scrimmages as we can where he plays against an outside team. I feel that this arrangement is perfectly sound and that we must hold to it. I also made up my mind to have the backs begin to do a little fair catching this afternoon so as to get them ready for any work of that kind, and so that they will know what a fair catch is. I am going also, in order to get rid of monotony in falling on the ball, to let the men line up and call anybody's name so that no man may feel sure that he is going to be called on until his time comes.

The coaches have been coming more on to the field than I intended they should and I shall tomorrow tell the Manager to keep the men off unless they are asked by other coaches to come on.[28]

I have got to get some men to report to me every day what is going on in Penn, Dartmouth and Yale, if possible, so I can keep track of the progress of each of the teams.

Just as soon as I get [the] squad fairly picked I shall give each man a list of his weaknesses which he is to work on to see if he cannot get them corrected.

I also made out a list of 15 or 20 men for Bowditch to look over for ends, since if a man cannot play in one position I shall want to play him somewhere else. As new men are continually being added to the squad, I am taking pains to find out if they ever had bad ankles and if they have not, I am giving them light work at the start so that they may get in first class condition. I am sorry that Waters is not out oftener than he has been, but it is because he is sick and cannot come out.

Afternoon:

We had the men out at 4 o'clock as usual, and after running them around the field, sent squads A & B through signals, and then lined them up against each other. We played two 7-½ minute halves, and squad A taking the ball from the kick off, took it to their own 20 yard line across the goal line for a touch down. We put in Capt. Hurley at right half back to start off with and in the first chance he had to carry the ball he tried to get around the end and then tried to hurdle, when he was tackled and his leg gave him a set back. I sent him right in, and Dr. Nichols says that Hurley will be very fortunate if he is able to do anything at all for two weeks. It must be remembered here-

---

28. Harvard and other schools traditionally allowed former players to come back periodically to help the regular coaching staff. Sometimes the number of these periodic coaches seemed to approach the number of players.

after that the Capt. must be given enough work so that he is not simply crazy to play. If I had given Hurley a lot of running before I had put him in he would not have felt quite so frisky, and would probably have not tried such unfortunate hurdling.

Squad B did some kicking and when we found out that both teams were not defending the kicking, some having their kicks blocked, we gave both teams a chance to do a good deal of punting so to give the kickers more experience in this line.

The playing was good and hard and we tried out some more men at end, and then sent the squad in.

Thursday, September 28, 1905

Morning:

As to-day was the day when my family was to move up from Cohasset,[29] I spent the entire morning and until practice time in the afternoon in helping get things in order.

Afternoon:

The squad reported as usual at 4 o'clock and were given five minutes dumb bell work and then were trotted around the field to limber them up. I then gave half of the squad, composed of the poorest material, to R. Brown and he gave them work on the Freshman field where we have usually had our practice, while I took the rest of the squad on to the stadium and lined them up in two squads (A & B). Squad A had on it O'Brien, right end; Squires, right tackle; Peirce, right guard; White, center; McFadon, left guard; Brill, left tackle; Blair, left end; Starr, quarter back; Foster, left half back; Hanley, full back; Wendell, right half back.

Squad B consisted of Hall, right end; Fultz, right tackle; Brown, right guard; Cunniff, center; McLeod, left guard; Montgomery, left tackle; Green, end; Quigley, quarter back; Nesmith and Lincoln, half backs; and Lockwood, full back.

The air was very embracing and we rehearsed the plays which both squads know, consisting of the full back dive between guard and center, half back straight dive on his own side, cross bucks, and the end runs, besides the kick. After the preliminary signal work we lined up for two 7-½ minute halves beginning with a kick off.

29. Bill, his wife, Christine, and their two children (William T. "Patrick" III, two-and-a-half, and Edith Williams, ten months) lived with Christine's parents, Mr. and Mrs. Albert Lincoln, in their summer home at Cohasset before returning to Brookline in the fall.

I am sure that heretofore our teams have not had as much endurance as they ought to have and I am going to make the line men keep out a little longer than they have been doing, with a little preliminary work. Already they are playing at Penn, Yale, and the other colleges some considerable longer than we are, and I want to get our men into suitable condition for an equal amount of work.

In the scrimmage, neither side was able to score and we spent much time on kicks, Leonard, Foster, Hall, and Brill doing most of the work. We seem to be unable to get good safe kicking formation and we want to get it settled as soon as possible, as well as to give our men who are doing the kicking and who are green a chance to get a little accustomed to men rushing through them.

In the talk which I had with Owsley, the Yale coach, some few days ago, he said that at New Haven the[y] rarely ever played their best men more than half of the playing time of the year, that they drilled them carefully in signals and in their duties and then got their wind in such condition that they could play on and last through the game. Putting this statement to a little closer examination it occurred to me that we have done too much playing of our best backs against each other; that is to say, the playing of the first 11 backs on the second 11 where they had to stop the rushes of other backs of equal ability coming through with the impetus which the Varsity line provided. By this plan all of our backs have had to play every day with almost no rest, the result being that they have soon gotten broken up. It is my plan to put the best backs on the Varsity, and to play them on alternate days, spending the days when the different sets do not work in getting fundamentals well cleared up in starts, in running through signals, in putting out ends, and in doing other fundamental work of backs. For instance, if I take Foster, Wendell, Lincoln, Nesmith and Leonard, whom I am now trying at half back instead of quarter back, and who will never make quarter backs, and keep them for Varsity backs and play them in alternation I think that the men will last better and play better foot ball because they will not be all tired out. The same principle seems to me to hold true of ends. The ends cannot be played every day and forced to run up and down the field on kicks without getting into slow ways or losing their fight. The first and second teams ought to have, each of them, several sets of ends and they should be laid off occasionally so as to keep them in fighting trim. The line men of course ought to be laid off too, occasionally, although, being slow, there is not the necessity for quite so much dash in them as in the backs, and therefore not quite so much need for so frequent rest.

In the scrimmage the Varsity line played very high and lacked charge and drive.

After the practice was over I took up the question of the steps the backs should take in starting, and found that in case they are running, say, around the right end what they have a tendency to do is to pivot on the right foot until their body is far enough around to enable them to take a step with their left foot. This is wrong, since in thus pivoting the opponent gets an instantaneous idea as to where the play is going before it is really under way. The impression given one looking on is that the runs rather hang fire temporarily. I discussed this at the coaches meeting after the practice, with Lewis, Waters, Dunlop and Brown, and we were unanimous in thinking that in case a run should be around a right end, a back's first step should be with his right foot so that his right toe is almost parallel with the rush line and so that if he swings his body he can get in a considerable drive to the right as he starts off. The steps of course should be short at first and gradually lengthened, but the men should try to get off at full speed. The men have been playing with their hands on the ground to start with, but I am requiring them now to start from an upright position in order to enable them to learn how to poise themselves on the balls of their feet and be able to start one way or the other rapidly. The instructions I am giving them are about as follows:

"Stand with your feet comfortably well apart, with your waist pretty well on the balls of your feet, with your heels touching the ground but without any weight on them, and the bulk of your weight being on the inner sides of your feet and your knees turned in towards each other. One foot of course may be a little back of the other, but at all events the knees should be best slightly in, thus enabling a man to push himself to the right or left and getting a good leg drive at the start.["] Later on in the season, after this balance has gotten pretty well secured, I shall give the men a chance to put one hand on the ground to steady themselves with, but I believe it is part of the fundamentals of a back's work that he should start standing up without his hands on the ground early in the season.

Capt. Hurley was not out this afternoon, having gone to the hospital after yesterday afternoon's accident to his leg. We are going to let him get absolutely well this time before taking any more risks with him. He knows foot ball enough to be able to get into condition at almost any time and to play his usual game.

I am giving the backs special work on the matter of holding the ball for end runs and for buck plays, so as to clear up the fumbling which has been so prevalent in the last year or two. If we work the quarter backs and centers enough there ought to be very little fumbling between them. Then, the quarter backs should be able to get the ball to their backs so that there is very little opportunity for fumbling there, while the backs should be able to hold the ball safely after they once get it. These are the three points where fumbles occur, and too much time cannot be spent in trying to remedy this. Lewis is still rather undecided as to how the ball should be passed back for the quarter backs, which I am a little worried about, because that matter ought really to be well settled before this period of the year. We ought to be able to give our quarter backs and centers absolutely definite instructions at this time. It is a time when much practicing can be done in getting the ball back and where much individual coaching can be done, and where too much other work cannot be done because the men cannot stand it. Another year I advocate having the question of the half backs from center to guard definitely settled so that the moment the men come on to the field we shall know exactly what we are going to teach them.

There were 102 men out to-day and in looking over the list after the practice, with Mr. Lewis, we decided that there were 33 possible men in the lot, with 30 questionable men, the others invariably being second rate. I shall give the team tackle around tackle play tomorrow if possible and will, at any rate, give them the assignments for it. We must also, have fake kicks in order to make our regular kicks effective. It will keep men from coming through anywhere near as fast if they have heretofore done, and that in itself will give the line men time to make the kicks safe.

I have arranged to have the second team have its training table at the Union and propose on Saturday night to give out the list of men who will go to the table. This will enable the first and second teams to be present for the talks which we expect to have and will make it possible to get hold of second team men without having to send out of the house for them. They have heretofore had their meals at the Quincy Lunch in the Dutch Room, and there is no privacy or pleasure in it.

Bob Brown, the Andover end is trying to get in here now and I hope that he will be able to as we shall need ends again next year. I sent out several of the men to have their pictures taken this afternoon for one of the papers and got that out of the way.

Immediately after the regular practice was over I put every man on the squad, who hadn't had any work up to that time, through signal practice using [Robert] Guild, who is a crew man, as full back. He seems to be fast and I have hopes that he may do something at full back, although most of the coaches think he never will.

I have told the men that I do not wish them to spend the time between their meals and practice in the afternoon, or games, as the case may be, in playing billiards, as the doing so invariably takes the edge of a man's activity off, and is likely to slow him up very decidedly.

I received a letter from Yost, the Michigan coach, to-day in answer to an inquiry I made concerning the detail of the method he uses in passing the ball back from center. I turned it over to Mr. Lewis.

The Williams team is apparantly pretty strong this year, and I have felt a little uneasy as to the probable outcome of the game. Our ends are so green that I very much fear trouble in that way, and our kickers are very slow also, which is an added disadvantage. We shall spend part of tomorrow improving the kicking game as much as we can. The worry is beginning to take hold of me and it is mighty uncomfortable.

Friday, September 29, 1905

Morning:

I spent the morning in Boston talking with Mr. Burr, the father of Freshman Burr who is the best kicker on the squad, weighs 200 lbs. and will probably make a good guard. The father has been unwilling to allow him to try for the Varsity because the boy had typhoid fever exactly one year ago, and because he feels if the son tries to play it will worry him so he will not be good for anything, and may perhaps be good for nothing next year. If he plays on the Freshman this year, he will be a good man for the Varsity next year. Mr. Burr was very pleasant about it but told me that the boy's two uncles and the family physician joined with him in feeling that it was more than the boy ought to attempt this year, and therefore, he did not wish him to try. Personally, I think that Mr. Burr is pretty nearly right, but I am going to try and see if I cannot bring it about so that the boy may have sort of a preliminary trying out to see how things will go. What I expect to do is to give him breaking through work with the Varsity squad but not to line him up except on [the] Freshman team, and then to give him, if his father is willing, later on, a chance for Varsity experience.

I tried to see Waters and Cabot, neither of whom have been out to speak of since the season opened, but missed them both. I did, however, have a good talk with Malcolm Donald in which I urged him to come out and asked him when he could come out. He tells me that he can't tell when he will be out or for how long, and is so undependable therefore, as to make me give up any thought of getting any help from him.

Afternoon:

The early part of the practice was the same as usual to-day. Waters, Lewis, Bowditch, Cabot and Daly were on hand and Bowditch put the ends through various steps for the benefit of Cabot, while Waters watched the line men and gave them some points on blocking for kicks and getting away down the field. We finished up with some considerable signal work for both squads A & B and for those who did not belong to either. I had some of the men do some goal kicking, and we had quite a little punting, although Kernan was not able to be out. Starr wrenched his ankle a little yesterday but did not tape it until to-day, and I thought it wise to lay him off over the Williams game and hope that by Monday he will be all right. Newhall will have to play tomorrow. The line-up we talked over and discussed and got it in shape so that we may make the substitutions which we hoped for in the proper order, especially from the standpoint of having a kicker on the team all the time.

Saturday, September 30, 1905

Morning:

This morning I accomplished very little as I got pretty well worried over the game. I spent a portion of the morning at home making over various notes that I had taken and trying to keep my mind off the game. I had luncheon at home and went down to the Locker Building early in order to see the men and look them over and talk with the coaches. The game began at 3 o'clock and we played a 15 and a 10 minute half, the weather being fairly suitable. We sent the team in in the following order to begin with:

O'Brien, left end; Brill, left tackle; McFadon, left guard; White, center; Peirce, right guard; Squires, right tackle; Leary, right end; Newhall, quarter back; Foster, left half back; Wendell, right half back; Hanley, full back.

Just before the men were sent on to the field I got Mr. Lewis to make them a short talk to urge them to do their best. He made them an exceedingly good one, which ran about as follows:

"Up to the present time you fellows have been getting ready for the opening of the foot ball season. You have been practicing for your first opportunity to play; to-day you are to have that opportunity and we want to urge you to make the most of it. What are you going to write on the first page in the book containing a record of the foot ball team for 1905? Are you going to allow a blot or are you going to allow the page to be kept clean?

["]The men on the squad are almost all of them untried and there are a good many of such men. Every man on the squad cannot be given as many opportunities to do things as we should like to give them. It is necessary then, that whenever any man has an opportunity that he should make the most of it. Those of you who go into the game to start with this afternoon have your opportunity—see that you *do* make everything of it that you can.

["]When you go on to that field remember that you are Harvard men and that your opponents are men from Williams. Go out there with a little pride of place in your bearing and play up hard against your opponents from start to finish. Remember that no team is stronger than its weakest man, and that if one man on either team is stronger than his opponent in that same position, there is a basis for winning through that position alone. Outplay your opponent individually; keep at him.

["]Now line men, the backs can gain in only two ways, around the line and through the line. The question is where they can gain the best, and that depends in a large measure and almost wholly on what you do in giving them a chance to play. Open up holes, charge your opponents back, help your line men to keep their feet, play hard and fight."

I am sorry that I cannot think of the other things that Lewis said because it seemed to me that they were very excellent, but I think his talk was an exceedingly good one for a start. I added a few remarks about as follows:

"Remember that Harvard graduates all over the country and Harvard people in general are going to turn their faces toward Soldiers Field to-day to see what you fellows are doing. Everybody is watching, waiting and hoping. What message are you going to send back as a result of the game? What is played to-day can never be played over again. This time will leave you never to return. You have got to face what you do to-day so long as foot ball history of Harvard College lasts. Make that history something that you can look at with pleasure. Williams has come down here to-day not to tie you fellows, but to beat you and she expects to do it. Are you going to let a small college come down here and do anything of that kind? If you are, we might as well stop now as any time.

["]I want you to go out on that field, take that ball and never let it go until you put it across that goal line. As Mr. Yost says, here is the foot ball, it is an express package, I deliver it to you and expect you to take it to its destination, which is behind that goal line, without delay or derailment. Remember if you are tired, that the men on the other side are just as tired and you must keep everlastingly at them."

After this I asked several individuals if there was any reason why there were not ready to fight. They said there was not and that they would fight, whereupon I gave the quarter back several instructions. In the first place I instructed him to kick always inside of our own 25 yard line and to kick on first or second down so as to be sure that a poor pass or fumble might not end in a serious situation. I told the quarter back to stop and look at the opposing team and see what the defence was and keep his eyes open and think. As Starr had wrenched his ankle I sent in Newhall, the quarter back, to take his place and try him out.

I found on weighing myself after the game that I had lost six pounds since the beginning of the season, weighing now only 159 pounds. I am, however, having all my meals regularly and go to bed on time so that I feel as though I were doing everything in my power to stay in good condition. This was one of the points that I made in 1901, and I want to see if I cannot do better than I did then, when I worried myself into a state of practical uselessness.

I had the manager make a plan of the game as it progressed in order that we might have a record of it to study afterwards and to criticise with the men.

Williams won the toss and took the wind, giving us the kickoff. Brill, who kicked off for us, kicked the ball to the Williams 5 yard line, where the man was down with only 4 or 5 yards gain. Williams then made a first down[30] and then kicked from her 10 or 12 yard line to her own 40 yard line where we took the ball and with straight dives and cross bucks scored in 4 min. 20 sec. White kicked the goal. Brill kicked off again, this time kicking over the goal line apparently forgot that the opponent might run it back if they didn't yell "down". Williams tried to have the kick made over again but our men refused and Williams tried to force them to stand on the 30 yard line allowing Williams to kick out from the 30 yard line, which our men again refused to do. The kick out which followed went to our 45 yard line, where Hanley after allowing the ball to bounce picked it up and ran it to the opposing 49 yard line, from where the team again carried the ball over in steady rushes; White again kicking the goal. During these rushes I replaced Foster with Nesmith, Foster having gotten out

30. In 1905, a team had three attempts (downs) to make five yards or relinquish the ball to the opposition. In 1906, the rule was three attempts for ten yards, and in 1912, the current rule of four downs to make ten yards was instituted.

of his head from a blow on it, and seeming not to know what he was doing. We kicked off again, the ball going to Williams' 15 yard line, and being brought back 10 yards since the kick was low. An end play brought the ball to their 45 yard line, Leary being easily circled on a fake kick. Harvard was held for three downs and on the fourth down was penalized for off side, which gave Williams the ball first down on their own 51 yard line.[31] They lost 4 yards in the next play and then kicked 30 yards to our 35 yard line, when Newhall fumbled and Williams recovered the ball. Williams then advanced the ball to Harvard's 20 yard line with the assistance of 5 yards as penalty where Harvard got it and were given 15 yards for holding, after which they carried the ball to our own 42 yard line only to lose 15 yards because the quarter back ran with the ball beyond the line of scrimmage. We immediately kicked 45 yards 10 of which were run back, when time for the first half was called. With penalties, fumbling in the back field and more penalties, the latter part of this half was very poor foot ball. We allowed the men no water during the line-up and simply allowed each man to rinse his mouth out between the halves.

We started off the second half with Grant in O'Brien's place; Cunniff in White's place; Hall in Leary's place; Leonard in Foster's place, Nesmith in Wendell's place; and later on I sent Quigley out in Newhall's place; Boyd in Hanley's place.

Williams kicked off to us on our 15 yard line. The ball was brought back 15 yards to our 30 yard line, from which place Leonard kicked almost 60 yards including the roll of the ball, Hall touching the ball on the bounce on Williams['] 22 yard line. Williams then tried a kick, but the pass was high and the full back was downed on Williams' 7 yard line. Instead of blocking the kick Harvard allowed the kick to be made and the ball was recovered on Williams' 25 yard line. From there with small plays the ball was carried to Williams' 11 yard line, when Newhall made a poor pass to Leonard and Williams got the ball. Williams was forced to kick and we recovered the ball just about at the center of the field. Hall was called upon to kick for us here and his kick was blocked, Williams getting the ball. Harvard took the ball from Williams on downs on our own 45 yard line and carried it to the 50 yard line, where a distance penalty was given which forced us to kick, the kick being about 55 yards 10 of which were recovered by Williams' catcher, who got around outside our ends. Williams was held for downs and

31. The playing field had been 110 yards long since 1881. It was reduced to a hundred yards with a fifty-yard midfield line in 1912 and a ten-yard end zone in which a forward pass might be caught. The final score was Harvard 17, Williams 0.

Harvard got the ball on Williams' 45 yard line, where she was penalized 10 yards. At this junction Nesmith took the ball on an end run for 37 yards, placing it on Williams' 25 yard line. From here it was rushed to Williams' 11 yard line, when time was called.

Williams had only a fair team and we ought to have scored at least twice more. In all we lost 40 yards by fumbles, a kick in the back field, an equal amount by having one of our kicks blocked, besides a total of 45 yards on penalties of one kind or another. Those penalties were due to over anxiousness on the part of the players, who seemed to be working with pretty good spirit. The quarter backs did not use very good judgment and tried to get buck plays instead of carrying the ball over long distances of the field by end runs, which could have been played pretty effectively. On the whole the game was a very good chance to try out a good many men and to see that in all probability neither Leary nor Hanley will do.

Immediately after the game I formed two teams and went through signals with them and had line-ups, with Waters, Lewis, Marshall, Cabot, Lawrence, and several other coaches on hand to witness it. The work was very fierce and there were several injuries, though they were not serious, much chance to see ends running down on kicks, and further chance to see back field work. Somes, a substitute full back, showed up in good form and I shall watch him on Monday. After this work was over we had a coaches meeting, at which Dr. Nichols, Waters, Lewis, Cranston, Dunlop and Brown were present. We discussed the work in general and the program for next week. We decided to have Monday a day largely of drill, and Waters and Lewis have both promised to be out ready for it. I will not attempt here to give an outline of the detail of the work, since that will come in Monday's account.

I took the 8:13 train for Cohasset where I spent Sunday in trying to rest up and forget the worry.

Monday, October 2, 1905

Morning:

I came up from Cohasset on the 9:11 train this morning and went at once to see Edgar Wrightington in order to talk over with him several questions on the season. We talked over different individuals on the team and I think we agreed pretty well as to the capabilities of the different men. He agrees with me that it is practically out of the question to make a kicker, that the men of kicking ability must be forced on to the team somewhere and by thus doing be given a chance to exercise their natural ability, rather than to try to develop that ability in a man who can otherwise make the team. Hoyt, who kicked for Yale last year, was, I am told the poorest player that they have had there in some time, and he was kept on the team entirely for kicking.

We talked over the advisability of playing the guards four yards back instead of 3-½ in order to help in the end runs and also in order to give the quarter back a little longer time to develop foot work in the passing of his position. He thinks it is a good plan. I told him about running a tackle around tackle in preparation for getting our tackles limbered up and he thought that too was a good thing, but he urges running the tackle in the tandem formation as soon as possible also.

After this I came out to Cambridge where I had some considerable talk with Ted Meier on the question of coaching the Freshmen. We went over the plan of work pretty thoroughly and the whole Freshman squad will be called out to work this afternoon. I went home for lunch.

Afternoon:

I had the backs down and dressed at 3:30 to-day in order to give them practice in kicking and catching and the centers practice in passing. The day was rather hazy, and the men muffed a good deal. I spent considerable time showing them how to go about it. Starr, Foster, Wendell, Lincoln, Nesmith, Leonard, Hanley, Guild, Somes, Dignowity comprised the squad.

Immediately after the main squad appeared on the field, I ran them through signals, squads A & B twice up and down the field, and then we had a line up of a 10 and a 5 minute half. We gave the team the tackle around tackle play in signal practice and rehearsed it pretty carefully. In the scrimmage White passed so poorly for punts that I put him off the field and brought Cunniff over in his place. The punting was fair although we did not have so much of it as I had hoped for, since Kernan did not show up. We had Parker running through signals, but did not let him play because he has an iron protection on his leg which is not yet properly padded. I tried out Spear, tackle, for a few minutes, and his leg gave out. I also gave Guild a little work at full back. In the midst of the scrimmage he had to retire from a crack which the Doctor said had done him no harm.

Just previous to the line up I had Brill kick off several times and had the line men catching the kick off in the back field in order to get them accustomed to handling the ball. The practice was hard but neither side was able to score, each side knowing the other's signals and playing to a certain extent for them.

Dunlop, working with the backs a little while before the scrimmage also, showed them how to start and run, while Bowditch took a bunch of about 20 men that I gave him to find out what there was among them in the way of material. Just as soon as I find a man won't do in one position I am trying to see if he won't do somewhere else.

After the scrimmage was over the line men reported for practice in blocking and breaking through, to Waters and Lewis, while I put two or three other teams through signals to try the men out somewhat. Newhall has been playing a splendid game particularly on the defence, and I expect he will make a hard fight for a place. We had some considerable kicking. I am trying to get out all the men in college who show any signs of being able to play, and have given the manager a list of men to hunt up. We are greatly in need of a full back and I am trying every man on the squad to see what we can do.

After supper I gave the squad a talk of about an hour and a half on the game, of Saturday. First I had each man who played in the game give me two criticisms of the game as he saw it and I got some very intelligent answers; among them were the following: the ends ran in too closely on the kick off and one of them got boxed in, there was too much consultation between the players instead of taking natural intervals of time for consultations, the ends played too far away from the tackle at times enabling plays to go between tackle and end, where if the tackle didn't get the man, the back was sure to gain something. The tackling was poor. We lost 45 yards on penalties, the line played too high, the passes were poor for kicks, the line men were over anxious, the spirit was good, Grant, the end, was fooled on a fake kick, there was a let up in the play immediately after one of our kicks was blocked and after one of our backs dropped a kick in the back field, the backs got off very slowly, the backs did not keep their feet, one of our kicks was blocked, and none on the other side, the fumbles from the back field were frightful, the line was too anxious to get off on kicks and did not hold long enough.

After this I drew out on the board diagrams of the play and showed the men where they had lost opportunities of scoring. As will be seen by the chart, the first opportunity came when Williams kicked from her own 5 yard line and got the kick off. For the rest of the time, until we had scored twice, pretty good foot ball was played except that end runs were not tried frequently enough. The first opportunity we lost was, then, in not blocking Williams' first kick; the next blunder came when Williams kicked and our back field man dropped the ball and Williams got it; then came several penalties for holding and off side and going beyond the line of scrimmage with the ball and the block kick. All of that happening in succession made a frightfully poor showing. Then penalties again in the second half where Harvard was unable to get moving. Among other things the men failed to follow the man over the goal line on a kick off which Brill kicked across the goal line and from which Williams made a touch back, not because our men forced it, but because they chose to. Our men knew where to play on the kick out after the touch back, but did not know how to line up to receive it. This point I straightened out, since they line up exactly as they do to receive a kick off. Hanley allowed the punt out to bounce which was poor foot ball. Then the quarter back fumbled in passing to Lawrence on the 10 yard line, where he lost the opportunity for a third score. These points I took up and also added the fact that White in making his goal kicked from the 17 yard line which was almost a good sized place kick. I called to mind, too, the necessity for giving the men more work in fundamentals—in kicking, catching, passing, etc. which we have been neglecting for the last few days. I want the ends to know how to box the opposing tackle, because that is one of the fundamentals of end work. I have asked Bowditch to take that up tomorrow.

After the talk was over, Lewis, Brown, Capt. Hurley, and I came down to the office and looked over lists of men to see what we could find in the way of other material to try out, and we also discussed one or two details in the play. At 10:30 we broke up and I went home.

Tuesday, October 3, 1905

Morning:

This morning the first thing I did was to look up Frevert, a big 220 lb. man, among the best sc[h]olars in college, who has not been out before. I found him in the Chemical Laboratory, and after talking with him a half hour succeeded in getting him out, at any rate for the next few days. I expect to make things interesting enough for him so that he will come out regularly from then on, as we need his brains very much.

Cavanee, a 206 lb. guard, who has not been out before and has never played foot ball before, and whom I got out Monday afternoon, and whom Waters said was the most intelligent and anxious man to learn he had run across. He came around to the office and I gave him some reading matter so that he might pick up all he could. He is taking hold finely and I am in hopes that he may be able to do something before the season is over. Waters and Lewis both spent considerable time with him yesterday and he shows very good spirit and is very enthusiastic about it, coming up into the room yesterday to find out what he could do in order to get himself in better shape. This morning he told me he had been doing the exercises and motions which Waters had showed him 150 times more than he needed to. If we could only get this response from other men on the team we should have a very effective product. I also got hold of Knowlton, who played here in 1904 and who is now back at the Law school. I urged him to come out and tried to persuade him in every way I could, but finally had to give him up for the day, although I mean to bring influence enough to bear on him to bring him out. He is in splendid condition, and after two years in an Iron Foundry, ought to play better than he has ever done before.

I had a long talk with Herbert White also, because I felt pretty blue over the situation and because he is always a splendid man to talk with under those conditions. We discussed the necessity for following up the Penn men to find out whether they were eligible, and he has consented to take the matter in hand. I gave him all the data that I know of and he is going to New York to see [Henry Beech] Needham, who is writing for McClures Magazine,[32] and who is said to have already material enough on hand to make it very uncomfortable for Penn. Mr. White is trying to find out about this before the article comes out, so that we can get evidence against the men before Penn is able to cover the situation up.

I have written a letter to [Edward] Coolidge[33] out in Colorado asking him to look up Lamson, who I am sure played on the Colorado college team and I shall write in a day or two to Collins, a teacher in my school,[34] to find out what he can tell me about Lamson or Zeigler, one or the other of whom he played on the team in Colorado with.

White says that the men on the squad are quite enthusiastic at the way things are going and say that they have never had foot ball presented to them in so pleasant a way before. I hope this is so and I shall try to keep it so.

After seeing these different men I dictated until lunch time when I went home.

32. Needham, one of the muckrakers of the Progressive period, had already written "The College Athlete," a two-part series for *McClure's Magazine* 25 (June 1905): 115–28, and 25 (July 1905): 260–73.

33. Reid likely is referring to Edward Coolidge, who played baseball at Harvard with Reid and was a letter-winner from 1900 to 1903. It is possible that he is referring to William E. Coolidge, a Harvard baseball letter-winner (1879–84) and a football letter-winner in 1882.

34. Reid probably is referring to his father's Belmont, California, preparatory school, the Belmont School, at which he was assistant headmaster before assuming the football position at Harvard.

Afternoon:

After lunch I was interviewed by a female reporter from the Boston Herald, whom I finally turned over to the manager because she was asking such foolish ignorant questions.

I went down to the field and was dressed at 3, when I took out the centers and backs for passing, kicking and catching practice. Kernan took charge of the kickers, and I took the kickers[35] with Dunlop. Dunlop took the men who were not actually catching and gave them some work starting. I gave the backs also, some practice in falling on the ball at different angles and in different ways. Starr and Newhall I find do not give enough with the ball as they catch it and find difficulty in changing the ball properly. Starr has been giving only with his arms and not with his body, and has, consequently, been having the ball hit him up on his chest. I showed him how by dropping one or the other leg back he was able to drop his body as far away from the ball as he needed to, thereby making up by the length of the backward step for any misjudgment in calculating the flight of the ball. In the matter of plain judging the ball, I showed them how to watch the flight of a ball so as to figure out how the ball is traveling. How when it does not travel according to physical laws it wabbles in the air. And I tried to instill into the men confidence in their ability to catch. Before the practice was over they were doing pretty well. I shall keep at this so as to make our quarter backs absolutely sure kickers.[36]

Just as soon as the main squad reported on the field I gave the ends in charge of Coach Bowditch for practice in falling on the ball, and the line men from tackle to tackle to coach Lewis for practice in tackling the dummy. Waters took Cavanee and one or two other green men and gave them some very elementary work. White kicked goals and Dunlop and I spent a little time in showing the quarter backs how to hold the ball properly for the kicker. After the various squads were done with their work, we put the squad through signal practice twice up and down the field, and then we lined the men up for a scrimmage of 10 or 12 minutes. They played hard and neither side was able to score. After the practice Waters took a portion of the line men to one side of the field and talked to them, and made them run about the goal posts to limber them up. Then I sent them in. Meanwhile I lined up a squad of substitutes and put them through practice and then we had quite a line up against a team which Bowditch put to-

35. Reid probably meant "catchers."
36. Reid again likely meant "catchers."

gether and which played very well. After considerable work of this kind, I took the men who were left and looked carefully through the whole squad for a full back. We are unable to find a full back, and I did not succeed in locating one this time out of the 10 men whom we t[h]ought might possibly do. I want if possible to get a line man so that we may be able to back up the center in good shape, leaving our two rush line half backs on the outside to do the more active work. We gave Foster no line up work in the afternoon because of his looking a little tired and I want to use him tomorrow.

Kernan and I went to the Freshman field and looked over the Freshmen and found no man there who would do for a full back.

Frevert came down to the field and Waters and Lewis took hold of him and he became quite enthusiastic over the work, he has a locker and plans to come out regularly. I hope he will keep to his resolution as I am sure he will make a good man for us before we get through.

I was to have had a meeting of the men on rules tonight, but after the very long practice which we gave them I decided it would be better not to fill their minds with any more foot ball for the day.

After supper, Capt. Hurley, Dunlop, Kernan and I went over the entire card catalog to see if we could not find a full back and found that there was very little on hand that looked at all promising. The loss of [Charles] Osborne is one of the most serious losses we have had. I got to bed at about 10:30.

Wednesday, October 4, 1905

Morning:

I did very little this morning except dictate and see Mr. Love about McLeod and MacDonald who are men we need badly on the squad, but who through technicalities of one kind or another are not eligible as yet and may perhaps turn out to be ineligible anyhow.

Afternoon:

Right after lunch I made out a list of the men whom I want to try out in the game this afternoon, and then went down to the Locker Building, and after running the gauntlet of half a dozen reporters and other men, I finally got up stairs. When the men were dressed and ready I gave them a little talk and so did Capt. Hurley, then we took them out on to the field. Before going out and before talking to our men, however, I went around to see the Bowdoin men to be sure that they were in comfortable lodgings.

The team started off with,—

Cunniff, center; Parker, left guard; Peirce, right guard; Brill, left tackle; Squires, right tackle; O'Brien, left end; Burnham, right end; Nesmith, quarter back; Foster, left half back; Hanley, full back; Wendell, right half back.

After running through signals we had something of a row with the Bowdoin men as to the length of the halves. We wanted to play two 15 minute halves, but they would not agree to it. The best we could finally do was to have two 12-½ minute halves. As the day was very hot, I did not press for longer halves, although hereafter we shall have to have them anyhow.

We lost the toss and Bowdoin took the wind, giving us the kickoff. The Bowdoin team was very light and in very poor condition. Brill kicked off [to] the 2-½ yard line where the Bowdoin man ran the ball in to the 25 yard line, where Bowdoin kicked the ball landing it on our 40 yard line, where our backs took it straight down for a touch down, a distance of 70 yards. Cunniff made a bad pass at the goal. The ga[in]s were not as big as they ought to have been and there was not the fight in the men. We gave them, to be sure, very hard and long practice yesterday, and they seemed, several of them, tired and I think tomorrow we had better give some of them a good rest. Bowdoin kicked off again, the kick being blocked by Cunniff since it went very low. It bounded back very nearly [to] the center, where the Bowdoin man fell on it. Bowdoin fumbled it once and Harvard got the ball. We fumbled it and Bowdoin in two or three rushes carried it to our 45 yard line where they kicked. Several very poor kicks were returned here of 15 yards until finally Bowdoin had the ball at the time the whistle blew on their own 15 yard line and we had scored only once.

It must be remembered in these accounts that under the rules the teams change goals after every touch down which would account for the apparent mixing up of the ball.

In the second half we put in:

Hall, right end; McFadon in Brill's place; Grant in O'Brien's place; White in Cunniff's place; later on I sent in Spear, tackle; Leonard, half; Somes, full back; Nesmith, half back; Kersburg as guard in Parker's place.

Bowdoin kicked off to us on our 20 yard line but the ball was brought back 20 yards, where after one play, we kicked 30 yards. Bowdoin tried rushing but was unable to gain; then tried to kick, the pass going high. Spear and Wendell got the man and took the ball away from him on Bowdoin's 5 yard line. Squires on tackle around tackle play took the ball over. White kicked the goal. Parker kicked off to

Bowdoin's 20 yard line; the kick was carried back 5 yards, Parker tackling the man. Harvard took the ball away on downs on the 25 yard line, where holding on the part of Parker caused us to be penalized 15 yards, where again holding by McFaden caused us to lose 15 more, which took away a chance to score. We kicked back and forth a couple of times and one of their backs fumbled the ball; Hall tried to fall on it but missed it and Bowdoin recovered it. Finally we got the ball on Bowdoin's 45 yard line and in six plays carried it over. There was a missignal on the goal line and Newhall having no one to pass the ball to stuck it under his arm and made a successful quarter back run for a touch down. The touch down was made at the extreme corner of the field and Leonard punted out,[37] after which White missed the goal,—Score 16-0. The chart appears on the opposite page [missing] where the game can be followed pretty closely. The encouraging things that happened were the line work of Parker, who constantly broke through the line and nailed his man for a loss, doing it no less than seven times in the game; the greater activity of Squires than he has shown heretofore, the work of O'Brien; the defensive work of Wendell; and tackles down the field by Grant and Burnham.

The unsatisfactory things of the game were lack of fight the men showed, the number of fumbles which happened both in the scrimmage and in the back field; the failure to fall on the ball successfully, the lack of drive in Peirce's work, Brill's absolute worthlessness, Foster's very poor kicking and the penalties.

After the game was over I lined up two other teams and set to work to try and find a suitable full back. I tried Carr, the tackle; [William] Corbitt, tackle; O'Connor, left half back; and [Clarence] Pell, tackle. Of these men, Carr did the best work with Corbitt a close second. Carr being especially effective in his defensive rushes, where he rushed continually into the line and filled up holes in it in the most effective manner. If he has the courage and fight which I hope he does I think he may help us out on our problem. Corbitt shows similar promise and I hope that out of the two I may get something worth while. Pell and two or three of the other men did not do very well. We had hopes that Phillip Mills[38] might possibly return, but I doubt if he will consider it since he has a seat in the New York Stock Exchange.

---

37. A punt-out could be made by the team that scored, from the place that the ball had been touched down, toward the center of the field. Then the team that scored could call for a fair catch of the punt-out and kick the extra point from that position. See James R. Church, ed., *University Foot-Ball* (New York: Charles Scribner's Sons, 1893), 117. The final score was Harvard 17, Bowdoin 0.

38. Mills was a 1905 Harvard graduate who was a football letter-winner (1902–4).

Bowditch tried out several of his ends and we found a new half back named Channing. He shows every promise of being a good man. All in all the afternoon taught us several things. In the first place, that Brill is probably not going to make the team, that Hanley is afraid of himself, that Carr stands a good chance, and that the men have had a little too much work. We shall try to remedy this just as soon as we can and hope tomorrow to be able to try out a number of other men and cut down the squad.

After supper, Lewis, Hurley, Dr. Nichols, Brown and I had quite a talk over matters and Connor, who is up at Exeter, told us considerable of what Hogan is teaching his men up there. We are certainly not having fierceness enough in our playing and we must get after this point at once. We must have some more work on fundamentals and must begin as soon as possible now to shape a team together. I had quite a talk with Lewis as to the method to be used in snapping the ball back from the center, and he and I are pretty well agreed that Yost's way will not do since it leaves the center after the pass in a very weak position and does not enable him to assist in making holes the way the other pass does. We shall probably go back to the style of last year, particularly after Lewis has gone to New Haven and has seen what Yale is doing. I would do a good deal to see Yale myself but cannot spare the time, although I hope next year, if I am here, that I may feel able to spare the time.

The matter of passing the ball back ought to be absolutely decided before the fall work begins so that the men may pass back from the start in the way which is to be finally adopted and not have to change around as is the case now.

Frevert has been out now for two days and is taking hold fine. A new man named Cavanee has also been out a few times and taking up the game fast.

I was very much worked up over the poor showing which we have made thus far and did not go to bed until quite late, working over the lists of men to see what I could find.

The quarter back used poor judgment to-day and we must get somebody else.

Thursday, October 5, 1905

Morning:

I spent the early morning to-day in looking up the eligibility of one or two men at the college office and talking with Dr. Nichols about laying the men off for a time, and in planning out the work for the afternoon. I tried to get one or two coaches on the telephone but could not, and finally dictated for a couple of hours on what has been happening during the last day or two. I also wrote out a notice for the [Harvard] Crimson asking for more men and better support. We simply have got to get more men out.

Afternoon:

I arranged to have Frank Hallowell and Norman Cabot out this afternoon and also arranged with Bowditch to give the ends a chance to show off their respective abilities. I also decided to try for a cut down of the squad as we have too many men out now and are not as effective in our coaching as we ought to be.

I talked over several matters with Dr. Nichols and it seemed wise to him and to me and later to McMaster, whom we consulted, to cut out practice for six or seven men who have been doing hard work and who have not had any let up thus far; these men are,—Squires, Foster, Wendell, Nesmith, O'Brien, Peirce, and Starr.

At 3 o'clock I went to the field where I saw a man named [Eleazar] Boynton,[39] a Harvard man, who told me that he thought he could prove that Levigne,[40] full back on the Yale Eleven, one of the best buckers in the country, is a professional. I shall follow up the evidence to see what there is in it. It is undoubtedly true and the only question is whether the man who can give the information can be persuaded to do so.

After this I set the kickers all at work, who were not laid off. We spent some time on Burr and a man named Harding, who is a new man, and a candidate for half back, and also some considerable time in getting the centers passing back for the kicks. Quite a high wind was blowing and the kicking was poor. R. Connor came down from Exeter to help somewhat and I gave him for the time being a squad of men whom I have picked out for quarter backs. To get this squad I went through the entire squad and took out every man who seemed a possibility whether he had ever played quarter back or not. I am not satisfied with our quarter back showing and I want to get more men tried out for the position.

Lewis spent some considerable time on White and Cunniff in passing back. Bowditch and Hallowell and Cabot took all the ends and sent them down the field on kicks and had them tackling backs who

39. This is likely Eleazar Boynton, a Harvard track letter-winner (1901–2).

40. The man is likely J. N. Levine, who played fullback for Yale in the 1905 Yale-Harvard game.

were catching kicks. This lasted until the end coaches had had all of that they wanted. Meanwhile Waters had the line men from tackle to tackle and with help from Lewis gave them some good work in fundamentals. I had Cunniff kicking a few goals and then we had a line up for about ten minutes. In this line up Burr, the Freshman from Andover played splendidly, as did Cavanee, a green man who is just out and who had been doing splendid work. I put in Carr at full back on the first then Guild, while on the second I had Hanley and two or three other men. Carr was altogether the best man of the lot and was especially good on the defence, where he continually nailed men behind the line and tackled fiercely on plays through it.

Previous to this work I gave the candidates for full back instructions on how to hold the ball for bucks and some instruction on how to run, and instructions on what the assignments are in the different plays.

I propose to play Carr full back in the game on Saturday in order to see what he can do. The practice was very hard and the men seemed to wake up to it with a good deal of vigor, and if I can only keep the regular Varsity men feeling that they want to play as the men felt this afternoon in spite of the great heat, we shall get a great amount of fight out of the team.

I am very certain that we are giving our men, the best we have, more than they ought to do and I am going to see if we cannot get their wind up and their endurance without giving them a chance to get worn out by it. Dr. Nichols agrees with me.

The Freshmen had their first line up this afternoon and came around safely. I am going to watch them pretty carefully from now on to see that they are used in a sensible way. They need all the care we can give them.

After supper I had a long meeting in my office at the Union which lasted from about 7:30 until about 10:30. At the meeting were present Lewis, Waters, Kernan, Daly, Brown, Hurley, and Bowditch, all of my assistant coaches except Dunlop. The first question that I brought up was that of Burr. His father will not consent to have him play on the Varsity this year. He is by all odds the best kicker on the field and one of the most intelligent guards. Lewis and Kernan both want him out exceedingly. The question was whether it was wise to try to get him. He impresses me as being a big, young pup, not fully developed or over strong, and with a seeming frailness in spite of his size. The question is whether it is wise to take a chance of breaking him this year because of the present need rather than to save him and be sure of having him for next year when he will certainly be good. Waters raised the same question that I do, while Lewis and Kernan both insisted that they must have him. We finally agreed to two things. First, to keep him on the Varsity squad and give him breaking through practice and a certain amount of line up, taking particular pains however, that nothing is over done and yet that he learns everything, this work to be continued for two weeks without trying him in any outside game. At the end of that time we shall ask his father, if the boy has made good, if he won't let us take him onto the Varsity squad permanently. It is our feeling that we can bring this about by exerting pressure at the right time.

The next question I brought up was the question of Brill. Brill's playing at the Bowdoin game was about the worst performance I have ever seen in a Varsity player; he didn't make a single tackle, didn't do much in making holes, talked a great deal, and thoroughly disgusted everyone. It is my opinion that Brill has not got the mental capacity for being a tackle and I want to put him off for a few days on the Second and see if that will wake him up. He apparently thinks that he is one of the best men out and is also one of the best men in his position playing a game.

Waters told of a talk he had with Brill the other night in which Brill said to him among other things,— "What do you mean Mr. Waters when you Yell out to me on the field there before the grand stand that I am loafing or a quitter and making other remarks of that kind? I don't understand you." Said Waters,— "I mean exactly what I say." Whereupon Brill said, "you can't tell whether I am quitting or not, nobody knows that but me, and I haven't yet." Waters said that he had and there was a little argument for a few moments on that point. Brill also said that he could not stand being called a name that he said Waters used last year, which Waters never used and moreover, has never used. This little glimpse of Brill shows a tremendous amount of personal pride on his part and a great deal of conceit. It was my suggestion that Brill be put on the Second and tried at either guard or center. Here Lewis said that he did not want Brill in any of the three center positions, saying that if he was not good enough for the tackle position he was not good enough for the team. He said if Brill had playing ability he ought to play at tackle, and if he had not playing ability or sand, it was poor policy to play him at all. To my proposal at playing him at center, Lewis said he was likely to sulk and be undependable and perhaps handicap us in that way greatly at the time of one of the big games, whereas White or Cunniff could be depended upon, at any rate, to that extent. To my proposal that Brill be tried at guard where his headless bulling through the line would be more effective than at tackle, Lewis said that the same bullishness might not do any good at guard either and that Brill would probably sulk if played at guard. After some considerable discussion, it was finally decided to put Montgomery on the first tomorrow and to play him first in the game on Saturday. Meanwhile, to give Brill careful attention at tackle and to tell him that he was in danger of losing his place. If by next Tuesday he does not show the desired response we shall put him on the Second team and at the Second training table and either make or break him. Lewis is going to tell Brill that the coaches doubt him and also tell him that Waters says that he (Brill) has got the making of a tackle in him if he will do as he is told, in order to keep Brill from feeling that Waters is unjustly prejudiced against him. If, under discipline on the Second next week, Brill quits, all right, he will have shown himself up and lost everything in the eyes of the college. As Waters says, Brill has a body which, if its possibilities could be realized, would make one of the greatest tackles in the country, and we must try in every way to handle Brill so as to get that effectiveness out of him, but it must come pretty quickly, as Brill showed last year that if possible, he would loaf through the early part of the season and then try to play up big at the end. This he is not going to be allowed to do this year and he must deliver the goods right along.

After disposing of the Brill matter I got a list of the entire football squad, and read the whole list over, dividing the men into first and second squads. We have now too many men on the field to make it possible for us to give as careful individual attention to the first men as we ought to. Going over the list I put a label opposite each man "first" or "second". We stopped and discussed several men as we went along. The following men were put on the first squad:

First Squad

G. G. Ball, '08	End
H. B. Barney, '08	Centre
E. G. Bartels, '07	End
H. S. Blair, '08	End
W. M. Bird, S '08	End[41]
K. F. Brill, S '08	Tackle

41. *S:* Scientific School; *Sp:* Special Student; *G:* Graduate Student; *L:* Law School; *M:* Medical School; *no notation:* Harvard College undergraduate. What *"sS"* and *"sC"* stood for is not known.

E. L. Burnham, '07	End
F. R. Boyd, 1 L	H-back
A. C. Blanchard, '09	End
J. C. Bailey, '06	Tackle
F. H. Burr, '09	Guard
W. Z. Carr, '06	F-back
H. Channing, sC '08	H-back
F. Clark, '09	H-back
E. R. Corbett, '07	F-back
H. K. Craft, S '07	End
J. Cunniff, sC	Centre
F. R. Dick, '08	End
J. V. Dignowity, S '06	F-back
H. Foster, '07	Tackle
G. Gilder, '08	Q.b.
P. Grant, '08	End
H. L. Hall, '07	End
W. A. Hanley, '07	F-back
H. Inches, '08	End
H. E. Kersberg '07	Guard
R. C. Leonard, '07	H-back
C. B. Lincoln, S '08	H-back
J. F. McDonald, '08	End
D. McFadon, 1 G.	Guard
M. McLeod, S '08	Guard
J. M. Montgomery, '06	Tackle
F. H. Nesmith, '06	H-back
M. L. Newhall, '08	Q.b.
J. S. O'Brien, '09	End
B. Parker, '08	Guard
W. Pierce, '07	Guard
R. A. Pope, Sp	End
R. A. Quigley, 2 M	Q.b.
H. R. Snyder, 1 L	H.b.
L. R. F. Spear, Sp	Tackle
D. B. Somes, '08	F.b.
D. R. Sortwell, '07	Q.b.
B. H. Squires, '07	Tackle
D. B. Starr, '08	Q.b.
J. H. Timmons, S '08	Q.b.
J. S. Wendell, '08	H.b.

F. H. White, '08	Guard
Witherby,	End
Cavanee, 2 L	Tackle

Second Squad

A. C. Blagden, '06	End
W. A. Brown, '06	Guard
S. Bowles, '08	H-back
J. J. Dearborn, S '07	F-back
E. F. Fish,	F-back
S. Fraser, '07	Center
M. B. Giddings, '08	End
J. B. Greenebaum, '08	H-back
R. B. Gring	H-back
R. F. Guild, '07	F-back
L. B. Harding, '08	H-back
J. S. Heilborn, s S	End
B. S. Horkheimer, 2 L	Center
W. M. Hurd, 1 L	End
G. Irving, Sp	Tackle
W. Mac K. Jones, '07	F-back
E. M. Keays, '07	Tackle
H. Kempner, S '08	Q.b.
H. C. Knoblauch, '08	H-back
J. D. Knowlton, S '08	H-back
L. H. Leary, 2 L	End
P. C. Lockwood, '07	End
H. F. Miller, s S	H-back
L. G. Morris, '07	Q.b.
E. F. Myers, '07	H-back
H. W. Nichols, '07	End
F. J. O'Connor, 2 L	F-back
J. B. O'Hare, '08	End
J. Palmer, '06	End
A. J. D. Paul, '06	Tackle
E. V. B. Parker, '08	End
C. C. Pell, '08	Tackle
F. R. Pleasanton, S '07	nd
J. F. Russell, '07	Tackle
W. M. Shoho, '07	H-back
H. R. Shurtleff, '06	End
H. Sibley, '07	Tackle

G. B. Simmons, '07	End
Metcalfe,	Q.b.
O. Smith,	End
B. T. Stephenson, S '08	End
R. H. Williams, '06	Q.b.
Whitney,	
Sargent,	End
Risley,	End

Having subdivided the squad in this fashion, we also changed some of the positions on the team. The question of using White at centre came up, and of Parker's playing guard instead of centre. After Parker's playing at guard at the Bowdoin game I felt that there was not much argument in Lewis' statement, that he certainly was too active altogether to tie down in the centre. That being the case, and it seeming likely that he might get hurt, also it seemed hardly wise to Lewis, and all of us agreed with him to put Parker in where he would not get laid up, thus leaving us at almost anytime in the season perhaps without a varsity centre or rush. With the new style appliance which Dr. Nichols has put on him he will last at guard as long as anywhere, and will make a good man for us as long as he plays. If White, however, plays centre, the chances are pretty small that he will get hurt, and he is a splendid man there for stubborn holding of the ground, which the centre is usually called upon to do. While as between Parker and White for guards there is no comparison between the two in mobility. Lewis thinks he could make a good centre out of White, and it seems wise for us at the present to keep him there. I do not feel at all satisfied with White at centre however, because he lacks aggressiveness, and I shall watch carefully to see if we cannot find somebody else who will do as well. Cunniff to my mind will never make a satisfactory man. Lewis wants Parker at left guard, and for right guard Burr, Peirce and McLeod. I have already talked over the Burr question, and it is now simply a question as to whether it seems wise to try to get him to play this year. Peirce has thus far been a great disappointment showing none of the fight for which he was so well commended last year. I am inclined to give him a try at tackle, since I think that he may feel too cramped up at guard.

McLeod is a man whose ineligibility is not as yet settled and he may or may not be able to play. I shall know by Monday, however. He looks like a pretty fair man. At left tackle there are Spiers, Montgomery and Brill. We have already discussed the Brill matter, and will now take up the Spiers and Montgomery.

Spier[s] is twenty-seven years old, weights 190 lbs., loves the game and plays it finely, but has a weak knee. We are having at present a steel brace made for it, and when it comes we shall put Spiers in and give him a thorough try out. I am a little uneasy about the prospects of his getting through safely.

Montgomery is a hard player and a fighter, muscle bound somewhat, but has a very good head and very fair possibilities for a man weighing 180 lbs. He is not altogether heavy enough for an ideal tackle, but for all that he is better than Brill as Brill has been playing lately. We decided to play him the first half of the game against Main[e] on Saturday.

A[t] right tackle there are Squires, Kersberg, Fultz, Cavanee and Frevert. Squires has a fine build, and Waters says that if he can get a good chance to talk all he wants to to Squires on the side, he thinks he will make a very fair man. He is a hard worker, strong but prone to getting overtrained. We therefore made up our mind to see that he was not overtrained, and to give him rather frequent lay offs.

Next to Squires is Kersburg, a man weighing about 196 lbs. and very aggressive. Lewis is working on him at present for the guard to[o], and it looks very much as though he might make something. At any rate he will make a very fair substitute. The only good quality about him is that he makes a splendid man carrying the ball.

Fultz is a 210 lb. man who has flat feet, and whom we have had under the doctor's care all of the spring. We have not seen him make a single tackle this season yet, and he has not been conspicuous in anyway, from which I have sized him up pretty well.

Frevert is a big strong man weighing 220 lbs. and pretty fairly awake for his build, but pretty green. He has a reputation as being an excellent boxer and is one of the best scholars in the university. He has only been out a couple of days, and it seems very probable that he won't be out much, as he says he is too busy. As he is an Austin Teaching Fellow, I judge that he really has all of the business he can stand, and I think he can hardly be considered a possibility.

At end we have on the left O'Brien, Bartel[s] and Grant. O'Brien is a freshman, green at his position, but who is doing very well. He weighs about 178 lbs.

Grant has football instinct, is a good tackle and does very well in boxing a tackle, but is impossibly slow in running. That being the case I do not see that it is much use spending more time on him. He looks to me like a second-class possibility.

Bartels does not weigh a great deal, but is otherwise pretty good. I am not satisfied to have him for the Varsity, not if it is possible to get anyone else any larger, as he only weighs 158 lbs.

Bill Reid as a sophomore fullback at Harvard, 1898. (Harvard University Archives)

Bill Reid, Jr. (right, standing) with his family, ca. 1901-2. Also standing are Reid's sister, Julia, and his brother, Charles Willard. Their parents, William T. Reid, Sr., and Julia Reid, are seated. (Thomas Stetson Personal Collection)

Christine Lincoln (on left), Bill Reid's fiancée, boards ship for Europe with her family, September 1900. (Thomas Stetson Personal Collection)

Mass tandem plays typified early 1900s football. Here, Bill Reid's 1901 team in tandem against Yale, a 17-0 Harvard win. (Harvard University Archives)

Walter Camp, "Father of American Football."

Harvard's tackle tandem play against Yale in 1905. (*Harper's Weekly*, December 9, 1905)

William H. Lewis (left), the first black All-American football player, became Bill Reid's assistant coach for the 1905 season. (Harvard University Archives)

Bill Reid demonstrates at the tackling dummy while trainer J. W. McMasters looks on. (*Harper's Weekly*, October 10, 1901)

Yale and Harvard before more than forty thousand spectators at Harvard Stadium, 1905. Yale won, 6-0. (*Harper's Weekly*, December 9, 1905)

Bill Reid during the 1905 Harvard football season. (Harvard University Archives)

On right end the men seemed to be Hall, McDonald, Burnham and Pruyn. Hall is probably the best end on the field but weighs only 158 lbs. I do not feel that he is big enough, and do not wish to have to play him unless it is absolutely necessary. He has kicking ability, which is one of the things we need on the team, but is slow in getting his kicks off. This I think we can remedy however. He is a fierce tackler, not afraid of anything and a pretty heady man. McDonald is in difficulty with the college office owing to a technicality. I am making every endeavor to get him released, because he is just as good as Hall in my mind and is quite a little bit larger.

Burnham is about 170 lb. man, is a hard player but hardly the build, being rather short and junky.

Pruyn, who was out last year has as yet done very little work, and I have not much of an opinion of his ability.

As I said, [I] am not at all satisfied with the ends, and I think there has got to be shift somewhere. We have got to have the eleven best men on the squad on that team somewhere, and if Hall has got to kick we will have to put him in at quarterback, where we have been trying him for the last day or two, even if by doing so we lose Starr. As I said to the coaches, it is all very well to carry a man on the team for his kicking ability alone, but it is absolutely out of the question to put a man on the rush line and carry him that way. We have got to have him capable of meeting anything on the rush line, while behind we may get along with one lame man for the sake of his kicking.

At quarterback Daly said the best we had were Starr, Newhall and Sortwell. He says that the fumbling that the quarters are doing now will certainly very quickly [end] and the quarters will hit their stride all of a sudden. I hope so. Newhall disappointed me very much in the Bowdoin game through his lack of thinking, and I am going to watch carefully to see whether he has the capacity for fighting. I rather think he has.

Quigley, who looked like a very promising man at the beginning of the season is probably not going to do owing to the combination of temperament and the lack of speed and general ability.

The left halves are Foster, Leonard and Channing. It is possible that Channing may not do, but we will find out as soon as we can give him enough playing to see. Foster I had hoped would be able to do the kicking, and therefore put him at left half. It seems likely that he will be unable to do it. This being the case it is a question of having Leonard play that position a good part of the time. I am teaching Leonard to go into the game. He is a very poor player thus far and with a peculiar disposition, and I question just what is going to come of him.

At fullback there are Carr, Cabot, Somes, Guild, Dignowit[y] and Hanley. Carr, by his work on the field this afternoon seemed to all of the coach[e]s to give the most promise for the fullback position, and we shall give him a try in the game Saturday. He weighs about 187 lbs. does splendid work on the defense, and pushes well. If he could only be taught to run with the ball and keep his feet and speed up I think he would do.

Corbett is another man of about the same type, although of a little less stockey build. He is, however, a good fighter, and may after the tackle experience pick up enough to play regularly on the team. It will be interesting to see how these two men work out. Personally I think if Carr does not get hurt he will prove to be the best man.

Somes is a pretty heavy man without apparently much head, who can be taught to push well and keep his feet especially well. That is the main reason he is in there.

Guild strikes me as being a man of fragile build with a great deal to learn. He is fast and plucky, but I believe is a man who will be getting constantly injured, and as such will hardly be dependable. This will, however work out.

Dignowit[y] is a big 190 lb. man, very slow in getting off and lacking push. He injured his shoulder in almost the first lineup, and I do not know yet what he can do.

Hanley has quit once or twice, and I have put him on the [second team] where he will be made to do or die. He played pretty well in the game against Bowdoin, but otherwise was only fair. His defensive work is poor, and he has not the confidence of his team mates.

At right half are Hurley, Wendell, Nesmith, Snyder and Lincoln.

Hurley needs no comment except that his leg is in poor condition, and I am very much afraid that he will not get through the year on it. The only thing to do is to give him a good long careful rest.

Wendell is next to Hurley the best back on the field. Stockey, strong, full of spirit and a good tackler and a good rush. He has got to be on the team somewhere if he has to go at end.

Nesmith weighs 170 lbs. and is a good hard player a good tackle and is going to make a tremendous struggle for the place. Just how we are going to arrange these backs so as to get the best out of them I cannot see, but something has got to be done. Snyder is a hard working, grittish spirited fellow of almost first-class ability. Just how he stands I have not been able to quite make up my mind.

Lincoln is light but has every other qualification for a back.

Having thus talked over the squad in detail I brought up one or two general points for discussion. In the first place the length of the practice. I have decided to have practice for the present begin at 3:30, feeling that in getting the backs out at 3:00 we are likely to tire them very decidedly and take the snap out of them, so until the darkness cuts us we shall begin at 3:30 with no early work for the backs who for that day are going to lineup. The backs must be kept full of life and spirit, and that means considerable rest.

The question of the programme of the afternoon came up, and Waters thinks that I am doing too much individual work on the field and that I can do better by doing more superintending. I think he is right, and I shall try to do this from now on. Another thin[g] that Waters suggested, and which I think was wise is, that in scheming out the afternoon[']s practice that we do a little on the various fundamentals each day, taking some days one portion of the fundamentals and on another others, so as to keep them all going and not have any of them neglected. This I shall do, and I shall begin it tomorrow.

We all decided we must have Knowlton out as a tackle, and Kernan and Bowditch are going to try to get him out at once. I want to get the team into as nearly its final formation as early as possible, so as to give the men every advantage that will come to them from playing regular in the same position as well as from the team work which comes from the association of one man with another as his neighbor.

Friday, October 6, 1905

Morning:

The first thing I did this morning was to have a talk with Herbert White over the telephone message that I had from Phil[a]delphia concerning a letter our Athletic Committee has sent to the University of Pennsylvania regarding our refusal to play a game with them next year. My idea in getting it off promptly was to see if I could not bring some pressure to bear on their Athletic Committee which should cause them to disqualify Draper who they are now playing on their team, and whom to my mind has no business playing there, it being a case like the Glass case which we disputed with Yale in 1901.[42] The letter which the Athletic Committee sent was simply a statement that we did not intend to be held for a game with Pennsylvania next year and that we proposed to be as free in arranging our game with them

42. Edgar Glass had played football for Syracuse in 1898 and 1899 before attending Mercersburg Academy, preparatory to entering Yale. He was ineligible by Yale's own rules, which required a year's attendance in such situations, but he would have played had he not been challenged by Harvard. See Walter Camp Papers, Box 22, "Cutts" Folder, Yale University Archives.

as we were with any other College. No explanation of any kind was given, but it was expected that they would gather what we were driving at.

Before I had left my house this morning I was called by McFadon of Phil[a]delphia, who said "Well Reid, the letter has come", making no statement of what the letter was or anything of the kind, but showing how greatly it had impressed him. He asked me if I would do him the favor to see that the facts were not given out to the newspapers, owing to the row they are having down there now with regard to the eligibility of their Captain. I did not give him much satisfaction, thinking I would let him stew a little while. He said to me, "Just what does that mean and how serious is it". I said I was not on the Committee and preferred not to discuss it. He then asked "Is it on the question of eligibility", and I said that I thought that might have something to do with it, whereby he said "If it is with regard to Draper, I do not see how the Committee here can possibly let him play".

I had a long talk with Herbert White over the thing, and we are going to get right at the matter of evidence against their men in combination with Cornell and any of the other Colleges that can help out. The political situation of affairs is splendid. Pennsylvania cannot get a game with either Princeton or Yale, and is hated by both. If we do not play her she will be dropped from the big four and her place will be taken by the team that play[s] in her stead. Realising this, they are very anxious that relations shall not be broken off. This gives us considerable leaverage on them, which we would be foolish to throw away. In my opinion we should always keep this game up for the power we have in the Intercollegiate circle, as so long as we have the Pennsylvania game Yale knows that we will not hesitate to break off relations with her (Yale) unless things go properly, whereas if we drop Pennsylvania and had no big game except Yale, Yale would have us in a pretty bad hole.

By getting Murphy at Phil[a]delphia, Penn has shown he[r] willingness to get ringers on her team because Murphy is a regular ringer getter, and as Dr. Nichols put it, Pennsylvania must be made to toe the mark or else be informed that Harvard does not consider her Penn contests worth while.

Herbert White was at New Haven yesterday and saw the practice, and aside from one or two little de[ta]ils, one of which was pretty good, I learned nothing new. One point worth keeping in mind is the fact that in catching kicks in the back field[,] number one back caught while the other said "high" or "low", shouting the position of the ball. This gets a certain amount of team work into these men while they are learning. I shall take that work up this afternoon. Another point which I had already felt was right was the fact that they did not have their backs catch a great number of kicks, but had them catching so long as they showed interest in it. The moment they began to lag they put in other backs. Herbert White commented on the greater system apparent on our field and the better economy of time than in New Haven, and says that he thinks that Sheldon has an awful swelled head. I hope he has, because every little helps.

I had something of a talk with Meier, the Freshman coach, about his work, and went to the College office to see about a couple of men. I also got Cavanee, the new green man that we have out, a chance to read some more football literature. He is picking up fast the points of the game, and shows good promise. From about 11 until 1 o'clock I dictated.

Afternoon:

At one o'clock I had luncheon at the Union, where I met Billy Garrison, who came out to talk over one or two things on the quarterback position. The two main points that he made were first, that the old idea of having the q.b. stand horizontal to the rush line was antiquated and no longer a common sense principle, that there was no reason why the quarterback should not face one way most of the time and thereby have a freer passage turning toward the runner at the same time and being able to get down much lower. The second point that he brought up was [. . .] that the ball should be caught by the quarterback [. . .] that it is handled more by the ends than by the middle, since it is difficult to handle a ball properly in the middle, whereas it is a very easy matter to handle it by the ends. These two points I told coach Daly at practice time.

After my talk with Garrison I went home for about three-quarters of an hour, and planned out the afternoon's schedule. I went down to the field at a little after three, having given the Managers several things to do. As soon as the squad came on to the field I divided them up into a first and second squad as we decided last night, turning over the second bunch of men to coach Brown, and divided the first squad up into three parts, giving Bowditch the ends, Montgomery a portion of the rest and myself the remainder. Then we had a lively practice falling on the ball, diving for it and going hard. This done I sent out to the dummy in charge of coach Dunlop and coach Brown the first squad for tackling work. Meanwhile I had Parker and Cunniff do some kicking off work, having several backs catching the kick offs. Starr was not able to lineup, so I had he and White kicking goals, spending a little time with each. Later on I had Cunniff kick some goals, and Brill several kickoffs. While I was doing this some of the second backs were set to work catching punts which Kernan's kickers were getting off, while Bowditch's ends ran down on the tackles. As soon as the main squad reported on the field I divided it into two teams, and Waters, Lewis, Marshall, Sargent, Bowditch, Kernan, Dunlop, Daly and I watched the various departments while our kickers were getting practice kicking with the line breaking through. Several kicks were blocked, but the line showed great improvement. The Varsity backs got into the back field and did much better than heretofore. We used a new ball in all of this work, since new balls are slippery and a good deal harder to handle. After this Lewis and Sargent worked on White and Cunniff, passing the ball back for kicks. After the breaking through work was done, in which Brill, who is on the second squad, showed more life, I sent the two teams through signal practice, and then lined them up for eight minutes of scrimmage work. The Varsity took hold in good shape, and carried the ball about sixty yards for a touchdown, Carr doing some excellent pushing for his backs and some fine work in keeping them on their feet. His defensive work was fine.

After the practice Dunlop took the rushline backs for a little talk on defense, and Waters took the linemen for a little, and then all of the men who had played were sent in. After this I lined up two other teams, sent them through signals and had another short scrimmage.

I had printed in the [Harvard] Crimson this morning the following appeal and two or three new men presented themselves as a result:

"The response thus far made to the urgent calls for more candidates for the University football team has been exceedingly disappointing. At present there are so few line men out as to seriously hinder the trying out of the men for other positions. Will not the student body take hold of the matter and see to it that every able bodied player reports at once? The prospects for a successful season are not bright and only the hardest effort on the part of the University at large can help us out of the difficulty."

After the practice I learned that Peirce had broken a small bone in his wrist and we shall lay him off for a time. I think that the laying off will probably do him good. Meanwhile we can give him some mental work.

Nesmith caught a fumble on the end of his shoulder in catching kicks, and being afraid that it might result in affecting the nerve, I did not allow him to line up and gave orders to have a special leather pad made for that shoulder for tomorrow's game.

Immediately after supper I went over in a three-quarters of an hour talk the game against Bowdoin, having traced it out on the board so every player could see it and see how every play was accounted for. I think the men learned a good deal from it and I hope that in the game tomorrow there may be some decided improvement. The points that we brought up in our discussion were, the kick offs were too low, that Parker broke through finely, that the backs ran blindly and did not keep their feet, that the line also lost its feet, that the end runs did not succeed, that in two or three occasions the men who went for the end did not get him, and kept on running out where they were no use at all. Hanley was pushing back on a buck because there was nobody to help him, Bowdoin got off several kicks before our men realized that the ball was about to be passed, the goal kicking was poor, the falling on the ball vile, and the penalties again altogether too prominent, and we did not use the wind to advance the ball. The tackling was poor and was altogether too high. Hall on his kick punted the ball over the goal line for a touch back instead of kicking it high up and trying to recover it on a fumble by opposing backs or by taking it away from them that close to the goal line. There was one case of missignals combined with poor judgement in calling the signals that were given. There was also too much slugging. I told them that I did not blame them for pitching into the men opposing them if they held them. I told them if they were going to try to take it out of their opponents they must do it when it was in the open and where they would not be disqualified for it.

We had a little singing at the piano and then Coach Daly took the quarter backs, first and second, off and gave them a little talk on generalship.

Dr. Nichols urged that just as soon as we found a man who is able to make the team that we do not keep hammering him against the next best man for the same position, but that we should change the men about so that they got drill and practice without getting worn out about it. Dr. Nichols said that we had always over worked rather than under worked our men, and that he was in favor of watching that point very carefully this year. He gave the men a little talk himself emphasizing these four points. The first thing he said was that any man who has diarrhea should report at once, that any man who had this trouble could not expect to take anything but milk and should keep quiet for a day or two, that in case of a scratch or bruise of any kind the greatest care should be taken to keep it clean no matter how slight the bruise was. The next thing he said was that in case any man in any game got hurt by a hit on the head so that he did not realize what he was doing, his team mate should at once insist that time be called and that a doctor come onto the field to see what is the trouble, also that every man on the squad must make up his mind in case he gets hurt, to have a friend with him from the time the injury occurred until noon of the next day, to prevent any serious results from beginning without anybody being around.

Hurley gave Cavanee quite a little talk on foot ball in general and reports that he knows a good deal even now about the game.

Saturday, October 7, 1905

Morning:

This morning I attended to correspondence and dictation all the morning getting my work up to date.

Afternoon:

I went down to the field just in time to get on my suit and make a talk to the men. I went over the main difficulties which they had had in the previous game and urged them to try and improve on them. Among other things, I laid particular stress on cutting out the holding, getting the ball in case of a fumble, hanging on to the ball when once it was in ones possession, blocking kicks on the other side and preventing any from being blocked on their side, more generalship, better work in the back field, no slugging, better goal kicking and more helping of each other along together with better keeping of the feet in rushing.

Capt. Hurley and I had a long argument as to the length of the halves. Anticipating that such would be the case, we went in and proposed two 25 minute halves, and as a matter of fact we really wanted a 20 and a 15 minute half. After my experience with the other teams we have played, I find it is necessary to make the proposition which may be torn down until one can get somewhere near what he wants. Of course we first asked the Maine Captain what halves he had thought of and he said a 15 minute and a 10 minute half, to which we would not agree. Finally, after much talking, we got the halves to 20 and 10 minutes, not insisting on the extra 5 minutes in the second half because the day was rather warm.

Squires was acting Captain.

Our team lined up as follows:

White Center. Parker and Kersburg, Guards.
Squires and Montgomery, Tackles. O'Brien & Hall, Ends.
Newhall, Quarter Back. Carr, Full Ba[c]k.
Wendell and Foster, Halves.

Maine kicked off to us and only kicked the ball 20 yards, Kersburg falling on it for us on our 40 yard line. With good judgment Newhall immediately tried two end plays, one on either side, in order to see if he couldn't make a long gain to the middle of the field. Failing in both, he ordered a kick and Hall punted to Maine's 35 yard line, a 35 yard kick. Maine started to rush here but fumbled and Wendall fell on the ball on Maine's 45 yard line. The team started off for what looked like a touch down and carried the ball to the 17 yard line when Parker held and we were put back 15 yards. We then had a fumble and Hall was called back to kick with the ball on the 30 yard line. Newhall reminded Hall not to kick over the goal line and Hall consequently kick[ed] the ball high up but without sufficient distance and Maine secured it after it had gone only about 8 yards. After three or four plays Maine fumbled the ball and a Harvard man got it on the 25 yard line, from which place it was put over. Parker then kicked off to Maine's 10 yard line from where the ball was brought back to the 20 yard line. After the plays Maine was forced to kick and we received the ball on Maine's 50 yard line, from which place the ball was taken over by steady rushes. Parker kicked off again. This time it only got to the 5 yard line, where Maine's back man fumbled and was downed in his tracks by Montgomery and Wendell. Harvard was held for downs, and Maine got off a kick although two or three men were almost on the kicker. It went 20 yards and O'Brien who was playing back attempted to catch it but was tackled and thrown back, and Harvard received 15 yards for interference, placing the ball on Maine's 10 yard line. A gain of 5 yards followed and on the second play the ball was taken over the line but Parker was holding and the ball was brought back to the 25 yard line where time was called before they had time to get it over.[43]

In the second half Parker kicked off to the goal line where Maine brought the ball back to the 16 yard line, where she was held for downs and tried to kick but Montgomery got through and blocked the kick and another score followed. Brill kicked off the next time to Maine's 5 yard line—the ball was brought back to the 15 yard line where Maine fumbled and Harvard got the ball. They carried it from there to the 6 yard line where Parker held again and the team was put back 15 yards. Under these circumstances Newhall called for a second kick and Leonard made all but 2 yards of the distance necessary to hold the ball. That gave Maine the ball on the 5 yard line. Maine was forced to kick and kicked 15 yards, the kick being almost

43. The final score was Harvard 22, Maine 0.

blocked. Harvard recovered the ball on the 21 yard line. A distance penalty in the first play put them back and we were finally obliged to give the ball to Maine on downs. Maine kicked to our 45 yard line after which Leonard tried to kick obliquely on the side line, but the ball bounced and rolled over for a touch down. A Maine man fell on the ball and our line men threw him hard, he dropped the ball and our men got it. Just then the whistle blew and as the Umpire refused to allow a touch down under the circumstances, the game was over.

We played, besides the first line up, Leary, at left half, Fultz, at right tackle because Squires broke a bone in his hand. We put in Burnham in place of O'Brien, who seemed logy, and Brill in the place of Montgomery, who seemed to be pretty well done up. Later on we put in Somes in place of Carr, and Nesmith in place of Wendell.

On the whole the game was something of an improvement, although if the men had handled the ball safely they should have scored twice more easy. Montgomery played a good game at tackle and I would give almost anything if he were only 10 lbs. heavier. Carr was rather disappointing at full back, but I believe he will improve as time goes on. The question of ends is giving me great concern as is the question of where to play Brill. He is a very promising man and it seems too bad to lose him entirely. I am going to force the coaches to decide this matter next week, because if Brill is to play tackle he needs all the work he can get there, and if he is going anywhere else he needs to same amount of work there.

Bowditch considers Grant one of his good ends, and I consider Grant an absolute impossibility, because he cannot run. The same is true of [Henderson] Inches, and it looks as though we should have to use a half back as end if nothing else turns up.

After the game was over, I put two more teams through signals, but had no line up on account of lack of men. Brown took his squad for work, Kernan took the kickers and gave them some dive work, also the backs, and Bowditch had the ends.

I went to Cohasset to stay over night.

Sunday, October 8, 1905

I did not do much on Sunday until late in the afternoon, when, since Dr. Nichols and I were to go to Washington to dine with President Roosevelt,[44] I wrote out a careful schedule of our work for Capt. Hur-

---

44. Theodore Roosevelt called a meeting of the athletic Big Three (Harvard, Yale, and Princeton) after Endicott Peabody, founder and headmaster of the Groton Prepa-

ley's guidance tomorrow. I wrote out in detail what I thought ought to be accomplished and mailed it before my train left. Dr. Nichols got on at Back Bay station, we taking the Federal Express which left at 7:45. On the train we found Burgess,[45] the Exeter man and a former substitute end, and had quite a talk with him over three or four men out on the squad. He says that Carr has good fight, is a hard worker, good spirited, and willing. He said that Brill had not very much life at Exeter and was not thought very much of. We talked over foot ball situations in general, and I went over a list of the ends with him so that he might tell me what men he thought best. He had however, seen so little of the men that he didn't know much about it. We talked until after 11 over various men and then went to bed. Our discussion was of a very general nature and I do not think it would be worth while to try to put it down.

Monday, October 9, 1905

Morning:

This morning just as soon as Dr. Nichols and I had had our breakfast we went over very carefully the Yale system of defence, reading over all notes and literature which I had covering it. I explained our defence and Yale's defence to Dr. Nichols and he agrees with me, that the Yale defence is much the stronger.

We reached Washington at a little after 9 and put up at the Cosmos Club where some Harvard graduate had very kindly put us on the list of guests. After washing up and getting dressed, we went out for a walk; then went to the top of the Washington Monument, where we took in the view until it was time to go to the White House for our luncheon, which came at 1:30.

Afternoon:

When we went into the dining room, Walter Camp sat at the President's right and Mr. [John] Fin[e] at his left, while I sat opposite to Mr. Fin[e] and Mr. [Elihu] Root's right and Mr. Nichols sat on his left.

---

ratory School, suggested that he do so. The idea was that if the academic and athletic leaders in America would agree to play ethically and cleanly, other schools and colleges would follow their example. See Roosevelt to Walter Camp, 24 Nov. 1905, in *The Letters of Theodore Roosevelt*, ed. Elting E. Morison (Cambridge: Harvard University Press, 1952), 5:94.

45. Reid is probably referring to James Burgess, a letter-winner on Reid's team in 1901. He graduated in 1904.

The two short ends of the table were occupied by Mr. [John] Owsley and Mr. [Arthur] Hildebrand.[46]

The President discussed the question of foot ball in general and made a few remarks on unfair play, giving an example of what he remembered of each college's unfair play from several things that had happened in previous years. He spoke of Lewis' coaching the Groton team on one occasion how to break the rules in the rush line without being seen; also one man's being padded up because of a supposed injury, when as a matter of fact the man playing in the corresponding position on the same team was the man that was hurt. This was simply to see if they could not get the opposing side to attack the well man rather than the injured man. After sighting points against each of the colleges, Mr. Roosevelt said he thought the position was one to be deplored and he wanted to see if there was not some way in which the feeling between the colleges could be improved and the training of the players made more effective in the right way.

Camp made some considerable talk but was very slippery and did not allow himself to be pinned down to anything. The Princeton and Yale men both disclaimed any knowledge of any man's having been hurt purposely in any of the games, although I have seen it myself in a Yale-Princeton game where Princeton tried to injure deSeaulles by tackling him hard when it was known that he had a very weak ankle.

The conversation changed from one subject to another along the same general line, and we finally went out on the porch of the White House to continue the talk, while the President attended to a little business. When he came out again on further talk, he finally asked the three older men to draw up some kind of an agreement on the matter while on their way home on the train together. This they agreed to do, and the following was the result:

"At a meeting with the President of the United States, it was agreed that we consider an honorable obligation exists to carry out in letter and in spirit the rules of the game of foot ball relat-

46. Meeting with Theodore Roosevelt were Secretary of State Elihu Root; Walter Camp, the leader of Yale athletics; John Owsley, Yale's head football coach; John Fine, head of Princeton's Athletic Committee; Arthur Hillebrand, Princeton's head football coach; and Nichols and Reid, the two Harvard representatives. The *New York Times* (10 Oct. 1905, 1) reported that Roosevelt had fought the railroad industry over rail rates, had successfully negotiated an end to the Sino-Japanese War (for which he won the Nobel Peace Prize), and was now ready to tackle football reform.

ing to roughness, holding and foul play, and the active coaches of our Universities being present with us pledge themselves to so regard it, and to do their utmost to carry out these obligations.

Signed:

Walter Camp
John Owsley
J. B. Fine
A. R. Hillebrand
Edw[ard] H. Nichols
W. T. Reid, Jr."

On this same train Hillebrand, Owsley and I talked over the matter of a more definite understanding as to what roughness, holding and foul play consists in and we drew up a sketch which I brought home with me for further consideration as soon as I have it in anything like good shape. I shall, of course, talk the matter over with Waters and Lewis and see if we cannot get something that will be worth while. I must say that I do not feel that Yale and Princeton were wholly in sympathy with the idea, although they professed to be, and I shall not be willing to stand by any agreement with them which I cannot feel certain that they intend to carry out in spirit and in faith.

After all, the way in which the game is played depends largely on the way in which the coaches take hold and the way in which the officials rule, and I think a good stiff official would do more in regard to this matter than anything else.

After the talk was over on the train, I had a talk with Walter Camp on foot ball in general, and got several things that I think are worth while. In the first place, I asked Camp what he thought of Brill, and he said that it seemed to him that our position would be that he was too powerful a man to lose. This seems to me to just about size up the situation. I think Brill will have to be on the team somewhere—if not at tackle, perhaps at center or guard, but he has too much rushing strength to make it wise to lose him entirely unless he proves to be an absolutely quitter. I also found out that Owsley, the Yale half back, did not play last year in but eight scrimmages during the entire season, which shows how well Yale looks after her men who are likely to be hurt but who are known to be good. Yale is already having her tackle behind the line carry the ball, and from what Kernan told me, they seem to be playing fast. I learn that they have a couple of big mattresses buried in the ground under their tackling dummy to prevent injury, and I think we shall do the same. The mattresses in this way give a good deal and prevent accidents to the shoulders in learning how to tackle. I talked over with Camp the necessity for having a provision in the rules next year whereby in case a man breaking through the line knocks down the kicker there shall be a penalty of ten or fifteen yards awarded. The penalty at present consists of disqualification where the bumping is intentional, but there is no provision where it is unintentional, and there is no excuse for a man bumping into another at all. I shall probably suggest this to the Rules Committee next year if I am here.

Camp, in speaking of the Penn team, said that he felt that we should have to make some special provision in our Penn game this year to prevent Stevenson from getting around the ends, such a plan involving perhaps the assignments of Stevenson, the Penn quarter, to two men to watch, which is, I think, a very good suggestion and one which we will look into with great care. Penn's most dangerous game last year, from what I am able to see, was the long runs of Stevenson, which brought the ball down in the neighborhood of our goal line, where she was able to put it over. This year I hope to be able to stop those plays in such a way as to make it necessary for Penn to gain almost entirely through the line, where we ought to be able to stop her.

These, and a few other points, were what I got that were most worth while, but I think they are well worth thinking over.

Dr. Nichols and I reached Boston on Tuesday morning.

I had previously written out instructions for Hurley for the Monday afternoon practice and I shall ask him to give an account of what he did. It is as follows:

I have tried a number of times to get Hurley to write this account up but he has not done so and so I am going to do as well as I can by writing it up myself.

What follows as an account of the work done from October 9th through October 14th is done in the same way.

Monday, October 9, 1905

Afternoon:

The work of the afternoon followed pretty closely the general results that are obtained on Monday afternoons. Very few of the Varsity men were allowed to do much owing to injuries and lay-offs. It turns out that Squires has a broken thumb, Peirce a broken wrist, Foster two broken ribs, and Guild a very sore collar bone. O'Brien, Hall, Montgomery and Wendell were laid off—Montgomery because of a loosened tooth received in the Maine game, Starr got back into signal practice. C. Blagden who was tackle on the 1901 team was on the field and did some coaching of the tackles and also played on the Second. I want to say right here that Blagden's spirit has been excellent all through. He is here for two weeks and has given up a two week's vacation trip to help us out. That is the kind of spirit with which he goes into things and the spirit which he exhibited on the team here in '01.

The work of the afternoon consisted of a long preliminary period, in which about twenty men, mostly line men, were given work in tackling the dummy. Lewis supervised the work. This tackling work we put especial emphasis on as the exhibition of tackling in the Maine game was very poor. The ends were sent down under punts against opposing ends in an endeavor to make our ends shiftier and more able to get past opposing ends who were trying to block them going down the field. This practice to my mind should be made a regular part of the fundamental work of the team. If we do not give special practice in this work we certainly cannot expect to get the best of men, such as Shevlin of Yale, just by a supreme effort at the last moment.

McDonald the end is trying hard to get off probation and I very much hope he may since he shows promise of becoming an excellent man. He took a petition up to the College Office today and I learned that Mr. Love of the Scientific school had indicated that favorable action on it is likely to be taken.

The line men after their tackling were given hard practice in blocking and breaking through—in charge of Blagden and Andy Marshall.

A great deal of time was spent on Cavenee, the green man from the Law School, who is most enthusiastic about the game, and who cannot seem to learn fast enough to satisfy his own cravings.

There was, also, falling on the ball for the ends, in charge of Bowditch, and for the line men in charge of Hurley. Time was spent also on handing the ball to the backs for line bucking in order to give the quarter backs practice in getting the ball in just the right place.

Newhall and Starr were coached by Daly and were given a good deal of attention in drop kicking, while Parker and Brill tried for goals.

Kernan had charge of the kickers and devoted a good deal of time to Channing, a new man who is fast and something on the type of Don Nichols and to my mind with much the same impossible temperament. I do not think he will pan out, but Kernan is enthusiastic about him and I am willing he should have every chance.

Following the preliminary work the First and Second line up for a scrimmage of 10 minutes. The team lined up as follows:

VARSITY		SECOND	
Burnham, Lockwood,	l.e.	Craft,	r.e.
Brill,	l.t.	Cavenee,	r.t.
Parker & Paul,	l.g.	McLeod,	r.g.
White,	c.	Cunniff,	c.
Kersburg,	r.g.	Brown,	l.g.
Fultz,	r.t.	Blagden, Irving,	l.t.
McDonald & Leary,	r.e.	Blanchard,	l.e.
Newhall,	q.b.	Sortwell,	q.b.
Channing,	l.h.b.	Mills,	r.h.b.
Nesmith,	r.h.b.	Bowles,	l.h.b.
Carr & Somes,	f.b.	Cor[b]ett,	f.b.

In order to try out the kickers we had a great deal of kicking work in which Channing got off some very good kicks, but in which he also showed great nervousness. Brill did some very fair work in the line, although when the Second had the ball Cavenee handled him pretty successfully. Cavenee played with great enthusiasm. Carr at full back did some very good work, although he had a tendency to take too short steps and appeared to have a hard time in keeping his feet. The best work of the afternoon was done by Nesmith, who blocked a kick or two, made several good runs, and was excellent on the defense.

The evening papers have announced that Reynolds, Captain of the Pennsylvania Football team, has been forced to resign owing to the fact that the Law School Faculty at Pennsylvania will not allow him to matriculate there. If this is true, it looks as though Pennsylvania were getting to have a little conscience for Reynolds' loss as Captain and kicker of the team will be a very severe one.

With Fultz having to play at tackle in Montgomery's place, Waters gave him a great deal of individual attention because he is a very weak player.

I got after Lewis on White's very poor passing for kicks and Lewis says that he will get White so that he will pass the ball well enough. It seems to me, however, that it is high time now that he should be showing some signs in that direction.

We took Bartels and Burr to the Varsity training table for supper and they will continue there until the end of the season unless for some reason they are dropped meanwhile.

As the men feel pretty well exhausted and tired out and begin to feel the nervous unrest that indicates worry and over work, I suppose I ought to let up for a few days to get them rested up a little.

What follows from here to October 23rd was written during the season, at the time when the things mentioned were taking place.

From October 23rd on what is written is supplied from my notes, which were pretty carefully made and which are reliable.

Tuesday, October 10, 1905

Morning:

I came down to the office quite early to-day in order to clear up the work that had accumulated while I was in Washington. During the course of the morning Blagden dropped in and I had quite a long talk with him, telling him how much we appreciated his coming and giving him so far as possible an outline of the present situation in football. I was very sorry not to have been on hand yesterday when he appeared but of course that was impossible.

Afternoon:

The entire practice this afternoon lacked life and spirit. In the preliminary work, Hall and Leonard did some very good work in kicking. The catching of the backs too was poor; the ends were slow and uncertain, and the blocking and breaking through was lifeless. Besides this we had falling on the ball and tackling at the dummy.

Peirce, Squires and Guild with their bandaged up injuries trotted around the field under McMaster's direction, and Montgomery, Foster and Hurley also did light work. Hall, Wendell, McFadon and O'Brien, whom we laid off yesterday, were put into the scrimmage. Starr was back at quarter back, his left ankle being much better. To make up however, for this good fortune, Hall in making a dive tackle hit on the point of his shoulder on the ground and injured it so that he will be out of the game for three weeks. It seems as though we could not possibly get away from this epidemic of injuries. Blagden again played on the Second against Brill and stopped most everything that came around his way.

We gave the team 15 minutes of scrimmage work before the afternoon was over, in which we played all of the men whom we expect to play in the game with Bates tomorrow. This scrimmage was on the whole very poor. The First team was able to score only once and was held for downs on the two yard line. If there were any bright spots in the play it was the work of Wendell and Nesmith, with the defensive work of Carr.

An amusing thing that happened in connection with the afternoon's work was the fact that Cavenee was given a try on the First and after one of the plays was not to be found. Upon looking around for him we found him lined up on the Second, he having lost his way through greenness. I think this little incident was the only amusing thing of the afternoon.

I do not know whether we are giving the team too much scrimmage work or not, but at any rate we do not seem to be able to get very much vim into the plays.

I had dinner with the team at the training table and at 7:30 addressed a mass meeting in the Union. Bart Stephenson, the Captain of the Nine, was Chairman of the meeting, and the speakers were Hurley and I. There were probably 1400 fellows in the room. The windows were down and the fellows hung over them from the outside. The balcony was full, men were standing on the mantel piece, and there were big bunches around the doors that could not get in. It was a most thrilling sight. I found when it came my turn to speak that I was going to have difficulty in controling my voice, as the enthusiasm was high and stirring up a great deal of feeling in me; to have as many fellows as were the[re] last night as hearty and as enthusiastic as they were gave me an impetus for further work that I have not felt for a long time. My talk was something like this: When I started to speak the fellows began cheering and the cheering lasted for over two minutes, leaving me standing on the platform ready to speak yet unable to and stirred up to such an extent that I didn't know whether I should be able to say anything when my chance came.

"I can't tell you how much I appreciate this magnificent reception which you have seen fit to give me—it takes me back to '01 when the student body marched down to the field with the band to cheer the team on the Wednesday previous to the Yale game. It fills me now with the same feeling that I had then. Standing on the field there I could hear the procession drawing nearer and when finally it marched in onto the field I thought to myself 'how I would like to make good for those fellows and for the University that they represent. They are doing all that they possibly can to help out and here I am willing to do all that I can but not capable of the work.' I am here with heart, mind and soul, and everything I can give to give you a winning team. You cannot appreciate my affection for this University, and the being away from it as I have been, and the seeing what has happened to our teams in past years (with not a bit of reflection of how the teams have been managed or coached, but merely how the other teams have handled our team, while we, owing to many handicaps, have practically had to handle our teams with one of our hands tied behind our back). At such a meeting I presume that you are expecting something optimistic. If so, I am afraid you will be disappointed because I have never been an optimist and am very far from it still—in fact I think I might be called a pessimist. Within the past week I have seen some of the best men on the squad laid up with injuries which will keep them from playing for several weeks and as a result there is not enough line material to sufficiently try out the backs. The material we have is not first class but the spirit in the men is all that could possibly be asked—there hasn't been a man taken out of a game this season who hasn't come out crying because of his desire to have a further chance to do better or because of his great personal disappointment. The prospects then, are not over bright and we need the sympathy and encouragement of the entire University for we shall do the very best we can. I wish to ask you to be patient of mistakes and not too quick to condemn—don't find fault too soon. It will take at least four years or one college generation to establish the system that we are trying to establish. If the men are beaten don't make them feel ashamed to come back to Cambridge—make them feel that every man who backs the college is backed by every man in it. We must show more spirit and fight as a University. We can no longer stand having it said of our Harvard teams that when Harvard gets to Yale's 5 yard line she 'may go over', but that when Princeton gets there she 'always goes over.' The fact that this comment has been made is something of a slap at us all. It is as much your fault as it is the fault of the players. This year we called back for the team 291 men—50 came, 100 answered. There were not enough men to give all the players a try out. If you really want to help the team make some sacrifice for it. Here is Crawford Blagden, member of the '01 team, who has given up two weeks of his vacation for the sake of coming back here to help coach. Very probably Mr. Blagden would much more enjoy a duck hunt in the Carolinas than to come out here and join in with the drudgery of football fundamentals, but he has not consulted his own feelings in the matter and will spend his first vacation since leaving college in helping out his football team. That is the kind of spirit that we all admire and the spirit that we most need here. There are men in this college, such as Knowlton and Don Nichols, who ought to be out—you fellows can get them out if you want to, the question is whether you will.

"We are going to have clean football even if we lose by it. If the rules are bad they should be changed, but as long as they stay in force they must be lived up to. That does not mean easy playing but it does mean the fiercest kind of playing so long as it is clean. The scores thus far represent the best work of the team; the team has not been coached to keep the score down.

"If you are down on the field and see a man trying to do something and he does it awkwardly, don't laugh at him but remember he is doing the best he can for you and the thing to do is to encourage and applaud him.

"And now one word as to my position here—some think I am a coach—I am not, I am here rather as a business manager to get men who know the game well to teach it to the players—not to do much teaching myself, although of course I am here to do anything in any way that I feel capable of doing it.

"We have a long hard row to hoe this year with many handicaps and we must stand shoulder to shoulder through it all and savagely and fiercely fight."

This is a very poor report of what I had to say, but it is the nearest I can come to the subject matter. It is not in the order in which I spoke it, but as I kept no record, I have nothing definite to go by. I think without doubt the meeting was the most enthusiastic mass me[e]ting that the Union or Harvard has ever seen, at any rate, since '01. The spirit of the whole meeting was like that of some of the great religious revivals of Sankey or Moody, or of the great Christian Endeavor Conventions.[47]

It does one an enormous amount of good to have such an experience as I had last night and I cannot see how a meeting of that kind can but help to bind the University wonderfully together. The singing by the fellows was the finest that I have ever heard—people two or three blocks away came to their doors to listen.

I found out after the meeting was over that one woman had heard the talk. It seems that she was up in the gallery looking at the Union having come from the ladies' restaurant, and the fellows came in so rapidly that she was separated from her escort and went into the gallery during the speeches. It came around to me rather indirectly that the girl had said to her escort on once more reaching him, that she was mighty glad she had been penned in and that although she did not know the two fellows who had spoken personally, she was wholly with them after the talks they had made and intended to watch the football season from beginning to end with greatly increased interest.

47. Ira D. Sankey (1840–1908) and Dwight Moody (1837–99) were Christian evangelists who often traveled together in America and Britain. Sankey wrote music that was played at evangelistic Christian Endeavor conventions. See J. Edgar Goodspeed, *A Full History and Career of Moody and Sankey in Great Britain and America* (New York: H. S. Goodspeed, 1876).

Wednesday, October 11, 1905

Afternoon:

This was the day of the Bates game and we sent in the following men:

O'Brien,	l.e.
Montgomery, Fultz,	r.t.
Parker,	l.g.
White, Cunniff,	c.
Kersburg, White,	r.g.
Spear, Brill,	l.t.
Burnham,	r.e.
Starr,	q.b.
Nesmith,	l.h.b.
Wendell,	r.h.b.
Carr,	f.b.

It will be seen that the team was made up largely of substitutes except for the backs, the numerous injuries in the line having made it impossible for us to play much of anything but substitutes. Brill is all right, but we laid him off for a part of this game owing to the loafing which he has been undertaking the past three or four days.

Harvard won the Bates game 34-6, being scored on by a 65 yard run following a double criss-cross. In the first half our team played very well, until it had scored its first touch-down, after which there was something of a let-up during which Bates got in her touch-down. Following this the team woke up and literally ripped the Bates team to pieces, the first half ending with the score 16-6, on one occasion the team carrying the ball from the 37 yard line over the goal line in six plays. Wendell did the kicking, what there was of it, because all of our kickers are laid up, and he got off one very good kick. Harvard was not penalized once during the whole game. Starr played a splendid game, especially in interference. Nesmith blocked an attempt at goal from the field, and Harvard blocked a punt which ended in a score.

In the second half I put Brill in in place of Spear, and his dispension from playing seemed to do him good. For example, we made the second touch-down from the 25 yard line in two plays. Montgomery broke his cheek bone by sticking his face into a tackle play. He is most unfortunate in the way he approaches play, and it is a big question to me as to whether a fellow who is so uniformly thoughtless as to the way in which he approaches a play should be allowed out. I sometimes feel afraid lest he may get seriously hurt. He is pretty well muscle bound, weighs only a little over 180 lbs., has a fine spirit, but is very slow, and is not what one might call a natural football player. Montgomery's injury will leave us very short of tackles because Fultz is rather weak.

The halves were 20 minutes and 9 minutes, the second half being called short a few minutes in order to save such injuries as seemed probable through the possibilities of collision in the dark. The team scored three times in this second half and certainly played the best game of the year thus far.

Nesmith played a fine game on the defense, although our defense in general was very weak. We must have some tackling practice at once and with it some live tackling. The backs kept their feet splendidly in this game and it was a game of dragging and helping the runner along. Kersburg at guard played a beautiful game, continually breaking through and making tackles behind the line. He was ruled off during the half owing to what seemed to be a blunder on the part of the official, who accused him of intensionally trying to injure an opponent. I saw what he did and did not think it was intensional or serious.

It seems to me that this game has demonstrated that we need to put more time on our defense at this time of the year. We should have out all our material and should have it pretty well sorted by this time. Bates' run and score was the direct result of a lack of team defense. Burnham on the end was easily fooled and Fultz didn't know where the ball was half the time. The rush line backs, and this is one of the most important criticisms of the game, stood altogether too close to the rush line and were frequently boxed with the tackle by one man; in other words, they stood too close to the rush line and hurried into the play so rapidly that they were very easily fooled. This accounted for Bates getting away with so many crisscrosses and double plays as she did. To me the score was a disappointment, but if it was disappointing, it was, nevertheless, a great satisfaction to see with what spirit the team gathered itself after the score had been made against them.

Bates had a light, active, fast team and came into the schedule at an excellent time.

Yale beat the Springfield Training School 29-0. The coaches whom I sent down to the game, Kernan and Dunlop, reported great speed in the Yale team and brought back to us considerable information on the special points for which they were sent, which was to find out how Yale plays her quick kick from close formation, which we are going to try next week ourselves.

The papers printed to-day a copy of the agreement which we coaches all signed as the result of our conference with President Roosevelt and which was drawn up by the older representatives of Harvard, Yale and Princeton while on the train on our return.

To my mind the week has been a pretty profitable one to us, and if we had not had so many injuries we should be vastly better off.

Thursday, October 12, 1905

Morning:

I had the managers go around to the college office to look up the marks of the men and their attendance, and found that with the exception of Bartels, all of them are doing very fair work. Realizing that a little later in the season we shall have to ask the men to do some cutting it is my policy during the early part of the season to have the men attend lectures regularly with a view to having a good record to stand on when cutting finally does occur.

I went in town and had a long talk with H. Livermore about Knowlton. It seems that when Knowlton left college a year or two ago he went into business and that business had not proven very satisfactory to him. During the summer he ran across Livermore whom he knew in college, and Livermore offered him a place in his law office as a partner, in case Knowlton would go to the law school and complete the course in two years. This brought Knowlton back. In trying to get Knowlton out, he felt that he had no business to come out unless he had Livermore's permission. This being the case, I went in as I said to see Livermore. Livermore was very pleasant to me indeed and said that so far as restraining Knowlton from going out he would do everything he could to encourage him, so that now what I need is to apply all the pressure possible to Knowlton himself.

After seeing Livermore, I went to see Mike Farley with a view to getting him to coach Knowlton after the season on the work that he is likely to miss during the season. Farley said he would be very glad to do this, so that thus far the Knowlton matter is very satisfactory.

I also called on Jim Lawrence to see if he would not agree to come out and work with the Freshmen, and at the same time give the Varsity goal kickers some coaching. He is very busy just now and says that he cannot except very occasionally.

I had lunch with Lewis and Waters at Young's hotel in order to draw up as water tight a rule to prevent holding as possible so as to submit it to Yale and Princeton in view of the agreement that we have while on the train after leaving President Roosevelt on our recent visit to Washington. Here is the agreement we came to:

Appreciating the good offices of the President of the United States, and his desire to promote good-fellowship and clean sport between the different Universities, and in accordance with an honorable obligation made with him 'to carry out in letter and in spirit the rules of the game of football relating to roughness, holding and foul play';

Now therefore it is agreed as follows:

Whereas, Rule 17 C provides in substance that no player of the side in possession of the ball shall use hands or arms except player running with the ball, we agree that there shall be no use of hands open, palm extended or with clinched fists. There shall be no use of arms extended at right angles with the body or curved so as to encircle or enclose in any manner or degree any part of opponent's body; there shall no use of arms to lift an opponent up in blocking, or to shove him one side. There shall be no striking of the runner in the face with the heel of the hand, in lieu of tackling.

Whereas Rule 27-C provides, that there shall be no unnecessary roughness, throttling, hacking or striking with the closed fist, we agree that there shall be no attempt in any way to injure another player, or to uppercut with clinched fist the underbody of a player, or to make any intensional rough play with the elbows.

I do not believe that this rule will allow much that is not fair, and if Yale and Princeton will agree to it I believe we shall clear up quite a bit of misstrust between us on the legitimacy of the coaching that is being done with the teams. I expect to submit this statement to Owsley and Hillebrand as soon as I can arrange a meeting.

New Haven, Conn. Oct. 14, 1905

Mr. Wm. T. Reid, Jr.,
Head Coach Harvard Foot ball Team
Cambridge, MASS.

Dear Mr. Reid:

I have just received yours of the 13th and contents.

The provision for holding seems to me to be much more detailed than anything we looked at on the train. As I remember, the arms could be used provided the hands were against the body. As to the use of the hand or straight arm instead of tackling the runner, I regard that as necessary to prevent a man from successfully hurdling the line. Your other provision as to rough

playing is all right. I think that these matters will have to be left
to the officials of the game, as they are all dealt with in the rules.

Very sincerely,

[signed] Jack Owsley

Princeton, N.J. Oct. 21, 1905

Mr. William Reid
Cambridge, Mass.

Dear Mr. Reid:
  In reply to your favor enclosing your interpretation of Rules
17C and 27C, would say, that your interpretation of Rules 17C
is not entirely satisfactory, and would suggest a meeting to discuss it further.

Very sincerely,

A. R. Hillebrand

I also saw a man named Atherton, '00, in regard to this man Draper
of the University of Pennsylvania and I got some very good points
from him.

Afternoon:

This afternoon as a result of much scurrying about on the part of the
managers and some of the fellows who seem to have been slightly
aroused after my talk in The Union, three new men came out for the
team; they were Preston Davie, Don Nichols and H. Whitman. I feel
rather dubious about all of them but we need men so badly that it is
going to be well worth our while to try these men out pretty carefully.
  Davie is a big fellow weighing close to 200 lbs. and strikes one as
being English; he has played before but never has done much. Last
year he hurt his shoulder very badly and so I sent him to the doctor
immediately before allowing him to come out. The doctor looked him
over and sent word that the fellow's shoulder was badly injured, but
that if he wanted to play he might just as well go ahead since unless
his arm dropped off there was not much else he could do to it.
  Whitman was end last year and belongs to the track team, is supposed to be a very fast runner, and as he is an end that speed just at
present would be very valuable to us, provided he has the other qualifications. Knowing the Whitman family slightly as I do, and knowing a number of fellows who knew Whitman, I doubt very much
whether he has the stuff in him to concentrate on football long enough

to get out of it what he needs. However, I shall turn him over to the end coaches and give him a thorough and immediate try out.

Don Nichols I have spoken considerable about in my writings of the preliminary season. He too has a bad shoulder, which he has used as an excuse for not coming out before. Whether he is not just like Putnam, rather erratic in his play, I do not feel at all sure; in fact I feel very dubious about his being of Varsity calibre. He has speed and size but lacks temperament.

Right here I would like to say that hereafter a coach should make up his mind to insist that every man is out on time, and put every effort forth to get out any men who have played but who are not out, within the first week or so. Having to readjust continually the working plan of the season to accommodate new men is a great handicap and retards development seriously. Another year I shall make a tremendous effort to carry this policy into practice.

After I had been out on the field a few minutes the Doctor handed me the report of injuries to the squad up to date:

Cavenee,	Fractured collar bone, 1 month.
Ball,	Dislocated elbow, 3 weeks.
Barney,	Inflam. Heel tendon, Any day.
Corbett,	Contusion Hip. (Not see for several days.)
Boyd,	Wrenched knee. (Not see for several days).
Dick,	Dislocated Rt. shoulder. Not all.
Foster,	Contusion side, Line up today.
Guild,	Separation inner end of collar bone, 3 weeks.
Hall,	Dislocated outer end collar bone, 3 weeks.
Hurley,	Ruptured hamstring, 4 days before Penn game line-up.
Leonard,	Sprained ankle, today.
Montgomery,	Fractured zygoma, 10 days.
Nesmith,	Wrenched knee, next Monday.
Palmer,	Joint mouse, not at all.
Parker,	Sprained back, Saturday.
Peirce,	Fractured wrist, two to three weeks.
Pope,	Recent appendix.
Quigley,	Water on the knee, 1 week.
Snyder,	Contusion hip, 5 days.
Squires,	Fractured finger, 2 weeks.
Keays,	Collar bone.

It will be noticed that we shall probably lose four men for good. Boyd, who has a very weak knee and who has stopped playing; Dick a loose jointed fellow of W. Kimball's type, who is continually throwing his shoulder or knees out of joint and that without pain. A fellow of this type is of no use on the squad because there is no telling when he will have a serious injury and be permanently disqualified and permanently disabled. Fellows like this ought not to be allowed to play at all. Palmer has a very bad knee too, of old origin, as is also true of Boyd and Dick. The doctor thinks he ought not to play any more.

Pope was operated upon for appendicitis as I have said elsewhere, only a little over a month before the season opened. He is one of the most persistent players I ever saw and with his wound hardly healed he has come out to play and on top too of a rupture. He is crazy for the game and I found out to-day indirectly that every afternoon after playing he comes in and goes off by himself and throws up, showing that the strain on his wound and rupture is very bad for him. The fact that he was willing to undergo this punishment every day shows more clearly than anything I can say how eag[er] he is in his desire to play. I would give a good deal to be able to reward a fellow of his type with a position on the team, but I shall have to tell him to-day to stop playing in order to do what seems to me to be the only right thing by him.

To go on now with the day's work, I had intended to go over to the Freshman field some time in the afternoon to be present at a cut down of the squad, in order to be sure that no good man escaped us, but so many unexpected interruptions occurred that I finally had to give it up.

For the practice to-day I laid off Carr, Kersburg, Nesmith, Brill, Wendell, and O'Brien.

Montgomery it turns out injured himself in the game yesterday, so that he will be out for two weeks, at any rate, until we are able to get a special head gear made to cover his cheek bone.

With so many of the regular team out of the line up we devoted much time to individual coaching. To begin with, the tackling in yesterday's game having proven unexpectedly weak, we devoted considerable time to dummy work, giving the men tackling at all angles and showing the principle of it very carefully. Waters and Lewis did most of the coaching on the First squad while Brown took charge of the Second. It turns out that the fellows have been having more or less fun out of this dummy work and that they have named the dummy Anna Held or Lillian Russell.[48]

48. Russell (1861–1922) was a singer and actress. In the summer of 1905, she signed

The usual amount of bad luck seems still to be with us. This afternoon Cavenee was trying to learn how to tackle and was doing very awkward work. Fearing lest he might hurt himself, I said to him "Stand aside there for a few minutes until I can get a chance to give you some individual work". He said he would and was apparently ready to wait. I had no more than gotten busy with someone else however, when he took a try at the dummy all by himself, missed it, hit on the point of his shoulder, and broke his collar bone, putting him out of the game for at least a month. This work was very disappointing and annoying to me, since I had attempted, by warning, to prevent the very thing that occurred. We had under the dummy any quantity of cut grass and the ground was very soft with loam, so that it was simply greenness in attempting to go at the work that caused the trouble.

Immediately after the tackling, I set Hanley and Leonard at work punting, while Parker, White and Cunniff did some place kicking, and Starr and Newhall drop kicking. I turned over the line men to Waters and the blocking and breaking through to Donald and Blagden, with Bowditch giving the ends some special attention in boxing the tackle in different ways. This has been one of the things that our ends have proven very weak on and which to my mind should be included hereafter in the list of fundamentals which we teach our team. We certainly cannot expect ends, unless they are pretty mature fellows, to work out the way of handling a powerful tackle all of his own initiative. I do not think we have given this half enough attention heretofore.

While this work was going on I devoted myself to the three new men who were out and tried my best to give Davie an idea of how to catch a ball and how to hold it for bucks and end runs because I want him to try it out at full back. We progressed very slowly.

After all this preliminary work was over we had a line-up of 16 minutes in which the Second easily beat the patched up Varsity on which was only one real Varsity possibility in the person of Newhall.

We shifted MacLeod from the Second Team to the Varsity in order to make it possible to get off kicks and plays. Leonard played at half back on the Varsity and got away for one pretty long run, but he is a poor football player. It looks as though now that we must have him on the team or at any rate on the squad for the sake of his kicking, and teach him whatever else we are able to.

---

a vaudeville contract for $4,000 a week at a fashionable Saratoga, New York, resort. Held was a British actress and singer who was popular in the United States. See the *Boston Globe*, 1 Aug. 1905, 7 and 23 Sept. 1905, 8.

The practice was very poor indeed and there was considerable fumbling until finally we had, in order to get any profit out of the afternoon at all, to spend most of our time in giving Leonard as much kicking practice as possible from behind the line of scrimmage.

Evening:

At supper time I dined at the training table where I talked over with Kernan and R. Brown what they had seen at New Haven yesterday when Yale played Springfield Training School. I sent them down to watch especially the starting of Yale's backs and to see how Yale utilizes her kick from close formation which they are using and with great effect. Both Kernan and Brown were most enthusiastic over the play and insist that we ought to adopt it as one of our plays at once. I am going to spend some time on it tomorrow, and if possible try it in the Springfield game which comes on Saturday.

After supper we went over the chart of the Bates game with the team and pointed out the mistakes and asked for criticisms. I also asked each man whether he had been in any play where he did not know what his assignment was and in which had had not looked after his assignment. I think the men knew pretty clearly what they were expected to do and had pretty generally done it.

Friday, October 13, 1905

Morning:

This morning I went in and had quite a long talk with Mr. H. Burr, the father of Francis Burr, to see if he wouldn't let Francis come out and try for the Varsity. I had a very pleasant talk with him and with his brother but was unable to gain his consent. To my mind though, I gained one point and that was that: Mr. Burr has agreed to allow us to keep Francis on the Varsity squad and at the Varsity training table so that we may give him Varsity coaching without, however, his being allowed to do any scrimmage work with the Varsity. This will give Mr. Burr a chance to see how the boy stands the work, will give the boy all the coaching that anyone else is getting, and will prevent him from being smashed up on the Freshman team, and will enable us, perhaps a little later, to get Mr. Burr to allow his son to get into the scrimmage in practice, if he does not play in outside games. In this way, if we are ever able to play Burr we shall not be handicapped through his lack of coaching. In case we cannot play him, he will at least be a good man for us next year.

Afternoon:

In anticipation of the game tomorrow, we gave the men light work consisting of signal practice, including running down under kicks, individual line work by Waters, starting of the backs by Dunlop, and coaching of the quarter backs by Daly. In the kicking work we undertook the close formation kick that I said we were going to begin on, and while we were working on it we allowed no one on the field. We found that about two out of every three kicks were blocked by the Second. Of course one reason for this was that the Second knew what was coming and did not have to hold off in uncertainty thereby saving the loss of time which would be the very thing to prevent successful interference with the kick. We did not make much progress but decided to try it in the game tomorrow. This kick and anything of a similar nature ought to have been worked out sometime before. It ought not to be given to the team the day before a game when [. . .] they have no confidence in it. However, since we have not had it ready the only thing to do is to make the best of it. I think it will be a great thing when we get it perfected, but will need a great deal of work in that perfection.

Peirce and Squires went through signals to-day with their hands bound up, and the line looked very much better with them in it. The problem at end is still a very serious one. At present Hall and Mac-Donald seem to be the best men we have although they really are too light for the place.

We tried out in running down under kicks Lockwood, Burnham, Whitman, O'Brien and Lovering, and none of them showed any special gift, although O'Brien did very well. We were all very much astonished at the speed with which Spear, at end, got down the field. It is possible that he may work into the position. If his knee were wholly sound, I should feel as though he stood a very good chance.

Saturday, October 14, 1905

Morning:

I have had so little sleep the last two or three night due to nervous worry that I found myself good for nothing this morning and although I tried to settle down to serious thinking on various things, I found I was unable to do so, and so I did nothing until lunch time except fool around. Just before lunch I went into the Union and met Dan Knowlton, the old Varsity tackle, and learned from him that he is now ready to come on. This was very cheering although I ought to have had him out long before. The difficulty with him was that he refused every time I have tried to see him, and it was not until I had taken around to his room five or six of the coaches that he finally promised to get to work on his mother and gain her consent.

Immediately after seeing Knowlton I had quite a talk with Kernan and Dunlop on the matter of the way in which we shall play our backs from now on. It seems that we must use Wendell as a kicker and Leonard, Brill and Hall also. Foster does not seem to be able to do it. Such being the case, it looks as though Wendell and Nichols must be shifted to left back, and that Nesmith and Foster will have to play the other back. Hurley is very uncertain, he being the worst injured man on the squad and I must have good backs on the right side in case of injuries. If, when he tries out his leg, it breaks down, then we shall have Wendell and Nesmith to step in. On the other hand, Leonard and Wendell must be at left half back because of their kicking.[49]

Afternoon:

The game began at 3 o'clock and it was exceedingly hot. We gave the men too much work yesterday afternoon and the result was that they seemed pretty logy. The Springfield Training School showed up in marked contrast to our fellows in the matter of speed. Our backs were slow in getting off. Owing to the heat we played a 20 and 15 minute half.

Springfield kicked off to us on the 5 yard line and Wendell brought it back to the 30 yard line, where, as he was tackled, he fumbled, but one of the other men got the ball. On the next play Wendell was again given the ball when he fumbled again. At this point Brill was called back to kick. He got off a 35 yard punt which the opposing full back ran back 5 yards. Springfield here made a first down, then were held and kicked about 13 yards. Fultz, who was playing right tackle for us, tried to catch the kick and fumbled it, but it was recovered by one of the men. He had no business, since the other side was in on side, to try to catch that ball, and it might have been pretty serious if we hadn't happened to get it. We immediately kicked again, Brill punting again and he got off a 40 yard kick to the Springfield 35 yard line. They made a first down here and then kicked about 17 yards to our 50 yard line where we tried a quick kick from behind the line and it was blocked, Foster doing the kicking. The ball rolled back 30 yards to our 20 yard line where Foster got it again by good luck. On the next play, which was Wendell's cross buck, Wendell fumbled and Harvard recovered the ball on her own 12 yard line. After a gain of 5

49. When kicking from a close formation, it would be easier for a right-footed kicker to kick starting from the left side than the right side.

yards Brill kicked again, this time 35 yards the ball landing on the center line, where Spr. fumbled and we recovered the ball. Starting from here, the team took the ball over the line in straight rushes.

Springfield kicked off over our goal line and Wendell fell on the ball for a touch back. The ball was brought out to the 30 yd. line and Brill punted it 40 yards of which 10 were run back by Springfield men. Starting on our 50 yard line they made a first down and then fumbled and were penalized 15 yards for holding, at which point they kicked, the ball going to us on our own 30 yard line. Starting from there we rushed the ball to the middle of the field where on an attempt at a quick kick from behind the line the ball went only 5 yards and Springfield had it at about the middle of the field. In a play or two time was called.

In the second half Harvard kicked off to the 15 yard line, and as Springfield allowed the ball to bounce, we got the man in his tracks. Springfield made a first down and then were held and we got the ball on their 22 yard line. After carrying it to the 12 yd. line we fumbled, when Springfield after a play or two kicked 35 yds., the ball going to the 50 yard line, where we started off for a touch down, but on the third play fumbled again, after which we took the ball over for a touch down. White kicked the goals although his kicking was very poor. I shall give some time to that right away so that we may be able to depend on the points. Springfield kicked off to us on the 15 yard line, the ball was brought back to the 30 yard line. After bucking the ball to the 45 yard line, Foster make a quick kick and with its roll netted 45 yards. Springfield gained the ball on her own 22 yard line. Being held for downs she kicked 20 yards to our 42 yard line, where we recovered the ball and started for a touch down. Time was called with the ball on Springfield's 20 yard line.

Three or four things stuck out in all this work. In the first place, the fumbling was frightful—out of the first six plays there were four fumbles and a block kick. This was caused by two things perhaps: the playing with an absolutely new ball, which proved quite slippery, the fact that the team seemed a little tired when they went on to the field, and probably very largely to the fact that in running with the ball, Wendell's arm moved back and forth on his body, and when he fell he stuck the ball out in front of him with his hands for whatever additional distance he could get. This was, of course, criminal. Then, I think that the Springfield men grabbed the man by the arm very frequently for the purpose of trying to force the ball out of the man's hands. They certainly were very effective. These fumbles and the trouble we had made quite a difference in our getting together. Parker was temporary Captain and the team did not seem to be at all together. There was too much talking by various individuals, the back field work was very poor and uncertain, and the tackles were not down the field on the kicks. Our defense needs looking over and the men must have a little coaching on that particular point. The backs were frightfully slow in getting off and did not run hard enough. We shall have to get after all these points at once.

The game did exactly what I had planned it to do on the schedule; that is, to give us a tougher game than we had had yet and to show us our main weaknesses.[50] The question of end and full back is giving me a great deal of concern. The right end is not at all satisfactory, and the full back is not either. Carr is very slow in getting off and does not seem to be a very good ground gainer.

Immediately after the game was over I got out the Varsity substitutes and lined them up against a team which Brown furnished. The substitutes did better than the regular men, much to my surprise. The starting was poor, but the men played with a great deal more dash and scored easily on the second three times.

I also gave Knowlton, Squires, Peirce and Guild some practice, in starting and running and it went pretty well. I had dinner with Dr. Nichols and Lewis at the Union, and we talked for two or three hours on several points:—the question of putting on at once a tackle back, which we had decided to do; the question of defense, which we are going to take up on Monday night; the question of the line's blocking on kicks; the question of what is to be done with the ends, and also the question of who is to play full back. Lewis and I are going to have a talk tomorrow, Sunday, on these points to see if we cannot get things a little better together. Our tackling is very poor and we have got to remedy it at once. We have also got to get a formation for receiving kick offs—the one we have now is very poor. This should have been decided at the beginning of the season, and I thought we had it decided.

I went home and to bed about 9:30 pretty much worried, and it is going to be a question of quite a struggle on my part to get myself up into shape again. I have done so much plugging this summer that I have not got much spare energy and I have drawn a good deal on that spare amount the last two or three weeks.

Sunday, October 15, 1905

This morning Lewis came around to see me and we had quite a long discussion on several things. In the first place he feels that the team should be given the tackle back, or at least a part of it, this coming

---

50. The final score was Harvard 12, Springfield 0.

week; that the line and back should be quickened up, and not allowed to go on slowly and carelessly, as they have heretofore done, up to the West Point game. I agree with him on this and one big argument in my favor is the fact that Yale's backs have been fast from the start and are kept fast. I think that it was a mistake not to have given the backs careful instruction in their starting—in sets of three as they play—for the first two weeks of the season, and every day to have given the whole team starts with a view to quickening them up. Lewis and I experimented with each other on the starts and I have finally come down to this idea of it, which I shall put into practice tomorrow.

The backs should stand at the beginning of the season without his hands on the ground. The feet should be spread comfortably apart with one foot or the other enough behind the other so that the toes of the rear foot are about on the line with the heel of the front foot, or thereabouts. Then both knees should be turned in and the weight of the body put on the ball of the feet although the heel is all the while touching. The weight should also be on the inner side of the ball of the feet, rather than on the outer. Standing thus, if a man wishes to go to the right, he is enabled to give himself a starting lunge off of the whole side of his left foot, although perhaps as he starts he lifts his heel a little bit off the ground, but hardly before he does start. If, on the other hand, the man should start to the left, he can get a corresponding drive of his whole left foot on the inner edge in a similar manner, his bended knee of his right foot assisting him in a drive to the left.

Now as to the question of going straight forward. Obviously the push for the forward motion must come from the foot farthest back. If that foot is placed back at right angles to the rush line, the start can be secured only from the toes, which is not a very broad base for a good drive. On the other hand, if the rear foot is turned to the right or left, as the case may be, so that it approaches in a measure a parallel position to the rush line, the runner has, as in the other two cases, a good chance to drive forward from the inside rim of his foot. Of course it is ridiculous to think of getting the rear foot parallel to the rush line, but what I mean is that the foot should be as nearly parallel to the line as the runner can get it and be comfortable.

Now as to the weight of the body; the men must not get down so far on their knees that the first motion they make has got to be an upward lift instead of a low drive in the direction in which they are to go. To remedy this, the backs should stand so that their weight is well above their knees and so that their first motion may be directly and without any raise to their body, in the direction in which they intend it to be.

Another point is the question of the foot work from this position on the start, and of the hand work. The rule that we have adopted is that a man shall step toward the direction in which the play is going with the foot nearest that direction, and not that he shall first pivot on the foot nearest the point he is to attack, afterwards to bring the farther leg over in front of the pivot foot for the first step. This point was taken up and argued among the coaches a year or two ago, and they decided that it was undoubtedly the right way. I have made up my mind, however, that if any man, such as Nichols, can get away the way Nichols does, his foot work ought to be left alone because of a chance of spoiling it. We must here, as in everything, make allowance for the individual.

In the matter of the position of the hands, I am not allowing any of the backs, except the full back, to have a hand on the ground, and even then he has his hand just touching the ground and no weight on it. The other backs are keeping their hands either hanging down their legs on the outside or bent up a little between their legs, an individual matter purely. The thing to be avoided especially is having the backs try to stand up straight this way and on their toes because they at once begin to teeter, lean and get unsteady. As the men start their tails want to be low and not high, and in case the backs are running to the right or left, the first thing they must do is to turn their body at their hips as rapidly as possible, almost with a jerk, toward the direction in which the turn is to be made. Simultaneously with this quick turn of the body must come the drive with the far leg. Do not concentrate the attention of the backs on the first step that they have to take with the leg nearest the direction that they are running, but concentrate on the quick turning of the body and the initial drive; following this initial drive the steps do not want to be too long but short and fast. From the experience I have had with the team since this talk with Lewis, I find that this is undoubtedly the correct way. Dunlop and I have lined the men up in pairs of three each and just had them turn their bodies and take one step, and the increase in speed has been exceptional.

Another point that Lewis and I took up was the question of the defense. We have got to get the team pretty well settled right away; in fact it should have been settled long before this. Let me say right here that I was at fault this year in not having several coaches meetings before the season opened and get these matters straightened out.

My idea of what the defense should be is that the tackle should hit nine out of ten times the opposing end who is, in all probability, blocking him, taking care to keep the opposing end in such a position as to be able to run around the outside of him and hit a hard play there, or to drive in behind the opposing tackle into a play on the inner side; at any rate, the principle being that this tackle shall hit the play and break it up.

The rush line back should play about directly behind the tackle and not go in too soon, he and the tackle to have an arrangement so that in case the tackle at any time decides, by way of variation, to run into the opposing line pretty sharply, the half back and end shall hang out for the safety of the play. In case, on the other hand, the tackle keeps pretty well out, then the half back's primary responsibility would be to guard the inside, reserving as a secondary responsibility a play on the outside. Instead of going into the play as our Harvard ends have usually done, the end should hang out so as to prevent anything getting clear around the end, and instead of going in right into the play, we shall expect the tackle to do this, and then for the end to catch any man who is forced outside by the tackles' interference. Lewis and I both feel that with ends such as we have this year, green and rather small, we must look out carefully for plays around the end, and cannot take the chance of sending in the line men to get all smashed to pieces.

Agreeing on this much of the defense, I decided to have a meeting on the defense on Monday night, when each coach of a position should make a statement of facts so that we can come to a regular understanding. This I shall do.

Lewis also criticized the fact that I have been doing too much general work about the field and have been spreading myself out too thin, and that Capt. Hurley has not been given a chance to do enough on his own account. The criticism is perfectly just and from now on I shall try to get Hurley into the game as the leader.

I complained to Lewis of White[']s poor passing and lack of spirit, and Lewis says that he does not himself consider White an A-1 center, but that he does think that by the end of the season he will be as good as we have got, barring Parker, who at present is probably the best guard we have. Lewis wants Burr, the freshman, out, and I am going to try and fix it so, although his father is apparently pretty much set against it.

We also talked over the question of a quick kick from behind the line of scrimmage and the question of how the steps in getting a kick off should be taken. Lewis suggested our having the man who is to kick take one backward step after he received the ball before getting off the kick, thereby not getting quite so near to the rush line. I think this is a pretty good suggestion and I tried the step. The question is whether in taking the backward step there is not danger of having the kick blocked by a man on the same side as the kicker. I shall, however, take this up on Monday and find out about it.

Mrs. Reid and I went over to Brookline for the rest of the day and I tried to get foot ball out of my mind. I have felt tremendously up in the air the last three or four days because of my habit of worrying and because of the lack of sleep which I have had through it. The Springfield game on Saturday was so disappointing in the way the fellows played that I am inclined to see a good deal more disheartening in the situation than there really is. However, I shall get together now in a day or two and expect to master the situation.

Monday, October 16, 1905

Morning:

This morning I had something of a talk with Prof. White about the eligibility of Draper, the Penn man, and it seemed clear to us that he is not eligible. I have a letter from a Mr. Henderson, who had charge of the summer camp in which Draper was paid for teaching classes in gymnastics,[51] and we shall probably force him out on this account, if not also on account of professionalism, which I think we can prove.

After writing several letters and telephoning to Waters and Jim Lawrence, to the latter about the matter of goal kicking which needs attention and which should have been given attention earlier in the season, I went down to the field with Newhall, Starr, Hurley and White and gave White work in kicking goals, also Cunniff. Kicking goals, if done right, is very simple. Aside from the way in which the quarter back holds the ball, the important things are aiming the ball correctly, picking out the spot on the ball to kick, approaching the ball with only one step, and watching it as the kick is made. What White has been doing has been to stand off about a step from the ball, take a step, and as he kicks brings his kicking foot up behind it with a backward swing of the leg. The result is that during the time that his backward swing is being made he is having to balance himself on his

---

51. Amateur rules generally rejected as an amateur anyone who earned money from teaching any physical activity such as gymnastics or any other sport. A common amateur rule was that "No student shall represent a college or university in any intercollegiate game or contest who has at any time received, either directly or indirectly, money, or any other consideration, to play on any team, or for his athletic services as a college trainer, athletic or gymnastic instructor, or who has competed for a money prize or portion of gate money in any contest, or who has competed for a prize against a professional." See National Collegiate Athletic Association, *Proceedings*, 1908, 78. About a week later, the Penn faculty declared Draper ineligible. *Boston Globe*, 27 Oct. 1905, 7.

other one leg clear through the whole swing, which of course upsets him. Instead of this I instructed him to stand back a couple of feet, to [sight] the ball, then to step up within one step of the ball, get the line of direction between the ball and the middle point of the cross bar, pick from the line of direction the spot on the ball that he intends to kick, then take about half a step forward with the foot with which he does not make the kick, at the same time bringing the kicking foot straight forward off the ground without any bend in the leg, but with the leg rigid, and then deal the blow, being careful as the blow is dealt to watch the ball and carry the blow through like a golf drive. If the men are not careful at this they will make a short, sharp snap at the ball without the carry-through, and miss. The kick should be made, for an ordinary straight goal, at a distance of between 12 and 15 yards, at the angle, possibly a little father.

In the matter of holding the ball, I had the quarter backs keep as much of their hands off the ball, either in the forward part or the back, as possible so that the kicker should have as clear a shot at the ball as possible. In case the kick is made at an angle, I showed the quarter backs that their bodies should be pretty nearly at right angles to the path of the kick, in order to keep their bodies from getting in any way in a line with the kick, thereby hampering the kicker. Further than this, I insisted that the men should lie down rather than kneel down as some of them are inclined to do, because of the added safety to the play. The quarter backs should, of course, scrape off any turf that is in the way and which is likely to tangle up the kickers' foot, and they should rest long enough after a touch down is made so that both men have their wind. After not having kicked goals for [y]ears, I was able in this way to kick 26 out of 27 after a few minutes of practice. Jim Lawrence is by far the best man to coach on this, and I had him out this afternoon.

Afternoon:

This afternoon I had the backs out at 3 o'clock with Dunlop and Kernan, and we gave them first kicking and catching, and then starts. The catching is very poor and we need to give a great deal of attention to it. I had the backs in pairs catching across the field, while Kernan took the kickers. It was very hot and muggy, and we were a little afraid of taking too much life out of the men, so we did not make the practice very long.

The back field work individually and as a team is poor.

In the last part of the practice I turned over the backs to Dunlop for a little live tackling practice. Our tackling has proven very poor up to date. The men took hold splendidly.

We also gave Wendell some practice in holding the ball correctly so as to get him out of the fumbling which he showed in the Springfield game.

As soon as the line men came out, I gave the backs to Kernan for [f]alling on the ball, which I took the line men. Then, Waters not being out, Blagden took the line and got a second team up against it and we had the backs practice getting off kicks. About every third kick was blocked, and Lewis and Dunlop, Kernan and I were pretty much dismayed, but after thinking the thing over, I came to the conclusion that it would be very wonderful if the kicks were not blocked, since lining up the second lined up their full back in the rush line, and a back at either end of the rush line, besides the two ends and the tackles, who played free. Against this on-rush it was impossible for the kicker to get a chance to get a kick off. The reason of course being that the other men knew there was going to be a kick, and laying aside all fear of fakes and plays of that kind, rushed headlong through intent on stopping the kick. Getting the first team together for a minute or two I gave them one or two fake plays to run as diversion, and that worked most successfully, although a kick or two was still blocked. I have come to the conclusion about this matter: In having the men break through it was our idea to give the kickers experience behind the line—this they could not get because where it was either a plain kick or also a disorganized fake, the second did not pay much attention to the fake, since the ball was brought right back and special point was made of it, while by blocking the Varsity kicks the Varsity kicker lost confidence in his line and in his ability to kick, and the kicking became poorer and poorer, so that hereafter in case we are to have kicking of this kind, I shall allow only the lines to block against each other, which will get the kickers accustomed to the scrimmage work in the line while they are kicking, and will at the same time give them confidence. I have determined also to work out tomorrow morning or to-night two or three fake kicks to make this kicking effective, a fake kick being directed at each of the spots where the opponents are most likely to get through successfully. By working these fakes I am in hopes of making the most dangerous blockers on the opposing side so afraid of coming through that they will wait and that, therefore, the kick can be safely gotten off in the extra time thus given the kicker. Fake kicks are the best protection in getting a kick off safely that there is, so I shall put this in.

Another thing that I decided was that in getting the quick kick off behind the line of scrimmage, our rush line must play close together, since the main danger of having a kick blocked is in having the opposing tackle, end or half back get through after a play starts.

After this work was over I had some goal kicking by Cunniff and Parker, some running down the field by the ends and tackles, and finally a short line-up of about 15 minutes. The weather was exceedingly muggy and hot and the play was fairly lifeless, although the backs and line did get off somewhat quicker.

It does one good to see the cripples begin to show up again. Peirce and Squires are doing a good deal of running now, showing that we are doing all we can to keep them in practice. They are also doing some falling on the ball, some kicking and some catching and signal practice. Hall's arm is out of the sling, Guild's arm is out of the sling, Ball is back in the game again, and to-night will decide whether McDonald, who is a good end, is going to be eligible this year. In case he is, it will give us in McDonald, Hall, and O'Brien three pretty good ends. We tried Spear out on end to-day, but put him on an end he has not been accustomed to playing on, and he did not do very well, owing to a great tendency to cut in too closely on end plays, thereby allowing the half back to get around on the outside. In as much as he was playing on the same side as Fultz, who is a very poor end, it was not surprising that the Second made a number of gains in that direction; they were, however, unable to make any distance whatever against the left wing, which represents the Varsity.

To my delight Burr's father has consented to have his son out for the Varsity, and he will be given careful attention.

Montgomery will be able to play against West Point on Sat. Knowlton is showing up pretty well for full back, and I hope he will prove to be the man we so much need. Carr is fair, but only fair.

After the scrimmage was over, which lasted for 16 minutes, the men who had played reported to McMaster and I put the substitutes through a good lively lot of signal work, playing everybody who had a chance.

Kersburg has a sore shoulder and was laid over a day or two, but with a shoulder pad, will probably be all right to play against West Point.

I was, as I have been, very much displeased at the practice, but made up my mind at the meeting of the coaches to try and get them to put a little more life into their work, with a view of quickening the team up a bit.

Tuesday, October 17, 1905

Morning:

I had Starr come down to the field at 11 o'clock for practice this morning, in catching, punts, and which he is at present pretty weak, and I spent about an hour and a half with him trying to limber his body up and get a sufficient amount of give to it in receiving the ball, and he certainly did better before he left the field. He has got to be made into an absolutely sure catcher and a sure handler of the ball in the back field in order to do anything decent against Yale's quick kicks and any other quick kicks that we may have.

The weather was much cooler.

Afternoon:

We had preliminary punting, running down of ends, and a little kicking with the two lines lined up. The first team lined up for practice consisted of Starr, left end; Brill, left tackle, Parker, left guard; Davie, left guard; White and Cunniff, centers; McFaden, right guard; Fultz, right tackle; McDonald, right end; Spear, quarter back; Foster, left half back; Wendell, right half back; Carr, full back.

The Varsity blocked two kicks on the Second and scored twice in about eighteen minutes of playing. The backs got off very quickly and ran hard, and were dragged and pulled along in good style by the line men. After the different men had had quite a little playing, I made substitutions, putting in Newhall, quarter back, Bartels, right end; Nichols, left half back; Nesmith, right half back; Hanley and Somes, full backs. After this scrimmage work was over, during which I allowed no coaching, I lined up the following men for signal practice: Pruyn, left end; Squires, left tackle; Kersburg, left guard, he being out of the regular practice on account of a bad shoulder; White, center; Peirce, right guard; Montgomery, right tackle; McDonald, right end; Newhall, quarter back; Nichols, left half back; Gring, right half back; Kersburg, full back.

I gave these men a great deal of signal work, and also gave the line some considerable practice in starting on a ball. We must quicken up the team and keep it quickened up from now on, as it is very slow, especially in the line.

Capt. Hurley was allowed to run to-day and he ran 10 or 12 laps flat footed without feeling it. This was encouraging and I think it had its effect on the squad.

After supper Lewis gave the men a good talk on fundamentals, an outline of which appears on the opposite page [see table].

I think this talk was greatly improved in form to what it has been heretofore. I think it should have been made a good while ago, and next year I shall recommend that it be given very much earlier in the season. There was one considerable singing before Lewis' talk and we had a meeting of the Offense Committee right after the talk. We took up the question of the offense and decided to put on four of the tackle

Football

Individual

Fundamentals

The Ball
Passing
    Straight
    Underhand
    Overhand
Catching
    Punts
    Passes
Handling
    Centre
    Quarter
    Backs
Kicking
    Punts
    Place
    Drop-kicks
Falling on the Ball
    Dead Ball
    Moving Ball

The Man
Position for Line
    Charging
    Starting
Position for Backs
    Charging
    Starting
Line on Defense
    Breaking Thru
    Tackling
Backs on Defense
    Reserves
    Tackling
Line on Offense
    Blocking
    Making holes   ⎱
    Pushing   ⎰ Charging
    Pulling
Backs on Offense   Fighting Spirit
    Taking the holes
    Following Interference   ⎱ Quick
    Keeping feet   ⎰ Starting
    The last inch

Position Play

End	Q.B.
Tkle.	Hf. Bk.
Gd.	F.B.
Ctre.	

Team

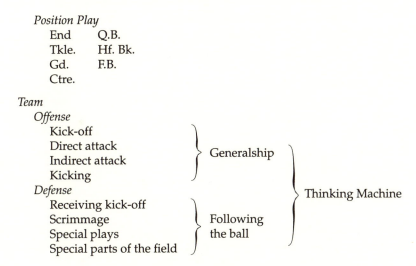

> *Offense*
>   Kick-off
>   Direct attack
>   Indirect attack ⎫ Generalship
>   Kicking ⎭
> *Defense*
>   Receiving kick-off
>   Scrimmage ⎫ Following
>   Special plays ⎬ the ball
>   Special parts of the field ⎭

⎫ Thinking Machine ⎭

back plays—"The straight tackle lunge between guard and center on the short side of the line", ["]the straight tackle lunge between guard and center on the long side of the line", and ["]the full back through the guard and tackle on the long side of the line, with the tackle facing into the guard-center hole on the long side". I shall have to accommodate the signals to these plays by tomorrow afternoon. We are for the present playing the far end up on the line of scrimmage instead of having him back, although it is quite likely that he will be back in the formation later on.

Wednesday, October 18, 1905

Morning:

I spent considerable time this morning in getting the assignments out on the tackle back plays that we have had, and in working out signals for them. I looked over the accounts of the previous Harvard-Penn games and found out that our lack of kicking had much to do with our defeat, other things being equal.

In putting on the tackle back to-day, I decided to have secret practice while we were giving the assignments, but to allow the crowd in later. Yale began secret practice probably on the same lines yesterday. Here I might say that I think we have made a mistake in not putting our tackle back on before this, at least in some measure. In my mind it should be run in signal practice at least, almost from the start of the season, and its going on should be planned absolutely before the season begins.

Afternoon:

In the afternoon Capt. Hurley and I planned out the work before we went down to the field.

First of all we had a little falling on the ball for the line men and backs, then some starts with the whole Varsity on a line, then we gave the backs to Dunlop for defensive work and a little live tackling, which seems to be a necessity. Meanwhile I took the backs that were not being worked and had them catch the kicks, with the ends running down, and occasionally tackling. The work improved a good deal. The weather was fairly muggy again—We have never had such a stretch of hot weather in a season before that I know of. Since Waters is to have the team to drive it on tomorrow, we made the line up this afternoon pretty short, only 10 minutes. The backs were not all as fast as they were yesterday, and showed a tendency to get off before the ball and to lean. We must correct this, and next year it should be taken up at the very start, along with goal kicking and catching punts. We had the backs doing some quick kicks behind the line for practice. Spear was in at right end on the Varsity with Fultz at right tackle. Fultz was an easy mark for the Second, and they made great gains through that side of the line, and they also got around Spear once for a considerable run, he running in close to the line in an endeavor to stop up the plays which Fultz was not handling. I hardly think Spear will make an end, particularly since he had trouble with his leg which seems unlikely to last any particular time.

After the practice and after supper, Daly took Starr and Newhall for a talk on generalship, and emphasized the fact that since the team is playing without a Captain, the quarter back must surely take more of the responsibility in his hands. He also emphasized the importance of the kicking game, the quarter back not having seemed to grasp that as yet. If we can only tide the team through the West Point and Brown games, and can get Hurley back as Captain, I think things will begin to round into shape. I constantly feel the great handicap under which I am working in that I have never before had a chance to see these different men play or to make up my mind as to where they ought to play. At any rate, when the squad is called back next year we should be able to lay our hands at once on the 50 candidates who have any possibility of making the team at the start, and thereby save ourselves the great amount of experimenting which we have had to do this year.

Thursday, October 19, 1905

Morning:

Before I came down to the office I spent considerable time at home going over the list of men that we have at present out on the field, trying to see if I couldn't make a better combination of men to play, and particularly to see if we cannot get a good full back. Carr cannot keep his feet, although he does good work behind the line on the defense. We need a rushing full back.

Of the possibilities on the field I put down the following men:—J. C. Bailey, 174; Burr, 195; Carr, 186; Craft, 181; Dearborn, 183; Fish, 171; Foster, 165; Gibson, 167; Gilmore, 180; Guild, 180; Hanley, 182; Inches, 175; Irving, 180; Kersberg, 197; Knowlton, 165; Lockwood, 170; Nesmith, 175; O'Hare, 172; Paul, 177; Pell, 181; Sholl, 175; Shurtleff, 168; Somes, 176; Wendell, 171; Whitney, 175; Stephenson, 171.

I am going to try to thrash out this list as soon as possible to see if we cannot get a good man out of it. At present we have no one who is satisfactory.

Having corrected the assignments on the plays we have thus far, I gave them to the stenographer to copy. I am going to drill each man carefully on his assignments and on the signals so that each man knows absolutely what his duty in every play is, and so that each man knows his signals without the slightest hesitation.

In thinking over the question of a kicker two things have struck me as being absolutely certain. One is that we cannot make a kicker out of a man who has never kicked, particularly in one year; the second thing is that if you want a kicker on the Varsity team, you have got to take a man who can kick and make him do the other things. In line with this we have as possibilities the following men as kickers:— Burr, Leonard, Wendell, Foster, Hall and Brill.

Burr is by all odds the best kicker out there and if he can stand the racket at guard, seems likely to be in the way to make a place. Next to Burr comes Leonard easily. He weighs only 160 lbs, and the only question is whether for the sake of his kicking we can afford to carry him as a back. He is the fastest man in our back field at present and the most elusive runner in an open field that we have. I am inclined to believe that with his open field ability in dodging and his kicking he must be given a place somewhere. He is not heavy enough and lacks driving power and life for quarter back. It looks as though he would have to go in at left half back. That will give us in addition to his possibilities as a kicker from the primary kicking formation, his possibilities as kicker in quick formation, which will give an added diversity to our plays. If Penn undertakes this year to block our ends on kicks, Leonard's playing is to be an absolutely necessary feature, since we cannot take any chance in letting Stephenson get loose on a kick down the field, such as would be very likely the case were the ball to go from the long formation directly into his hands. With Burr a possibility in the line and Leonard a kicker behind it, we have got two styles of kicking there to play, and then, I believe Leonard can be made into a drop kicker. We shall have to teach him what offense we can, and what defense also.

The next best kicker is Hall at end, who is pretty small, and as end, can hardly be depended upon for a great deal of kicking after he has banged into the opponents' offense for an hour or so, still he must be kept at it.

Wendell is an ordinary every day kicker without great possibilities, who probably will be unable to kick from close formation.

Foster is decidedly mediocre, and Brill has very small feet and no sense of study in his working out of a kick. He simply boots the ball, clubbing it rather than kicking it; as a general rule his ball simply fights the air and does not travel properly. Brill is heavy and thick and it would be impossible to work any fakes from the ordinary formation, which would mean that it would be a serious question as to whether an opposing team could not so concentrate on the kicks as to successfully block some of them. With Leonard they would find a mighty slippery man in runs on a fake kick. I believe with Kernan that Foster and Brill are practically impossibilities, and Leonard is the best of those left, provided Burr cannot play.

Afternoon:

This afternoon Waters was to have the team for 10 minutes of driving practice. The day was very warm and so we gave the men very light work until Waters arrived for fear otherwise of taking the life out of them. The men merely had falling on the ball, passing, and then a run up and down the field for signal practice, and then they lined up. The Varsity lined up with White, center; Burr and Kersburg, guards, Brill and Pell, tackles; O'Brien and McDonald, ends; Starr, quarter back; Carr, full back; Wendell and Nichols, halves.

The Second was unable to do much on the offense, while the First got along pretty well, although fumbles were altogether too frequent. No coaching was allowed and Waters went ahead by himself. This was all in secret practice. After the men had played some time, I took out Pell and put in Montgomery, who is now so that he is able to play, and put Bartels out in O'Brien's place, since O'Brien is a little bit banged up and slightly frail. I put Whitman in place of McDonald, put Nesmith in place of Wendell, and Leonard in place of Nichols, and Knowlton in place of Carr. The men did better than they have heretofore, although the weather was very hot.

Leonard got loose on a fake kick through the center once for a touch down, dodging beautifully. Knowlton did better at his work, but does not seem to me to be a first class full back. During one part of the practice Waters said to Brill—"Hurry up Brill, get into your place" and Brill turned around and walked up to Waters and said—"I am getting tired." Waters said afterwards that there were very few times when he was ever struck speechless on the foot ball field, but that he was then. He made no reply to Brill, but will talk the thing over with him on the way to West Point. From my standpoint, this little matter closed Brill out of my mind. He has an impossible temperament, and one which I do not think any one can handle. He is always likely to do some fool thing and you can never tell where you will find him. He is uncompanionable, and in his position on the field makes everyone on the team question whether he is playing his hardest, which, of course, greatly handicaps the morale of the team. I'm very certain that Brill will have to come off the team, and that we shall have to put in some other man as tackle in his place. Brill is not to be counted upon, this in spite of his great physique and would be fine rushing power if he would only give it. I am perfectly sure that we are wasting time on him, and just as soon as the West Point game is over I shall try to get Knowlton back into the line.

White, the center, passed the ball over Brill's head at one time and is as likely as not to do it on other occasions. He may have good spirit, and be a hard worker, but I am convinced that he is no center—what is more he is no athlete, and is very slow, and with feet almost approaching club feet, he has no possibility in the way of speed. He seems to me to be good only for a substitute center or guard, with Parker going in as regular center.

The team as I should pick it now would be:
O'Brien, left end; Knowlton, left tackle; Burr or possibly White, left guard; Parker and White, center; Kersberg and Peirce, right guard; Squires, right tackle; McDonald and Hall, right end; Starr and Newhall, quarter backs; Starr, Carr and some other man, yet to be found at full back; Leonard, left half back; Nesmith, right half back. That combines the greatest activity with the greatest kicking and proba-

bly the best defense, with unquestionably the best spirit. Brill might possibly be worked in at center, although Lewis does not want him in any of the center positions.

After this line up of 10 minutes was over, during which the First scored three times on the Second, I took Cunniff, center; Peirce, right guard; McFadon, left guard; Montgomery, right tackle; Davis, left tackle; Pruyn and Whitman, ends; Newhall, quarter back; Knowlton, Foster, and Snyder, half backs; and ran them through signals. Previous to this I had the Second eleven line up against the First eleven line in order to give Burr and Leonard some kicking practice behind the rush line. Burr got off several beautiful 60 yard kicks with perfectly tremendous height. Leonard got off some good ones too, although both men are a little slow in getting their kicks away. After this was over I got every man into signal practice and then sent them in.

There were out to-day among the coaches, Waters, Lewis, Dunlop, Daly, Kernan, Guy Murchie, Carl Marshall, [and] A. Marshall. C. Marshall came out to help the backs in their starting, but did not get a chance owing to the programme of the day's work. He was to have been out two days ago, when I had it planned that he should help. Murchie was also to have been out a day or two ago, and did not have a chance to do anything to-day, although he got in a few minutes with the quarter backs in catching.

After the practice was over I had quite a talk with Dr. Nichols and he says that Peirce and Squires will probably be able to get into the scrimmage during the latter part of next week, and that Hurley seems to be getting along very well, the doctors being unable to tell on examination last night which was his injured leg. One great difficulty with the team this year so far is the fact that it has no leader, and I think that at the beginning of the West Point game we have got to appoint a captain so that the men may have someone to rally around. The best men seem to be Montgomery, Parker, and Starr. We shall undoubtedly make one of those men captain. It is mighty hard for a team that has not yet gotten together owing to injuries, to have to play leaderless. Dr. Nichols feels more strongly than I do in the matter of the necessity for having a kicker, and on the necessity for dropping Brill and White. The Yale team is going to be speedy, and it is exceedingly sure that our team will be very slow if we keep these men on it, and what is more, it will lack in dash with men of that type.

Immediately after the West Point game we have got to put a combination together and keep it together for the rest of the time. We have got to walk through signals and assignments right straight along until every man's work is plainly cut out.

After supper I had the whole Varsity squad down in the first training table room where I made them a talk, going over the signals and the assignments for each play, and asking different men on the squad to explain certain things so as to make the men think. Brill and White, as was to be expected, proved the dumbest men of the lot. I took up the matter of the kicking game at length, and the combination of the kicking game and fake kicks. I showed the men the main reason why we had a fake kick run around the side on which the opposing team has the most of their men was because we wish to make those men less certain in breaking through the line, which would, of course, slow them up in their regular work to block kicks. Then in order to prevent the opposing team from putting their full back up in the line and trying to work him through the center and to prevent the guard and tackles from playing too far out, we have a couple of fake kicks through the line, and then so as to prevent the men on the non-kicking side of the opposing line from coming through too fast, we had planned a run of the tackle on the kicking side around the non-kicking side. I explained to the men that these plays were done for strategic reasons rather than for reasons of offense, and that they must not be disappointed if they gained nothing on them. The squad did not realize before what fake kicks were played for, and I think it rather opened their eyes, and I hope our fake kicks may prove more effective hereafter for that reason.

We considered sending a telegram to Penn of condolence over the unfortunate sickness of Zeigler, their best guard, who has typhoid and may not live. It was finally decided that lest such a measure should feel like crocodile tears and for fear that the papers should attempt to make a mean display of it, we decided not to say anything about it. At a meeting of the Athletic Committee to-night the matter of taking up the question of Draper's eligibility was taken up at the request of the Penn athletic committee, who want to know whether he would be eligible here or not. Our Athletic committee decided that he would not be for two reasons: First, because he played two years at Swarthmore before going to the Springfield Manual Training School, and in the second place, because he taught gymnastics and was paid for playing foot ball some year or so ago, of which I think we can get proof.

I forgot to say in connection with my account of the afternoon work that Dunlop, McMaster and I took the backs during the early part of the afternoon and gave them practice in starting, which I had planned out yesterday. As a result they got off very much quicker in the Varsity practice.

Immediately after supper I had a long meeting in my office at which were present Dr. Nichols, Lewis, Waters, Daly, Dunlop, Kernan, [and] Bowditch. The first proposition we took up was the question of the defense. I have given that to Lewis to look after, and I made him Chairman of the meeting. He then asked each representative what he thought should be done and put the ideas down on paper. The whole defensive ideas hinged about the play of the tackles. Waters is to play his tackles so that they are a little on the outside of the end or tackle of the opposing line. They are to charge the end each time, keeping on his outside, if the play is outside, and driving through between the interval formed by forcing the end back, and thereby leaving a space between the opposing end and tackle in case the play is on the inside. In any case the tackle is to hit the play. The whole style of Harvard end defense is to leave our end cut in early and hit the play hard, leaving the half back responsible for the play around end. This style of defense cannot be played here this year because we have not got heavy enough ends to do it, or experienced enough ends, in case they do do it, to make it improbable that a direct play around the end might not go successfully. With this point in view Bowditch modified the play of his ends whereby they should play out a little further than heretofore and come toward the play, aiming at the outside man of the opposing team, but not mixing up in the play, the ends to be responsible for plays around the side. The guard to play a little bit outside of his man so as to be able to slice through into the tackle-guard hole in case a play comes in that direction. His playing in this position will force the opposing tackle to play in fairly close instead of way out in order to keep our guard from going through and will thus give our tackle further out a chance to get through with only an end against him. The rush line backs must play at a little interval from the line so as to watch the tricks and see what is going on, then dive in. This seemed to be the general idea of what the defense is going to be, but Lewis is going to run it over. The coaches were ready to have both our tackle and end run through into the opponents' offense without having anybody, except the rush line back, stay out for plays around the end. This seems to me very weak and seemed also weak to Dr. Nichols, so between us we forced the situation of having the end responsible for outside plays, and in that to have him hang out to one side and watch for the runner.

After this very long discussion was over, I went over a short list of candidates to see what the different coaches thought were the best men we have. Lewis says that he considers White as the best center; he also says that White is not ideal, but that he thinks in the long run he will be the best man, and that he will not break, and believes that

Parker is the best guard and it would be too bad to waste him at center. Cunniff, in Lewis' opinion, is first substitute center. Parker, Kersburg and Peirce, with McFadon as a substitute, are the best we have as guards. At tackles the question was pretty much argued. Waters thinks that Brill will probably do and is to have until the West Point game to decide definitely. Squires undoubtedly, is the other tackle. Fultz and Montgomery would seem to be the best substitutes, with Spear if his leg holds out.

At ends are O'Brien, McDonald and Hall, who seem easily to be our best, with Pruyn, Bartels and Burnham and Whitman as substitutes. Spear is to be given further trial at end to see if we cannot get an end out of him, in which case if we fail, he is only substitute tackle.

At quarter back Starr, Newhall, and Sortwell are easily the best.

At full back Carr, Somes, possibly Paul, are the best, with Knowlton as a possibility.

At right half back, Hanley, Nesmith, and Wendell in that order.

At left half back, Wendell, Leonard and Peirce.

For kickers, Leonard, Burr, Wendell and Foster

Lewis made a good criticism, saying that we are not getting all out of Blagden that we ought to; that since he was good enough to come on here and give up his time, we should make the most of it, and that thus far we have not done so, which I think is true. We have not gotten out of him all we should have gotten, and I shall arrange to have him talk with the tackles in their rooms during the coming week.

It being very late after this discussion had taken place, we broke and went home.

Friday, October 20, 1905

Morning:

This being a very rainy morning, I did nothing but dictate until lunch time.

Afternoon:

I find that Meier is proving an utter failure as coach of the Freshman foot ball team, and at Eyres' suggestion, I had a long talk this morning with McDonald[52] in which I asked him to take charge of the Freshmen from now on. We must have a Freshman coach who will drill the freshmen so that next year we shall feel certain what men are

---

52. McDonald is likely W. V. McDonald, brother of the varsity end.

worth calling back, and so that we may also be certain that they are in good condition. McDonald is undoubtedly a good level headed fellow, and since he lives in Boston, can probably take charge of this matter for the next two or three years, which will mean a good deal to the possibilities of good development.

The following men are to be taken to West Point, and will leave the Square this afternoon at 3:55,—

Bartels, Brill, Burr, Carr, Cunniff, Foster, Fultz, Hall, Hanley, Hurley, Kersburg, Leonard, McDonald, McFadon, Montgomery, Nesmith, Nichols, Newhall, O'Brien, Parker, Peirce, Pell, Snyder, Spear, Somes, Squires, Starr, Wendell, White, and Whitman.

It rained all the morning so that we had a short signal practice in the cage,[53] which I had put in condition for the practice, fearing if the cage floor were left as hard as it naturally is, that the men might twist their ankles. I did not allow Kersburg to come down to the practice at all, as he looks a little bit thin in the face.

We left the Square at about 3:55 and went to Back Bay Station where we took the 4:15 train. We had a special car as far as Fall River, where the men were assigned state rooms. We had some discussion as to whether to give the men state rooms according to their relative positions—a tackle with an end, or a tackle with a guard—or whether to give them a choice to select room mates. We finally decided on the latter point. As soon as we were on the boat everybody had dinner, the men being divided into groups of four or five each at tables for that number. After dinner the men loafed around the boat listening to the music and finally went to bed. A good stiff breeze was blowing and around Point Judith several of us felt a little bit sea sick, I being the only one who succumbed. During the night Daly, Dunlop and someone else, I do not know who, went around to McMaster's room and beating on his door woke him up, to McMaster's great annoyance. They also woke up a couple of men on the squad. I do not know what they could have been thinking about to take a chance of troubling the sleep of fellows who were on such a hard trip, and I shall speak to them about it when they come out on Monday. The squad seemed to lack cohesiveness, and the men instead of getting together, rather hung apart. I shall try to get them together from now on so that they are more like a family. They had no singing together as has usually been the custom.

The air on the trip was splendid, and if there had been plenty of blankets, the men could not have had a more comfortable trip. There

---

53. The cage was an indoor practice area constructed for the baseball team.

was, of course, no fog with such a wind, and it was more quiet than the men could possibly have had on the train.

Saturday, October 21, 1905

Morning:

Several of the men did not sleep very well last night, but I know all of them had a better rest than they would have had on the train. We left the boat after breakfast and went to the Murray Hill Hotel, where the men lounged around an hour or so before the train left for West Point. Waters and I roomed together, and owing to the little experience the night before, did not get up until later than the other men, and had our breakfast at the Murray Hill Hotel. While we were eating the team slipped off on the train to West Point, and when Waters and I appeared we found that we were left. This made only a delay of a half hour or so, but it prevented us from going up with the team, wholly due to thoughtlessness on the part of the Manager.

Arriving at West Point, on the Garrison side, we were ferried across to West Point, where the coaches were all taken to the Officer's Club for lunch, while the men had their lunch in the Cadet Mess Hall. Immediately after lunch everybody went to the parade grounds to see the parade which was a beautiful sight. Following this the men dressed. I had asked the two officials, who were Dr. Stauffer of Penn and Langford of Trinity, to come over to our training quarters and see our aluminum pads, which I told the men to wear. To my dismay when I got there I found that after the experience of the team last year at West Point, none of the men were wearing them, having left them behind. This disgusted me, since the men simply decided that matter for themselves without any consultation whatever with me or with Capt. Hurley. I was very much afraid that leaving them off might disable some of our team with poops and would prevent us from getting the team together as soon as I had hoped, and would further delay team work. Hereafter the men must be told to bring all their clothes unless they are instructed not to. The matter of wearing the aluminums in the game does not lie with the other team, but rather with the officials. If the officials say they are safe, that ends it.

There was a great deal of discussion before going out to the field as to the length of halves. West Point only wanted to play two 15 minute halves, or a 20 and a 15, because they said their men were not in condition. We suggested a 25 and a 15 minute half, but they would not agree to that, and so finally we settled the question by tossing up, and we won. The halves were 20 minutes. Hereafter I would suggest in this game as well as in all other preliminary games, that the length of halves should be agreed upon before opposing teams come here or before we go to West Point. We had difficulty in getting the length of halves we wanted in the Bates, Maine, and Springfield games, and we must look out hereafter that those teams understand that they are to play at least such and such halves, and that there will be no reduction in them, unless the weather is very hot or for some other reason that may be good, so that we shall play halves of stipulated length anyhow.

The team lined up as follows:[54]

O'Brien, Left end
Parker, Left guard
Kersburg, Right guard
McDonald, Right end
Leonard, Left half back
Parker was temporary Captain.

Brill, Left tackle
White, Center
Montgomery, Right tackle
Starr, Quarter back
Nesmith, Right half back

The wind was blowing at a frightful rate straight down the field, and in tossing up we lost the toss, which gave West Point the advantage of the wind.

Acting under instructions Parker waited in kicking off until a little lull in the wind, and then kicked the ball off from the right hand corner, where West Pt. would have least advantage from the stand point of the wind, which was blowing diagonally across the field rather than straight down it. Parker made a very good kick off and the West Pt. man was downed on his own 5 yard line. West Pt. immediately kicked and the ball was allowed to bounce by Starr, and was finally Harvard's on the other side of the center. Starting with it here, Harvard took the ball right up the field to West Point's 11 yard line, where with about a yard to go, Starr called to Leonard for a cross buck. Leonard was playing on the team solely for his kicking, and Starr's lack of judgment in calling on him for the distance was simply inexcusible. As it was, Leonard all but made it and ought to have made it easily if he had gone at it hard. West Point took the ball and punted it down the field again, when we tried once again to advance it up the field. A fake kick by Leonard failed to yield anything, and finally we were forced to kick. West Point got the ball and began some heavy plays through the line from tackle back formation. The plays were very strong and at first made some distance through our line,

54. Omitted from this list was Carr, fullback.

Brill not doing his part. Then they shot a couple of end plays around for some distance and got the ball about to their 30 yard line or so. The reason the end plays worked was because the tackles were not in a position to hit the plays as they should because the interferers hit our ends too much in tact where the ends could not possibly get at the men. Leonard was no help on the defense, and so were short a rush line back there. Kersburg played a very pretty game at guard, and McDonald played a good game at end, except on the defense where he was unable to do any satisfactory blocking. Parker played well while he was in during the first half. Nesmith played well all through. Starr handled kicks in the back field very poorly as in most cases he let the ball bounce. The first half ended with no score for either side, although we had come the nearest to it.

In the second half we put Burr in place of Parker, who had difficulty at kicking; putting Foster in place of Leonard, our defense stiffened up a good deal, although West Point won a couple of long runs. We blocked a couple of drop kicks and two more place kicks were blocked. We had a quick kick blocked; one of Burr's kicks was tipped, putting our men on side and the ball went down toward the end line with several Harvard men close after it, and McDonald finally fell on it over the line for a touch down. Burr kicked pretty well, although his kicking was rather disappointing on the whole. Montgomery had to leave the game on account of a bad crack he got. O'Brien had to leave on account of a broken nose, and Spear had to come out, after he had substituted Montgomery, for slugging, which was ridiculous. There was no slugging of any kind and the officials came very near putting Starr off the field for the same reason that they finally ruled Spear off for. The officiating was very poor and it shows very clearly that neither of the two will do as officials for our Yale game, which was the reason we had them as officials at West Point.

West Point held a good deal and were penalized about 60 or 70 yards for holding, off side, forward pass, etc. We ought to have scored another touch down in the second half easily if the team had played hard enough, as they carried the ball to about the middle of the field after West Point fumbled a kick up to the 5 yard line. Since our team only had the straight three-men back plays, which directed the full back buck between guard and center on either side, and half back straight dive between tackle and guard on either side, and two cross bucks between half backs, the two end runs for the half backs, the tackles running around the opposing tackles, and the kick, a quick kick, and three fake kicks. Then from the tackle back they had the tackle carrying the ball straight through between guard and center, both as a cross buck and as a straight play, and the tackle straight through between guard and tackle and a straight play—three tackle back plays in all.[55]

At first our plays went very well, but after we got near the goal line and West Point realized that we had no variations to our plays, her backs got nearer the line on the defense and choked up our offense. Let me say right here that notwithstanding Waters, I believe that hereafter the Harvard team should have most of the tackle back plays on by the time of the West Point game, since it is out of the question to expect a Harvard team to play a stronger team than the West Point team with the playing between the back formations and a variation. Waters' point that the men should be made to fight for what they get is a good one, but it seems to me very clear, and also to Lewis, Dr. Nichols, A. Marshall, Daly, Dunlop and Bowditch, that there is no reason why the team should not have diversity enough to its plays to be able to score without calling upon the line to make pulls through an opposing line that is pretty well closed up and is stiffened by a strong secondary defense behind it. Yale always plays her tackle back against West Point and West Point has always had a tackle back against us, and it seems as though we were asking a good deal to expect our team to beat a team the size of West Point with only about six plays, and none of them strong enough to make any consistent gains at the tackle. I am very sure that I am right on this subject, and in case I am here next year, shall put my idea into practice. I think there is a great deal in what Waters says, in not hurrying the formation too much, and in making the team fight, but I think they ought to have enough plays so that the other fellow does not know all the time just what the play is going to be. If we had had a tackle back on with one or two split plays even, we should have beaten West Point 12 or 24 to 0, and just barely missed making it 18 as it was. The starting of the backs is much better and at times there was some considerable power in the plays. Then again, the backs should be getting off much faster than they are at first go.—another point to be kept in mind. Carr did carry much of the work at full back and showed as good a ground gainer as any of the backs, besides doing good work on the defense. [. . .]

The best things about the game were the playing of Kersburg, who tackled all over the field, behind the line, and who followed the ball good; the playing of McDonald at end, especially in running down the ball on kicks; the following of the ball by the whole team, so that in almost every case of a fumble the Harvard men got the ball; and

55. The final score was Harvard 6, West Point 0.

the fact that we must have a kicker on the team, even if he cannot do anything else. Leonard was very poor on defense and offense, but was worth all his errors for the kicks he got off, which averaged about 35 yards against the wind. Dunlop and I had a big argument on the boat about the kicking. Dunlop said that Leonard was of no use, to which I replied that he might be no use on the offense or defense, but that he could kick, and the team must have a kicker. He wanted to see Burr do the kicking, to which I agreed in case Burr could stand the racket and was good enough to play. With a kicking half back, however, the plays are certain to be more diversified, and the other side cannot tell whether there is going to be a quick kick at any moment or a regular play. This point I am sure I am right on, and it is a question of our having Leonard do the other things for the sake of having him as a kicker. We've often been caught without a kicker and we must now have one.

I shall call over on Monday afternoon all the kickers on the varsity squad to see if we cannot make something out of some one of them. If we can, it will help us out greatly. If we cannot, Leonard has got to play left half back regularly, and be taught how to play otherwise.

Starr did very poorly in the back field, and has got either to learn to catch kicks or give way to Newhall, as in some cases the ball went into play bounced and rolled 15 yards farther than they had ought to do if he had gotten them as he should. We have got to spend considerable time on our kicking formation this week in order to make it safe since one block kick in a game may change the whole aspect of the game. The quick kick from close formation ought to be given more attention than it has been and ought to be begun among the fundamentals at the beginning of the season.

The condition of our men was good, much better than the West Point men, and except for Parker's re-hurting his back, and Montgomery's blows, one of which he seems to get regularly in every game, we came through about as well as could be expected.

Several things were made apparent by the game: in the first place Leonard and Burr have both got to play at times on that team, unless a kicker can be found elsewhere. Montgomery will never make a regular varsity player, since he is altogether too liable to injury. McDonald will probably be right end regularly. It is a question whether Starr will make a quarter back; Carr will probably do as full back.

After the game was over we took the first train back to New York, and on the trip had a coaches' meeting, when we talked over the different problems much of the information which I have already given was considered at that time.

We had dinner in New York, and said very little to the men about their playing. After dinner we all went to the theatre and then went home and went to bed. I roomed with Waters and we had quite a discussion about Brill and Knowlton. I do not believe Knowlton will be a full back, and should like to see him put back into the line.

Lewis went down to see the Brown-Penn game which ended in a score of 8 to 6. I do not know what he thought of it.

There were, as usual, a number of Yale men at the West Point game, there being Bloomer, Bull, Hoyt, and Kinney.

Sunday, October 22, 1905

Morning:

We had breakfast and took the 10 o'clock train for Boston, arriving in Boston at about 4 o'clock in the afternoon. Let me say that this arrangement for the trip was the best that I have ever known for the West Point trip, and would suggest that it be followed again next year. It may be a little more expensive but the expense is more than made up by the good rest and general condition which the team returns in.

On the way back on the train I had a meeting with Dunlop, and A. Marshall and Capt. Hurley on offense, and we planned out the other plays from the tackle back, which we shall give the men on Monday. I also got the quarter backs together and we settled upon further signals for the plays. The arrangement was very easily made and the team ought to have no difficulty in learning it.

The team went home, or out to Cambridge, as soon as they got in, except the men who were injured who were taken by McMaster or Dr. Nichols to be looked after.

We allowed no separation of the men in New York, although they wanted to go home or make calls or something of that kind, but we simply told them they were there for foot ball and not for calls. They accepted it in very good part. It is no use to allow any liberty on the trips at all, or else there will be no end of difficulty in bringing the men together and in getting them to think foot ball.

Monday, October 23, 1905

Morning:

I went over carefully the assignments for the plays to be given the team this afternoon, planned out the work for the afternoon, and dictated an account of things up to date. At noon time I gave the team some of the plays on the black board, and afterward had a long talk with Lewis about Penn and Brown, and offense in general.

The substance of the talk was about as follows:

Lewis said that the game was a very close one, the score being 8-6. The closeness of the score, however, does not indicate the relative merits of the two teams, since Pennsylvania fumbled so badly that it was impossible for her to take the ball long enough distances consecutively to take advantage of many opportunities for scoring which she had.

Brown played a very quick and active game and Lewis says we will have to look out for her. Penn's rushline playing was very crude and slow, her general playing was very rough—indeed, Stevenson, the Penn quarter back, knocked out Russ, Captain and end on the Brown team, by a deliberate blow in the face. This means, of course, that we shall have to look out for trouble of this kind when we play Penn. Lewis says that the Penn full back, Folwell, is a very good one, and that Penn played the quarter back kick as usual a number of times and very effectively. Lewis thinks that we ought to have no trouble at all in disposing Penn, as he thinks we ought to be able to beat them with our rushline work. Lewis showed me a number of the Penn formations and the plays for them. I shall not attempt to reproduce them here, since Brown, the coach of the Second team, has written them all out and they will be found in the back of this book [missing].

Lewis and I then talked over our own defense and settled on a number of plays to give to the team while we are developing others. They are all tackle back formation and the same formation as the tandem of 1901.

Afternoon:

We had secret practice again to-day and shall continue it pretty generally throughout the rest of the season. Our reason for doing so is to get a chance to put the plays on very carefully devoting a great deal of time to having the men learn their assignments effectually and to see them walk through them. Of course, such practice if open would enable anyone to copy down the plays in the greatest detail.

I find that we did not get through the West Point game as satisfactorily as I had hoped. Following is the doctor's report:

Parker,	Strained back - one week
Montgomery,	Poop - one week
Squires,	Scrimmage last of this week. Friday
Hall,	Kick soon as harness is done. Scrimmage 1 wk
Guild,	As soon as harness is done scrimmage
Peirce,	Scrimmage Wednesday

Ball,	
Hurley,	Scrimmage next week Wednesday
O'Brien,	Fractured nose, play last of week
Quigley,	Knee - begin
Snyder,	Scrimmage now
Carr,	Slight poop, out in two or three days.

These injuries were very annoying indeed since they might have been avoided if the men had taken their aluminum thigh guards with them as I had expected them to do, and which they had not done because last year West Point protested against them and they took it for granted that they would again this year.

For the practice, in addition to these men who were injured, I laid off White, Kersburg, Starr and Foster, all of them having had pretty steady work of it.

The first thing I did on coming onto the field was to send over to the Freshman field for Clark, Kennard, and Gilbert, the best kickers on the Freshman team. I turned them over to Kernan to try out since we need a kicker badly. When Kernan got them going I went over and took a look at them myself and had no difficulty in deciding that none of them will do, at any rate this year. Meanwhile, Burr, Leonard, Foster and Wendell kicked, while Starr, Newhall, Nesmith, Foster and Lincoln caught. At the same time the line men were given work in making holes and the ends were shown how to block tackles. Parker, White and Burr tried some goals and place kicks. The line and backs were given starts in order to try and quicken them up. Then followed signal practice in which I had the team walk through the various tackle back plays and in which every man in each play had to tell me what his special duty was in each play. It was careful drill in assignments and precision. The line up which followed was the longest we have yet had this fall, lasting twenty five minutes of actual playing. In this scrimmage Brill was the only regular player who was used all the way through. [Walter] Harrison, '06, came out and joined the Second squad to-day. He was one of the men whom I made an [e]ndeavor to have attend the summer school last Spring hoping that he could pass off an entrance condition and be eligible. I saw him play a splendid game on the Second to-day and I wished time and time again that my efforts had only been successful, because he would make just the full back we are hunting for and might possibly make a linesman.

Knowlton having had a week of preliminary work I put him in at full back on the Varsity in order to see whether we can work him in there or not. The trial was very discouraging as he shows no aptitude for the place even after every allowance is made for the [aw]kwardness which follows after a man has been out of the game for two or three years. He has not the right build for a full back or the aptitude for the place. After I tried him out for some time, I tried out Paul as full back, he having been doing some very good work on the second team, and in many ways he did very well. He is big and willing but pretty green and fairly slow. He seems to be as good as anyone we have now except Carr. It looks as though Knowlton would have to go back into the line for he is too good a player to be lost.

In the scrimmage the Varsity fumbled a great deal but somehow managed to score three times even in its weakened condition. The defense of the Varsity team was very good and it frequently held the Second team for downs. The Second tried the quarter back kick and practiced putting two men on the Varsity ends on kicks, in the endeavor to give the Varsity ends good practice in that way.

I told Pruyn, Bartels, Whitman, Davie and Burnham to report to the Varsity training table. Knowlton is already there.

Tuesday, October 24, 1905

Morning:

This morning I went in town and talked over the Brown-Pennsylvania game with Robinson, the Brown coach, and he said he did not consider Penn much—that in fact he thought they were very lucky in getting off without being beaten in their game with Brown.

Following this I went in and had a talk with Stockton, the head of the City Trust Co., which ended in my getting [Percy] Haughton out for the afternoon to help in coaching the kickers.

I then went around and saw Mike Farley and got him out to help on the ends.

It is pretty plain that Bowditch and Kernan while willing as they can be and faithful, do not seem to be getting the results in their respective departments that they should be getting and I must call in outside aid. The feeling that the different departments are not being handled as I had hoped they would be is worrying me very decidedly and I begin to feel pretty much on edge. I know that I am getting somewhat overtrained but one in my position cannot help that.

Afternoon:

In the afternoon the preliminary work consisted in falling on the ball by the whole squad. This was followed by a long punting practice with Haughton in charge of the kickers, though he did little except look on with the idea of finding out what the men were doing by themselves before doing any coaching. This seemed to me very wise, and I am coming to believe that Haughton, were it not for his tendency to in a measure disrupt discipline by nonsense, is one of the best coaches that we have—he certainly gets more out of the kickers than anyone else because he is full of encouragement and enthusiasm and the men respond. Farley and Bowditch watched the ends go down under the kicks, a most discouraging sight as they over ran the men continually and when they didn't overrun them seemed to be brushed aside [with] ridiculous ease.

We tried Snyder, one of the substitute half backs, out at end and he seemed to do very well indeed, showing considerable of the intuition necessary in an end, and was fairly certain of his tackles. We put Knowlton back at his old place at right tackle and he showed up very well there. In our endeavor to get at the full back proposition I had Davie put at full back on the Second for a while and had a man named [Austin] Mason try for it also. Mason has been doing some good work on the Second and looks as though he might make a good full back, but Brown says he has no head and that it is a waste of time to give him a try on the Varsity. Nevertheless I like his build and spirit and shall watch him. I have made up my mind to try out every man who has a show for full back either on the First or Second, thus getting in a great deal more trying out at one time than would be possible if I had it all to do on the Varsity team.

Davie got through the Varsity line in good shape as a full back on the Second and did some excellent pushing, but on the defense his work was poor—he is very awkward and it hardly seems possible to consider him further.

Burr at left guard played splendidly and Lewis and Andy Marshall devoted a great deal of time to him. He learns very rapidly and is very anxious to play. Nate Hall was out today with the shoulder harness that has been made for him on. He tried to do some kicking but it was evident that his arm was pretty weak and that the jarring caused by the kicks was rather painful to him. Since Hall is pretty light at end but is a good fighter with a very good head, we decided to start him at quarter back. A good illustration of his nerve is well shown by the way in which he played in the championship pool tournament of the University. It seems he put a little money up on himself in this tournament and was badly behind in his score. Instead of trying to hedge in in any way[, he] went about the room and bet anybody who was willing to bet that he would yet win. A number of fellows took him up and then he set to work and won. He is one of the gamiest men on the field and if possible we must utilize him. He is also a good drop kicker.

Sargeant of the '01 team, and Lewis spend considerable time with the centers endeavoring to get them to pass back more accurately. The line men had drill in charging and starting, in which department they were exceedingly weak in the West Point game.

Following this preliminary work, which sounds longer than it really was, we had a long hard scrimmage consisting of two 14 minute halves in which the bulk of the time was spent on kicking. Peirce and Squires were unable to get into the scrimmage but did get into some of the signal work. I am anxious to get the team together now as quickly as possible, and were it not for the injuries I think we should have a very good team. Were I able to play the men I want, I should at present line up the team in this fashion:

O'Brien,	l.e.
Brill,	l.t.
Burr,	l.g.
White or Parker,	c.
Kersburg,	r.g.
Knowlton or Squires,	r.t.
McDonald or Hall (but preferably a larger man),	r.e.
Starr,	q.b.
Foster,	l.h.b.
Nesmith, Wendell,	r.h.b.
Carr,	f.b.

The day's work as a whole was very profitable.

In the evening there was another football mass meeting which was most enthusiastic. At it Lewis spoke, and it seems he spoke of me in a highly imprudent way, saying that in his eleven years of experience as coach the efforts that I am now making as head coach are the most tireless and energetic he had ever seen, which was all very nice. He went on to say "I cannot quite make out whether Coach Reid is really the Pinkerton's eye that never sleeps, or like cascaretts, does the work while he sleeps."[56]

Wednesday, October 25, 1905

Morning:

Having found that Ted Meier, whom I appointed as Freshman Coach, was not doing his work well through lack of coaching ability, I called in W. V. McDonald, a brother of the end, and a fellow who has

56. A "Pinkerton's eye" is likely taken from the Pinkerton Private Detective Agen-

coached Worcester Academy successfully for a year or two, to have a talk with him. I told him that Meier was as earnest as he could be and as faithful, but that he simply did not seem to have the [k]nack of teaching or of executive ability. I asked McDonald how he would feel about taking the work up and he said he would like to do it very much on condition that he be given sole control, subordinate, of course, to me. After talking over things with him I decided to give him the work and told him to be down on the field today so to look on in order to be ready to take up the work tomorrow. If he will only turn out to be the man I want I shall have one great load taken off my shoulders.

It seems that today is my birthday and that I am getting quite an old man, twenty-seven years old—I feel about fifty. The worry has taken it out of me so.

Afternoon:

I tried to celebrate the day by assuming a more cheerful air than I have been able to assume for the last few days and succeeded fairly well.

Before I got dressed I met Ted Meier and told him how I felt about the Freshman team. He took everything I said in the finest spirit and said that he would not only be glad to turn the work over to Mc-Donald if I thought best, but would continue under him as an assistant coach if I wanted it. Meier's spirit in the whole thing was simply excellent. I told him that I would suggest that he resign on the ground that the work was taking more time than he could give and that he appoint McDonald in his place. He agreed to this and so announced to the squad before they went off the field that this change would be made. In this way I got over a rather disagreeable point.

This afternoon we had no scrimmage work at all. The bulk of the time being spen[t] on live tackling by the backs and ends in charge of Dunlop and me. We gave some of R. Brown's squad the ball to carry and had them run slowly toward the Varsity men who tackled them with the side dives. The improvement this afternoon almost warrants me in saying that a few days of this particular tackling is vastly better than almost any amount of the dummy.

Wendell and Foster took hold in a fine spirit and I think that Wendell has mastered our style of tackling in one afternoon and Foster about the same. Nesmith already tackles well. Leonard also did well.

---

cy, which advertised that it followed people day and night. "Cascaretts" likely refers to laxatives.

While this was going on we had live tackling also for the line in which Lewis and Waters had charge. This work lasted a little over a half hour. Following this we had some catching and kicking for twenty minutes and then careful signal practice by the First against a dummy Second which lined up opposite it but made no attempt to stop the plays, giving simply the Varsity men an opportunity to indicate clearly that they understood their assignments. At times the plays worked in this manner seemed rather congested, but as a whole the practice was very satisfactory. After thirty minutes of this work we spent some considerable time in working up interference at the kick-off. We also got the starting signal going. After this work Jim Lawrence gave White and Parker some work on goal kicking, Jim and I agreeing absolutely as to method.

Dr. O. N. Taylor who used to coach me at school and who is staying in Cambridge for a while was out on the field watching the work, as was [Thomas] N[elson] Perkins, a member of the Corporation.[57] [William] Garrison,[58] a former quarter back was out too and gave the men a little attention on the side in the live tackling practice that I spoke about.

I see in the morning papers that Draper of Pennsylvania, has been disqualified. It is just as well for Penn since I have a letter in the safe here which would have disqualified him later if present action had not been taken.

As soon as the practice was over I went over to Brookline with Mrs. Reid, had something of a birthday party at the Lincoln's and spent the night there.

While this was going on, Waters made the team a talk on the West Point game and I understand that it was a very good one.

Thursday, October 26, 1905

Morning:

I spent the morning in going over the assignments of tackle back plays very carefully and in trying to decide other ones to add. I am feeling so nervous however, over the Brown game that it is very difficult for me to concentrate enough on the work.

In order to give the college a chance to see the team play before the Brown game, we decided to have open practice to-day, though

---

57. The corporation was the governing body at Harvard. Perkins was a "Fellow" of the corporation from 1905 to 1924.
58. Garrison was a letter-winner in 1897.

we had a few minutes of secret practice before we let anyone into the stadium. In the preliminary work we had 5 yard starts for the line and backs and spent considerable time on running in kickoffs. Following this we had a signal practice of about 15 minutes, and then the line up, which consisted of a 15 minute and a 22 minute half. The work of the Varsity was both good and bad. The most satisfactory feature of the practice was the work of Nesmith, Burr, Starr and Newhall. We gave Guild, who is once more ready for scrimmage, a try at full back. In the first rush or two he hit himself again on the collar bone and it was apparently sore so I took him out and put in Somes who is about the only truck horse full back we have left. W. Peirce got into the scrimmage again for the first time since he was hurt but did not do very much.

Harrison played a splendid game at tackle on the Second, and if he were only eligible I should not hesitate to put him in Brill's place. Toward the end of the practice I put Nate Hall in behind the Varsity line to allow him to practice drop kicks and he got two out of five of them over. So far as possible I played two men in each position in order to prevent any one man from getting too much.

After the scrimmage was over I turned the kickers, Brill, Burr, Hall, Foster and Leonard, over to Haughton for drill in kicking. At the end of the afternoon I asked Haughton which of the kickers he thought was the best and he mentioned all but Brill. He agrees with me in regard to Brill—that he has not the nature and the application ever to make a good kicker or even a passable one. It takes a man of some considerable patience to learn to kick well and Brill has not this quality.

Norman Cabot was out to look over the ends with Bowditch, and I allowed Bowditch and Cabot to put men onto either the First or Second at end as they saw fit in order to let them be seen by comparison.

Friday, October 27, 1905

Morning:

I have felt so on edge all day that I was able to accomplish very little this morning, and spent most of my time at my house reading over the notes on my '01 season.

Afternoon:

Tomorrow being the date of the Brown game, we had no scrimmage this afternoon. We did, however, do considerable fundamental work. From 3:30 to 3:45 we had starting for the line and backs; from 3:45 to 4:00 we had live tackling in which Leonard got a great deal out of the coaching; from 4:00 to 4:15 we practiced on the kick off; from 4:15

on we had signal practice for two teams, the Varsity and the substitutes. During the signal work we put some considerable time on working up our kicking game. I laid off Brill and Carr owing to the work that they had had. I gave Guild and Hall work at quarter back.

After supper we had a meeting of the squad at which Lewis made the fellows a fine talk on fundamentals. I took down a few notes while he was giving it and follow here with those notes and also with an outline of the talk. The substance of the talk has been given before but it was presented in a very different way this time, the best we have yet seen it.

Lewis said in part, "If I had only one rule for defense what would it be" and then he asked different members of the squad to tell him what they thought it might be. One fellow said "break through and get on the ball" and then said "use your hands and get the ball", another said "keep the ball" another said "get low and go hard and get the jump on your opponent", and still another said "tackle hard." After listening to these various comments Lewis said "The one rule is 'follow the ball', we would need no rule if every man would do this. The best player on the offense and defense is the man who is right around the ball. Follow the ball is the underlying principle of any defense—on the offense if all men follow the ball we have team play—on the defense if all follow the ball we also have team play, and a team with perfect offense will probably always win. If, on the other hand, the defense is perfect, we never could lose, but it is impossible to prevent the other fellow from getting the ball, and so we must have some way of getting it away from him."

Then followed quite a long talk on the Harvard and Yale season with general applications such as are indicated in the diagram that follows, if I can get a copy [missing]:

I should like to mention here that this talk ought to be given very much earlier in the season than it has been this year.

Saturday, October 28, 1905

Morning:

In order to overcome so far as possible my nervousness over the Brown game to-day I went in town this morning and had quite a talk with Robinson, the Brown coach. He told me some considerable about the Penn game and something also about Dartmouth, and asked me to come in next week in order to talk over Penn in detail. Before I left him I asked him how he felt about our game, and he said that he expected us to win by some two or three touchdowns. I believed what he said because he was very open about it and I felt very much relieved. When I put Brown on the schedule where she now is I did so with the assurance of Robinson that he would not attempt to develop a team of such a nature that it would reach a climax at our game. He declared that he was after Dartmouth and could not afford to take chances of having his team out of shape when he played Dartmouth in order merely to make a good showing against Harvard. That he kept his word is evident from what happened this afternoon.

Afternoon:

We defeated Brown 10-0 in a good clean [h]ard fought game. The work of the past week showed in the playing of the team and I left the field greatly encouraged. We made one touchdown in each half and did almost no fumbling whatever. The first touchdown came after about ten minutes' of play, the halves being 25 and 20 minute periods. It happened in this way: Burr kicked off to Brown and the ball was run in to the 20 yard line; Brown gained 3 yards but was penalized 15 yards for holding whereupon Brown punted the ball[,] it being received by Foster on Brown's 45 yard line and being run back by Foster 25 yards. Because of holding the run was not allowed and the ball was put back to the 50 yard line. From there the team took it over Brown's goal line in thirteen plays, Nesmith, Foster and Carr doing the bulk of the offensive work. Knowlton finally scored on a tackle back play but Burr missed the goal. The remainder of the half was spent in a punting dual between Burr and the Brown full back. After a considerable amount of kicking[,] time was called with the ball in Harvard's possession on her own 25 yard line.

In the second half Brown kicked off over our goal line; Burr punted out to Brown's 40 yard line where the ball was run back to Harvard's 40 yard line. Adams of Brown, punted the ball to Starr on the Harvard 12 yard line; from there the team carried the ball the whole length of the field by strong rushing, a distance of 105 yards[59] including one penalty and one loss. There was no fumbling and the score was the result of one of the cleanest pieces of strong straight football that I have ever seen. The punt out for a goal[60] was spoiled by a Brown

59. One must remember that the length of the field at the time was 110 yards rather than today's 100 yards. The field had been 110 by 53 yards since 1881.

60. The punt-out for a goal was a method of getting the ball toward the center of the field for the extra point. If a player touched the ball down in the end zone (a touchdown), the ball was brought out perpendicular to that spot, and the point after the touchdown was then tried from that angle. With a punt-out for a goal option, the ball could be located more in front of the goal posts. The ball was punted from the point of the touchdown and had to be caught by a teammate, and an extra point attempt then followed.

man and so the score was 10-0. Shortly after this the half ended, with the ball in Harvard's possession in the center of the field.

I was greatly pleased with the work of the team as it seemed to be really shaken together, a thing that I had planned to bring about in as large a measure as possible during this week. The defense of our team was very good for Brown tried tricks of all kinds but was unable to do much with them owing to the magnificent defensive work of Foster, Carr and Nesmith. The team lined up for the game in the following order:—

O'Brien,	l.e.
Brill,	l.t.
Burr and Peirce,	l.g.
White,	c.
Kersburg,	r.g.
Knowlton,	r.t.
McDonald,	r.e.
Newhall, Starr,	q.b.
Foster, Leonard,	l.h.b.
Nesmith, Wendell,	r.h.b.
Carr,	f.b.

Leonard played very well. He made one tackle that may have saved us from a score; a Brown man got free when he came running down the field. Leonard picked him up with a good, straight tackle which he had only learned yesterday in practice, and threw his man back 10 yards.

White's passing for kicks was very poor and we shall have to get right at this weakness. O'Brien at left end did practically nothing during the whole game. I shall put him on the Second team or lay him off on Monday next. Carr played splendidly, keeping his feet well, pushing men along and doing good work on defense. He looks certainly to be the first choice.

We had our usual crop of injuries. Knowlton has developed water on the knee; Nesmith broke a small bone in his leg; and Newhall sprung his collar bone. We cannot afford any more such losses as this and be much of anywhere on our big games. I have never known a team to have so many injuries happen in the games with outside teams. Usually the accidents we have come in our scrimmages.

After the game I saw Starr and some of the men after they had had their baths. Starr was grinning from ear to ear. I knew the reason why and was delighted because he felt as he did. Carrying the ball for 105 yards without losing it is a might exceptional piece of work, and it was not surprising that Starr felt pleased over the fact that under his direction the team had done this. I gave him a good pat on the back and told him to take good care of himself between now and Monday. Such a performance as the team made to-day in carrying the ball cannot help but increase the confidence of the men in their own ability, and confidence is what they need. We have, I am afraid, overdone matters in getting the newspapers to rather black eye the team and its chances, I think it is high time that we began to encourage the team. Yale has been talking nothing except about her great team and I know she hasn't as good a team as we had last year. That talk is being given for the sake of its effect on the team and I believe it is wise.

I saw Robinson the Brown coach after the game and he was very much pleased with the result and spoke in a very complimentary way of our team. He thinks that we ought to be able to beat Penn without much trouble, particularly if the men can keep up their standard.

SUNDAY I did nothing but loaf.

Monday, October 30, 1905

Morning:

I went in town and had quite a talk with Robinson the Brown coach in regard to the Penn team and gathered some valuable information from him. He has promised to come out one of these days and watch the practice and give me his frank opinion about it.

Afternoon:

We had no scrimmage for the regular First Eleven this afternoon but played a team made up of substitutes against the Second eleven, and got considerable team play out of the combination.

The Doctor's report shows a number of men on the injured list and it is discouraging enough. Carr seems to have received a bad poop in the Brown game which will keep him out for some time.

Carr,	Poop—needs a rest
Cavenee,	Fractured clavicle, 3 weeks out yet
Guild,	Trots, Play short time tomorrow
Montgomery,	Poop, out a week
Newhall,	Injured shoulder out 7–10 days
Nesmith,	Fractured fibula
Starr,	Contusion hip, no scrimmage

Squires,	Fractured thumb, doubtful if fit
Knowlton,	Twisted knee, 7 days
Hall,	Play tomorrow.

The preliminary work consisted of punting practice and the line men were coached in breaking through on kicks. Parker spent some time in goal kicking with Jim Lawrence. Lewis gave the ends some blocking work with the line men, while Dunlop and I gave the backs starting practice. When we came to the signal work I took the Varsity squad and ran it through signals while Dunlop took the substitutes. Following this I took the Varsity and Substitute squads and lined them up opposite each other with Burr doing the kicking for the Varsity and Leonard for the Second, Lewis taking charge of the defensive work of the lines in preventing the kicks from being blocked. The work was on the whole pretty poor because the Second team knowing that there would be nothing but kicks rushed through with great speed and succeeded in blocking the kicks without difficulty. I do not believe it is worth while trying to practice getting kicks off under these conditions because I think having kicks blocked tends to hurt the kicker's confidence, and a man like Burr needs all the confidence he can get.

I gave the ends, including any man on the squad that the end coaches saw fit to take, to Bowditch in order that he might work them before Frank Hallowell who came out to give what help he could, largely owing to Lewis' urging. The brightest work of the whole afternoon was the return of Hurley to signal practice. He has been gradually warming up during the last few days until today the doctor said that he might get into the signal work, at any rate, for a time. The reappearance of the Captain seemed to give life to the squad and the practice went off with considerable dash.

After supper Hurley and I drew up a protest to send to Penn giving the names of Lamson and Zilligan as being men who really ought not to be eligible. Lamson we know has played two years at Swarthmore, two at Penn and two at Coe College, Colo., although while playing on the Coe College team he was attending a high school. Zilligan is well known as a professional.

Tuesday, October 31, 1905

Morning:

I felt so done up all day that I finally went in and took lunch with Dr. Nichols in an endeavor to get my mind off the place. I am badly overtrained I know and while I struggle against it as hard as I can, I have not got enough vitality left to struggle sufficiently. I simply go around in the morning so nervous that I am unable to apply myself to anything.

Afternoon:

There were two distinctions in the practice this afternoon; one was the fact that Hurley lead the squad out onto the field for the first time this year since he was injured, and the men went out with a great deal of vim. He was allowed in the scrimmage for about five minutes and came through it all right and feeling well. It was a great relief to me to have this happen because I knew if he didn't get through all right he would be unable to play again this year and we would then have to count on Wendell as a regular. The other remarkable thing of the day was the fact that I turned the team over to Waters for driving. We tried Carl Lincoln, the light but good half back, at quarter back in the endeavor to get a substitute for Starr, now that Newhall has a bad shoulder. I am hoping that both Hurley and Squires will be able to get into the game against the [Carlisle] Indians on Saturday. If they do this, we will be able to get the right side of the line pretty nearly into its final shape.

After practice I had something of a talk with Dr. Nichols and Herbert White and they have persuaded me to go to the theatre this evening and to go off for tomorrow and the next day in Herbert White's automobile.

Wednesday, November 1, 1905

Morning:

I got up late this morning and went down to the office to attend to some odds and ends. On my way back I met Herbert White who was in his auto with Mrs. Reid. I got in with them and we went out to Sharon. I was astonished to find how easy it was for me to lay aside my football worries. White made a rule that I could not talk any football on the trip and promptly put off any discussion I tried to raise. At Sharon we had lunch at a delightful little Inn and then came home, stopping at one or two places on the way. We reached Brookline just in time for dinner at White's house. Dinner over, we went down to Marblehead for the night. We stopped at the Cliff Club, and a very delightful place it is, and had a nice lunch before we went to bed. I had a telephone call from Hurley and he said practice had gone off finely.

Afternoon:

Although I was not at the practice, I got a careful report of it from Lewis who was in general charge of the work. It was Water's second day at driving the team and they went at it splendidly. With the scrimmage a long one of 16 and 23 minute halves, the team had a very little time for preliminary work. Hurley got into the game and the Varsity made five touch-downs and a safety against a strong Second. The special happenings of the practice were the end work of Snyder, who showed up splendidly, the dragging done by the whole team, Leonard's 80 yard run, and the good kicking of Burr. Hurley spoke most enthusiastically of the work, as did Lewis, who said that the playing was the best that the team had shown during the entire year.

Prof. White has had to make a statement to the Press regarding the situation between Harvard and Pennsylvania on eligibility. The papers are doing their best to stir up ill feeling and Prof. White had to clear the matter up as far as he could. His statement to the papers follows:

> In view of statements appearing in the public press regarding Harvard's protest of certain Pennsylvania players the chairman of the athletic committee desires to make the following statement of Harvard's position:
>
> By the articles of agreement between the University of Pennsylvania and Harvard[,] lists of players are to be exchanged at least three weeks before the game. Any objection to the eligibility of [a] player must be made within ten days after his name has been received. One graduate of each university is to be appointed to act as an arbitration committee to decide all questions arising under the agreement. This arbitration committee is to act upon the objection within four days. In case of disagreement the arbitration committee has power to appoint a third person to act as umpire.
>
> When the Pennsylvania list was received at Harvard the names of two players were noticed whose eligibility seemed questionable to the Harvard football management. Exercising his undoubted right, Capt. Hurley at once forwarded a respectful protest. The name of one of these persons is apparently to be withdrawn. Regarding the other person, the question of his eligibility turned upon a perfectly legitimate difference of opinion with respect to the application of the eligibility rules. The protest implies no charge of bad faith in the matter and is one which

ought to be discussed and settled in an entirely friendly manner. The arrangement for settling such cases provided by the articles of agreement gives no occasion for arousing bad feeling or recrimination.

Harvard proposes to accept the result of the arbitration without further discussion. There is absolutely no intention or desire on Harvard's part of withdrawing from the game.

Thursday, November 2, 1905

Morning:

This morning we all got up late and had a delicious breakfast. At about 11 o'clock we went out for a sail in Mr. White's sail boat; then Mrs. White took the train for home, while Mr. White, Mrs. Reid and I rode home later, stopping a while at Reading enroute. We got back just in time for me to see the end of the practice. After practice and after supper Mrs. Reid and I went into town to the theatre. I give the details of my little excursion because nothing could have done me so much good as this trip, and in case anyone else comes into such a condition as I was in, the remedy is right here.

Afternoon:

Following the two day's of driving which Waters has just given the team, we gave them this afternoon fairly light practice. The schedule follows:

2:35[61] to 3:45	Starting of the line and starting of the backs
3:45 to 3:55	Tackling
3:55 to 4:10	Line work
4:10 to 4:30	Signals
4:30 to 4:45	Kicking practice and end run by the scrub.

When I arrived on the field I was wearing a big fur coat and was approached by the manager who wanted to know of me while my back was turned who I was and what right I had on the field. He was greatly surprised when he recognized me. I found the work going on in good shape. Frank Hallowell was on the field working with the ends and he was doing most valuable work. The Second was given the ball and told to play end runs. Whenever they were successful

61. This likely should be 3:35, not 2:35.

the Second was told to play the same play over again more slowly, thereby giving the Varsity ends a chance to size up the plays, which they did, and which ended in their getting the end offense pretty well in hand. Then followed a scrimmage of 42 minutes, devoted however wholly to punting practice, Burr and Hall doing the kicking; Lewis superintending the starting of the men to protect the kicker. The work of Squires and Starr was good, Leary at end played good too, and looks now like a Varsity possibility.

In the signal work which closed the day, I took a hand and, feeling as though I had been off on a vacation for about three weeks, put a lot of spirit into the coaching and was greatly delighted with the result. I find it is most fascinating to me and that I am fast gaining in real affection for all the men. I cannot remember another time when as coach or Captain I had quite the same feeling toward the squad that I have toward this one.

Friday, November 3, 1905

Morning:

I got up pretty late to-day and drove over to Cambridge with Mrs. Reid just a little before lunch. I immediately telephoned in to Lewis about the afternoon's work and he told me what he planned and said he would bring out schedules for the coaches.

Afternoon:

Tomorrow being the day of the game with the Indians, we had no scrimmage work, though I had the first and second teams lined up against each other in order to perfect our kicking game so far as possible. We had in a number of substitutes in the line and gave Brill and Peirce a lay off. After the kicking work was over Lewis spent some considerable time walking the second team through such of the Indian plays as we know. The actual schedule of the work follows, and it was carried out in a pretty thorough manner, although the time allowed to each division was not quite followed:

3:35 to 3:45	Kicking and catching punts for backs and kickers
	Ends going down, but not tackling
	Goal kicking
	Line men incidentals
3:45 to 3:55	Walking through the defense
3:55 to 4:05	Receiving kick off

4:05 to 4:25   Signals—First ten minutes slow, particular attention being paid to assignments, and last ten min-
utes fast.

4:25 to 4:35   Kicking behind rush line
Everybody goes into the Locker Building.

After the Varsity had gone into the Locker Building I got together
the Second Varsity and had Daly, who was down here to watch the
Carlisle game with a view to getting points for West Point who is to
play them next Saturday, to walk the Second team through the West
Point plays in order to show us the formation. I wanted this done especially since we are at present trying to find a formation which will
do as a final formation against Yale. There are a good many things
about the West Point formation that appeal to Lewis and to me. In
the first place, you can use line men to great advantage through two
or three different spots, and there is more opportunity for diversity
of play than there is from our own tandem formations. On the other
hand, it is very lopsided formation and the question with Lewis is
whether a perfectly adequate defense could not be found for it. Daly
is most enthusiastic about it and thinks that with a good team playing it it should not be stopped. I got Daly during supper time to plot
out the various plays so that I could study them over a little more
carefully.

During the supper hour I decided to accompany Lewis to Philadelphia to-night to see the Lafayette-Penn game tomorrow. At first I
questioned very much whether I ought to go, but soon got over this
when I considered that I had not seen Penn play, and when I realized that our game with her takes place next Sat. The coaches thought
it a good scheme and so I left with Lewis on the midnight for New
York.

Before leaving the training table I arranged to have Waters take
charge of the team tomorrow and arranged to have Dunlop and
Brown go to New York to see the Yale-Columbia game. I also told the
managers to arrange a meeting for me with [Arthur] Hillebrand and
[John] Owsley [the Princeton and Yale coaches] at New York on Saturday night. Then I got the team together and told them that I wanted very much to go down to see Penn play and I felt a little appre-
hensive about the Indian game, and that unless they would promise
to win the game, I would not think of going. Brill, who was standing
in the back of the crowd, spoke up and said—"You go home and have
a good sleep Mr. Reid, and we will attend to those Indians." Many
of the other fellows said that I need not worry and so I went off feeling as easy as I could under the circumstances. The Indians this year

are supposed to be stronger than for several years and claim to have some very effective tricks, so I felt pretty dubious about the outcome of the game.

Saturday, November 4, 1905

Morning:

Lewis and I had breakfast at the Murray Hill hotel[62] and then took the train to Philadelphia. The night before, however, I went around to the New Netherlands hotel and had quite a long talk with Owsley, Shevlin and Camp[63] over the matter of officials. It is plain that Yale wants Dashiell very much and it is equally plain to me that we do not want him and we are in quite a muss as to whom to get. I found that I could have the conference this evening all right and told Owsley that I wanted to bring up the question of holding.

The Yale team was lounging around the hotel and looked in very good condition, although the men did not look to me like as formidable a lot as I had expected to see them.

Arriving at Philadelphia, Lewis and I went immediately to the field having had our luncheon on the train, and got some very satisfactory seats near the middle of the field and pretty well up.

Penn tied Lafayette 6 to 6, the score at the end of the first half being 6 to 0 in favor of Lafayette. Penn fumbled badly and ought to have scored twice more at any rate. They finally scored on a block kick. Penn's line played high and her offense was very slow in getting off, but had, nevertheless, a great deal of power in it. Her line men stood with their feet well behind them and their weight on their hands, a very awkward position, and seemed to use very little head work. Lamson is undoubtedly the best man Penn has. Stephenson played a dirty game again and was finally disqualified. His loss made no difference with the team, because he was playing a very poor game. I heard to-day that he has gonorrhea and his stomach has gone back on him. If such is the case it explains his poor work to-day. He was constantly fumbling in the back field and his passing seemed to lack

62. The Murray Hill Hotel in New York City was the site of the original meeting in late December 1905 of what became the National Collegiate Athletic Association. Sixty-eight colleges gathered to reform football, both in playing rules and in ethics.

63. John Owsley was coach, Thomas Shevlin captain, and Walter Camp chief advisor of the Yale team. Camp had written to Reid on 30 October 1905: "I also feel that Dashiell, in view of the fact that of his interest as a member of the Rules Committee, and personally, as well as from the fact that he has officiated in all our games since we renewed relations, would certainly be the wise choice. Furthermore, I understand that Harvard has taken him now for some of her other games." Walter Camp Papers, Box 20, Folder 572, "Wm Reid," Yale University Archives.

life. Penn showed several good fakes which Lewis and I got down and which will be combined with notes which Brown took in connection with an article on Penn's offense in the back of this book [missing].

I felt extremely uneasy all during the game because the report was megaphoned across the field that the score of the Indian game was 5-5. This was, of course, very startling. I felt a little better, however, when the report came later that the Indians had missed their goal and the score was 6 to 5 in our favor. When the score finally came in 11-5 in Harvard's favor for the first half I felt easier but still greatly worried at the fact that the Indians had scored. I was able to get very little out of the second half of the game because I felt so worried. When we got back to the hotel we learned that Harvard had won 23-11. This made me feel very uneasy about the Penn game in spite of the fact that Brown and Lewis said we ought to beat Penn by two or three touch downs. It seemed to me that there was a great deal of power in the Penn team which is greatly to be feared if it gets loose. We were not at all encouraged when we learned that Yale had beaten Columbia 53-0, although we realized that Columbia must have been off her feet to say the least.

Arriving back in New York about 8 o'clock I had a conference with Owsley and Hillebrand as previously arranged, and we talked over the article on holding which I had sent to them some little time ago, to which they said they could not agree. The conference was very unsatisfactory, since neither Owsley nor Hillebrand would agree to anything. The result was that we parted with the understanding that the interpretation of the rules would have to be left pretty much in the hands of the officials. We had something of a discussion as to the question of locking legs, which Yale is doing pretty generally. Hillebrand stood with me against it, while Owsley took the ground that it was allowable. The result is that that matter too, will have to be left to the individual officials for our games.

When I got to my room I found a note there from Dunlop stating that he had gone to the theatre but that I should not worry about the Yale-Columbia game, since he never saw anything quite equal to Columbia for playing.

Sunday, November 5, 1905

Morning:

Lewis and I got up to-day in time to get the 10 o'clock train for Boston and were joined on the train by Dunlop and Brown who, as I said before, had been down watching the Yale-Columbia game. We got a state room and spent the entire time in talking over a new offense. Lewis suggested a triangular form of offense something like one used last year as being just full of possibilities and particularly adapted to our team with its numerous line men capable of carrying the ball. We went over carefully and worked out all the plays that we could develop as possibilities from this formation and then took up the West Point offense in the same way, utilizing all that we had been able to glean from Charlie Daly on last Friday. Further than this, we reviewed the position plays from the formation which Yale used in the game against Columbia. Each system offered some very good points. All of them are strong on straight plays. The West Point formation seeming to provide with straight plays, however, a little greater diversity. The West Point formation with only a guard on the short side of the line is so lopsided, however, that we all felt considerable hesitation in giving that serious consideration, although the straight plays are undoubtedly extremely powerful. Realizing that something must be done and done quickly, if we are to have any further plays, I telegraphed to Boston to have Charlie Daly and Waters meet us on our arrival in Boston to join in consultation.

As soon as we arrived in Boston we went to the hotel Lenox and got a room and set out to work out plays. First of all, I got from Waters a brief account of the Indian game, he having had charge of the team on Saturday. Waters did not seem to be at all depressed at the showing, but said on the other hand, that for the most part the team had played about the best ball that it has yet shown. He said the offense was first class though a little slow. The team showed lots of fight and life, and with a little bolstering of the defense everything would be all right. It seems that Harvard scored her first touch down with ridiculous ease. The team never lost the ball after receiving it on the kick off. First came Starr, who received the ball with a run 5 yards the other side of center, from which point the team took the ball over the line in thirteen plays. The Indians in their turn which followed carried the ball from our 40 yard line over the goal line by bucking. This was followed by another touch down by Harvard, from the Indian's 45 yard line.

The great trouble in our game when the Indians made their touch down was with the work of Squires and Hurley, both men being in the game for the first time in over month. The result was that Squires played with very little head and played at least twice as far from guard as he had any business to play, and almost three times as far as he could successfully cover. This resulted in the Indians throwing a number of quick mass plays in the gap between tackle and guard, which had, therefore, to be met almost wholly by Hurley alone. This of course he was unable to do, with the result that the Indians made constant progress through this space. When Squires was kept in where he belonged, which was only occasionally, the plays were stopped readily. One of the plays that the Indians used most effectively was the old play of the tackle running around the other tackle from his position in the line. This play, so Waters says, seemed to absolutely bewilder Squires and Kersburg. The guard was unable to do much since the Indians put two men on him[,] leaving only one for Squires who was so far out as to need almost nobody. The score at the end of the first half was 12-5 in our favor. In the second half Harvard carried the ball from the Indian's 40 yard line of the goal for a first touch down, and from the Indians 50 yard line over the goal for the second touch down. The Indians scored their last touch down in the very last minute of play on the run back of a kick of 45 yards by Mount Pleasant, the Indian quarter back, who put the ball on the 10 yard line, from where it was carried over in three or four plays. The run was the result largely of an error in judgment on the part of the quarter back who signalled a quick kick with the ball on the Indian's 40 yard line, coupled with poor covering of the kick in the darkness by the ends. The scored ended, as I said before, 23-11.

The Harvard line-up was:

First half		*Second half*	
Hall,	l.e.	Leary,	l.e.
Brill,	l.t.	Brill,	l.t.
Burr,	l.g.	Peirce,	l.g.
White,	c.	White,	c.
Kersburg,	r.g.	Kersburg,	r.g.
Squires,	r.t.	Squires,	r.t.
McDonald,	r.e.	Snyder,	r.e.
Starr,	q.b.	Guilder,	q.b.
Foster,	l.h.b.	Leonard,	l.h.b.
Hurley,	r.h.b.	Wendell,	r.h.b.
Paul,	f.b.	Lockwood,	f.b.

The halves were 25 minutes.

Other comments that Waters made on the game were that Brill had shown some signs of a weakening but carried the ball in good shape. That Guild had played good at full back until he hurt himself, and Paul had done very well too.

The game was an absolutely clean played one and the best of spirit prevailed. The attendance was very large. How badly hurt the men who had to be taken out are remains to be seen tomorrow by the Doctor's report.

Following this we got to work, as I said, on the offense and Daly argued strongly for his West Point formation. After going over carefully the assignments for the various West Point plays with him and after going into as much detail as possible on Lewis' formation as we had worked it out on the train, we all went home, having decided to think the matter over and if possible to take action tomorrow definitely.

Monday, November 6, 1905

Morning:

This morning I went in town and got hold of Lewis, he[,] Waters and I having something of a conference in Water's office over the afternoon's work. We planned it out together, figuring in the weaknesses which Waters had noticed in the game Saturday. Then I went over to Lewis' office with him and we went over again the plays from his formation. I feel very uncertain as to whether it is going to be wise to attempt the putting on of another formation between now and the Yale game, seeing that we already have a lot of injured men who have not had as much practice as they ought to have on this formation, and the question seems to me to resolve itself into whether it is possible to give them enough drill to perfect the plays that we already have and at the same time learn new ones. I very much doubt it myself. The other coaches are unanimously in favor of adding the plays and so if we can get a satisfactory formation I think that is what we will do. Lewis and I then met Waters by appointment at Young's hotel and had lunch there for the purpose of talking over several points. In the first place, I raised the question about putting Knowlton back into the line in place of Brill. Waters was strongly opposed while Lewis was in favor of it. This makes a very difficult situation since it is taking a good deal of responsibility to over rule a man of as much experience and practice as Waters has had in the selection of men for particular position in which he coaches. I finally came to the conclusion that it would be better to make the mistake of sticking to the man that we had spent our time on all the season, in trying to utilize the other man somewhere else, perhaps at end—for he certainly will not do at full back. Our discussion lasted until it was time to leave for the field, when I went out with the other coaches in the automobile.

It being Monday, we gave the men light work which was also a good thing because of the rain and soggy condition of the field. The doctor's report that Paul has hurt his shoulder so badly as to be out of the game for the rest of the season. This injury made me rather angry because before I left for Philadelphia last Friday, I particularly instructed Hurley to see to it that every man who went onto the field was provided with leather covered shoulder pads with felt lining, which, by recent experiment, we have found to be the best shoulder pads we have ever had. In fact no men who have worn them have hurt their shoulders. The fact that Guild played without one was very probably the reason for his injury. This means that with Carr probably out of the Penn game, and Paul now hurt, and with Guild out with a weak shoulder, we have got to find another full back in the limited number of candidates which remain for that position, and it looks as though it would have to be Lockwood. I accordingly called Hanley and Lockwood over from the second varsity squad and put them at work. We laid off Burr, Starr, Hall and Kersburg, because they looked pretty tired after the hard work they have been doing the last few days. In addition, Starr has also got a sore shoulder. Cavenee who was hurt early in the season by improperly tackling the dummy began running today, and [Jimmie] Kerans,[64] who was quarter back for the second varsity last year, was on the side line, and wants to come out. Whether he will be allowed to report by the doctor I do not know.

The preliminary work consisted of work in handling the wet ball, some starts on the slippery field, some falling on the ball and some tackling. Following this the regular players who were left were given individual attention, Waters and Lewis devoting a great deal of time to the individual line players with the tackles and guards on defense, especial attention being paid to Squires, Kersburg and Hurley in blocking up the hole which developed on the right side of the line in the game on Saturday. Following this the line men were sent in. The ends who had been trying to get through two blockers in running down the field under kicks were carefully drilled in blocking

64. Kerans evidently had verneral disease. According to starting guard Harry Kersburg four decades later: "I remember a notation about Jimmie Kerans whom I knew very well. He was not a fellow who went out with women but the first time he did he contacted syphilis. You mentioned how he pleaded with you for a chance to play even going so far as to promise not to eat at the training table if he made the team. You pointed out to him that should he get a cut and any of his blood came in contact with one of the players who had a cut that the contacted player would contract the disease. Those were the days!" See H. E. Von Kersburg to Bill Reid, 26 Aug. 1948, William T. Reid Papers, "Correspondence" Folder, Harvard University Archives.

tackles and then sent in. This blocking by the ends we took up for two reasons; first because Penn last year put two men on our ends on every kick, and I thought it might be possible that they would do the same this year. I am determined, however, to make public the fact that we are practicing against this play, as well as developing the quick kick where any practice that Penn may be doing in blocking our ends will be useless, in the endeavor to bluff Penn out of trying it if possible. I think that by having our ends carry the two blockers out toward the side line as far as they will go we shall have a splendid chance to work one or two fake kicks, which we played in the Indian game for the express benefit of the Penn man who was looking on. If in the game Penn carries her double blocking system into operation and her two men do not follow our men out, the end will of course get free without any trouble. If they do follow him out, then one of our backs is almost certain to get in a long run through the unprotected territory. The practice ended with a line up of 25 minutes between the varsity substitutes and the second. The substitutes did very good work and carried the ball some considerable distance by bucking, although Guild's work at quarter back was very inferior and uncertain.

I forgot to say that the Varsity had 15 or 20 minute[s] of careful signal drill.

At the conclusion of the practice I told Hanley and Lockwood to report to the Varsity training table immediately.

After supper Reggie Brown put on the board a diagram of the Penn plays, our plan being to leave them there during the rest of the week for the men to study and learn. Meanwhile the second team is being coached in the plays and has already played them for some ten days. These diagrams will give the Varsity a good chance to see what they have been trying to meet.

While this work was going on the fellows had a good time singing at the piano, something that they do very frequently now in the evening:

Tuesday, November 7, 1905

Morning:

This morning I went in town with Herbert White and we got Dr. Nichols at the City Hospital and then went to Young's for lunch with Sullivan of the Boston Globe. At this dinner we talked over the wording of a letter which I am going to publish in which I intend to make the statement that football needs revision, and in which I ask the graduates Athletic Association to appoint a Committee to take the matter up at the close of the present season. The idea in writing the letter is this: In the first place the governing Boards of the University are, I understand, getting pretty uneasy about the present game of football, and spurred on by President Eliot,[65] are considering abolishing the game. This same feeling is to a certain degree prevalent among other College Faculties. Further, Walter Camp has been spending two or three weeks up in Canada studying the Canadian game, where they have to make 10 yards in three downs, with a view to getting points to incorporate in the revision of the game, which he, too seems to feel is now inevitable. By getting this letter printed now, and particularly before the Penn game has been played, Harvard will be on the front seat of the band wagon and some of Yale's fire will be stolen.[66] Dr. Nichols and Sullivan, who are in pretty close touch with the feeling of the governing boards, agree that this is a wise thing to do.

At lunch we got out a letter, a revision of one which we had formerly drafted and turned over to Mr. Sullivan for careful consideration, since it is very important that the wording of the letter should be precise and wise. After thinking it over, Mr. Sullivan is going to let us know what he thinks and then I am going to publish the final draft some time this week.

Immediately after lunch was over I took the car for Cambridge where I spent the time before practice in working out the day's work and in looking up the statistics of the weights of the Penn players.

Afternoon:

It was wet and sloppy on the field but nevertheless we had one of the best practices of the year, playing two 20 minute halves against the Second, which played the Penn plays whenever they got the ball and the Penn defense as nearly as we could give it to them when the Varsity had the ball. The Varsity scored six touch downs with ease, which the Second scored once after being presented with the ball by the coaches on the Varsity 5 yard line.

65. Charles W. Eliot, president of Harvard from 1869 to 1909, had been opposed to the brutality and questionable ethics of football players for more than a generation. He opposed football in 1905 as he had done in the mid-1890s, when he wrote: "The game of foot-ball grows worse and worse as regards foul and violent play, and the number and gravity of injuries which the players suffer. It has become perfectly clear that the game as now played is unfit for college use." See Report of the President of Harvard College, 1893–1894, 16, Harvard University Archives.

66. More than two decades later Reid, for the first time, revealed the plot to save football at Harvard. See *Boston Herald*, 17 Oct. 1926, E7.

I gave Lewis a great deal of opportunity for his defensive work and the team took hold in good shape, Squires seeming to have cleared up the trouble of Saturday. Lockwood, whom we played at full back, did very good work and kept his feet well. We tried Knowlton at right end and he did good work, getting every fake that was tried around his end and very effectively helping out Squires.

The photographers are beginning to worry me a good deal now as they want pictures of some of the men almost every day. To offset this I have about decided to appoint one day this week on which I will devote half an hour to the photographers giving them a chance to take pictures of any men that they see fit, only, however, on the condition that they will promise not to ask any more.

Hurley did some good playing on the offense and the practice was almost as ludicrous as a contest. The second team could not seem to stop the plays at all, Wendell making a touch down from the kick off.

Following the scrimmage work the ball was given to the second team at different parts of the field, such as the 40 yard line, the 20 yard line, the half yard line, 10 yard line and the 5 yard line, the latter being the only occasion on which the Second could get the ball over. After the practice I told Gilder, Leary, Gilmore and Snyder to come to the Varsity training table and we took a number of other men to the second training table.

The adding of so many different men to the training table is injuring our team feeling at the table since every new man that comes has to become to a certain amount acquainted with the other fellows and their way of doing things before he feels perfectly at home and before the other fellows feel quite as free toward him as they do toward the others. As the training table now stands, I have never seen such a mixed up lot of temperaments in my life. It seems as though they varied indefinitely. This is one of the problems in trying to get the team together.

After supper Dunlop went over the alterations in the assignments of our plays made necessary by the Penn defense showing the men what plays would have to be cut out and what ones would probably be the most effective, also what slight changes in assignments are necessary. Meanwhile Leo Daly had the quarter backs[,] running over with them the possibilities of the various plays and of the various men so as to get these things pretty fairly in mind by Saturday.

There has been much talk in the papers about Hanley's not getting a chance to try for the first team. The talk seems to be confined largely to the Post which is usually the paper that does the most complaining. It puts me all out of patience because Hanley had three weeks of steady work at the beginning of the season during which time he did not come up to scratch. Since then he has on two occasions not appeared for practice at all for two or three days, and then has reappeared without offering any explanation for his absence. Furthermore, he has had a weak ankle which has given away every time we have tried him. At least no man on the entire squad believes in him. I don't either, nor do the coaches. Our sole reason for bringing him to the Varsity training table and playing him now is because we have practically nobody else.

Wednesday, November 8, 1905

Morning:

It turns out in the papers this morning that no agreement exists between Harvard and Pennsylvania and that therefore, unless Penn chooses to take notice of the protest which we have made against certain of her players we have no appeal. It seems that the agreement which Harvard supposed she had with Penn was terminated two or three years ago by Prof. [Ira N.] Hollis,[67] but that no record of the termination being kept, the present Committees here and at Penn thought that the agreement was still in existance. This enables Penn to play whoever she chooses to play regardless of any protests that we have made.[68]

I am feeling so much in suspense over the Penn game and the situation in general that I am unable to do anything in the morning that amounts to anything. The main question in my mind is how to pass the time without worrying. My house seems very dreary to me because one of the rooms is pretty large and I am alone in it a good deal of the time. Whenever possible, I get someone to be about with me in order to have someone to talk with.

I had luncheon today with Dr. Nichols and talked over the whole situation with him. I told him that I was about all in and asked him

67. Hollis, a professor of engineering, had been on the Harvard Athletic Committee fron 1895 to 1903, becoming chair in 1897. He had been instrumental in the construction of the Harvard Stadium, the first steel-reinforced stadium in America, in 1903. The stadium was the gift of the Class of 1879, which gave a twenty-fifth-year graduation present of $100,000, inaugurating the practice of twenty-fifth-year gifts by Harvard alumni. See Samuel Eliot Morison, *Three Centuries of Harvard, 1636–1936* (Cambridge: Harvard University Press, 1946), 418, and "Professor Hollis Resigns," *Harvard Bulletin*, 17 June 1903, 1.

68. Harvard had threatened to break relations with Penn previously, but the Lamson eligibility controversy increased the desire to do so. See the *Boston Globe*, 1 Nov. 1905, 11, 2 Nov. 1905, 16, and 9 Nov. 1905, 8.

if there was not some tonic he could give me. He said he did not know of any that would be beneficial and told me I would simply have to put the thing through. I thereupon tried to grit my teeth to it and think I can get through the game in pretty fair shape now. I had quite a talk with the doctor about the letter which I spoke about yesterday and which I have received back from Mr. Sullivan. I felt like letting him know because I am so worked up that I do not like to spend any time on any outside matter. Dr. Nichols thought it would be very unwise for me to let it go and so I published it this evening.

I came out to the field in the automobile and we got out in good time; in fact promptly. This is something that has been a ban on the whole thing. The getting out later on the part of the doctors, largely due to the lack of promptness on the part of the college fellows who drive the auto, ought to be stopped. Another year, whatever else happens, the auto service should be arranged so that the doctors get out early without fail. Toward the end of the season they should be there by 2:30 in order to look at the men before practice, and thus give the coaches a chance to see what they have got to meet and thereby prepare for it by adjusting their plans. As it is, the lateness on the part of the doctors constantly keeps the whole squad waiting before going onto the field, because we do not want the men to do any more work than is scheduled and if we sent part out early they would have to keep on after the others came out in order to give the late ones their share. I cannot emphasize this point too strongly and it should be brought out with great care at the beginning of the season. Nothing should prevent the management from arranging to get the doctors out when wanted.

Afternoon:

This being the last day of hard practice before the Penn game, we gave the men a good scrimmage and it went very well. The men were dressed to play at 3 o'clock. We then had 10 minutes of preliminary work for the line men with Waters in charge, also Lewis, much of the time being put on Squires. At the same time this was going on there was punting for the kickers with Haughton directing, with the backs catching the punts and the ends going down under kicks. Then came the scrimmage which consisted of two 20 minute halves. The first half was subdivided as follows: The first 5 minutes, offense; the second 5 minutes, kicking; the last 10 minutes, defense; Between the halves we had a 5 minute rest; during the second period of 20 minutes Hurley took charge of the team and no coaches except myself were on the field. We did this in order to give the team as much confidence in itself as we possibly could. Both the offense and defense was well done. The only blot on the afternoon was the injury of McLeod, who on becoming eligible for the team to-day for the first time immediately broke his hand the way Squires did, putting him out of the game for a considerable time. On the defense the team did exceptionally well and continually stopped the Second when given the ball in the neighborhood of the Varsity goal line. If we can only get the team to play with its head in the Penn game I have hopes, although this team does not begin to compare with the team of '01 and Penn's team is stronger. Most of the coaches are absolutely over confident but I cannot see it that way.

It looks as though Lockwood would have to go in at fullback because Carr's poop will not permit him to run at all. We kept Starr out of the scrimmage because of his shoulder but hope it will be all right on Saturday.

Newhall is still out of the game and as Starr is hurt we have nobody but Guilder to put in there and he is very inferior.

We posted a list of the men who are to go tomorrow, and they are as follows:

Bartels, Brill, Burr, Carr, Cunniff, Foster, Fultz, Guild, Hall, Hurley, Kersburg, Knowlton, Leonard, Leary, Lincoln, Lockwood, McFadon, McLeod, Montgomery, Nesmith, Newhall, Nichols, O'Brien, Parker, Peirce, Spear, Squires, Starr, Wendell, White.

———————

Drs. Nichols and Smith, McMaster, and Ryan (the shoe maker), myself, Goodhue, manager, and Reynolds, Asst. Manager.

At the last minute I decided to add Hanley because Guild is not in first class condition and the chances are that Lockwood will not last through. I do not remember having taken such a squad as a first squad anywhere before, but it is due wholly to our numerous injuries. I had a row as usual with the managers over the number of second eleven men who are to go. I want to take the whole outfit as a small expression of our gratification of their valuable work which they have done during the season. I was not able to bring this about however, though I got most of the men along all right.

After supper Dunlop went over all the alignments of all the plays on the board in order that any man who had any questions might clear it up.

Following this I went down to the [Harvard] Crimson office and gave out my letter, having first, during the afternoon, showed it to Waters, Lewis and the other coaches. They all agreed that it could do no harm at all, though they could not see much necessity for it. After I had had the article in the Crimson office for some little time, Lewis came around to m[y] house and said that on thinking it over it was evident to him that there was one sentence in it that he wanted to talk with me about, because he thought it a little injudicious, particularly the sentence referring to the fact that I personally considered the game to have a bad influence not only on the College but on the public. Lewis asked me whether that would not be just as well left out. I agreed and immediately telephoned down to the Crimson office only to learn that the matter had already been given to the Associated Press. I thereupon got hold of Grilk and two or three New York correspondents and they promised to do everything they could to correct the mistake. I immediately revised the mistake and gave them a corrected copy, thus insuring so far as I could against the first copy by giving the newspaper something to print. In my desire to have the change made I went down to the Crimson office and hung around until midnight waiting until the efforts to cancel the first account had been successful. It turned out afterwards that only one paper in the whole lot published the sentence that I didn't want, and that was one of the New York papers. The letter follows:

John D. Merrill, Secretary Harvard Graduates Athletic Assn.

Dear Sir: After several years' experience with intercollegiate football, after careful consideration of the criticisms which have been made of the game, and after many honest but fruitless efforts to change it so that the criticisms could be avoided, I have become convinced that the game as it is played today has fundamental faults which cannot be removed by any mere technical revision of the rules.

Although I am willing to admit that the necessary roughness of the game may be objectionable to some people, that appears to me to be much less serious than the fact that there is a distinct advantage to be gained by brutality and evasion of the rules, because they are committed when the player and the ball also are hidden from the eyes of the umpire. For these reasons I have come to believe that the game ought to be radically changed.

I therefore respectfully request your association, which represents the alumni of the University, immediately to appoint a committee whose duty it shall be to make a careful investigation of the game as will remove the unfair advantage now obtained from violation of the rules, will put a higher premium on skill, make mere weight and strength of less value, and will produce a more scientific and interesting sport.

Very truly yours,

W. T. Reid, Jr.

Thursday, November 9, 1905

Morning:

This being the day of leaving for Philadelphia, I was of course very nervous and in order to occupy my mind as well as possible I went in town with Mrs. Reid in the morning while she did some shopping. Before leaving Mrs. Reid I went down to the South Station with her and got her a ticket and accommodations to Philadelphia, then I went to luncheon with Mr. Lincoln at the Exchange Club. After lunch I went out to Cambridge, got my bag and went down to the field where we had our final practice, which consisted only of running through signals for an hour, followed by a rub-down. The men went through their plays smoothly and in good spirit.

At 4 o'clock the men left in a special car from the Square, being cheered off by five or six hundred students. The send off was a most enthusiastic one and pleased the team greatly.

To my delight just as the car was pulling out [David] Campbell[69] appeared, a man whom I have longed for for the past month and whom I had given up trying to get. He told me that Coolidge,[70] the old Varsity Ball Nine player, in whose employ Campbell now is had written asking Campbell if he could not come on to coach. Coolidge had waited a little while and then telegraphed Campbell that he had business for him in Boston that needed to be attended to immediately. Campbell immediately left for Boston and when he arrived here Coolidge told him that the most pressing business lay out on Soldiers Field. I got him into the car with the fellows, then we had songs, etc. on our way in to the train. We had a car by ourselves on the train to Fall River, in which the fellows discussed more or less the letter which I had written and seemed to think it was wise.

At Fall River we gave the fellows rooms, having settled the rooming question on the way down. The question came up in connection

69. Campbell was a Harvard all-American end for three years (1899–1901), being captain in 1901 when Reid first coached.

70. Reid is probably referring to William H. Coolidge, a six-year letter-winner in baseball (1879–84) and a football letter-winner in 1882.

with that which I settled in this way. The question is whether to allow the fellows to room with the ones they want to or whether to put them in rooms by position—in other words, a center with a tackle, a guard with one of the tackles, or a tackle with one of the ends. At first I thought they should go by position, but finally came to the conclusion that the best thing to do would be to let the fellows choose for themselves which would insure good feeling.

Shortly after we got on board we had our dinner.

After dinner the fellows usually have done a great deal of singing or have done more or less nonsense, but on this occasion there was very little. The only thing they did was to get together and sing a few of the Harvard songs. I was disappointed in this because I had hoped the men would get together a good deal and sing more. Many of them went to their rooms and played cards, others loafed around or read, and still others went to bed early.

I roomed with Campbell. After I was in bed I told him to come into the state room with me, and we went over the ground pretty thoroughly. I told him that I felt some of the departments had not been well handled, not, however, through the slightest lack of interest or earnestness on the part of the men who were in charge but simply because they would not have the [k]nack of teaching. I mentioned, for instance, the end department, which Bowditch has. Here we are within two days of one of our big games without a good pair of ends and with the head of the department arguing that men such as Hall and McDonald are good enough for the Varsity. Then, I took up the matter of kicking in the same way and told Campbell about the lack of companionship on the squad, also the failure on my part to have the offense prepared early enough to insure its being safely in hand. Campbell was most encouraging in every way and while he said he could not say much to the team because he had not seen it play, still he said to me,—"don't worry about the end proposition because I will take that off your hands and will guarantee you two good ends for the Yale game.["] This was a great relief to me and took a big load off my mind. Then too, Campbell was so confident that we had done everything we could do that that eased me up and I finally got to sleep.

Friday, November 10, 1905

Morning:

We reached New York and had breakfast on the boat, going from the boat immediately to the Philadelphia train, on which we had a parlor car to ourselves. We arrived in Philadelphia at about 11 o'clock and spent the time between 11 and luncheon in getting the men assigned to rooms and in resting. We stopped at the Aldine hotel as usual and I told the men to be very particular in their actions since I understand the Aldine would not take our fellows for the last two years because of some very questionable things they did two years ago. The rooms we had were excellent and we cannot do better in Philadelphia than at the Aldine.

After lunch I played billiards to pass the time away and talked somewhat with members of the Harvard club, who were very good in their attentions toward us. To all such men who wanted to know what the prospects were I said that I could not tell—that while the coaches felt we should win, I felt considerable doubt [about] it although I acknowledged that I was so nearly overtrained that my opinion was not worth much. I had any amount of cards to various clubs and was asked to speak at the Harvard Club, but I did not feel like accepting. At 2:30 the men went out to [the field]. We went in special street cars since it was pretty cold and the drive was quite long. Arriving on the field we went to the gymnasium and were given comfortable quarters where the men immediately dressed. Following this we had an hour or so of signal practice supposed to be secret, but as a matter of fact almost all of the buildings around the field were filled with Pennsylvania rubber necks, so that in order to protect what few formations we had we kept our substitutes around the players so that nobody could see what was going on. We ran the team over the field and found that the cleats went well. The men were in excellent condition and good spirits. Following the signal practice the men had a shower bath and then we went home. As soon as we got in[,] Dr. Nichols gave me the following list of injuries which will show just what the situation on the squad is at present:

White,	Signals[71]
Parker,	Signals, try him out
Leary,	No signals, probably no good for game
Hanley,	No signals, probably no good for game
Starr,	Signals
Spear,	Signals, poor condition
Guild,	Signals, use as 2nd string
Newhall,	Signals, cannot play game

71. *Signals* means that an individual may practice the given plays (signals) but may not srimmage or do any rough work.

Carr,   No signals, cannot play

McLeod,   Signals, cannot play for 7–10 days at least.

When the men got back to the hotel I allowed them to go for walks or [d]o about anything they pleased. At the regular hour we had our dinner and the fellows were told that they might go to the theatre, so long as they did not go in a body and so long as they returned in good time for bed and for their rubs.[72] Instead of speaking before the Harvard Club I got Lewis to do it and I went to the theatre with Waters, Campbell and A. Marshall to see the Rogers Brothers in Ireland, which was a pretty poor show but helped pass away a good bit of time.

When we got back to the hotel I sat up for a long time in order to get so utterly tired out that I could sleep. Dr. Nichols had me take some Hot Scotch and a warm bath in order to help the good work along.

Saturday, November 11, 1905

Morning:

I made no attempt to get up with the rest of the squad but slept as late as I could, the latter part of my sleep amounting largely to a doze.

The first thing I heard was that Penn was planning to play Reynolds, who some time ago was declared ineligible, and whom the papers said had since been declared eligible by the Penn Faculty. The coaches talked the thing over somewhat and we decided that the chance of their playing Reynolds was very small. Dr. Nichols was positive they would not. About the middle of the forenoon McMaster took the whole squad out for a walk and afterwards the men returned to the hotel where we tried to keep them out of the lobby to prevent them from being interviewed by newspaper men and Harvard fellows who had come down on the midnight. Before lunch I got the squad together up in one of the rooms, and got Dr. Nichols and Lewis to say a few words to them, after which I made a few remarks myself. Dr. Nichols' remarks were something as follows:

> You fellows have now come to your first big game and you want to remember that if you feel nervous, the other fellow is

---

72. It was common practice for players to be rubbed down after practice and before and after games. People doing this were generally called "rubbers" or "rubbers down."

just as badly off. You want to remember also that nobody expects any man to do a miracle. All you are expected to do carry out your instructions as you have been told. The men against whom you are going to play have no license to beat you and they won't if you will keep your heads about you and do your best.

Lewis then made some remarks, to the line men and the team in general, telling each man to do his utmost, and then I followed saying to the men that I realized that they all expected to win and that a good many of the coaches felt so too, but that I had seen Penn play and didn't feel so sure. I told them the fact that Stephenson had gonorrhea, and gave that as an illustration of the kind of men they were going to run up against. I warned the fellows not to get in any brawls, and I also urged them to use their heads—suggested that probably the game had better be largely a bucking game. The men were very sanguine, and the feelings rather helped me along. While the team was having its lunch, I saw Mrs. Reid and my room mate and had a word or two with them, then left for the field with the team. Arriving there, the men were rubbed down and got into their suits. The day was a bright, clear one, with something of a wind blowing down the field, but not much. It was largely a diagonal wind, that came up and then flickered out. Before the team was ready I had quite a talk with Dixon, the head coach[,] and with the Referee and umpire, in which I said that there would be no sideline coaching on our part, or anything else unfair. They said they would do the same, and when the game began we were all in pretty good spirits. There was a good sized crowd on hand.

Harvard lost the toss and Penn chose the kick off, giving us what little wind there was. The first kick off went to Hurley on the bounce. He picked it up and ran back quite a distance but slipped and fell. A Penn man was off side on the kick off however, and so the ball was kicked over again.

On the second kick off the ball went to Lockwood, who fumbled; Starr got it on the 4 yard line, on the 9 yard line he slipped and fell. It was then that those of us on the side line realized that the field inside the 25 yard line had been soaked during the night making it slippery and hard for our men to get a foothold on. I found out after the game that Penn had put on long and new cleats in order to enable her to get over this muddy field, thereby hoping to handicap us. This happened in 1900 and in 1901 I wrote down to the Athletic Committee in regard to it, but it never occurred to me yesterday to do the same thing, as in recent years our team has had no trouble.[73]

However, it was Harvard's ball on her own 10 yard line. Instead of kicking as Starr should have done, he called for a straight buck play in the ordinary three men back formation, and then repeated the same play giving the ball to Hurley. Hurley fumbled the ball on the second play and the ball was Penn's on the 10 yard line from which spot Penn put the ball over, and then kicked the goal, leaving the score 6-0 against us.

Burr then kicked off for us, the ball going behind the goal line but being caught by one of the Penn backs who went after it but who fumbled on the 7 yard line, Lockwood getting the ball for us. Here Harvard should have scored at once, but in three downs lacked half a yard of the distance and Penn took the ball on downs. Penn then punted to Starr who caught the ball on Penn's 45 yard line and who slipped on the 40 yard line. From this point Harvard carried the ball straight down the field for a touch down, made the punt out, kicked the goal and tied the score.

Penn kicked off to Hurley who caught the ball on the 4 yard line and carried it back to the 41 yard line where Harvard started in with her offense but was penalized when fairly under way for holding, whereupon Harvard tried a fake kick, Hurley getting the ball but dropping it on being tackled by Folwell and losing the ball on our 53 yard line. In the next two or three plays Parker was disqualified for slugging Torry the Penn center and Captain, who hit Parker, White went in in his place. Here our offense seemed to get going and the ball changed hands once or twice after this with Harvard on the offensive all the time but wearing herself out in an endeavor to score from more than half the length the field. It is frightful to stand on the side lines and see these Harvard attacks go for 35 or 40 yards and then have the ball go to Penn only to be kicked back the full distance. I made up my mind not to do any coaching from the side lines, but I realized that our men were getting worn out and yet I could very well prevent it. All told in this half Harvard rushed the ball over 160 yards, to Penn's 10 yards.

At the end of the half it was evident that our men were not in good physical condition and that there was going to be a hard fight, so we sent the men in and had them lie down, then we fanned and rubbed

73. The watering of the field was likely the incident that caused Harvard to break relations in football with Penn until the 1920s.

them so as to give them all possible strength. The color in the faces of the men was very poor and I was very much afraid of them when they went out for the second half, although they seemed to be very determined.

The second half was pretty much of a kicking contest with Burr doing some excellent work, but with little opportunity for our men to get the ball into Penn's territory. Three times Penn had a chance to score, and the third time with only 10 min. left, she finally put the ball over. Lewis and Waters both felt that the team had quit. I did not feel that way, for it seemed to me that the men were in poor physical condition and had worked themselves out during the first half and lost all power of head work. Hurley seemed absolutely to be in the air, what the matter was I could not tell.

We lost 12-6 and Penn certainly earned her victory. Their team was in better physical shape than ours, was made up of older men, and was better generally, but it was not a great team at that.

The teams lined up as follows:

HARVARD		PENNSYLVANIA	
Leary,	l.e.	Scarlett,	r.e.
Brill,	l.t.	Lamson,	r.t.
Burr,	l.g.	Robinson,	r.g.
Parker,	c.	Torney,	c.
Kersburg,	r.g.	Holson,	l.g.
Squires,	r.t.	Rook,	[l.]t.
McDonald,	r.e.	Levine,	l.e.
Starr,	q.b.	Stephenson,	q.b.
Foster,	l.h.b.	Greene,	r.h.b.
Hurley,	r.h.b.	Sheble,	l.h.b.
Lockwood,	f.b.	Folwell,	f.b.
Our line averaged 190 lbs.		Penn's line about 185 lbs.	

Back of the line Penn's backs were heavier, while on the team Harvard was about 4 lbs. to a man heavier than Penn. Penn has older men than we have too; her team is made up largely of men, while ours is made almost entirely of boys.

One of the greatest handicaps to our success was the number of penalties inflicted by [Bill] Edwards[74] against us. We were penalized con-

74. Edwards was one of the better known officials. He had played football for Princeton in the late 1890s, making Walter Camp's second all-American team at guard in 1899.

tinually for holding, and for holding which Dashiell considers perfectly legitimate. In one case, having taken the ball 42 yards in 6 rushes, we were set back in the last three plays 15 yards at a time, actually placing the ball back of the mark where we had first started and putting us on the defensive when within five minutes before we had Penn well on the run. The curious thing about it all was that the penalties were all of them inflicted against the side of the line about which the plays were not going and where there was no excuse for holding if the men had wanted to do any. For instance, Brill would be penalized for holding when the play was going around Squires' side.

During the game Lewis remarked to me on the sideline, as did Bowditch,—"You are perfectly right in determining that McDonald and Hall are too small for the game", for McDonald was incapable of checking the Penn tackle. This was something that I had felt all along would happen, but something in which I was ready to hear to the opinion of those coaches, who, being particularly interested in their position, ought to be able to give better advise than I, although Lewis had stood with me pretty much on this point. His comment was—"You see we cannot do anything with such little men for ends!"

Leary on the other side of the line played a good game and tackled on all parts of the field. Penn could do nothing with his end. Burr played a good game, but we had to take him out before the game was over because he was so badly done up.

Lockwood, at full back, was a failure, being altogether too light for the bucking which he was called upon to do. He got hurt and we had to put in Guild, who was worse than Lockwood. Neither of them did any defensive work that was worth anything, showing very clearly that the middle rush line back, who would have been Carr if we could have played the man of our choice, is the most important of all the rush line backs.

Had we had Carr in the game and had Parker not been disqualified, I believe that Penn could not have scored, although we might have scored more than our one touch down. Carr's loss to us was the worse one we had. Peirce took Burr's place and did very well. We put Knowlton in a few minutes in place of Squires, Snyder in for McDonald toward the end of the game, and they both did well. Nichols and Foster did well too. We put Nichols in when Foster was tired out to get advantage of his speed and directed him to tell Starr to try some fake kicks and other plays, with a view to getting Nichols free around the end. He got free nicely once, and but for one man would have scored. On the next occasion he got free too, but fell over his own feet and lost his chance.

Immediately after the game I went in and congratulated Torrey and then went into the room with our fellows and did all I could to buck them up. Most of them were crying. Then I got into a Cab with Dr. Nichols and Campbell and we went back to the hotel.

After dinner we got the team together in a room up stairs and told them that I was ready to accept the blame for the whole thing and that the generalship has lost us the chance and that I was at fault in giving such positive direction in regard to generalship. I was interrupted constantly by protests from the players and was cheered in the middle of my speech. The men said they would not allow me to take the blame, but that it was all theirs. Starr, Kersburg, Hurley, Lockwood and Parker were in tears the whole time and some of the other men were on the verge. Nevertheless, I felt exactly as I spoke, that the team had not been properly generalled and the blame for that lay on my shoulders for having prepared the team for the game in too much of a cut and dried way, instead of leaving the team to apply general principles for itself. For example, we told the team that Penn's defense would be so and so, that probably the best play would be through such and such a place. The team adopted these suggestions and when Penn shifted her defense, took no notice of it and tried to make the same plays go through a reinforced portion of the line. In the first half when we were held for downs almost on the goal line, Starr called for Brill to take the ball through the line. He did it two or three times and then Penn massed her entire rush line back defense in front of Brill, leaving the short side of the line without any rush line back defense at all. Instead of at once making a fake play with Brill and sending the full back on a split play against the short side, Starr sent Brill through the same spot and he could not get through, so we lost the ball. That is one illustration of the poor judgment displayed. For this I take the blame because I had not insisted that the team should use its own brains enough.

Immediately after speaking to the men, I dictated the following statement to the [Boston] Globe correspondent, which was published in Boston.[75]

Without in any way wishing to detract anything whatever splendid fighting game which Pennsylvania played, it seems to me that Harvard lost a very fair chance for victory through the very poor generalship exercised in the first half.

For this poor generalship I take full responsibility.

75. See the *Boston Globe*, 12 Nov. 1905, 17.

The team was instructed to play a rushing game and carried out the instructions to the letter. As a result Pennsylvania secured her only chance of a score in the first half owing to a Harvard fumble on the 10 yard line. Obviously, the play under those conditions should have been a kick.

When it was early seen in the first half that Harvard was holding the Pennsylvania attack, Harvard should have played a kicking game and was fully prepared to do so, except that instructions were followed too much to the letter.

Without any special data to go by, I can say that Harvard must have carried the ball 10 yards to Penn's one in the first half; in fact, the Harvard team in attempting to buck Pennsylvania down the field on every occasion caused Harvard to use up her strength in the first half. Since the attack was directed largely outside of Penn's tackle, it was her ends and secondary line of defense that received the brunt.

The result was that in the second half Pennsylvania's line men were comparatively fresh and Harvard's line men were less so, owing to the tremendous amount of energy that had been expended in the first half.

In the second half, when Pennsylvania got the ball she was enabled to use her offensive strength, which she ought to have been made to distribute over the first half. Had Penn been forced to buck during the first half, she must have entered into the second half with much less potential energy than she did.

Many will probably feel that the defeat was due to overconfidence, which I do not think was the case, since Harvard went into the game expecting a mighty hard tussle.

The work of Edwards of Princeton as an official showed him to be the best official in the country today. Ever watchful and all over the field, he made decisions which any one interested in the future of football could not help but admire. Certainly, if any question remains in the mind of any one as to the work he did last year in the Pennsylvania game, when he was subject to considerable criticism, he has shown himself impartially just and fearless.

[. . .] Lockwood came up to me and said: "I want you to know that while your taking the blame on yourself is not right, the fact that you are ready to do it is the whitest thing I have ever known, I would give one of my right arms for you." All this with tears running down his face. Then Hurley came up, threw his arms around my neck and began to cry. He wanted to take all the blame himself and tried to make me agree not to make any statement such as I had made, to which I would not agree. He felt bad because of his fumble and because of lack of generalship, but I did all I could to comfort him and finally got him quieted by telling him that as Captain of the team it was his duty to keep up his courage and that of the other fellows, and that he ought not to give way to his feelings. Meanwhile, White[,] who had a bad crack on the eye which had closed it[,] was lying on the bed in the room waiting for his turn with the doctor. After lying there for a while he got sight of my room ma[t]e who was standing there. Getting up on one elbow he said "Are you Mr. Reid's room mate?" Whereupon my room mate said yes. "Well, said White, "I think he is one of the whitest men God ever made." A minute or two later Starr came up and took hold of me[,] his face all wrinkled up with grief, begging my pardon and begging that I give him another chance to show what he could do and an opportunity to make up for what he had not done. These [were] samples of the scene about the hotel during the early part of the evening. I never felt so sorry for a set of fellows in my life. They are such a good square earnest lot of fellows that I felt as though there was nothing I would not give to make them happier. A feeling of affection came over me which I never felt in connection with other teams and which is bound to last.

Later on the team took the Federal Express for Cambridge, while I went to New York with Mrs. Reid to the home of my room mate, to get away from everything over Sunday. This disappointment was so great that it made the experience one that I shall never forget, an experience that stirred me up to a remarkable degree and made me anxious to get out onto the field again in order to try and make up in coaching for my failure. The other coaches felt the same way. It was a sad experience all around.[76]

Sunday, November 12, 1905

Morning:

I got up late this morning and spent an hour or two reading up the newspaper accounts of the game. Then my roommate and his wife, Mrs. Reid and I went for an auto ride ou[t] about 25 miles from New York. It was a fine day and the crisp air, the beautiful foliage and the fact that we were in a different neighborhood proved a great tonic to

---

76. This was the first loss Reid experienced as a head football coach in 1901 and 1905. He had won the previous twenty games.

me, the effect of which was greatly added to by the thoughtfulness and sympathy of everybody else who was along. It was treatment of a kind that I shall never forget and I do not expect in a long while to be in a physical condition where the bottom seems to fall out of things as it did at this time—completely down and out. The ride and the fresh air, however gave me a good appetite. We got back to East Orange, where we started from[,] in time for a very delicious supper, after which Mrs. Reid and I took the midnight from New York for Boston. On this train almost all of the New York-Harvard men who had been to the game and stopped off at New York were, on their way back to Cambridge. I dreaded to meet these fellows because I felt that no criticisms they could make of me could be too harsh, but I did not hear a single reproach although several men spoke to me for some minutes—no compliments, simply sympathy. Nor did I catch any glympses that conveyed to me the slightest hostility. That feeling of support which this action on the part of these fellows, unwarranted it seemed to me, stirred me up greatly and gave me a great amount of determination and strength for I made up my mind that if the College is going to stand by in such a fashion as this, I am going somehow to make good as being the only means of my appreciation. I did not sleep much on the train, I was so anxious to get to work.

The football team arrived in Cambridge on Sunday morning and had breakfast at the training table, after which they all went out automobiling. This was one of the best things that could have been done, for returning tired out and glum as they did and wishing to keep out of the way of their college mates so far as possible, at any rate for the time being, the fellows naturally looked upon each other as their best friends, which in turn tended to draw the men more together than ever before. It reminded me of that little line of poetry which runs something like this:

A touch of adversity,
makes the whole world akin.[77]

It certainly had that [e]ffect in this case. The Managers reported to me that the men came back from their ride very much cheered up and with their minds made up to make things good during the next week. So that the effect of the Penn game on players and coaches was alike—the determination to bend too all the harder and to make things come

---

77. This line is likely adapted from William Shakespeare's *Troilus and Cressida*, Act 3, scene 3, line 175: "One touch of nature makes the whole world kin."

out right, much of this feeling being due to the manner in which the University stood behind the team after it had sorely disappointed that University. It is a peculiar experience for Harvard teams and a peculiar experience for the undergraduate body, it being one of the first times that I have ever known Harvard to stand as a body behind a beaten team through thick and thin.

Don Nichols it turns out sprained his ankle when he fell during the second half of the Penn game.

Monday, November 13, 1905

Morning:

Arriving in Boston this morning we took a cab out to Cambridge where we had breakfast. I got Campbell to come up to the house and we talked over the situation pretty thoroughly. He is not in the least discouraged and says he considers the team a pretty fair one and that in the two weeks that are left we can get a pretty formidable aggregation out of it. At 11 o'clock I went in town with Lewis and Dunlop and went over the new formation and got ready certain of the plays to give to the team, figuring out also, signals for these plays. At noon I gave the team the assignments for some of the plays we are to use against Yale changing them from what we played against Penn. We put these plays on the board where the men could study them pretty carefully.

Afternoon:

This afternoon the doctor handed me the following report:

Carr,	4 laps, play next week
Starr,	Laps
Parker,	O.K.
Montgomery,	Laps, play next week
Nichols,	Can't run for three or four days
Leonard,	Cold, can play
Davie,	Play in two days
Guild,	Lay off, probably cannot play this week
Hanley,	Laps, play 2 or 3 days
Paul,	Out for good
Foster,	Laps
Leary,	Can not run for two days.

Carr, as will be seen, is not able to line up; Starr can run; Montgomery can run; Nichols cannot; Guild cannot play; Paul is out of the game for good; Leary cannot run; Newhall cannot play; and Lockwood cannot play, at any rate until an X-Ray of his arm comes out, as he seems to have hurt it badly in the game. Burr's father telephoned me that he had a bad cold and was in bed, so that he will not be out until tomorrow anyway. With this condition of the squad, and it being Monday and that too a Monday following a defeat, it was not to be wondered at that the practice was discouraging. The men did not appear really discouraged, but showed serious determination. We gave the regular Varsity men practically no line up at all, except in the case of such men as Snyder, Peirce and Parker, who had been in for a very short time anyhow.

With Starr and Newhall unable to line up and Guilder a failure at quarter back, we had to do the best we could with Sortwell, who was, however, so uncertain in his passing as to make fumbling very prevalent. The only work of the day that really amounted to much was that done with the ends by Campbell, who sent the men down on kicks continually in the preliminary practice and frequently ran off down the field with them. He told me that one trouble with the ends in their failure to get down the field quick enough, was due to their getting a very poor start, and to illustrate it he had Hall and McDonald and Snyder stand on a line with him and go down. In spite of his lack of practice, Campbell was always there first and yet he cannot run as fast as any of the other men. This set the ends to thinking. We had a very profitable afternoon's work for them. Campbell put a great deal of life into his coaching and did not hesitate to speak pretty sharply at times, if the men did not carry out his orders promptly. Knowlton did some good work at right end. We had a scrimmage between the first and second but it did not amount to anything except as an object lesson to the members of the Varsity who were not in the play but who were told to follow right behind it.

Tuesday, November 14, 1905

Morning:

I spent the morning in conference with Lewis in fur[th]er detail of the new formation and then came out and worked further on the signals for it.

Afternoon:

In the afternoon the men who reported seemed pretty tired and so we put the afternoon in on signal work without any scrimmage.

To begin with it was rainy and wet and so in giving the team the new plays we took them into the baseball cage where the floor had been so prepared as to prevent the men from turning their ankles. In there we put the men through the plays very carefully, both the Varsity and the substitutes, then we went out onto the field.

Signs of the Yale game are beginning to show from all sides—the end stands[78] are almost done and as the men go through the timbers to the field it keeps before them the nearness of the game.

Burr was out on the field this afternoon, did some kicking and then went in. Harrison who has up to this date been playing on the Second and who is now eligible for the Varsity we put in at full back in Carr's place for signal practice,—more work for Campbell and some also for Haughton.

We put the whole afternoon on signal work.

The teams lined up as follows:

VARSITY		SUBSTITUTES
Leary,	l.e.	Pruyn
Peirce,	l.g.	McFadon
Parker,	c.	White
Kersburg,	r.g.	McLeod
Squires,	r.t.	Cavenee
Knowlton,	r.e.	McDonald
Starr	q.b.	Sortwell
Foster	l.h.b.	Leonard
Hurley	r.h.b.	Wendell
Harrison, Somes	f.b.	Harrison

We walked the men through their plays, trotted them through them and ran them through them, working to get speed and precision in what reparatorial plays we have and endeavoring to get our assignments re-arranged so as to successfully meet Yale's defense.

The doctor's report was as follows:

Lockwood,	Draining ankle discharge
Harrison,	O.K.
Snyder,	Signals
Leary,	Strap knee, signals, not kicks
Guild,	Signals
Newhall,	Signals

78. The Harvard stadium was constructed in a "U" shape in 1903 with an open end. That end was filled in with temporary stands for the Yale game to bring the capacity to more than forty thousand.

Brill, No signals
Nichols, No signals.

After supper Waters and Lewis spoke to the team about the Penn game. Both of them determined that the team had quit in the Penn game. For instance, [Waters] said that Foster had quit when he dropped the punt in the back field, and Parker had quit when he so far lost his temper as to be sent off the field for slugging, and so on wherever he had a point to make with the team.

Lewis' talk was something the same although much milder, both Lewis and Waters bringing out the point that they were being laughed at all over Boston at the display which the Harvard team made, for which they were partially blamed. They both said they had taught the team enough football to win, that they had expected the team to win, but that it had not done so and that in many instances the team had simply quit. These two talks were the results of a talk with Waters and Lewis yesterday afternoon, when both of them said they would have to stop coming out to coach unless they could tell the team what they thought of it, because they thought in trying to coach a set of fellows it was impossible to do them much good unless one was perfectly frank and told them just what he thought of them. Dr. Nichols and Dunlop were against the idea, but Campbell was for it. I finally decided to let Waters and Lewis go ahead and I asked the other coaches if they wanted to come in. Dr. Nichols came in, also Dunlop, A. Marshall and R. Brown. Dr. Nichols was much wrought up as was Dunlop, over what was said. I dreaded, too, to have the thing said, but felt that such measures were necessary and that I did not have the strength to do it myself. Some of the members of the team were very decidedly bitter over the talk, Parker and Kersburg among them.

After the meeting Campbell and I rode home and spent the night with Herbert White in Brookline.

Wednesday, November 15, 1905

Morning:

Campbell and I arrived in Cambridge about 10 o'clock this morning and went down to the training table for lunch. The men were fairly recovered from what happened the night before, and after lunch I got them together and spoke to them something in this fashion:

Now you fellows know that you are not quitters and you feel pretty indignant at being called such. On the other hand the work you did down at Philadelphia is bound to call forth all sorts of criticisms and you have got to meet it, and the way to meet it is to get closer together than ever before and play with almost vindictiveness.

I finished by making a personal appeal to each fellow there to respond in the afternoon's work and they took hold of it in excellent spirit. I told them that we were going to send them hard in the afternoon and I should expect each man to do his level best.

Burr's father telephoned that he is sick in bed and won't be able to come out until the end of the week. This is pretty discouraging since we have shown Francis every possible consideration in order to keep him in good shape. I telephoned to the family doctor, who is pretty much of an old fogy, and he won't let Burr out, so I made up my mind to play the team as though I was not expecting to have Burr in order to meet such a possibility if we had to.

Afternoon:

In a talk which I had with Dr. Nichols before the afternoon's work he told me that Harrison had injured his shoulder and would not at any rate be able to line up today or tomorrow. I never saw such luck. First he was ineligible, then two days after he was declared eligible he injured himself making it impossible for us to use him. Dr. Nichols said that the men should be kept on the field the shortest possible time each afternoon, that they should get out promptly and be through the work and undressed within an hour. This is good policy and I shall adopt it.

In the work that followed we gave the team very little signal practice but started them out in a scrimmage of two 20 minute halves. Almost as soon as they got out, the Varsity scored five times on the second, while the second scored once on a fumble by Squires. Foster and Starr ran through signals but did not line up. We played Knowlton at end again and he did very well. I had intended to have Waters drive the team because they need such a drive but with the feeling so strongly against Waters after his talk yesterday I thought perhaps I had not better do it and thereupon attempted to do it myself. I am unable to be severe enough to do this as well as I ought to because I feel too much of an affection for the men, and am afraid my drive did not amount to so much as it should have.

Dr. Nichols said to me in the course of the practice that he thought what the team needed was precision and speed and that we must avoid injuries by having a little less scrimmage and must get the men off the field as soon as possible. Furthermore, he urged that the team should be left by itself as much as possible or in the hands of some one man. The doctor, besides this, asked the rest of the coaches if they didn't think Hurley was a little queer in his mind. I was unable to notice it and I watched him very carefully. The doctor says he thinks he is a little out of his head, so we are going to keep a close eye on him from now on. The only thing that looks at all like it is the fact that Hurley is not a[s] prompt at the training table as he should be and I cannot seem to make him any more prompt by any complaints I make to him.

After supper we had some singing and then I spoke to the Freshman class in the Union at a mass meeting that they were having and in anticipation of their game with Yale on Saturday. I had very little to say but urged the class as a whole to back up their team and give it all possible support. After this I went home with Herbert White, taking Lewis with us. We played checkers and I had various concoctions. I learned after the season that White had put one or two sleeping powders in my drinks, with Dr. Nichols permission, and that was what made me feel so sleepy when bed time came.

Thursday, November 16, 1905

Morning:

I came over to Cambridge and spent the morning in trying to write out the assignments of all the plays with a view to having one copy typewritten off so that I could file it somewhere where the team would come and refer to it in case of any misunderstanding of assignments. This scheme I think is an excellent one although I found myself too nervous to keep at the work long enough to do more than indicate the assignments by symbols on paper without writing out what each man had to do. I would suggest that next year and hereafter it would be a good scheme to carry this plan into complete operation early in the season; soon in fact as possible after the offense has been planned. There is no reason why the team should not start off the season with such a book, even for the very earliest preliminary plays.

Having got the plays diagrammed out in this fashion I went down to the training table and had lunch and put them on the board so that the men might ask me questions about them. I had this board turned to the wall when the men went out so that no one who did not know the plays were there would think of looking for them.

Reports of the Dartmouth team indicate that they are very strong, and in spite of reassuring remarks by Andy Marshall, formerly a Dartmouth man, I think we are going to have a mighty hard struggle. Dartmouth beat Princeton 6-0 on the day we played the Indians and Yale played Columbia. It is queer when anyone is pretty well worked up he is ready to take in some of the big tales which the newspapers publish regarding the strength and speed of certain individuals or of certain teams. So much do the newspapers take hold of me nowadays that I have given up reading them any longer and have advised the whole squad to give it up also. Another thing that I feel rather annoyed about is the gloomy aspect with which the newspapers here are clothing the situation at Cambridge. It is true that I have encouraged newspapers to this policy, but I did not expect them to run the team into the ground, and now I shall speak to two newspaper men about cheering things up in every way possible. I think that there is a good deal in what Jack Parkinson, center of last year, said when he complained to me that a man was almost always cursed out in the papers or by the coaches without credit enough to him in case of a good job. I have carried this in mind during the present season on the field and have commented more often than I have criticised, but it has not been true enough of the newspaper situation. Grilk as press censor is a good fair fellow and I know that by speaking to him it will be all right. I am bothered by newspaper men wishing to take pictures, as well as photographers from Harpers, Colliers and Leslies,[79] who wish to get groups and pictures of motion for their magazines. I had a few days ago to let some of the men into secret practice for a few minutes in order to give them this chance.

I want to adopt on the field as cheerful a bearing among all the coaches as I can bring about. I realize that I am not much of a person to talk on this subject but I feel that I am in some ways more fitted to speak about it than anyone else. For instance, nobody has a harder time keeping cheerful than I do, and therefore no one is more sensible of the fact that it is difficult than I. Lewis has been going about the last few days looking glummer than I look and I got after him at noon today on this point and told him he would have to cheer up. This remark on my part caused a great deal of laughter among the other coaches, but even if I am unable to carry out my own instructions at least I try as hard as I can. Haughton is one of the best jolliers in the whole bunch of coaches, and so I arranged to get him out in the afternoon, and told him to make just as big a fool out of himself as he felt like.

79. Reid is referring to *Harper's Weekly, Collier's Magazine,* and *Frank Leslie's Illustrated Weekly.*

At lunch I told the football team that Waters was going to drive them today and that he was going to do everything he could to try and rile them, and I told them I wanted them to be sure and keep their tempers through it all. Then I told Waters that I did not want him to use the word "quitter" in any of his remarks, whereupon he said if he was going to be limited in the use of his expressions he would prefer to have somebody else do it. I finally yielded to him.

Afternoon:

Some of the men were a little late getting down to the field this afternoon and I got after them. Brill it seems came down fifteen minutes late having been attending a lecture which he said he was afraid to cut. Knowing as I do that the marks for November hour examinations will not be in until after the Yale game, I knew that he could not be put on probation and so I told him to cut whenever it was necessary in order to be on time for practice.

The doctor gave me the following list of injuries:

Lockwood,	Signals
Parker,	
Foster,	Signals
Montgomery,	Signals
Hanley,	Laps
Snyder,	Can play
Guild,	Cannot play
Carr,	Laps
O'Brien,	Can play
Harrrison,	Cannot play today
Nichols,	Laps
Guild,	Nothing.

Following my scheme of giving the men their work as promptly as possible, we had a brief signal practice and then sent the strongest Varsity team we have into the game against the second with Waters in charge. The Varsity scored three times with considerable ease, while the second was hardly able to make any impression. Besides, we gave the Second orders to kick constantly in order to give our back field men a chance to catch and in order to give Campbell a chance to coach the ends in going down on the kicks, because he put some of the Varsity ends on the second in order to give them much needed practice. The men took hold well and I really felt quite ashamed of myself for having told them how Waters was going to drive them because my little protest had quite an [e]ffect on him and he was milder than I have seen him for a long time, though the men worked for him in good shape. Burr was not down to the field and the Doctor will not let him come out until after Sunday, much to Francis' disgust. The scrimmage was of 30 minutes duration.

Immediately after the line up we sent the men in and followed them up after they got in to see that they stayed under the showers only a short time and that they got dressed and moved out of the water as soon as possible.

Immediately after supper Dunlop went over some of the plays with such of the men as wished to do so.

Friday, November 17, 1905

Morning:

Campbell and I spent the morning talking over the squad and discussing the end problem in particular. Campbell thinks that Knowlton will do as an end, and that Leary looks like the next best man, with Snyder pretty nearly as good as either. He thinks that the ends are improving rapidly and that by the time of the Yale game we shall be better than we have been for several years.

At about 11:30 I went down to the field and coached Starr in catching kicks and gave Parker and White and Newhall work in kicking goals.

Afternoon:

This being the day before the Dartmouth game we sent the whole Varsity team off for an auto ride out around by the Wayside Inn. Meanwhile I took the substitutes and gave them very careful work on signals and formations. I arranged to have Reggie Brown, Lewis and Waters go to see the Yale-Princeton game, while Dunlop and I stayed to take care of the team in the Dartmouth game. We shall not be able to play our strongest team tomorrow because some of the men are not in the best physical condition and we do not intend to run any risks.

The team will play as follows:

Brill,	l.t.
Leary,	l.e.
White,	l.g.
Parker,	c.
Kersburg,	r.g.

Squires,   r.t.
Knowlton,   r.e.
Newhall,   q.b.
Leonard,   l.h.b.
Hurley,   r.h.b.
Lockwood,   f.b.

At the same time we are playing the Dartmouth team the Freshmen will play Yale on the Freshman field. The Dartmouth team is reported in good shape and we shall undoubtedly have a very stiff contest.

Saturday, November 18, 1905

Morning:

I stayed at home until lunch time when I went down and ate at the training table with the team. I found the men in fine spirits and Kersburg spoke to me in the most enthusiastic way of the auto ride. It was true that the entire squad looked rested and had some color.—a vastly different looking outfit from the one that went in against Penn which looked all done up.

Owing to the fact that it is getting dark so early nowadays we plan to begin the game at two o'clock, and so the men had to have their lunch earlier.

Afternoon:

After lunch while the men were dressing I went around to the Dartmouth dressing room to talk with the Dartmouth coach, Folsom, and to offer Dartmouth men any little courtesies that I could. I had a very satisfactory talk with Folsom and also had quite a talk with J. Bowler, the Dartmouth trainer, whom I made it a point to meet, since if we change trainers next Fall, as I certainly hope we shall, he looks like a good man and I plan to see him again when he comes to Boston with the Dartmouth track team.

When our men were all ready, Hurley came around to arrange for the length of halves and found great difficulty in getting Dartmouth to consent to as short halves as we wanted to play. Finally Hurley called me around and the two of us finally secured what we wanted, namely 25 and 20 minute halves, it being our idea with the few substitutes that we had to play as short a game as we could consistently play with the hope of getting through without injury. This turned out to be what happened so that although the game was a tie 6 to 6, it served the very purpose for which we had planned it.

I shall not attempt to describe the game in detail, but will confine myself largely to the remarks on the playing of the men and the work of the next week.

In the first place Dartmouth took the ball on the kick off and by various speedy plays in line bucking formations carried it 3/4 of the distance down the field, only to lose it on a penalty for holding which forced them to kick. Newhall received this kick on our 15 yard line, was thrown back to the 12 yard line by a powerful tackle by Glaze, the Dartmouth end, who threw his body at Newhall so that as he went through the air his body was near the ground. From the 12 to the 33 yard line Harvard carried the ball, after which Leonard kicked it a little beyond the center. From here Dartmouth started once more for our goal and in fourteen plays brought the ball to our 15 yard line. From here Dartmouth carried the ball over in one rush going on a tackle back formation just outside of Knowlton and drawing Hurley off who was backing him up, and dragging Newhall, who tackled the runner, over the line. On the punt out a very pretty catch was made by Dartmouth and the goal was kicked, leaving the score 6-0 in favor of Dartmouth.

Dartmouth was playing a very quick game and was doing considerable damage by having one of her players start before the ball was put in play, a thing of which Hurley complained to Dashiell [the official], but of which he took no notice. Glaze and Swazey, the two Dartmouth ends, were down the field promptly on every kick and were very effective—we haven't anything like them in college. After kicking off, Harvard finally got the ball on Dartmouth's 47 yard line, from which point, she took it over with Brill and Squires doing a good deal of work. Knowlton helped greatly by picking up a fumbled ball and carrying it forward 15 yards. Parker kicked the goal, making the score even.

At about this time I had to take out Lockwood, whose arm was hurt again, and put in Harrison. Harrison and Knowlton did good work, catching everything that came around the end of the line. The half ended with the score a tie.

In the second half I took Parker out because he was pretty well done up, and put White in at centre and Peirce at guard. White had been the mark of the Dartmouth attack during the first half, playing very high, and was repeatedly put back. He is no athlete and I think we have made a mistake in working so much with him all the time, still he does not get hurt and it is a good deal to know that a fellow will certainly be on hand throughout the season.

The second half was largely in Dartmouth's favor, she having the ball in our territory a good deal of the time, while we never once menaced her goal. I was afraid at one time that they were going to score and pulled out Leonard, who was doing poor work as rush line back, and put in Foster, who I had not intended to play. He immediately stopped up the hole and Dartmouth was forced to try a place kick, which was almost blocked and which went wide of the mark. The half ended with the ball in Dartmouth's possession in the middle of the field.

Had Dartmouth played us 30 minute halves I think that unless we had put in our full strength we would have been beaten. They had the fastest attack of the year and I am certain that nothing Yale has will prove any speedier. A good deal of the speed I understand is due to the use of the "bucking strap", an invention of Folsom's and something I intend to look into immediately after the season is over.

I forgot to say that after Lockwood got hurt I tried Hanley but he hurt his ankle and had to come out, after doing nothing the short time he was in. He is one of the only men on the squad for whom I feel a disgust, and I hope, in case I am not here next Fall, anybody else who has charge will not spend any time fiddling with this impossible man, to which statement every coach on the squad will say "Amen"!

To my delight, we got through this game without anybody being hurt. This was a most gratifying thing to me, especially since Harrison, who Dr. Nichols had said had hurt a nerve in his shoulder so that the chances were he would not be able to play again, went through the game, thirty minutes of it, without noticing it at all, which means he can play in the Yale game, in case Carr does not come out all right. That settles the full back problem.

About twenty-two thousand people came out to the game and it was well worth seeing, as only one thing in the whole game marred an absolutely clean contest. When Parker kicked the goal which tied the score a Dartmouth Freshman threw his head gear at the ball in an endeavor to spoil the kick. He was severely called down for this and I am certain his act did not represent the coaching he had received or meet with the sympathy of the large body of Dartmouth men present. I learned that on one occasion when Dartmouth had the ball and Harvard was penalized for holding, a Dartmouth cheer leader stifled an attempted cheer with the statement "We don't want to cheer unless we have earned something" which showed good spirit. I could not help thinking, however, at the same time, how much it was like the story told about Capt. Evans during the battle at Santiago, where, when one of the Spanish ships was sinking, his Crew started to cheer, the Captain yelled out "Don't cheer fellows, the poor devils are dying."

I had as a guest on our side lines Robinson, the Brown coach, largely as a compliment to him for the very kind way in which he has treated us in the way of suggestions and in the game that Brown played with us.

At the close of the game the returns from the Yale-Princeton game were almost all in and I waited on the field until the final score was passed, 23-4, the score at the end of the first half being 6-0 in favor of Yale. I was not wholly surprised at this and felt that we would do well if we staved off as bad a trouncing. Of course I was eager to hear the reports of the coaches who had gone down [to see the Yale game].

I forgot to say that a good portion of the game today we tried the formation which we have been working on the past week, and it went well—not especially because it is a superior formation, but because, being new, the men had taken hold of it with zest and confidence and had really made it go because of their confidence in it. I had not intended to use this play unless we had to, but we had to and so went ahead. I learned after the game that Dartmouth had been practicing a defense for our tandem plays as they had been able to see them played in open practice for a whole month and that the new formation upset them and enabled us to get through their defense when we probably could not have done so with our ordinary offense.

Leary played a very pretty game.

Taken all in all we had a most satisfactory game and I was extremely glad that we came through it so well.

Before going home for the night I left orders with McMaster to put in all his spare time tonight and tomorrow in getting the men into the best possible shape for next weeks' work.

Sunday, November 19, 1905

Morning:

I spent the morning in reading over the newspaper accounts of our game and the game between Yale and Princeton, and in listening to what Lewis had to say about the Yale-Princeton game. He said that Yale was very quick and had good team work, with their men in apparently good condition. Lewis seemed pretty well down in the mouth and I could get very little encouragement from him, especially in view of our showing against Dartmouth on Saturday.

Mrs. Reid and I went to Brookline for lunch and while over there I arranged for a meeting of the coaches at the B.A.A. [Boston Athletic Association] at 7 o'clock. We had dinner there also, because we felt that men would be able to come earlier if their supper were provided for. At the dinner I succeeded in getting Campbell, Dunlop, Haughton, Lewis, Dr. Nichols and Herbert White. I tried to get Brown, Andy Marshall and Leo Daly also, but was unable to do so for various reasons. Before we sat down Herbert White told me that Yale had a rattling good team and our chances against them were pretty small it seemed to him; also that the Yale team reminded him very much of a big, lean, hungry pack of wolves. However, the meeting was not at all glum, as everyone pitched in and did his best.

During the supper we talked over the make up of the team by position and settled on the order of substitutes. It ran as follows:

l.e.	Leary	Snyder	Bartels	
l.t.	Brill	Montgomery	Spear	
l.g.	Burr	Peirce		
c.	Parker	White	Barney	
r.g.	Kersburg	MacLeod	McFadden	
r.t.	Squires	Knowlton	Fultz	
r.e.	Knowlton	Pruyn	McDonald	
q.b.	Starr	Newhall	Hall	
l.h.b.	Foster	Nichols	Nesmith	Leonard
f.b.	Carr	Harrison	Somes	
r.h.b.	Hurley	Wendell	Lincoln	

This was agreed to by everybody.

Dr. Nichols contributed an interesting piece of news, that Brill had very probably cracked a rib in the Dartmouth game, but said that so long as he (Brill) did not know it he could probably play all right, but that he would not be able to go into a scrimmage before the Yale game.

Foster is in like condition, having hurt his knee during the few minutes he was in the game against Dartmouth, as a result of kicking the ball.

But the worst piece of news was that Dr. Nichols is afraid Hurley is a little out of his head. None of us will believe this, but are all going to watch him carefully from now on. What makes me uncomfortable about the thing is that the fellows who were in the Dartmouth game complained that Hurley was blaming men for not being where they ought to be, when, as a matter of fact, they were doing just what they ought to do. I could see something of this in the Dartmouth game, but could not quite grasp what it was all about though it was very apparent that the team was playing practically without a leader. If Hurley has to drop out, Wendell will have to take his place, and

I am not sure but it would be a good thing for the team for Hurley is not playing much of a game, having had little practice and being in very poor form.

After supper we went into a lengthy discussion of the schedule for the week's work.

Monday we were all agreed upon as follows:

Doctor out at 2:30—men dressed at 3.

3:00 to 3:15,	Kicking and catching by the backs, with the ends going down, Goals, Cross blocking by Marshall in the line. Waters with Squires.
3:15 to 3:30,	Starting practice for the whole squad, Lewis taking charge of the line; Dunlop and I the backs.
3:30 to 4:00,	Brisk signal work, the second and third formations being run through fast; tackling for Leonard and Knowlton.
4:00 to 4:15,	Kick off and receipt of kick off.
7:00 P.M.,	Lewis on defense, with Reggie Brown explaining the Yale plays. Lewis running over the Yale defense and assignments for the ends and backs, not to last over three-quarters of an hour.

When it came to Tuesday, we had a very lively discussion. Lewis wanted a long scrimmage, since he felt that the team was under done; Campbell favored a long scrimmage too, while the rest of us favored a shorter one. Dr. Nichols was especially anxious for a short scrimmage—said he "Yale is going to send up a basket full of rosies to play against your team, and you have got to send a basket full of rosies out against them—that is your only chance." He argued further, that every scrimmage we have this week is chancing more injury to the men and he maintains that we cannot afford to lose any more men and still have a respectable eleven to play with. He also urged that the team should be taken by one man, preferably myself, and that the rest of the coaches should keep off the field except during lulls in the work. Finally as a basis for making my decision I asked each coach for what he thought the program should be.

CAMPBELL thought that we ought to have fifteen minutes of scrimmage, then some signals and then fifteen minutes more of scrimmage, divided in ten minutes of defense and five minutes of offense.

DUNLOP wanted 15 minutes of signals with two halves, one of 15 minutes for scrimmage and 5 minutes for defense.

HAUGHTON wanted 20 minutes offense.

LEWIS wanted 15 minutes of signals and two halves of 25 minutes and 15 minutes, the 15 minutes divided half to offense and half to defense.

DR. NICHOLS wanted 15 minutes of scrimmage all told and did not care how we used the time.

HERBERT WHITE wanted two halves of 25 minutes and 15 min.

After much discussion I finally decided on the SCHEDULE FOR TUESDAY, as follows:

3:00 to 3:15,	Catching, kicking and quick kick offs.
3:15 to 3:30,	Starting practice, with Lewis in charge of the line and Dunlop and I in charge of the backs.
3:30 to 4:00,	Scrimmage—15 minutes for offense in which I would have charge of the team and 15 minutes of defense in which Lewis was to have charge, both of us to encourage fight, accuracy and speed.

On WEDNESDAY, after getting everybody's opinion, I decided upon the following:

3:00 to 3:15,	Catching and kicking, goals, punt-outs and kick-offs.
3:15 to 3:30,	Starts, Lewis taking the line, Dunlop and I the backs.
3:30 to 3:45,	Fast offense.
3:45 to 3:50,	Rest.
3:50 to 4:00,	Lewis alone with the team.
4:00 to 4:30,	Fast signal practice and all in.

In the evening Hurley and the quarterbacks to go over the generalship of the Yale game.

THURSDAY we decided to take the team into the country if it could be arranged, there to give them starts and signals and to rehearse the defense.

FRIDAY, Starts and signals.

With this plan made out we disbanded for the evening, and I came out to Cambridge feeling very much relieved at having the weeks' work so well planned out.

Monday, November 20, 1905

Morning:

I had Starr down at the field at about 11 o'clock today to give him about an hour of careful coaching in back field catching. I have a great dread of fumbled punts and intend to prevent any such thing if possible. Starr is pretty uncertain in his work, although he usually manages somehow to hang onto the ball even if it does send a shiver up ones back to watch him.

When we got through with this work I telephoned in and got Mr. Deland to agree to come out to the practice to get his opinion of things, since he has not been out here at all this Spring[80] and will have a p[er]spective of the team which none of us can have.

Afternoon:

In the afternoon we followed out our schedule pretty carefully though I did one or two things we had not planned. It seemed to me that Carr was looking a little worried as to whether he was going to be allowed to play or not and since he is a very conscientious player and we had decided to play him as first string man I told him so on the side, knowing full well that he would not lose any of his conscientiousness. I also told Kersburg that he was to play, my idea in doing so being that there were worries enough at this time of the year without having the additional worry of competition for places, particularly when a fellow is laid up so he is not able to compete. I believe this is the proper thing to do and do not feel that either in '01 or this year I have made a mistake in so doing. It is, of course, unwise to tell some men because they will let up, but where you have a real earnest fellow it is altogether the best thing for him.

After a conference with the coaches, we finally decided to accept Dashiell because the men whom Yale suggested in his place were not as good as Dashiell and we had no others to substitute, so I told Goodhue to go ahead and telegraph Yale to the effect that we would accept Dashiell. This official business has been hanging fire ever since last Spring and here it is in the week of the Yale game before we have been able to come to any agreement. It ought not to be allowed to drag on in this way again and I would suggest that if Yale cannot show a little more of a disposition to settle things more promptly next year, that we simply send her an ultimatum.

I had rather a curious side light pass on Brill by a story which one of the men told me about him. It was this: While coming down to the field this afternoon one of the men was talking with Brill and got to talking about the Yale game, when Brill said "I would much rather get an "A" in Calculus than to score a touch down against Yale." This shows how little Brill has thrown himself into this work. I don't

80. Reid must mean fall.

care how much of a student a fellow cares to be at other times—four days before the Yale game he ought, and I don't see how a man can help feeling that hardly anything is more important than to beat Yale. This remark of Brill's coupled with the fact that he was late coming down to the field in spite of an appeal that I made that the men should all be prompt makes me think Brill one of the weakest spots on the team, and also makes me thoroughly disgusted with him.

We had only the lightest work this afternoon. We had starts, punting and catching practice, a short preliminary practice for the line under Lewis and Waters, with substitute signal practice. Burr came back and looked in very good condition, taking hold most earnestly.

Newhall went in at quarter back, Nichols was able to get into the signal practice. We got the men in on schedule time and things went with a rush. One of the great things of the afternoon was Haughton's jollying the men along. He began it in the dressing room and kept it up all the afternoon and it became quite contagious to the extent that everyone pitched in enthusiastically.

The detail work on signals which I placed in the hands of Haughton and Dunlop was excellently done. Deland said he thought the work was good but that it was really too late in the season for the detail work we were giving. I grant that this is true, that it is later than we ought to be at this sort of thing, but since it is needed it is one of the best things we could possibly do.

When the men came off the field they had calves foot jelly and cherry, a bath and rub down, when we sent them out of the house. They were feeling in good spirits which was shown by the singing in which they very generally indulged.

Brill coming out late as he did exasperated me so that I stuck him in among the substitutes for the afternoon, first, however, not noticing him at all for some time, until he was forced to report to me, whereat I said "I cannot stop for anybody who is late—you will have to report to the other squad" which took him down some considerable as I intended it should.

Dr. Nichols told us to watch Hurley very carefully and see if we could not discover something wrong with him, but we could not see how he was off at all, as to us he seemed perfectly rational.

After supper I spoke to the Freshman football team at its beer night, and then went down and had about a two hour talk with Dr. Nichols. I shall not attempt to cover the ground that he and I discussed, but in general it was that we should do very little work in a scrimmage way but should devote our time in getting the men into the best possible shape for Saturday's game, on the basis that if the men are under done we cannot get them along far enough in the remaining two or three days to pay for the risk we would run, while if the men are over done the two or three days will do them a great deal of good. He further told me that he did not expect Hurley would be able to play, and told me that I had better give Wendell all the practice possible, as he considers Wendell now to be playing a better game than Hurley. I do not feel so much the possibility of the loss of Hurley, except for the fact that it will be hard for the team to go into the game without a Captain, although, of course, they have been doing this the whole season.

I told the manager to see that Haughton's employer had tickets to the game and that Al Eyre was given some, for Al helped out a good deal this year, even though we had not been able to allow him quite so much freedom as he would like. We have decided to have no open practice this week, feeling that we need all the time we can get for the regular every day work.

I forgot to mention last Thursday or Friday that Lonagan, one of the teachers of my school and coach of the Stanford Univ. football team had come east here to get what points he could to help him out. I have given him admission to all secret practice and have introduced him to all the coaches and intend to give him a big a chance to get points as possible. He is not in the least obtrusive and that makes me the more anxious to help him.

I went over to Herbert White's after all this was over and spent the night there with Dave Campbell. Dave is the greatest help imaginable. Were it not for him, I should have a hard time to keep going owing to the worry.

Tuesday, November 21, 1905

Morning:

Campbell and I had a little talk this morning and then I went down to the field and gave Leonard some coaching in catching kicks. In case we have to use Leonard, I shall, if possible, arrange so that he won't have to go back in the back field, but I thought if we had absolutely to use him, I would get him into as good shape as possible. He is very [ph]legmatic of temperament and it is very difficult to teach him anything, but I think I got something out of him this morning. When I got done there I went up to White's office to talk over the rumpus which he has stirred up at New Haven in regard to Lavigne, a ringer full back at Yale. We know perfectly well that he is neither an amateur nor a student and that he came to New Haven simply to play football, but we are able to get absolutely nothing that could be used as absolute proof. White had a man go up to Maine to gather information, but we could not get affidavits from the men who could really give us one. White told me that he had wired down to New Haven that he had evidence which made it plain that Lavigne[81] was not eligible, with a view to bluffing as far as he could. He showed me the letters and telegrams that he [has] and said he was going to carry the matter on as best he could. I hope that we can prevent the man playing. There is no doubt in my mind but that he is crooked.

I just got up to the training table in time to have a bite, Campbell and I eating most of our lunch with Hurley who was also late and who for the first time acted queerly in my presence. He frequently repeated sentences that he had said two or three times one after the other, and urging him as best I could, I was unable to get him to eat anything but prunes for lunch, and that three days before the Yale game. Besides this he was late at lunch and I could not seem to impress on him the necessity of promptness.

Afternoon:

Our practice for the afternoon was much the same as we had planned it, except that the scrimmage was not over twenty minutes. The listlessness of the squad was all gone and there was a distinct get-there spirit in the efforts of everyone. It did ones' heart good to see the team playing almost as it will in the Yale game. Carr at full back played as well as he has ever played before, and Burr did splendidly too. Starr, at quarter back, helped things out, and even Leonard woke up. Brill, Leary, Parker, Foster and Hurley were not allowed to go into the scrimmage, Brill on account of a cracked rib; Leary on account of a stiff knee, Parker on account of his back; Foster on account of his knee and Hurley on account of his leg ostensibly, although really on account of his head. We had good officiating, getting Evarts Wrenn and Mr. Lonagan to act, urging them to be strict which they were. Wrenn told me after the practice that the team played much better than he had expected from what he had heard.

It turned out after the practice that Dashiell had telegraphed back that he will be unable to officiate, but that Yale had telegraphed to him urging him to accept and that he had finally reconsidered. In order not to have the urging all seem to come from Yale, since we had accepted Dashiell, I immediately telegraphed to Dashiell, urging him to officiate and got Waters and Goodhue to telegraph also. We hope

81. Reid evidently was referring to J. N. Levine, a Yale fullback.

in this way to rather counter balance the action of the Yale men. It is my feeling that Dashiell is likely to be pretty impartial Saturday because we have intentionally kept him doubtful as to whether he would be the official almost up to the end and he knows why. Then too, Dashiell has a tendency to coach the teams that he is officiating for, and our team this year needs all such coaching they can get since Brill and Squires are repeatedly off side without any good reason. Then too, Dashiell committed himself on the locking legs question by telling me after the Dartmouth game that he would not stand for it, and that McClung, the referee, would not stand for it either, and therefore, I expected in the Yale game that this would put an end to Yale's antics of this nature, and if it does, I think that Dashiell will be as satisfactory to us as he is to Yale, although many people urge that Dashiell has a blue streak[82] running down his stomach.

At the last moment this afternoon word was brought to me on the field that Brill was in great danger of being put on probation, so I came at once up to the college office where I found that his record was such up to date that there was not much doubt but that he would go on probation at the meeting of the Board next Monday, but that there was no danger really of his going on until then, since at the Board meeting on Friday his name will not be acted upon owing to the fact that his record is not all in. I felt mightily relieved to get out of that fix.

Every afternoon now after the practice we have the field covered with straw to prevent it from freezing, this especially at Yale's request. We made everything at the training table just as lively as we could and to my delight Burr ate good. In consultation with Dr. Nichols, I allowed Burr to go home and sleep and stay home to breakfast if he chose. I also told Burr that he was going into the game.

After supper I went down to the Athletic office and found that Hurley had just been down there for some tickets to the game, and that along with them he had asked for a bowl of crackers and milk. I reported this to Dr. Nichols immediately and he saw to it that wherever Hurley went some fellow went with him, in order to prevent any possibility of accident through the chances of temporary insanity.

The team was given some coaching after supper, but not much. I was not present. I went over to Brookline with White and Lewis and we had a very pleasant time playing checkers, eating and drinking until bed time. Somehow or other I am beginning to feel very much encouraged over things and there is certainly a great increase in con-

82. Yale's school color.

fidence among the men and in the college. Yale's team was certainly at its best some little time ago, and our fellows may surprise us yet.

Wednesday, November 22, 1905

Morning:

As the work is practically all done now, I passed the morning in any way I could to get through it. I had lunch with the team and we joked as much as we possibly could. I always ask each fellow when I go to the training table how he feels, in an endeavor to show each man that I am interested in him, and I threw in a little nonsense today to limber things up all I could.

Afternoon:

We had our scrimmage again much as it was planned last Sunday and the men did well, especially on the defense where Lewis coached them carefully in their assignments. The defense was largely one of a man for a hole, and each man was told to "chug" into the hole low down as quick as the ball was put in play.

At the start of the scrimmage which was, of course, preceded by starts and some kicking, Kersburg and Squires seemed to be having great trouble in getting into a strong position, so I called Lewis' and Waters' attention to it. After some considerable experimenting Lewis said he thought the trouble was that Kersburg was down so low he could get no leg drive and no direction, while Squires took a position with both feet on the same line, making it hard for him to get started and very easy for an opponent to block him. After a few minutes work with these two men the defense on that side straightened up. It is strange that Lewis and Waters have not seen this fault before, because I have noticed it for a week or more but supposed there must be some reason for it. That is one trouble with coaching—we don't work with the individuals enough in an analytical way, and our individual coaches do not watch their men careful enough through the scrimmage to see into what blunders they fall. The coaches apparently watch the game too much from a spectators' standpoint instead of a standpoint of the individuals for whom they are supposed to be looking out. This is what Yale does more than we do and it certainly shows.

In the preliminary work the catching was very poor, almost everything slipping through the men's hands. I was very worried at this and spent a considerable amount of time with the backs myself. Foster, after a slip in the Penn game, seemed to have lost confidence and so I did not allow anybody to curse out any man, no matter how bad a showing he made. Instead, we simply encouraged the men and I greatly built up confidence on the part of the catchers by having the kickers, without the catchers knowing it, kick the balls low so that they didn't offer the same difficulty that the high ones did, and when the catchers could handle those all right, then we raised the height of the kicks and they were still caught. We had the kicking and catching the long way of the field instead of crossways because the sun is getting very low in the stadium these days and is almost directly in the catchers' eyes in one direction down the field. To get our men accustomed to this we made them catch the ball with the sun in their eyes. The shadows, too, creep up the field very rapidly so that by the time our practice is over every afternoon there is no sun light on the field at all, making another problem in catching. The sun will certainly have a bearing in the game Saturday and will be a factor in the choice of goals.

Both on offense and defense the playing was a great improvement today, as in fifteen minutes the Varsity carried the ball from the kick off over the Second's goal line without losing it, and although the Second were given the ball three times on the Varsity 15 yard line they could not make a first down, even with six downs to a try. In fact they were actually put back from the goal line twice the distance from which they started—in other words, if they began on the 15 yard line they ended up on the 30 yard line in the other direction.

Immediately after the Varsity had had its work we sent them in and then gave the substitutes a scrimmage. Today was the last practice for the Second team and they went at it with light hearts, and at the close of practice were given big cheers by the Varsity, who were in turn cheered. Leary, Foster, Brill and Hurley were not in the scrimmage owing to the doctor's instructions, but they all had signal work except Hurley.

After the practice Dr. Nichols came to me and said he was certain that Hurley was off and that he intended to have him examined by a specialist during the afternoon.

Haughton was again out and very jovial, as were most of the coaches, looking down on the practice from seats up in the Stadium. The work was pretty smooth and will certainly be better when we get the five men in who are at present not allowed to do anything more than signal work. Carr is playing a good game at full back and we shall start him off.

When we got up to the training table Dr. Nichols told Hurley to come to one side and sent in for a specialist to see what was the matter with his head. The specialist came out and almost immediately announced that Hurley could not hope to play. What was more he would have to go right in town and be kept quiet. Hurley seemed to suspect that something was wrong and begged us to tell him, so Dr. Nichols told him he thought he better go in town, at any rate for the night, and let the Dr. look him over.

Immediately after this I had a short meeting in the training table room to discuss generalship of the Yale game.

The first question I brought up was that of whether we should choose the kick off or the wind. We decided unanimously to kick off, since we felt pretty certain that Yale could not carry the ball the length of the field and we would probably get possession of it about the middle, in case she were at all pressed to make her distance after receiving the kick off. We decided that in case we did kick off to kick well to the left since the weakest Yale players are on that side and since it will give Shevlin an opportunity to run through the strongest place on our side, in case he gets the ball as he goes after all the kick offs. Figuring that we would be certain to carry the ball out at least 15 yards, we decided to kick, and on second down allowing one down for a buck play in order to get the center and players steadied before undertaking a punt. We determined to try for that first play a play from the third formation, which might possibly net us considerable distance, but in which there was no risk. We decided that of the first formation plays, that is, the ordinary three men back, the full back through center and cross buck were the only two we cared especially about. We also decided that the one of the best chances for ground gaining would be inside or outside of Hockenberger or Erwin, as well as inside of Forbes, the tackle, who was the mark of the Princeton team and who seemed to be in that game really thick headed. I raised the question as to whether our line men should not notify the quarter back in case they found some plays very weak. Some of the coaches thought that the quarter backs would be more annoyed than helped and so I determined to leave that to the quarter backs, asking them about it some time before the game. We shall try the quick kick from the third formation whenever we have occasion, since it affords an excellent chance of getting the ball away safely. We also decided to warn the team of a trick that Yale has played on one or two occasions when they have been near the goal line. For instance, if Yale needed the distance badly the quarter back would give a signal to which Shevlin would stand up and say "Wait a minute, what was that?", apparently intending to question the play, thereby causing the opponents to be off their guard for an instant. At just this instant the ball would be snapped back and a good gain usually resulted.

The talk was not a very profitable one, as it was clearly the sense of the meeting that, barring a few very general instructions, the game should be left pretty much to the players themselves, to prevent us from falling into the same trouble we did in the Penn game. However, I shall get hold of the quarter backs before the game and run over some of the general points carefully with them. There was so much disagreement at this meeting that I did not try to prolong it, deciding to get the matter into my own hands.

Immediately after this meeting I had to speak before the Mass meeting, the final one of the season. I had told Stephenson, who was in charge of the meeting, that before I spoke I would like to get the Varsity players in the training table room, and so shortly after the meeting on generalship had been broken up all of the football men who were able came into the training room where I told them of Hurley's injury and the fact that he would not be able to play. The men did not seem quite to know how to take it and they seemed pretty glum, but I had a little talk with each one and with all of them together and finally succeeded in getting some determination in them. I then went out and spoke at the Mass meeting. Of course, under the circumstances, I did not feel especially enthusiastic and so I made my remarks very short and earnest. The room was absolutely packed there being fully two thousand fellows on hand. I never saw such an enthusiastic Harvard crowd before. I think everybody considers the meeting unprecedented in enthusiasm. Men stood in every corner, in the windows, hung around the doors, and even looked in from the outside, not being able to get in. McMaster and I were cheered as we came in and the singing burst forth in great volume. McMaster made a few remarks and then I got up to make a talk which was a great strain on me. I said that I had never seen such enthusiasm before, that I had never known Harvard to be so much behind a team, that the team needed all the encouragment it could get because it must do without its captain. After I finished this remark a hush came over the whole room that was most impressive—it extended all through the building. I then explained as best I could the reason for Hurley's inability to play, placing more emphasis on his leg than I did on his head. Since football is being severely criticized just at present, a case of concussion on the brain would be very serious.[83] "But" said I, "If the team plays on Saturday without its captain, it will nevertheless, play for its captain and for the University." I then made a few remarks on the rapid progress of the team during the past few days, and said

83. That same day, a debate between Harvard and Yale was scheduled: "Resolved that the intercollegiate football in America is a detriment rather than a benefit." The day before, President Roosevelt stated that he "emphatically believes in continuing the game." *Boston Globe,* 22 Nov. 1905, 5 and 21 Nov. 1905, 5.

that if the team could only keep up a sustained effort throughout the game such as they had been showing recently, we should stand a very good show. I ended up with "the team needs your whole hearted support, will you give it?" There was quiet for a moment or two, then cheers for Hurley—a great burst of enthusiasm. I left the room amidst great cheering and went down stairs and played billiards with Dr. Nichols until White's auto came back from carrying Hurley in town. The singing up stairs kept growing stronger. I finally went outside and listened to it, and here also I found crowds of people—not content with singing in the building, the fellows all got up and sang through the street, the enthusiasm was contagious and the sight one I shall never forget. What has taken hold of Harvard this year I do not understand because we never had such enthusiasm and such loyalty before. I believe that most of it is due to the fact that the college believes pretty much in the way things have been handled and believing in the management are ready to give their support.

Campbell, White and I then went over to Brookline, where we played checkers as usual, and I had my usual lot of peculiar drinks.

Thursday, November 23, 1905

Morning:

This morning I got everything all packed up ready to go to Marblehead[84] and then went down to the training table for lunch which was a little earlier than usual. Immediately after lunch I came home and got my clothes and we started off. In the [Harvard] Square as we started off was the biggest crowd of college fellows that has ever cheered a team off and the cheering was continuous and most hearty. There was cheering at the U[n]ion too, before the men got through dinner. It was worth almost any price to sit in the car as we started and look into the faces of the crowd of fellows. The interest, loyalty and enthusiasm in every face was a certainty. During a lull in the cheering the whole car gave a cheer for the University which caused renewed enthusiasm in the large crowd. I could see an increase in determination in the team as they saw the feeling of the University and I knew perfectly well that more than one man there had pledged himself inwardly to play until he had no strength left. On the way in town we sang a good deal and cheered Hurley,[85] sending him a message before we got onto the train, also receiving one from him before we left.

84. Marblehead is on the Atlantic Ocean about twenty miles northeast of Cambridge, close to Salem.

85. The team sang an old Harvard song to Hurley on its way to North Station; see the *Boston Globe*, 24 Nov. 1905, 1.

We had a special car to Marblehead and on arriving there went immediately to the Cliff Club, where the proprietor, Mr. Wainwright, was ready to assign rooms. Before anything was done, however, I called a meeting of the men, at which by unanimous choice Knowlton was chosen captain and cheered. The men were then put into the main building where they put on sweaters and football shoes. Following this we had signal practice for 15 minutes on a lawn, into which the men entered with great vim. As soon as the regulars had had their work I sent them in and put the substitutes through. After this the men hung around the town, bowled, went for walks, etc. until supper time, when we had a most delicious supper, the men eating at tables on the glassed piazza overlooking the ocean. The change took hold of the men and they ate heartily. After supper they sat around in the main room and read and sang, or went to their respective quarters and played cards. The fellows named the different quarters to which they went—Randolph, Westmorly, Dunster, Claverly and Holworthy.[86] This is an ideal place for such a trip, and whenever any coach wants an excellent place to go to, this is the place. The men went to bed at the usual time and there was no fooling.

I received a telephone message from Cambridge in which I was told that the fellows at Cambridge were having a big time in celebration. They had a mass meeting with singing and started to march down to the stadium, but ended up by marching through the yard calling everybody out and marching two thousand strong clear into Boston with enthusiasm which has never been equalled. The place seems wild.

Friday, November 24, 1905

The men were up promptly most of them reporting a good sleep, and all had a good appetite. Immediately after breakfast I got the men all together and had each fellow give me a list of his recitations for the day in order to decide on what man to send up to lectures in order not to have too many cuts and in order to keep the good will of the

---

Here's to you, Dan Hurley,
Here's to you my jovial soul,
Here's to you with all my heart,
And now we're in your company,
We'll have a drink before we part,
Here's to you Dan Hurley.

86. These were privately owned dormitories at which the wealthier Harvard students were housed.

Faculty.[87] I sent about ten men up, among them some of the best and some of the poorest students. During the morning those of us who were left spent the time in various ways. Wendell and Starr went for a sail; Carr, Nesmith, Squires, Kersburg, Peirce and several others went for a launch ride; Hall and Leary went fishing. We had a graphophone[88] brought down from Boston last night and had that going. It afforded a good deal of amusement although the pieces were not the best that might have been chosen. The men are looking fine.

At Noon[,] Dunlop, Campbell, Kernan and Bowditch appeared to see the final practice, Haughton came along later. By the courtesy of the Golf Club here, called I believe, the Tedesco Club, we had our signal practice on the golf links some little distance from the hotel. We drove out there in barges and found a great number of people there. We had them stand some little distance off and then went ahead. Ayers Boal, guard on [William] Burden's team[89] in '99, one of the teams on which I played, came down to see the practice. The practice of the Varsity was splendid, and that of the substitutes equally good. We had difficulty in getting the men off the field after we had allowed them the short half hour that we had assigned for signal work—that is just the way that we want them to feel—anxious for more with a great amount of vigor. During the practice Haughton grew very enthusiastic and exclaimed "Just look at them, they are a rattling good team." And really as we looked at them they were a fine looking outfit. At the close of the practice we allowed Burr to take a few kicks which he went at with great vigor. After he had kicked about four with Haughton and I looking on, a tremendous smile came over his face and he called for Haughton and I to come where he was, not realizing that we were standing near at hand. When we asked him what the matter was he said "I have got it" referring to his kicking, "I have found out what the trouble was" and we had to stand by while he showed us and show us he did by booting the ball farther than ever before and keeping it up. He was perfectly delighted with himself and said that he would do much better work tomorrow than he has ever done before.

When we came back to the hotel the men had supper and a good

87. The *Boston Globe*, 22 Nov. 1905, 5, reported that Harvard football management chose a place off campus but close enough to Cambridge so players could get to the university for classes.

88. A graphophone was a phonograph for recording and reproducing sounds on wax records.

89. Burden was the captain of the 1899 team and a third-team all-American guard that year.

deal of singing and another message was sent to Hurley, this time by telegraph. I was greatly surprised and delighted to find a testimonial from the New York Harvard Club waiting me with the signatures of over three hundred graduates of New York. Pretty nearly every signature was that of a prominent man, including Ex-Senators, Bankers, Presidents of Corporations, Clubs and what not. The sentiment of the letter was: "We don't care what has happened or whether you win the Yale game or not, we believe in you and are with you." This sent thrills up my back. To have this come on top of all that I have already had just about filled my cup full, and after feeling all the season that we were going to have a hard row to hoe and that the chances of our winning were small whereupon I expected a crash, but to have the Undergraduates take this position was a gratification too great to be expressed. I immediately wired a reply to the effect that I was gratified beyond expression at the vote of confidence and that I would stick to things until I was able to show in more than words how much I appreciated their kindness.

We shifted some of the players about for the night because the main house is noisier than the quarters and it turned out that it was well we did so for a crowd of men and women came along in an auto, had something to eat and drink, which ended in the women losing their heads and singing and almost dancing in their delight with themselves. It was very amusing to all of us, but not especially quieting to the football men and at 10 o'clock I asked the manager of the Club to quiet things down. He approached the people and they were most violent in their attitude toward him for presuming to interfere, and finally left in a high rage, vowing vengence the next day.

After this the coaches and whatever other Harvard men were there sat around and told stories until quite late, when everybody went to bed.

Saturday, November 25, 1905

Morning:

When we went to bed last night there was quite a wind and it was raining a little. We expected a wet day, but this morning the air was clear and crisp. The men all slept well and were in fine spirits. We took the 9 o'clock train for Boston and at 11 had lunch. I went home immediately after I got back and saw my room mate and his wife who were staying at my house. Right after lunch, too, I had quite a talk with Owsley, the Yale coach, about playing Levigne, and he told me that unless we had some definite proof he would play him if he had to, although he did not expect to have to. I told him we considered him ineligible at Cambridge, although it was up to him as to whether he was really eligible to play or not. The result was that I left Owsley in doubt as to whether he would play or not.

Afternoon:

At one o'clock we went to the field and had a hard time getting through the crowd which poured in in an endless stream from the Square, filling the street and so crowding the little bridge the police would only allow a certain number at a time and would allow no autos or carriages at all. When we got to the field, while the men were dressing, I had a long discussion with Owsley again over the matter of locking legs. I took the position that I had assumed earlier in the season and said I thought that was a matter to be left to the officials, who had not at this time come along. Owsley said the center should be allowed to lock with the guard if he wanted to according to the wording of the rules. I said he ought not to be allowed to because of the spirit of the rules, which I knew was against it since I was on the Committee at the last meeting when the matter came up. While we were thus arguing Dashiell came along and we at once got hold of him and started the matter up with him. We were not getting much of anywhere in the discussion when I saw [Frank] Hinckey[90] coming along. Realizing that he would probably undertake to get in a word, I suggested to Dashiell and Owsley that we go over to the Harvard side to avoid the curious. In this way I evaded Hinckey, and got Owsley into a room with [T. Lee "Bum"] McClung,[91] Dashiell and myself on the Harvard side of the house. Owsley argued with the officials, saying among other things "Well, if you want to undertake to interpret the rules and forbid something the rules allow, of course that is your privilege, but it is something I would not care to do if I were an official." I enjoyed the situation very much and kept saying to

90. Hinckey was one of the greatest players in the history of Yale football, playing end from 1891 to 1894, being captain in both 1893 and 1894, and making Walter Camp's all-American team at end all four years. Weighing only between 146 and 157 pounds, his competitive spirit was second to none. A New York newspaper once described players like Hinckey as being "brutal fellows, born sluggers, without the smallest pretension to gentlemanhood," as quoted in Thomas G. Bergin, *The Game: The Harvard-Yale Football Rivalry, 1875–1983* (New Haven: Yale University Press, 1984), 59. Hinckey was head coach at Yale from 1913 to 1915.

91. McClung was a starting halfback against Harvard for three years (1889–91) and one of the greatest backs in Yale's history, a two-time all-American. He became treasurer of the United States from 1909 to 1912, under the administration of William Howard Taft, a Yale graduate.

Owsley, "Why Owsley, you said yourself just a little while ago that all matters of this kind should be left to the officials, and now you don't want to do it." Owsley was finally instructed to tell the Yale team not to lock legs. I then went up to our dressing room and got our men together and told them about it, and then had Lewis and Dr. Nichols say a word or two to them, and then I had my last word.

The squad then went onto the field, the regular players[92] preceding the substitutes—I walked on behind. As our team came onto the field Yale was just having a little signal practice down at the end at which we came in. As our men came onto the field I overheard the delightful sentiment expressed by [George] Sanford,[93] a Yale coach, who, addressing the Yale team, said, "There goes the sons of bitches now." This shows pretty much Sanford's idea of sportsmanship.

After a short signal practice Knowlton toss[ed] up and won the toss, taking the wind and leaving Yale the kick off with the sun in her eyes.

The Yale team did not strike me as anything more than a very ordinary team and I felt considerable confidence in our own team as it prepared to receive the kick off.

The stadium was filled to twelve or fourteen rows built on top of the boulevard around the top and extending to within 10 yards of the field.[94] The cheering and singing, the colors and enthusiasm were a sight never to be forgotten. I shall not attempt to describe the game, but suffice it to say that we had the better of the first half which ended in a 0 to 0 score, and the game was one of the prettiest I have ever seen. Burr out kicked the Yale back easily, and the sun being in the Yale mens' eyes, our men recovered all the distance each time, our defense worked splendidly, and Yale lost the ball on downs several times, once on our 11 yard line with only a half foot to go. This was

92. The Harvard team averaged 186 pounds, the line 195 pounds, and the backs 170 pounds. The Yale team averaged 186 pounds, the line 193 pounds, and the backs 173 pounds. Harvard's heaviest man, Parker, weighed 220 pounds. Yale had two men at 205 pounds. The Harvard men's heights ranged from five feet, eight inches to six feet, one inch; the Yale men were from five feet, nine inches to six feet, three inches. See the *Boston Globe*, 25 Nov. 1905, 1.

93. Sanford had played against Harvard in 1891 and later coached Columbia from 1899 to 1901, defeating Yale in 1899, the first time a Columbia team beat Yale playing modern football. At the time he was probably the highest paid coach in America at $5,000 a year. His questionable ethics, including paying athletes to attend Columbia, brought about his departure from the university.

94. The desire to be one of the overflow crowd of nearly forty-three thousand was so great that $2 tickets were scalped for $10 to $30, according to the *Boston Globe*, 25 Nov. 1905, 8. It was probably the largest crowd to witness a football game to that time.

an attempt through Burr. There were no fumbles at all in the first half and no penalties were given although Yale did some bad holding, it seemed to me. Parker's passing for kicks was very poor, and how Burr got off some of them I do not understand, since after taking the ball on the kick off, he would kick the ball seemingly through the arms of the various Yale players and put it from 50 to 55 yards every time. Brill and Squires went through the Yale line without much trouble. Carr's defensive work was excellent, and Wendell out played himself. The one trouble with the first half was the failure of our team to use the wind, especially when they found that Harvard was able to hold Yale whenever she got the ball. Our plays went at times for 5 and 10 yards at a rush and through any part of the Yale line.

Just at the end of the first half, after a 40 yard run by Roome (how he ever got by I do not know since Leary was right after him) Harvard held Yale for downs. The enthusiasm on the Harvard side was perfectly tremendous and after the half ended a great wave of enthusiasm swept down the whole Harvard side of the field. Yale's great end running game with which she was going to kill our team had not materialized, and with the exception of Roome's run, she was not able to do anything with us.

Following the men into the Locker Building, we had them all lie down on mats, wash off their faces, while we told them a few things and made them keep quiet. Parker was all done up so I decided to put in Barney who had been doing much better passing than White. That was the only change we made at the beginning of the second half.

Shortly after the half began our fellows got the ball and seemed on the way to a touch down, When Dashiell penalized us for off side on Yale's 25 yard line. This ended in Yale's getting the ball on a kick, and kicking it to us on our 45 yard line. A poor kick by Burr, which went outside, gave the ball to Yale on her 45 yard line. At this point I sent Nichols in in place of Foster who was all in. I told Nichols before he went in, if he was sent back in the back field, to get back on the side on which the kicker would be most unlikely to kick the ball, that is, on the left side of the field, leaving Starr to take the other side and to catch the ball. What is more, I had told Starr and Knowlton of this on the way up from Marblehead. To my great amazement, however, Yale kicked and Nichols went back without protest from Starr and took the most responsible position. Yale kicked, Nichols fumbled, Forbes caught the ball on our 30 yard line, from which position Yale rushed it up to our 10 yard line, where Brill was apparently hurt. McMaster told me that Brill was hurt and he ought to be taken out.

Having only a moment in which to decide I sent in Montgomery on the ground that if Brill were hurt Yale would be able to score anyhow. If he were not hurt, it would be well to keep him in, although I could not be certain. But I hoped Montgomery might be able to ward off the attack that had been driven at Brill so steadily. To my surprise Brill ran off the field apparently all right. Yale soon after scored and kicked the goal. That ended the scoring of the game. I sent Newhall in in Starr's place, in an endeavor to get some trick plays off, but he did not use them and I doubt if Newhall improved the play much.

Yale made eight substitutions, using all the full backs she had, two sets of backs, two quarter backs, two ends, three left guards opposing Kersburg, and two centres.

Had Nichols not fumbled that kick, the score would undoubtedly have been a tie, as there was less than 10 minutes to play and Harvard was able to hold her own for the rest of the game, the ball never being in danger territory.

There were two things during the game which caused a great deal of discussion, one of them the disqualification of Morse for striking Wendell. I do not think that Morse hit Wendell intentionally, unless Wendell was doing some holding which he had no business to do. The other case was that of Burr and Quill, which happened in the first half. In this half Yale had kicked out once and Burr had tried for a field goal but missed it. A few minutes later Yale had to kick out on a touch back and Burr himself caught the ball and made a fair catch distinctly. As he caught the ball Quill, the Yale back, came along and struck him square in the face; whether with his fist, the heel of his hand, or his open hand, I do not know, but at any rate he struck him a hard blow, knocking Burr senseless for a moment and breaking his nose. A perfect storm of hisses came forth and Major [Henry L.] Higginson[95] told me to take the team off the field at once, which I did not do. To my astonishment, Dashiell did not rule out Quill[,] and McClung did not recognize the fair catch, which may perhaps have lost us the game, as the ball was caught on about the 40 yard line and almost directly in front of the goal post.[96] Whether Burr would have

95. Higginson was an influential Harvard man, a member of the Harvard governing board, the Corporation, from 1893–1919, who had given his alma mater thirty-one acres for an athletic field fifteen years before.

96. After a fair catch, a team could attempt a field goal from that point unhindered by the opposition. This little-known rule is still in existence. Referee "Bum" McClung claimed that no heel mark was left, a rule for making a fair catch. Following the game, McClung said of Quill's hit: "It looked ugly, but was within the rules of the game." *Boston Globe*, 26 Nov. 1905, 30.

gotten it over or not is a question, of course, but there was at any rate a good chance of it. It was the failure on the part of Dashiell to penalize this foul that I think caused him to penalize Morse's small act in the second half, in an endeavor to square himself if possible.[97]

In the second half the Yale players used their fists a great deal more than they did in the first half. Wendell said he was struck squarely in the body at the very kick off. Other men complained in like way. Not one of our men lost his temper and we had the satisfaction of having all the blame credited to Yale, who before the game had been boasting that Harvard had been criticizing Yale's players too much and had better look after her own, that Yale had not had anyone disqualified in seven or eight years. When Morse was disqualified Shevlin tried to get Knowlton to agree to let Morse stay in, which Dashiell would not allow, and of course, which Knowlton would not have agreed to. This was an interesting side light on the remark that Camp and Shevlin made to me regarding the not having of Edwards as an official. They could not think of having anyone as an official who would do as Edwards had done the year before in the Penn game, allow two men one of either side, who were disqualified, both to remain in the game; yet here they were trying to have their own man stay in when none of our men had been disqualified. I am rather sorry for Morse, but [there] was so much banging on the part of the Yale team made me quite willing that anyone of them should be disqualified as a punishment for the illegal practice.

In this game for the first time in a long while I saw a Yale team apparently "up a tree" and there were numerous consultations on plays and Shevlin was running back and forth very much disturbed at the signals and plays, and apparently very much upset because things were not going the way he expected them to go.

When Nichols dropped his kick a great sigh came from the Harvard stands and many people broke out crying—I felt like it myself.

---

97. Reid was so angry at Dashiell's failure to call the penalty that he told Dashiell that he would never officiate another Harvard-Yale game—and he never did. President Roosevelt, upset that his Harvard team was shut out by Yale for a fourth consecutive year, called Reid to Washington to explain the controversy. Roosevelt also wrote to Dashiell to get his side of the story. Dashiell, up for appointment as professor of chemistry at the Naval Academy, an appointment Roosevelt controlled, replied: "I am deeply sorry, Sir, from every personal feeling, that the matter should have been brought to you in so unfavorable a light. . . . I regret the injury to the game, now in so critical a condition." Roosevelt in return held up his appointment for six months. Dashiell continued to serve on the Football Rules Committee, as did Reid. See Dashiell to Roosevelt, 7 Dec. 1905, in Charles W. Eliot Papers, Box 244, "Theodore Roosevelt" Folder, Harvard University Archives.

At the close of the game Walter Camp came out and congratulated me. I was not in the mood for congratulations because I thought the game ought to have been a tie. On all sides as the crowd moved out I heard expressions of admiration for our team's work, and many expressions in which the speaker said that he would rather be a Harvard player than a Yale player after the mean game which Yale had played.

We got into the Locker Building after a time and the whole college came around it and cheered, showing the greatest enthusiasm. The team inside was heart broken and many of them were crying. I stayed until I had spoken to them all and had seen some of the coaches and then went out with a newspaper man from the Globe and drove home where I dictated the following story [missing]:

Immediately after this I went in town to say a few words to the team at their banquet. The men were pretty quiet, but Waters, Lewis and I jollied them up all we could and after they had eaten something and had had a little Champagne they began to liven up. Kersburg came up to me with tears in his eyes and handed me a piece of blue jersey which he had torn off from Shevlin and which he told me to keep as a souvenir of the game.

Before leaving I shook hands [. . .] with each of the fellows and I found it hard to get out of the room. Nesmith said that he had had a most delightful time of it and so did Carr, Newhall, Starr, Kersburg, Parker and others. Poor Dan Nichols did not come in. He was so frightfully done up after his fumble. The players had sent a special message to him to be sure he was on hand because none of them were disposed to blame him. I made a few remarks, clearly showing that I had no feeling and urging the fellows, who did not need the urging, to let it make absolutely no difference with them. At the end Nichols was cheered and a number of the men are planning to go around and see him tomorrow. The feeling toward Waters, whom the men disliked for some time following his talk after the Penn game, has absolutely turned around and he is now very much liked, almost loved by the men. It turned out just as Waters said it would. He said "These fellows may not like me now but you wait until the season is over and you will see that they will come up and speak to me telling me that what I said was all right and that they would not have played so well if I had not said it."

After the game while the men were dressing, Waters came in and said to the men that he was proud of them all and Kersburg and Squires and some of the other men came up and thanked him for what he had done and for a talk he had given them, and said they could not have done so well if he had not given it. At the supper Waters said he wanted to take back everything he had ever said, and that he was proud to know all of them and always would be; that they had played all they knew, and that he never asked any more of anyone.

I must say before closing up that for the first time in years Yale played a special defense bringing her tackle around to the side on which our tandem attacks were made in the endeavor to strike that side. This, of course, left the short side of the line weak and we were able to go through there for big gains although the quarter backs did not apparently appreciate the fact even though we told them between the halves. This is the first time I think that Yale has done anything of this kind and I learned from Camp that it was only on special occasions that Yale ever thought of such a thing.

Hurley was kept posted on the proceedings of the game by a special wire to the hospital, and although disappointed at the result of the game, was not at all discouraged, but on the whole was delighted with the showing.

Thus ended the work of the year, not in a wholly satisfactory way to me, because we lost our two big games, but we have laid a foundation for an excellent start next year and will have almost a veteran team, composed of a good many fighters and players with excellent spirit, with confidence in each other, and with the confidence of the University in them. A number of the men are pretty fairly old, between 23 and 25. I have felt continually during the season that never has Harvard had such an athletic spirit as this year. I have realized that we had an excellent chance to beat both Penn and Yale, but I also realized that things were in such a condition that it was impossible to reach out and take things which were almost within easy grasp, and which we could certainly take if we could have this same team next year with what work we could give them. Not knowing the players, or the coaches, the style of game or the general situation, we have not been able to get as much out of the season's work as there was in it, but if we didn't, it was not because every coach and player connected with the football eleven did not put his heart and soul into the work and give all that he had.

Afterword

Bill Reid continued to coach the Harvard eleven in 1906, but not before becoming embroiled in the most important reform movement in intercollegiate history. Following the 1905 season, a committee of the Harvard Overseers, one of two Harvard governing bodies, called for either a radical change in football rules or its abolishment.[1] To create such new rules, the Harvard Graduates' Athletic Association formed a seven-member committee, headed by Reid, with LeBaron Briggs, dean of Harvard College, serving on it as an established voice of the university, and five former coaches. After a month, Reid's committee proposed nineteen new rules to reform the game. In the meantime, the death of a Union College halfback in the New York University game caused Henry MacCracken, chancellor of NYU, to call for a meeting of institutions that it had played over the years to determine if football should be abolished or reformed. Out of that meeting, a call for a larger conference arose. The meeting that began in late December 1905, was the beginning of the National Collegiate Athletic Association and a new football rules committee.[2]

The "Old" rules committee, on which Reid sat, had been dominated by Walter Camp of Yale for a generation. The fledgling NCAA group formed a "New" rules committee. After a tense fortnight, the two rules committees merged into one. At this point Reid brought out his nineteen rules, and he told members of the "Old" rules committee: "Either these 19 rules go through or there will be no football at Harvard; and if Harvard throws out the game, many other colleges will follow Harvard's lead."[3] The new rules for 1906 contained the

1. Records of the Overseers of Harvard College, 13 Dec. 1905 and 10 Jan. 1906, Harvard University Archives.

2. For a fuller explanation of the 1905–6 crisis, see Ronald A. Smith, "Brutality, Ethics, and the Creation of the NCAA," in *Sports and Freedom: The Rise of Big-Time College Sports* (New York: Oxford University Press, 1988), 191–208.

3. Reid told, for the first time, his version of the events of 1905–6 in a lengthy article in the *Boston Herald*, 17 Oct. 1926, E7.

essence of the Harvard rules. Among the rules suggested were the expansion of the number of yards needed for a first down to ten; the introduction of the forward pass; the abolishment of interlocking arms at the line of scrimmage; the creation of a neutral zone between the opposing lines; and the outlawing of interference with a player attempting to make a fair catch. Both the Harvard Overseers and the Harvard Corporation, in close votes, agreed to continue the game— against the wishes of President Charles Eliot.[4] Following by a day the birth of their third child, Christine, Bill Reid wrote jubilantly that "I felt as though I'd had twins."[5]

Before the Harvard football controversy was resolved, Reid had to determine whether he would return to California. His father wrote to him about returning as assistant headmaster of the Belmont School. If Bill would return, his father said, "I should want to turn affairs over to you as quickly as possible, yet I must have a serious interest in things until all debts are paid off."[6] Turning over the school to Bill was difficult for a commanding figure such as William Reid, Sr. At one point in the deliberation process, Bill told his father, "You and I have regarded each other largely as father & boy."[7] That would have to change, and so would Christine Reid's attitude toward returning again to California. Christine had not enjoyed her first two-year stay in the West, and Bill's father knew it. Now, the Senior Reid said, Christine had agreed that "it was her business to fall in with whatever you wanted to do and make the best of it even if it should happen to be something that she did not wholly like."[8] The contentiousness of Christine falling in line with Bill about California was to be tried again, but not for another year. With the vote to keep football, Bill stayed for a second year with the Crimson team.

Although Reid's team had lost to Yale to conclude the 1905 year, he knew that his material for 1906 was outstanding. It consisted of "five men all ready, big & strong & all over 23 or 24 years of age, a mature team such as a coach delights in & gets about once a decade."[9]

4. Records of the Overseers of Harvard College, 9 May 1906, Harvard University Archives.

5. Bill Reid, Jr., Harvard, to Harriet Thompson, Providence, R.I., 9 May 1906, Thomas Stetson Personal Collection. All documents cited hereater in this chapter are from this collection unless otherwise indicated.

6. William T. Reid, Sr., Belmont, Calif., to Bill Reid, Jr., Cambridge, Mass., 1 Feb. 1906.

7. Bill Reid, Jr., Harvard, to William T. Reid, Sr., Belmont, Calif., 26 March 1906.

8. William T. Reid, Sr., Belmont, Calif., to Bill Reid, Jr., Cambridge, Mass., 1 Feb. 1906.

9. Ibid.

But his own Athletic Committee did him in by agreeing with Yale to prohibit participation by all graduate students, as well as freshmen, beginning in 1906. By eliminating graduate student participation, Reid said that he lost six regular varsity men in addition to fifty other promising candidates.[10]

He nevertheless looked forward to his 1906 season, with the same salary as the year before, $7,000, appreciably over the $1,500 he might receive for returning to his father's school. The schedule was similar to the 1905 season. This time Harvard won its first ten games, being scored upon in only three games before the Yale game. Yale was also undefeated, being tied in a scoreless game with Princeton and having given up only six points the entire season. Against Yale, with the incomparable Walter Camp advising the team, Harvard lost again, 6-0. Reid's team gained only one-third as much yardage as Yale, which scored its only touchdown on a new forward pass play.

The disappointment for Reid was total. "I looked upon the two years as a failure," Reid wrote a quarter century later, still remembering them as "very difficult ones."[11] This, despite his record of eighteen wins, three loses, and one tie. The lack of success was solely due to the two loses to Yale, the only game that really mattered. He thus returned to California considering himself a failure, coming back to a position at the Belmont School, where both he and Christine had difficulties early in their married life. To Bill, who exuded a pessimistic ambience, and Christine, who much preferred life in the East, the transition would be difficult and strained.

Christine and the three children remained in Brookline for several weeks, while Bill returned to California in March of 1907. Less than a year after the great San Francisco Earthquake, which did a couple thousand dollars of damage to the Belmont School, Bill wrote, "Papa is letting me do things my own way, and I am enjoying the work immensely."[12] But his mind was continually on Christine. "I shall see that you are happy," Bill wrote to his wife, "You are to have things as you want them—and if I can't get them, then we'll come East."[13] Their love, as expressed in their frequent letters, was strong, passionate, and explicit. "If you were here now you would be mostly undressed lying in my lap in front of the fire," Bill graphically wrote, "getting hugged & kissed & squeezed & felt—Then I'd take my lovely

10. Ibid.
11. Harvard College, Class of 1901, 25th Anniversary Report, 1926, 501–2, Harvard University Archives.
12. Bill Reid, Jr., Belmont, Calif., to Christine Reid, Brookline, Mass., 14 April 1907.
13. Ibid., 6 March 1907.

bride to bed, and we'd both taste the fruits of a perfect union."[14] And Christine responded. "Take care of yourself, for I want you and 'tinker' to be in good shape when I get there. 'Tinker-bell' is feeling 'right pert.'"[15] It was not their love for each other that would cause problems, but rather living in California and their relationship with Bill's parents. And there was always the lure of the East and of Harvard.

When Reid left Harvard, he did so with a parting shot about its needs if it wanted to beat Yale. Harvard needed a permanent coach Reid believed, "a paid coach of the right type and self-respect, or charity coaching and a loss of self-respect." Harvard, he said, had a permanent coach in crew, baseball, and hockey, and the sports were consistently winners. "We have tried the charity method on football for 15 years," he noted, "and it has failed."[16] Reid opposed the appointment of his successor, Joshua Crane. He told Christine soon after the appointment that "We will lose all we've gained I'm afraid, & I'm looking for a good licking next Fall already. It's too bad."[17] Just that happened as Harvard lost its last three games including a convincing win by Yale, 12-0.

Reid was almost coaxed back to help coach Harvard the next fall, when peerless Percy Haughton began Harvard's greatest years of football success against Yale. In the spring of 1908, Haughton offered to pay Reid and his family all expenses if he would drill the squad and take care of the defense. By the summer, Haughton was nearly pleading for Reid to return. "If you want Harvard to win next fall, don't say no," he wrote to Reid, concluding the Californian was "absolutely essential to our success."[18]

Bill proposed going back East to his father, calling it a "vacation after having been here two years."[19] Both his father and mother strongly opposed the move, however. "You could not make a greater mistake," Bill's mother advised. "Important as athletics are they surely are regarded as belonging to the 'childish' things to be put away or put in the background by mature men who have serious interests."[20] Reid likely did not heed her borrowed biblical injunction, for he seldom listened to his mother, but nevertheless he reluctantly turned

14. Ibid., 1 April 1907.

15. Christine Reid, Brookline, Mass., to Bill Reid, Jr., Belmont, Calif., 3 April 1907.

16. William T. Reid, Jr., "Football and Coaching," *Harvard Graduates' Magazine* 15 (March 1907): 400–401.

17. Bill Reid, Jr., Belmont, Calif., to Christine Reid, Brookline, Mass., 24 March 1907.

18. Percy D. Haughton, Harvard, to Bill Reid, Jr., Belmont, Calif., 7 July 1908.

19. Bill Reid, Jr., Belmont, Calif., to Christine Reid, Lake Tahoe, Calif., 24 July 1908.

20. Julia Reid, Lake Tahoe, Calif., to Bill Reid, Jr., Belmont, Calif., 23 July 1908.

down the offer. He did so, in part, because his father believed that returning and being associated with the inevitable loss to Yale would not bring credit to his son.[21] Without Reid, though, Harvard went on to an undefeated season, beating Yale in the season's final game, 4-0.

Bill's decision to remain did not create harmony at the Belmont School. During the summer of 1909, when Christine made her annual pilgrimage back to Massachusetts to be with her family, she wrote Bill that remaining at the Belmont School was not "the right or best thing for you any longer, or for the rest of us."[22] Christine would not forget her father-in-law's biting comment that Bill had been a "hindrance" in running the school.[23] Bill, who felt great loyalty to his father, had once told Christine's parents that "life at Belmont was impossible under the conditions there." Christine's father, Albert Lincoln, saw "no probability" that Bill and Christine would ever be continuously happy at the Belmont School.[24] By the summer of 1910, Christine had made up her mind that she could not remain in California. She and the children returned East for an extended "vacation" with her parents.

Bill was in a dilemma. He could stay at the Belmont School in a poorly paid position and be without Christine, who he said had "stood by me out here in what was almost a 'hell'" to her.[25] Alternatively, he could return East to be with her and abandon his aging parents and the school he would inherit. He wrote himself a stream-of-consciousness memo, attempting to clarify the situation. Bill claimed that he was not literary or scholarly, did not have love and affection for the school boys, lacked the missionary spirit, disliked dealing with condescending parents, and did not like the parsimonious life of a schoolmaster. He asked himself whether he should "choose a distasteful work to gratify one's parents." Yet, he wrote, "Where is Papa to get a letup, such as he should have if I took his place?" Tugging him eastward was Christine, whose "friends, family & interests" were there as were most of Bill's friends. If he left, though, he would have to start in business at the bottom, with no house as he had at Belmont, and the "problem of maintaining a family."[26]

For well over a year, Bill and Christine wrestled with the problem

---

21. William T. Reid, Sr., Lake Tahoe, Calif., to Bill Reid, Jr., Belmont, Calif., 21 July 1908.

22. Christine Reid, Cohasset, Mass., to Bill Reid, Jr., Belmont, 10 Aug. 1909.

23. Ibid., 24 July 1909.

24. Albert L. Lincoln, Boston, to Bill Reid, Jr., Belmont, Calif., 12 Jan. 1910.

25. Bill Reid, Jr., Belmont, Calif., to Christine Reid, Brookline, Mass., 22 Oct. 1910.

26. Undated note, ca. 1910.

of severing relations with the Belmont School and starting anew in the East. Bill reached the depths of despair in October 1910. He wrote: "I have been tired, blue, discouraged, and harassed and had a haunted feeling which has born down on me so that at times I felt as though I didn't care a continental what happened." Reid told Christine that he felt as if he would "burst with pressure," feeling worse than before the final game he coached against Yale.[27] As he reached his thirty-second birthday, Bill looked back and concluded that his life had been "largely a story of 'might have beens' and does not for ten years seem to have amounted to much."

A decision to break with Belmont and return East gave Reid new strength to return to Christine and make a new life in business. By November 1910, Bill had received a definite offer to be a bond salesman for William A. Reed & Company in Boston, and within a month he was headed East to be with Christine. "I am in this to win and win I will," he wrote to his wife.[28] He was resolute on turning around what he considered a failed life. "I am determined that your home shall be the dearest one that ever was," he wrote Christine. "Wait & see if I don't put those other fellows in the shade."[29]

Just before taking the rail to Boston, Reid had a pleasant sendoff from townspeople, the Belmont School faculty, and its football team. "It makes me feel for the first time as though I am as capable as the next man," Reid told his wife. "With my half finished football at Harvard and failure staring me in the face here for two years I began to wonder whether I wasn't a failure."[30] And he made peace with his parents, for as he told his mother, "If any conscience were not clear I could not stand it, for my going is a severe wrench. . . . I have never been very affectionate to you or Julia [his sister] or Papa," Reid confessed, "but I have felt a great deal & my heart goes out to you all."[31] Reid had mended his California fences, and he was ready for a new start in the East.

Life in the East, though, never quite worked out the way Bill had planned. Neither the bond sales job nor the joys of their marriage would reach the level that either Bill or Christine expected. Bill went on the road throughout New England selling bonds for the Boston firm. In May of 1911, he wrote discouragingly to Christine from North Adams, Massachusetts: "Not a sign of a sale today. . . . I haven't even

27. Bill Reid, Jr., Belmont, Calif., to Christine Reid, Cohasset, Mass., 7 Oct. 1910.
28. Bill Reid, Jr., Belmont, Calif., to Christine Reid, Brookline, Mass., 14 Nov. 1910.
29. Ibid., 23 Nov. 1910.
30. Ibid., 15 Dec. 1910.
31. Bill Reid, Jr., note to Julia Reed Reid, Belmont, Calif., 17 Dec. 1910.

had a toehold anywhere, and have come to the conclusion I am a big dub."[32] On another occasion he told Christine that "I know that you want a masculine man and that it must be a humiliation to you to see other's earning so much more."[33] There is no indication from the letters that their love life retained the spark of the first decade together. In fact, the spark that Bill tried to kindle apparently never returned completely to Christine. "Your greeting at the door tonight and once before," Bill wrote Christine, "warmed me up—it's what I need & want. Don't force it but let it come when you feel it."[34]

The faults of the two, which may have been glossed over during the first years of marriage, evidently became the causes of later friction. Christine had told Bill many times when they were courting that her temper was a shortcoming. Then, too, she had periodic bouts of depression. Bill's penchant to criticize, to want to make Christine perfect, must have led to discomfort when they were together, although almost never was it found in his frequent letters. Bill's mother may have been correct when she attempted to analyze their marital problems. Christine, she said, "has ill temper to contend with & you have a disposition to sulk & to upbraid in tone if not in words that you have to contend with."[35] The marriage continued, but it seemed to be more one of convenience than of love and passion as it had been. For a short period, Bill apparently took out some of his frustration with the marriage by drinking and smoking to excess.[36] Bill Reid's older sister once asked about the marriage: "You are a household aren't you?"[37] They were, and they even had a fourth child, Charles, in 1914.

When the United States entered World War I, both Christine and Bill became involved. Christine took a course in war cooking so that she might cook at a military camp.[38] Bill was involved in the Secret Service and evidently helped drill enlisted men in Cohasset in the early months of the war effort.[39] The war seemed to have less effect

32. Bill Reid, Jr., North Adams, Mass., to Christine Reid, 23 May 1911.

33. Bill Reid, Jr., to Christine Reid, 8 May 1911.

34. Ibid.

35. Julia Reid, Belmont, Calif., to Bill Reid, Jr., Brookline, Mass., 19 May 1912.

36. See, for instance, William T. Reid, Sr., Belmont, Calif., to Bill Reid, Jr., Boston, 20 June 1914; Julia Reid Willard, Coronado Beach, Calif., to Bill Reid, Jr., Brookline, Mass., 30 Dec. 1916; and Bill Reid, Jr., Hartford to Boston RR, to William T. and Julia Reid, Belmont, Calif., 13 April 1917.

37. Julia Reid Willard, Santa Barbara, Calif., to Bill Reid, Jr., 21 July 1913.

38. Bill Reid, Jr., Hartford to Boston RR, to William T. and Julia Reid, Belmont, Calif., 13 April 1917.

39. Ibid.; Billy Reid III, Cohasset, Mass., to William T. Reid, Sr., Belmont, Calif., 1 Aug. 1917.

upon the Reid family than on most. Even the flu epidemic did not appear to reach Bill, Christine, or their children. When the war began, Bill was too old to be inducted and Billy was only fifteen. The war may, in fact, have brought a degree of prosperity, for there is little reference to financial concerns in Reid's correspondence after the middle of the decade.

Somewhat surprisingly, Bill and Christine invited Bill's father to live with them after Bill's mother died early in the war and his father sold the Belmont School. Perhaps inevitably, Bill went back on his word not to coach once he moved East. The spring following the armistice, Harvard, in midseason, paid him $1,000 to take over a faltering baseball team. Although the team beat Princeton, it lost to Yale as it had done more than a dozen years earlier in football.[40] The war was over, but Bill Reid's battle with Yale remained.

What happened to the Reid family in the 1920s is unclear. On December 13, 1924, Christine evidently took her own life while she was at the Weld Farm Homestead in West Roxbury, Massachusetts. Her eighteen-year-old daughter, Christine, affectionately known as "Poo," had written a cheery letter the day before from Boston, saying that she wanted to write because she hadn't seen her mother "for so long and I know you'll like to hear all the news."[41] Three years later, she wrote of her mother in her diary. "Things will never be the same again. How could they be?" her daughter recorded. "She was the center of our family life, and the staunch mainstay of our existence. . . . She was too good for our world."[42] Bill was left to care for his four children, only one of whom was past the age of schooling.

Life was rather lonesome for Reid, and existence as a bond salesman probably never excited him. He remained single until 1931, when he married Cornelia Hinchman. They lived in Brookline, where Reid became somewhat involved with conservative Republican politics, belonging to the Brookline Taxpayers Association and opposing what he called "crackpot" New Deal programs of Franklin Roosevelt's presidency.[43] A friend wrote shortly before World War II: "You were right to say that life was lonely. . . . You can readily understand what emptiness there is when your children marry and leave your home, your

40. Bill Reid, Jr., Boston, to William Reid, Sr., 16 May 1919, W. T. Reid Papers, vol. 3, "June 1896–Sept 1907" Folder, University of California Archives; Harvard Athletic Committee Minutes, 26 May 1919, Harvard University Archives.

41. Christine L. Reid, Boston, to Christine L. Reid, West Roxbury, Mass., 12 Dec. 1924.

42. Christine Lincoln Reid Diary, 1 Jan. 1927.

43. *Boston Globe*, 30 Sept. 1976, 75.

wife gone, your father—the last touch gone too—nothing to cling to but trouble."[44] His eldest son wrote during the war that his father "looks miserably & is head over heels in some zoning law, running his 40th reunion [Harvard], & writing all the big shots in Washington. . . . If you want peace," he wrote to his younger brother, "for god's sake keep out of that house next year."[45]

Another decade later and approaching his fiftieth Harvard graduation reunion, Bill wrote to his daughter, Christine, telling her "how far short I have fallen from the hopes of 50 years ago," sometimes feeling "pretty low." Yet he felt good about his children, whom, he said, would bring satisfaction to their mother. "You children," he told his daughter, "are her heritage to me."[46] He had looked out for his children's financial station by starting a trust fund for all four when they were young. By the 1960s, the collective value was about $1,200,000.[47]

As Bill grew into old age, athletics and Harvard remained meaningful to him. He remained active with the Harvard baseball team well after World War II, assisting the coaching, especially of catchers. His football accomplishments came to be recognized on a national level. In 1970, when he was ninety-one, the College Football Hall of Fame voted him in as a Pioneer member.[48] As he reviewed his career in athletics, it is likely that his grandest memory was saving football at Harvard during the crisis of 1905 and 1906. When Reid was interviewed by the *Washington Post* in 1970, only six years before his death, he remembered the 1905 season almost as if he had been reading his diary of that year.[49] If he only could have beaten Yale in football in 1905 and the following year, all would have been well.

44. Edmund Zacher, West Hartford, Conn., to Bill Reid, Jr., Brookline, Mass., 5 Aug. 1941.

45. William T. Reid III, Cohasset, Mass., to Charles W. Reid, U.S.S. *Joseph Dickerman*, New York, N.Y.

46. Bill Reid, Jr., Brookline, Mass., to Christine Reid in California, 17 June 1949.

47. Bill Reid, Jr., Brookline, Mass., to Christine Reid, Berkeley, Calif., 4 July 1964.

48. *New York Times*, 1 Oct. 1976, 4:13.

49. *Washington Post*, 13 Sept. 1970, C13.

Appendix: Timeline

Prelude to the Diary (1878–1905)

October 25, 1878	William T. Reid, Jr., was born in San Francisco, the second child of William T. Reid, Sr., and Julia Reed Reid.
Summer 1881	The Reid family moved to Berkeley when William Reid, Sr., was elected president of the University of California.
January 31, 1885	The elder Reid resigned as president of the University of California (effective August 1).
August 5, 1885	The Reid family moved to Belmont, California, where the senior Reid opened the Belmont School, a preparatory school.
June 1893	Reid visited the Columbian Exposition in Chicago.
June 1896	Reid took entrance examinations at Harvard.
September 1897	Reid entered Harvard as a freshman.
July 2, 1898	Reid was starting catcher as Harvard lost the best of three series in baseball to Yale.
November 19, 1898	Reid scored two touchdowns as Harvard beat Yale 17-0, the first victory since 1890.
December 17, 1898	Reid's football picture placed prominently in the Christmas issue of *Harper's Weekly*.
March–April 1899	Reid in controversy with Percy Haughton, captain of the baseball team.
May 20, 1899	Reid accused of dirty play in baseball game against Princeton.
July 1, 1899	Reid was catcher on winning Harvard baseball team in series with Yale.
July 1899	Reid's expenses for junior year at Harvard were $1,794, including transportation.
November 18, 1899	Reid played in scoreless tie game with Yale as a substitute fullback.
December 25, 1899	Reid's father offered him position at the Belmont School if he was interested.
February 24, 1900	Reid began corresponding with Christine Williams Lincoln of Brookline, Massachusetts.

Spring 1900	Reid captained Harvard's baseball team, which was victorious over Yale.
Summer 1900	Reid and Christine became informally engaged.
September 12, 1900	Christine Lincoln began a seven-month trip to Europe with her family.
October 1900	Reid decided not to play football, in part because of a baseball injury but primarily in opposition to the football coach and captain.
November 24, 1900	Yale defeated Harvard, without Reid, 22-0.
December 1900	Reid offered the head football coaching position at Harvard for 1901.
December 18, 1900	Reid elected Class Day officer, second marshal at Harvard.
June 25, 1901	Harvard won baseball series from Yale in two straight games under Reid's captaincy.
September 24, 1901	Reid appointed Harvard proctor while working on A.M. degree, 1901–2.
November 24, 1901	Reid-coached Harvard football beat Yale 22-0, concluding an undefeated season at 12-0.
May 18, 1902	Reid, after delay, agreed to become assistant headmaster at the Belmont School.
June 1902	Reid received A.M. degree at Harvard.
July 2, 1902	Reid and Christine Williams Lincoln married in Brookline.
July–December 1902	Bill and Christine Reid honeymooned in England and Europe.
February 1903	Bill and Christine Reid arrived in Belmont, where he became assistant headmaster at the Belmont School.
March 17, 1903	Bill and Christine Reid's first child, William T. (Patrick) Reid III, born.
Summer 1903	Christine Reid indicated some dissatisfaction with life in California and being away from her eastern family.
January 4, 1904	Harvard captain Dan Hurley offered Reid the football head coaching position at Harvard for 1904.
February 2, 1904	Harvard's Athletic Committee voted against paying Reid $3,000 to coach football in fall 1904.
May 21, 1904	Reid's salary of $1,250 at Belmont School raised to $1,500 for 1904–5.
December 1, 1904	Bill and Christine Reid's second child, Edith (Didie) Williams, born.
December 27, 1904	Reid traveled to Harvard to consider the call to coach.

January 1–11, 1905	Reid met with influential football men and key Harvard figures, including Charles Eliot, Dean L. B. R. Briggs, Dean Hurlbut, and Major Higginson, as well as the football team.
February 24, 1905	Reid's return to coach announced publicly.

Year of the Diary (March–November 1905)

March 14, 1905	Reid arrived in Cambridge as Harvard's first paid head football coach.
March 1905	Reid attempted to get Harry LeMoyne back into Harvard's Scientific School.
March–April 1905	Reid worked diligently to get Harvard football players academically eligible.
March 30, 1905	A Harvard dinner honored the 1904 baseball team and Reid's return.
April 4, 1905	Reid met with former Harvard football players to discuss line play at guard.
April 5, 1905	Spring football practice began.
April 6, 1905	Reid met with former Harvard football players to discuss line play at end.
April 7, 1905	Reid met with former Harvard football players to discuss backfield play.
April 12, 1905	Reid met with former Harvard football players to discuss line play at tackle.
April 28, 1905	Spring football practice ended.
April 29, 1905	Reid met with former Harvard head football coaches.
May 3, 1905	Football schedule announced, with nine home and two away games.
May 4, 1905	A Harvard graduate suggested the use of the forward pass to open up the game.
May 8, 1905	Reid wrote to a Princeton professor, opposing any "allowance of the forward pass."
May 10–11, 1905	Reid met with Glenn "Pop" Warner, Cornell coach.
May 11, 1905	Reid met with former Harvard football players to discuss line play at guard and tackle.
May 26, 1905	Practice called for kickers only.
June 1905	Muckraker Henry Needham published "The College Athlete," criticizing big-time athletics.
June 10, 1905	Reid appointed as Harvard's representative on the Football Rules Committee.
June 28, 1905	Yale beat Harvard in baseball, for the first time since 1898, before thirteen thousand spectators. Yale beat Harvard in each major sport in 1904 and 1905.

June 28, 1905	President Roosevelt spoke at Harvard's Commencement, advocating rough games.
July 1905	Roosevelt invited muckraker Henry Needham to his Oyster Bay home.
July 11, 1905	Reid wrote to Roosevelt, attempting to get West Point graduate Charlie Daly assigned to Boston Harbor so he could coach at Harvard.
August 14, 1905	Reid completed the first 114 undated pages of his diary.
August 29–30, 1905	Reid met with Fielding H. Yost, Michigan coach.
September 10, 1905	Reid called for football candidates to end smoking, drinking, and other dissipations.
September 13, 1905	Football practice began.
September 26, 1905	First scrimmage.
September 30, 1905	First game played against Williams College, Harvard winning 12-0.
October 9, 1905	Roosevelt invited the Big Three (Harvard, Yale, and Princeton) to the White House to discuss ethics and brutality in college football. Reid attended.
October 10, 1905	Reid spoke at big pep rally Harvard students held to get behind the football team.
October 11, 1905	Text of Big Three agreement released to the national press.
October 12, 1905	President Jacob G. Schurman of Cornell suggested a football reform congress.
November 3, 1905	President Nicholas M. Butler of Columbia called for a new football rules committee.
November 7, 1905	Reid met with Dr. Edward Nichols, William Sullivan, Bertram Waters, and Herbert White to combat a possible football ban by Harvard.
November 8, 1905	Reid released a letter condemning college football as then played and calling for a Harvard graduate committee to reform football.
November 11, 1905	Harvard played its first "big" game against Penn, resulting in 210 yards of penalties. Penn watered the field to gain a traction advantage, and a Harvard player was removed from the game for slugging in the 12-6 loss.
November 11, 1905	President Eliot viewed a rugby game between two Halifax, Nova Scotia, teams in Harvard's stadium while Harvard played football at Penn.
November 24, 1905	Captain Dan Hurley reported to have a brain blood clot just before the Yale game.

November 25, 1905	Harvard played "The Game" against Yale; "Burr-Quill" incident created controversy.
November 25, 1905	Reid closed diary with the statement that those associated with Harvard football put their "heart and soul into the work."

Postlude to the 1905 Diary

November 25, 1905	Harold Moore, Union College halfback, died of a cerebral hemorrhage in a game with New York University.
November 25, 1905	Chancellor Henry M. MacCracken of New York University requested that President Eliot of Harvard call a conference to reform or abolish football. Eliot refused.
November 28, 1905	Columbia faculty and president abolished football.
November 28, 1905	President J. S. Schurman of Cornell recommended a New England and middle states conference on football, with presidents and alumni represented.
November 28, 1905	MacCracken invited each school NYU had played football against since 1885 to a conference to discuss reforming or abolishing football. He also suggested the need for a national meeting at the end of December.
December 1, 1905	*Harvard Graduates' Magazine*'s inflammatory article about Yale's "athletocracy," created strong bitterness between Harvard and Yale.
December 4, 1905	Reid went to the White House to confer with Roosevelt on the football question.
December 8, 1905	The MacCracken meeting of thirteen institutions voted 8-5 to reform rather than abolish football.
December 8, 1905	The conference called for a national conference in New York City on December 28 to reform football.
December 9, 1905	The Harvard Athletic Association Committee to reform football announced, with Reid as chair.
December 13, 1905	The Harvard Athletic Committee voted unanimously to continue football if new rules acceptable.
December 13, 1905	Harvard Overseers committee regarding sports recommended banning football, which it called "essentially bad in every respect."
December 20, 1905	Harvard's Athletic Committee allowed Reid

	to meet with the national Football Rules Committee.
December 21, 1905	Roosevelt wrote to Eliot: "I do not agree with you that the game should be stopped."
December 28, 1905	A new National Intercollegiate Football Conference of sixty-eight institutions met in New York City (beginning the National Collegiate Athletic Association). A new football rules committee asked to meet with the Old Rules Committee.
December 29, 1905	The New Rules Committee went to Philadelphia to attempt an amalgamation with the Old Committee.
January 10, 1906	Harvard's Board of Overseers voted to ban football until Harvard's reform rules accepted as official.
January 12, 1906	The two football rules committees agreed to meet in New York City after Reid withdrew from the Old Committee and joined the New Committee, replacing Walter Camp as committee secretary.
February 6, 1906	Harvard Faculty of Arts and Sciences favored abolishing football.
March 7, 1906	Roosevelt said privately that Eliot was doing the "baby act" in opposing football.
March 26, 1906	Reid offered $3,500 to run a summer camp in the White Mountains if football banned at Harvard.
March 31, 1906	New football rules agreed upon that included a neutral zone between teams, requiring six men on the offensive line, ten yards in three attempts to maintain ball possession, and the introduction of the forward pass.
April 2, 1906	Harvard Athletic Committee sanctioned football for 1906 based on reform rules.
April 2, 1906	Reid's salary again set at $3,500, with an additional $3,500 to be subscribed.
April 18, 1906	The Great San Francisco Earthquake damaged the Belmont School.
May 8, 1906	Bill and Christine Reid's third child, Christine (Pussy, Poo) Lincoln, born.
May 9, 1906	Harvard governing boards voted 15-9 and 17-6 to continue football, over Eliot's opposition.
September 1906	Reid began his final football coaching season at Harvard.
November 24, 1906	Harvard lost its final game to Yale, 6-0, after

winning its first ten games. Reid considered his thirty wins, three losses, and one tie record a failure.

January 18, 1907	Harvard Athletic Committee thanked Reid for serving as football coach.
March 1907	Reid returned to the Belmont School as assistant headmaster.
March 8, 1907	Dean L. B. R. Briggs of Harvard favored Reid's return to coach football.
July 7, 1908	Percy Haughton, new Harvard football coach, asked Reid to assist him in the fall. Reid declined, to the relief of his parents.
October 3, 1908	William and Julia Reid's home in Belmont burned.
July 24, 1909	The senior Reid's statement to Bill—"you have been a 'hinderance'" at the Belmont School—hardened Christine against staying in the West.
August 18, 1909	Reid apologized to Christine for their meager life-style with "absolutely no bank account."
January 12, 1910	Christine's father wrote to Bill: "I see no probability that you & she will ever be continuously happy in Belmont."
August 31, 1910	Christine Reid and children left Belmont for the East, forcing Reid to decide between his position and his family.
September 25, 1910	Walter Camp visited Reid at the Belmont School.
October 16, 1910	Reid's depression over Christine leaving greater than "my worst football days."
October 26, 1910	Dr. Edward Nichols asked Reid to return to coach baseball. He refused.
November 11, 1910	Reid told his wife: "I am absolutely through with coaching of any sort."
November 13, 1910	Reid accepted a job as a bond salesman with William A. Reed & Company of Boston.
December 17, 1910	Reid began the journey East.
May 11, 1911	Reid, eking out a living as a bond salesman, felt unmanly and humiliated before Christine.
November 10, 1911	Reid's father asked if he wanted to return to the Belmont School.
May 19, 1912	Reids's mother attempted to help him through marital difficulties.
June 1913	Reid and children traveled to Lake Tahoe to visit the elder Reids.
December 17, 1914	Bill and Christine Reid's fourth child, Charles (Chilly) Willard, was born.

April 1917	Reid served with the U.S. Secret Service during World War I.
April 21, 1917	Reid's mother died.
December 1917	Reid visited his newly retired father, missing Christmas with his own family.
May 26, 1919	Reid paid $1,000 to coach the Harvard baseball team for the remainder of the year.
December 17, 1922	Reid's father died.
December 13, 1924	Christine Reid ended her life at age forty-four.
June 1926	Reid's twenty-fifth Harvard Anniversary Report noted his "failure" as a coach but success at having "saved the game at Harvard."
October 17, 1926	Reid first recounted his effort to save football at Harvard in the *Boston Globe*.
August 20, 1931	Reid married Cornelia (Connie) Hinchman.
June 17, 1949	Reid felt that he had "fallen from the hopes of 50 years ago."
July 4, 1964	Reid revealed a $1,200,000 trust fund for his children from which each received interest.
1970	Reid elected into the Football Hall of Fame as a Pioneer member.
September 28, 1976	Reid died in Brookline at age ninety-seven.

Index

Books in the Series Sport and Society

Cowgirls of the Rodeo: Pioneer Professional Athletes
Mary Lou LeCompte

Sandow the Magnificent: Eugen Sandow and the Beginnings
of Bodybuilding
David Chapman

Big-Time Football at Harvard, 1905: The Diary of Coach Bill Reid
Edited by Ronald A. Smith

REPRINT EDITIONS

The Nazi Olympics
Richard D. Mandell

Sports in the Western World
Second Edition
William J. Baker